THE ART OF SAMPLING

THE SAMPLING TRADITION OF HIP HOP/RAP MUSIC & COPYRIGHT LAW

SECOND EDITION

AMIR SAID

Superchamp Books SB

New York City

Published by Superchamp Books

Copyright © 2015 by Amir Said.

A Superchamp Books Second Paperback Edition

Print History:
Augutst 2015: First Printing.
January 2016: Second Printing.

The Art of Sampling: The Sampling Tradition of Hip Hop/Rap Music and Copyright Law — Second Edition / by Amir Said
1. Sampling—Music and Digital. 2. Copyright Law. 3. Beatmaking 4. Hip Hop/Rap—Production 5. Hip Hop—Histroy 6. Rap Music—Performance Practice 7. Rap Music—History 6. Hip Hop—Producers 8. Music—Technology 9. Music—Popular 10. Music—Social Aspects 11. African Americans—Music—History and Criticism 12. Popular Culture—United States 13. Music History I. Title

Library of Congress Control Number: 2015911652 (Paperback)
ISBN 978-0-9749704-1-7 (Paperback)

Photographs:
Front Cover photo by Amir Said Copyright © 2002 Amir Said
Back Cover photo by Amir Said © 2002 Amir Said
Author Back Cover photo by Amir Ali Said © 2014
Cover, Design, and Layout by Amir Said

For my son, Amir Ali Said.
Amir, nobody can be a better you than you.
("When the door opens for opportunity, walk through.")
Insha'Allah…Al-Humdullilah.

CONTENTS

x

Preface

The idea for *The Art of Sampling* was born more than 18 years ago, back before I wrote and published the first edition of *The BeatTips Manual*. I'd been collecting vinyl records for 15 years, been DJ'ing for 7, and making beats for 10. I was enamored with the art of sampling and the culture that emerged from it. Weekly trips to used vinyl record stores all over New York City were a big part of my routine. Journeys to fellow beatmakers' production "studios" throughout the Bronx, Queens, Manhattan, and Brooklyn were common. And, of course, late nights (early mornings) hunched over beat machines felt mandatory.

This time, ca. 1990-1995, was special. I was a teenager, and the sampling tradition of hip hop/rap music, which first popularized the art of sampling, was rising to its zenith. Sampling pioneers like Marley Marl, DJ Premier, Large Professor, Pete Rock, The Bomb Squad, Q-Tip, and The RZA were all creating great music and carving out signature styles and sounds. And the beatmaking community was just beginning to blossom.

Eager to examine and document the roots and rise of the beatmaking tradition — not just the art of sampling — of hip hop/rap music, I embarked on an ambitious undertaking that would eventually result in the creation of *The BeatTips Manual*.

Though *The BeatTips Manual* was the bigger endeavor, the more immediate calling — my deep interest in and focus on the art of sampling — always remained. In fact, much of what is presented here in *The Art of Sampling* is based on the sampling chapters that I published in various editions of *The BeatTips Manual*. It was always my intention to break out and extend those sampling chapters and sections and turn them into a book that was distinct from the much broader focus of *The BeatTips Manual*. Specifically, I wanted to create a study where I could further expand on the discussion of the art of sampling exclusively, without necessarily covering all of the key areas of the beatmaking tradition. Also, I wanted my examination of copyright law, and the implications it holds for the art of sampling, to share equal space in one combined study. Thus, what follows is a comprehensive and detailed examination of the art of sampling — as it's best articulated and observed in the hip hop/rap music tradition — and United States copyright law.

Who is This Book For?

The Art of Sampling is for anyone interested in the art of sampling, especially as it's articulated in the hip hop/rap and beatmaking traditions and the encompassing hip hop culture. Though this study is geared towards beatmakers and other musicians, it should be noted that this information is also for many others as well. Certainly, I trust that students, professors, cultural and copyright scholars, music lawyers, music writers, hip hop/rap aficionados, and casual hip hop supporters alike will find *The Art of Sampling* equally valuable.

About the Slant of This Book

This book is an examination of the art of sampling as it's articulated within the hip hop/rap music tradition — on its own terms. It has been conceived and written from the up-close perspective of a sample-based beatmaker and life-time practitioner, one who's deeply connected to and entrenched within the traditions and culture of hip hop.

This book is not a typical academic jaunt. Academic texts are usually written for and by professional academicians; and as such, they carry the language, feel, motives, priorities, and predilections of the members of that community. Thus, I've taken great effort to construct this study with a language and feel that is equally appealing and accessible to beatmakers, academicians, and everybody in between. All the while, I've kept my focus first on the needs and interests of sample-based beatmakers.

This book is not the work of someone who spent time doing "fieldwork," admirable as that is, but rather it is the product of someone who's *lived* in this particular field all of his life. In other words, my own musical knowledge and experiences in this area means that I didn't have to rely on a bevy of interviews to be introduced to or understand all of the material presented in this study. However, I have interviewed a number of acclaimed sample-based beatmakers. Therefore, it's inevitable that some of their insights have helped to sharpen my prior understanding of a number of topics covered in this study.

Further, *The Art of Sampling* is not meant to be a standard ethnographical look at beatmaking and/or hip hop culture. That being said, most of the elements of this study will certainly appeal to both ethnomusicologists and musicologists alike. And although this book relies on more than two decades of research, it must be noted that the *The Art of Sampling* is more musician's guide than it is research study. Fundamentally, my aim is to teach the art of sampling of the hip hop/rap music tradition and to inform sample-based musicians about the copyright implications of their work.

It is also fair to say that this book is not an anthropological study of a culture for which I only have a fleeting interest in or enthusiastic (but perhaps shaky or incomplete) understanding of. I have not watched beatmaking and the art of sampling from the sidelines; I have fully participated within these traditions for more than 23 years. And my studies in beatmaking began — though I didn't know it at the time — when I was just 11 years old, the same time I first knowingly participated in the hip hop/rap music tradition. Moreover, I did not just recently become aware of the art of sampling, nor did I just recently become familiar with beatmaking as a legitimate music compositional method; I knew it was legitimate back in 1986 when I first heard Eric B. & Rakim's seminal classic, "Paid In Full."

Of equal importance is the fact that I have not merely attempted to make beats simply to publish my findings on the processes of beatmaking, nor have I attempted to make beats due to some residual provocation from writing this book. I didn't decide to acquire an Akai MPC drum machine/sampler at the end of my research for this present study. I've made beats — with a professional level of skill and understanding — for more than 20 years now. In fact, while writing this manuscript, I took many impromptu breaks to make beats, all of them sampled based of course. So the heart and soul of beatmaking is embedded in this study. Further I've owned various MPC models and other electronic music production instruments (EMPIs) since 1992, years before I even considered beatmaking as a possible literary topic.

Any and all participation that I've had within the hip hop/ rap music tradition has not occurred expressly for the purpose of gathering data for this study. But that said, I make no apologies for my penchant for keeping a journal of notes, memorable photos, historical party flyers, vinyl records and cassette tapes, and even old sneakers! There are a number of my personal experiences within hip hop that have contributed substantially to the production of this manuscript. Therefore, I think that there are several key facts about my background that I should mention up front.

Since I was 9 years old, I have consistently collected vinyl records of all sorts. Both of my parents were pseudo record collectors. I took my cue from them, along with my grandmother and my uncle, and I went to another orbit with it. I have listened attentively, at times obsessively, to more than 1,500 hip hop/rap songs, ranging in release year from 1979 to 2013. I have personally conducted, taped, and transcribed more than 75 interviews with beatmakers (critically acclaimed, well-known, and underground), engineers, label execs, accountants, lawyers, and other music insiders. In the past 15 years, I've been to numerous beatmaking sessions and attended more than 50 live performances and showcases at local clubs, as well as large-scale concert/tour series, in New York City and as many as 10 other states in the U.S., as well as France, the U.K., and Austria. I have made/produced and recorded music in more than 70 different recording studios of all varieties, sizes, and scopes — from high-end commercial labs to mid-level professional outfits, to the most bootleg, grungy bedroom setups. Finally, since 1994, I have made/produced, recorded, engineered, and mixed more than 2,000 beats (well, at least 2000 that I care to admit to).

It's also worth pointing out that my aim with this study has not been to be politically correct, but to be fundamentally accurate. I deal with what was, what is, what may and what will most likely be. I do not, however, deal in what should have been, what it should be now, or what it should be in the future.

Finally, so that there is no confusion, I must give readers some more critical context: This book is not concerned with the fringe musical developments of hip hop/rap music, such as the hip hop-R&B hybrid or the alternative "rocker rap" or so-called "mashups". This study is unequivocally concerned with and centered around the art of sampling as it's best articulated and observed in the hip hop/rap music tradition in its truest, most fundamental meaning. Thus, it should be clear that the beatmaking compositional methods and concepts that are explored in this book are those that are utilized by beatmakers for the purpose of creating music (instrumentals), first and foremost, for rappers to rap over. But this does not mean that these methods can't be used for the purpose of creating music for other performers (i.e. non-rappers).

What's in Here?

I have designed *The Art of Sampling* to serve as both an examination of and instructional guide to the sampling tradition of hip hop/rap music. Thus, this book contains a wealth of information on the sampling tradition of hip hop/rap music as well as beatmaking in general. Along those lines, I have intended for *The Art of Sampling* to be a portal or a gateway into the vast world of beatmaking. In this study, you will encounter methodical, technical, and stylistic examinations of the art of sampling. This means that this book contains a detailed examination of the most crucial compositional, cultural, historical, and legal components of the art of sampling. Also, within these pages there are stories of my own experiences and those of people like you.

The Art of Sampling ambitiously approaches three broad areas: history (and tradition), instruction, and copyright law. These areas are further organized into three parts: **Part 1: History; Part 2: Instruction: Aesthetic and Compositional Analysis, Performance, and Philosophy of the Art Of Sampling; and Part 3: Copyright Law.**

Helpful Icons

In this book, there are two important icons to be aware of. First, the **BeatTip** icon. I have inserted this icon as an aide to help notify readers of an especially important point and/or tip. Second, the **Check This Out** icon. I have inserted this icon as an aide to help notify readers to either a personal story of mine or an extensive discussion that further personifies the particular topic, theme, or idea that is currently being examined.

How to Navigate through This Book

This book is a practical tool that can be easily navigated. It's not a rigidly fashioned, cold-numbers, point-by-point-style, tech-heavy text book. It's not designed to overload you with fancy technological jargon or tricky algorithms or the like. I've organized and broken down the parts, chapters, and sections of this book into an order that is both logical and consistent with the time line of a typical beatmaker's progression and development. Thus, if you know nothing at all (or very little) about the art of sampling or beatmaking (or even hip hop/rap music), you can start with Part 1 and progress confidently through this book at your own pace. Still, if you prefer to skip around, I recommend that you do so by Part rather than Chapter alone. For instance, if you feel that you already have a solid grasp of *how* to make sample-based beats and you're more interested in learning about copyright law — or if you're a lawyer or policy wonk — then starting with **Part 3: Copyright Law** is perfectly fine. Just make sure that at some point you carefullly read through **Part 1: History** and **Part 2:**

Instruction. There's a wealth of knowledge in those parts that I'm sure you wouldn't want to miss.

Note on Nomenclature and the Use of Some Cultural Slang In This Study
The Use of "Hip Hop/Rap," Hip Hop (no hyphen), Beatmaking, and EMPI

So that readers have an understanding as to why I use certain terminology in specific areas within this study, I thought I should offer some brief explanations.

As for the term, "hip hop," it must be recognized that throughout the past 15 years, the terms "hip hop" and "rap" have been so misused and misrepresented that without context, it's very hard to determine what the average person actually means when they use them. For instance, there are some who attempt to distinguish "rap" as something purely commercial and not indicative of so-called "real" hip hop — this despite the fact that by 1983, all of the pivotal pioneers regularly referred to the music as "rap," as well as hip hop. In fact, between 1984 and 1995 "rap" was the most commonly used term to describe the music of hip hop culture. But after 1997, around the time when beats first began to be used more prominently by other music genres that did not include rappers, e.g. the merger of hip hop and "R&B," the term "hip hop" became the primary means for describing the music of hip hop culture. This created a disconnect between the paramount role that the art of rapping has played and continues to play in the music of hip hop culture. Moreover, the misuse of "hip hop" not only narrows the culture of hip hop down to just its musical expression, it takes focus away from the fact that hip hop culture is actually comprised of four distinct artistic expressions: graffiti, b-boying, DJ'ing, and rapping.

Also, the word "rap" has always had several distinct usages in the black community. In the 1960s and 1970s, "rap" was used to describe "talk," in particular, a heavy, intellectual (enlightening) form of speech. "Rap" could also be used to describe the slang of the urban black community. And "rap" was (is) also commonly used as a word to describe the courtship language used by many black American men in their social pursuit of women.

In this study, I use the term "hip hop/rap" as a means to reconcile the misunderstanding of these terms and their subsequent use. "Rap" is embedded and interlocked within hip hop. Rap explicitly means hip hop music. So identifiable is rap to hip hop that it's impossible to seriously discuss hip hop without recognizing the interweaving connection of rap to the music of hip hop culture. Thus, I prefer to defer to the original use and intent of these two phrases. "Hip hop," in its original context, encompasses and covers the entire cultural expression. However, I recognize, for better or worse, how contemporary lexicon employs both "hip hop" and "rap." That is to say, today, "hip hop" is often used synonymously with "rap." Thus, in an attempt to reconcile these two phrases, and to literally show their deferential link, I use the term "hip hop/rap" when referring to the music of hip hop culture. Also, in some areas of this study I only use the term "rap," as it is sometimes necessary to be distinguished from the hybrid of R&B and hip hop, which does not often include rapping. Finally, I use "hip hop" — no hyphen — because that is the way the original architects and pioneers of hip hop wrote it; my deference is to them.

Next, the terms "beatmaking" and "production" are often used interchangeably to describe the same thing, but depending on the context, they're actually not. Producing does not always involve actual beatmaking (the making of beats). That being said, most of those who make beats refer to themselves as "producers," perhaps because the term presumably holds more prestige. But the fact is, in the annals of hip hop/rap music lore, the "beatmaker" is more prestigious, more hands-on. Beatmakers literally make beats! Moreover, the term "beatmaker" itself is a unique name for a different kind of music composer. Because of this, and the fact that I defer to the essence and scope of the originators and architects of beatmaking, I prefer to describe those who actually make beats as "beatmakers," first and foremost. This is also why in this book I primarily use the term "beatmaking" rather than "producing." However, throughout this book, I may indeed link these terms and their variations, e.g.: "beatmakers (producers)." In those cases, I'm confident that given the topic and context of discussion, readers will know which term applies more appropriately. Also, wherever the terms "beatmaking," "production," and the like appear, I am only referring to the compositional methods of hip hop/rap music.

I should also note that within this study there is some slang, cultural jargon, and similar expressions mostly known to members of the beatmaking and hip hop/rap communities. Deliberate effort was made to preserve the authenticity of these expressions, along with their actual, or in some cases, intended, meanings.

Finally, in this book, I use "EMPI." It's an acronym, pronounced: em-pee, that stands for Electronic Music Production Instrument. Throughout this study, all beatmaking or electronic music production gear is routinely referred to as EMPI or EMPIs .

Case Study Production Setup:
Akai MPC 4000/Akai S950/Akai MPC 60 II/ Roland Fantom S 88/Propellerhead Reason Setup with Digidesign Pro Tools DAW

With a book such as this, there must be a primary beatmaking (music production) setup through which the various technical and theoretical components and principles of hip hop/rap beatmaking can be examined. For this purpose, I have chosen to use my own production setup. Because my setup is a hybrid composed of hardware (both classic/vintage and contemporary pro audio gear and equipment), and software, it is particularly well suited for the task at hand. The individual EMPIs within my setup include:

- Akai S950 Digital Sampler (maximum memory).
- Akai MPC 4000, Akai MPC 60 II

- Roland Fantom S Keyboard Workstation (88-note)
- Mackie 32/8 Analog Mixing Console
- Apple Power Mac G5 1.8 GHz/6GBRam/150G
- Digidesign 002 Rack (not Control Surface)
- Pro Tools LE version 7.1
- Properllerhead Reason
- Numark DM 1200 DJ/Stereo Mixer
- Technics SL-1200 MK2 Direct Drive Turntable
- Mackie HR 824 self-powered Studio Monitors
- Tascam 302 Dual Cassette Deck (with pitch control)

The setup I use offers a variety of particular nuances that permit me to apply many different methods and techniques. But the compositional and procedural aesthetics of beatmaking are nearly universal — for the most part (or in principle), they can be applied to any setup. Moreover, sampling can not be restricted to any particular hardware and/or software. But the methods and techniques which a beatmaker is able to use can vary depending upon the setup. Furthermore, the setup that I use offers a number of sound and technical effects that are unique to this particular gear and software combination.

No two digital samplers, drum machines, sequencers, keyboard workstations, or even software applications are identical. There may be many similarities at their core, but each piece in any setup performs in line with its design and function capability; and different EMPIs combine to produce various effects. What one beatmaker may be able to do on a particular setup, other beatmakers may not be able to accomplish on yet another. Likewise, where one beatmaker is limited by a particular setup, another beatmaker may discover unlimited possibilities using that same setup. The compositional possibilities within the hip hop/ rap beatmaking and production process seriously depends on how beatmakers use their gear and other production tools. Finally, in no way is this book about or an endorsement of a particular setup or EMPI. The center of this book is grounded upon the study of the art of sampling (and by extension, the beatmaking tradition) and copyright law.

Introduction

The fundamental purpose of this book is to help people gain a better understanding of both the art of sampling — one of the most creative, indispensable, and, unfortunately, polarizing processes of modern music — and United States copyright law.

In terms of the aesthetic and compositional component of this study, I want to distinguish the sampling tradition of hip hop/rap music and present it accurately on its own terms. Hence, within this study, I offer a more enhanced and nuanced understanding of the art of sampling, hip hop/rap music, and the broader hip hop culture.

As for the copyright component of this study, I address the main critics of the art of sampling while offering a sobering look at what copyright law actually says on the matter. Copyright hawks, lawyers, and musicians who do not see the art of sampling as an art form at all, but rather an activity of theft that's as criminal as it is uncreative and unoriginal, have been largely successful in the framing of the public debate about sampling. In fact, one of the greatest travesties involving the art of sampling is that its description to the public has been framed largely by lawyers in a (flawed) legal and technological context rather than in a cultural and artistic context, the context which reveals sampling's true pedigree. This book suggests that the art of sampling, particularly as it's articulated in hip hop/rap music, is a dynamic, well-developed, and complex music process that serves as a public good and honors the fundamental purpose of copyright law: to Promote the Sciences and useful Arts.

The art of sampling in the hip hop/rap music tradition is a form of sound collage, certainly, but it's also a continuum of some of the most common elements of the African American (Black) music tradition. However, because mainstream debate has focused on the legal implications that the art of sampling raises, sampling's true meaning, value, and history has been overshadowed, if not outright ignored by those who have mostly framed the debate. And when you consider the reality that the purpose and meaning of U.S. copyright law and policy is lost on most people, what you have is a woefully misunderstood art form that is heavily criticized by so-called legal experts who are insensitive to what sampling really is, and who rely on a willful mis-interpretation of key sections of the United States Copyright Act.

Because a work that includes music sampling routinely receives an unfavorable appraisal of the constructive purpose of the overall work, this low regard for (and estimation of) the overall value of sampling — the secondary work — overshadows the creativity and usefulness of the art of sampling. Thus, by examining the history and compositional practices of the art of sampling, this book aims to show exactly why sampling is an art form. Further, by exploring the history of United States copyright law, this book seeks to demonstrate why sampling is an activity that is encouraged and protected by copyright law, rather then discouraged and unprotected.

In addition to the fundamental purpose of this study, there are a number of auxiliary goals that I hope to achieve with this book. First, I want to provide the most crucial, comprehensive, and widely useful information on the art of sampling and the implications it holds for copyright law. In doing so, it is my hope that this study helps remove the negative stigma that's often attached to the art of sampling.

Second, I want this book to establish some basic uniformity and consensus regarding the core aesthetics, concepts, and terminology of the art of sampling. Thus, in this study I have included a great deal of clarity on both the well- and little-known terms, methods, practices, and themes of beatmaking that are regularly passed around with little consistency. Though there is no such thing as a bad or wrong way of making beats, there are indeed a number of standards — creative and ethical — that have long been recognized within the sampling tradition of hip hop/rap music. In this study I identify and examine these standards.

Third, I want *The Art of Sampling* to act as a gateway book, a conduit that further leads to learning more about the processes that define the beatmaking tradition as a whole. Sampling is inextricably linked to beatmaking, yet the broader beatmaking tradition includes a vast number of dimensions that are worth examining (most of which I cover in *The BeatTips Manual: The Art of Beatmaking, the Hip Hop/Rap Music Tradition, and the Common Composer*). Therefore, it is my hope that this study encourages people to further broaden their understanding of the entire beatmaking tradition and culture.

Fourth, I want to provide sample-based beatmakers with the information and know-how they need to make transformative sample-based music, without the fear of being sued for copyright infringement. Transformative sampling, the form of digital sampling best articulated within and most commonly associated with the hip hop/rap music tradition, is often more than likely a case of fair use. Also along these lines, I hope that *The Art of Sampling* contributes to the larger discussion about copyright law, specifically in terms of how it better reflects the reality of sound collage.

Finally, an important purpose of this book is to restore the art of sampling to a more prominent position in mainstream hip hop/rap music. (There should always be a prominent place for the art of sampling in mainstream hip hop/rap music.) Sample-based beats played a vital role in the rise and expansion of hip hop/rap music, and they helped catapult the careers of many of hip hop/rap's biggest icons and cherished artists. So it's paramount, particularly to the preservation of hip hop/rap music, that sampling maintains a prominent position in mainstream hip hop/rap music.

Other Studies on Sampling

Hip hop/rap introduced sampling to popular culture. And since its rise, most studies covering the art of sampling in the hip hop/rap tradition have tended to be either devoid of a comprehensive examination of all of the mechanics of sampling, or narrowly focused on the implications of copyright law. Some studies have done a commendable job of using an ethnographer's lens to observe some of the creative and social aesthetics of the art of sampling; here, Schloss's (2008) fine work comes to mind. While these observations may have mentioned or even highlighted some of the foundational points and aesthetic characteristics of sampling, they have not included (perhaps they never intended to) a comprehensive examination and analysis of the various methods, processes, and styles that collectively define the art of sampling as a compositional process. Likewise, such studies have not included (again, perhaps they never intended to) an instructional guide for sample-based beatmakers or anyone interested in learning *how to actually make* sample-based beats.

Further, some studies on sampling have focused solely on the implications of copyright law, using a discussion of the actual art of sampling in hip hop/rap music as just one component of a larger "remix" culture. By the way, I understand the remix culture coinage (i.e. Lessig, 2008), how it includes the art of sampling and sample-based music, and how it presents a collective force for change in copyright law. But that said, a *remix* (or *remixing*) is not sampling in the same sense that it's commonly understood within the beatmaking and hip hop/rap music traditions.

So-called "mashups" do not fall under the hip hop/rap tradition's common rubric of sample-based beats. Furthermore, a "remix" is not equivalent to a "sample." A remix is a version, a variant of an original sound recording. A remix involves using the core of the original sound recording, and it always includes the lyrics of the original song, along with additional elements. Therefore, a remix is a derivative work of the original song. Sampling, by contrast, involves the transformative use of snippets from sound recordings — a sample is just a small excerpt from a sound recording that's used in an entirely new song, one with a completely different core and new lyrics. Therefore, the new song that contains the sample is not a derivative work of the sound recording which it sampled.

Thus, we should be careful in how we situate "remix," "sample," and "sampling" in discussions of sample-based beats. Likewise, the work of most mashup artists should not be compared to the work of the likes of DJ Premier, Pete Rock, J Dilla, et al. To do so is, at best, inappropriate; at worst, it's intentionally misleading. Nonetheless, recent sampling studies have curiously (or perhaps not so) began their sampling discussions with an introduction to Girl Talk (Gregg Gillis), the musician widely considered to be the figurehead of mashups.

If some music and copyright scholars believe that Gillis is the best entry point to the art of sampling, so be it. But I find that the term mashup is an unfairly narrow description of what Gillis actually does. There is a conceptual aesthetic that he applies to his work, and he displays a deftness for mining both old and contemporary source material (plus, his recent work with rapper Freeway shows that he's moved away from mashups and deeper into traditional beats). Both things, having a clear and deliberate conceptual aesthetic and a knack for diggin' in the crates (so to speak), are important traits of sample-based beatmakers. Still, what Gillis does — with regards to his mashup works — is not exactly parallel to what sample-based beatmakers traditionally do. Any assertion otherwise demonstrates a lack of fundamental understanding about the sampling tradition of hip hop/rap music.

But forgive my digression....

In those studies that have focused solely on the implications of copyright law, the ability or inability of the current copyright statute to effectively deal with the implications of sampling is the central thrust, and rightfully so. For the broader purposes of these studies, a comprehensive examination of the art of sampling in the hip hop/rap tradition is not warranted.

But in both cases described above, these studies have not been written or lead by beatmakers, sample-based or otherwise. Of course, there is nothing inherently wrong with this. But I argue, and I hope that many would agree, that a voice from a beatmaker, especially a sample-based beatmaker deeply rooted and actively engaged in beatmaking culture, is valuable to any examination or discussion of the art of sampling. Therefore, *The Art of Sampling*, which draws upon portions of my previous work found in editions of *The BeatTips Manual* (2002, 2003, 2007, 2009, 2013) is my second formal entry into the ongoing dialogue about sampling and copyright law.

And considering the fact that most studies on the art of sampling have chosen to focus on one tract or another, usually either the aesthetic tract or the copyright law tract, I wanted to bring forth a study that thoroughly examined the art of sampling, in equal parts, from its methodology, to its historical and aesthetical characteristics, to the implications that it holds for copyright law. More importantly, I wanted to provide an instructional guide for sample-based beatmakers, or anyone interested in learning how to actually make sample-based beats, in terms of the mechanics and nuance of the compositional process. And with regards to copyright law in particular, I wanted to more thoroughly present what implications the art of sampling holds for the interpretation, and perhaps rethinking, of copyright law. Within this trajectory, I wanted to discuss historical concepts of creativity and originality, offer a set of guidelines for a compulsory sound recording license, and provide a plausible framework on how to successfully make beats that meet the fair use threshold.

For those not familiar with the art of sampling, the general presumption is that it is not a musical process; that there isn't any creativity, originality, ingenuity, or skill involved in it; that it is simply the non-discretionary act of "taking other peoples' music;" or that it's not a substitute for traditional musicianship. Partly for this reason, *The Art of Sampling* concentrates on the sampling tradition of hip hop/rap music as its own wholly developed musical process, complete with its own aesthetics, nuances, tropes, principles, and priorities, as well as standards of creativity, ethics, and quality. The analysis in this book debunks the presumption of sampling as a non-musical process, as it provides a highly detailed description of the sampling tradition of hip hop/rap music, both from a musicological and insider's perspective, and shows not only why sampling is a musical process, but why it's more complex than many people realize.

My familiarity with the art of sampling and the beatmaking tradition in general, as well as the African American (Black) music tradition and twentieth-century American popular music, has convinced me that the negative presumptions about the art of sampling, which are born out of the prevailing conventions of Western music theory and issues of race, class, and cultural identity, can only be addressed with evidence that clearly demonstrates sampling as a fully functioning musical process and tradition. That the art of sampling is a musical process, and that sample-based beatmakers represent a new and highly valuable kind of musician, are two central preoccupations of this book.

Part 1
HISTORY

The central problem in analyzing the art of sampling in the hip hop/rap music tradition without first examining, however briefly, hip hop's artistic cultural roots is that you miss the critical aesthetic priorities, sensibilities, and attitudes that are deeply woven into sampling's foundation. Without an analysis of the connection between the four artistic elements of hip hop culture, you can't understand how hip hop is actually a *culture of sampling*.

In a culture of sampling, everything from language to fashion to the fine arts — dance, painting, music — is fair game for borrowing. In a culture of sampling, if it can be converted and flipped (according to the predilections and priorities of a particular community), it will be. This culture of sampling sensibility permeates throughout the entire hip hop culture. For example, there's the b-boy fashion, which took sportswear and casual attire and combined them into a new style of dress that was celebrated for its comfort, flexibility and style. And then there's hip hop terminology, which often converts different words (even tragic ones) into terms of triumph, words like "dope" and "sick" become impressive expressions of magnificent creativity and authenticity. Certainly, all of hip hop culture involves sampling and "flipping" something.

Thus, before I begin a broader examination of the art of sampling in the hip hop/rap music tradition, it's important to first look at the four founding artistic elements of hip hop culture and how they all featured a different but commonly practiced form of sampling. Though each of the original elements (artistic expressions) of hip hop culture represented its own distinct tradition and subculture within the broader hip hop tradition and culture, it must be noted that the development of each of these elements overlapped and cross-fertilized throughout the 1970s and early 1980s. It's widely recognized that all of the early hip hop pioneers participated in at least two (if not all) of the four elements of hip hop. Therefore, here it is necessary to spend some time exploring the origins and development of each element as well as the development of hip hop overall. So what follows in this chapter is a brief historical breakdown of each of the four original artistic elements of hip hop culture, along with an examination of the aesthetics, tenets, priorities, values, and principles that underscore all of the elements of hip hop collectively.

Chapter 1

A Culture of Sampling
An Overview of the Four Elements of Hip Hop

There is a culture of sampling that underscores communities that are forced to undergo catastrophic circumstances. In fact, one prominent result of an oppressed people and their isolated, fragmented community is that its residents learn to incorporate (salvage) any element within and outside of their environment that they see fit to forge and fortify their culture. The fragmentation caused by the South Bronx Disaster[1] directly led to a culture of sampling in which residents of the South Bronx (and other similarly hard-hit cities across the United States) learned to take pieces from the mainstream American society, then convert them in accordance to their own needs and values.

"Where They Jamming At?"
Street and Party Cultures Collide

Partying is one of the most vital cultural events that take place within ghettos.[2] In ghettos, parties serve two very important functions. On one hand, parties allow for a temporary relief or

---

[1] The South Bronx Disaster refers to the harsh socio-economic backdrop of hip hop's origins. The South Bronx Disaster was created by a combination of socially disastrous events that took place in New York City between the 1950s and 1970s. For a thorough examination of the South Bronx Disaster, see The BeatTips Manual, chapter 1.

[2] Hip hop culture did not grow out of the street gang era of 1970s New York City, as some writers and historians have implied. The street gangs, in particular, the organization of the street gangs, served as one conduit (there were others) for which hip hop was able to travel and mobilize into one formidable force. They represented a street level organization of would-be party goers. Street gangs may have committed crimes and acts of violence, but their favorite past time was partying.

escape from the harsh realities of an impoverished environment. On the other hand, parties form a celebration of the resilience of the human spirit in the face of hopelessness and despair. Thus, aside from the conditions of the South Bronx Disaster itself, the other two primary sources of consistent familiarity for its residents were parties and music. Throughout the burning and destruction of the Bronx (1969 to 1979), impromptu parties or "jams" and music provided much needed healing and entertainment.[3]

But what is particularly important and distinct about the 1970s South Bronx party scene is how it was further bolstered and unified through the arts and talents of its party-goers. To be sure, there were parties before that fateful day in 1973, where the first official hip hop party (or coming together) took place, as legend has it. There were parties held at other community and recreational centers, ballrooms, churches, school gymnasiums, and street blocks. In fact, even by DJ Kool Herc's own admission, he played nothing new at that initial "hip hop" gathering, that he simply gave the people what they liked, and all of the partygoers took to the floor, knowing exactly how to *move* to it. But it was this one party, and many others like it (especially the ones given by Grandmaster Flash and Afrika Bambaataa), that soon followed that served as the initial breeding ground and force that would merge the individual art forms together into one mighty sub-culture that would soon come to be known as hip hop.

The Unification of the Four (Original) Elements of Hip Hop Culture

The culture that would eventually be dubbed "hip hop" was actually brewing before the Sedgewick Rec Party in 1973. But historians love clear benchmarks and timelines. Moreover, historians adore the prospect of assigning definitive historical developments to key figureheads. And so it would seem, the fewer the number of key events and figureheads, the easier it is for historians to draw

---

[3] In fact, it is this curious dichotomy, "fun" for black and Latino youth *within* the context of survival, that helps fuel the "hip hop sensibility."

a clean narrative. This is why the story of hip hop, for better or worse, always *neatly* begins with the Kool Herc/Sedgewick Rec Party storyline. Accordingly, the story of Kool Herc DJ'ing at the Sedgwick Rec Room on August 11, 1973 has been offered up by hip hop historians, prime hip hop architects, and common fans alike, with such reverence that it has risen to the level of romantic legend.

But even if one does just a surface read of the 1973 Sedgwick Rec party storyline, it's clear that the event didn't emerge as if Kool Herc had said, "Hey, I'm going to throw a 'hip hop' party." And according to Kool Herc, the party wasn't even his idea, it was actually the idea of his older sister, Cindy Campbell. As the story goes, Cindy hired her brother (Herc) to DJ the party, which was either a birthday celebration or back-to-school affair (or perhaps both). So one of the biggest misconceptions about hip hop culture is that it was the initial product of one lone force: hip hop music, and one lone person: Kool Herc.

Though the music of hip hop did indeed drive the entire culture as it further developed, hip hop/rap music did not spawn *each* element of hip hop culture. There were many simmering creative impulses leading up to that first hip hop party. The hip hop movement formulated with a wide range of expressions that were moving parallel to one another in the South Bronx and other areas around New York City (most notably Brooklyn) at the same time.

So it should be understood that hip hop culture is not the story of a single event or invention of a single person. Instead, it's the story of the coalescence (unification) and formalization of seed elements that were already present within a community devastated by the South Bronx Disaster. B-boying (later more commonly known as "break dancing" or "breakin'"), DJ'ing, rapping (MC'ing), and graffiti writing, all sprang up from the same cultural and social conditions. And the development of each of these elements overlapped and cross-fertilized.[4]

---

[4] The notion of "cross fertilization" is particularly important, as nearly all of the earliest pioneers participated in more than one of hip hop's artforms. Many were DJ's and b-boys, graffiti writers, *and* rappers. Thus, all of the pioneers had a keen awareness of each of the art forms that eventually came together to comprise the collective hip hop culture. It's important to note that Kool Herc was first a graffiti writer *before* he became a DJ. This fact is significant for two reasons. First, it demonstrates that Herc, like all of the

Graffiti[5]

In New York City between the 1950s and late 1960s, graffiti was mostly used by street gangs to mark their turf (territory) or by some political activists to make statements. However, the underground art form that would take hold in New York City actually had its roots in Philadelphia, PA in the late 1960s. The two writers from Philly who are credited with the first "conscious bombing efforts" are CORNBREAD and COOL EARL. It's unclear exactly how the Philly concept of graffiti made its way to New York City. But by 1971, it was apparent that the form was rising.[6]

In 1971, the *New York Times* published an article on TAKI 183, a teenage graffiti writer from Washington Heights. The article was very influential in that it not only made TAKI 183 (real name Demitrius) the first graffiti writer in New York City to be recognized outside of the newly formed subculture, it also helped push forward an already growing underground New York City graffiti movement. As the article noted, TAKI 183 worked as a foot messenger who, being on the subway frequently, wrote motion "tags" in subway stations and on subway cars as well as buildings all across New York City.[7] But TAKI 183 certainly was not the first graff writer in New York City, nor was he even considered to be one of the graffiti kings. During this time, JULIO 204 was most widely credited as being one of the first writers of significance. After noticing JULIO 204's tag, TAKI 183 took up writing his name and street number (with a wide marker) wherever he went. Other significant writers

---

early hip hop pioneers, was skilled in more than one of the four original elements of hip hop. Second, it demonstrates that as a graffiti writer, something distinctly American at the time, Herc found his first real artistic apprenticeship in the underground New York City art form of graffiti, not DJ'ing. This fact is crucial because it clearly indicates that by the time Kool Herc took up DJ'ing (some seven years after arriving in the Bronx), his direct musical influences were American, not Jamaican.

[5] The common technical definition of graffiti is described as images or lettering scratched, scrawled, painted or marked in any manner on something, typically walls, trains, and subway cars. Graffiti itself is centuries old.

[6] For an extended history of graffiti see: @149st (http://www.at149st.com/history.html). Also, see: *Subway Graffiti: An Aesthetic Study of Graffiti on the Subway System of New York City, 1970-1978*, by Jack Stewart; also see *Subway Art* by Henry Chalfant and Martha Cooper; and "History of Graf," daveyd.com.

[7] *New York Times*, "'Taki 183' Spawns Pen Pals," July 21, 1971.

who appeared in 1971 were LEE 163, SLY II, and PHASE 2, LEE 163's cousin.[8]

Between 1971 and 1974, the first pioneering period of graffiti, hundreds of new graffiti writers emerged, and the art form continued to grow in volume and, more importantly, style and complexity throughout the five boroughs of New York City. Tags were the norm for most writers, and competition was a major driving force. Writers competed with each other all over the city, seeing who could get the most tags up as possible. At first, buses, handball courts, schoolyards, and other locations were hit, but as graffiti grew more competitive and writers grew more daring, subway cars became a favorite target. Not long after, the concept and method of "bombing," painting subway cars as they sat parked in train yards, was born.

During this time, writers experimented with script and calligraphic styles. Flourishes, stars, crowns, and other similar designs also marked the earlier part of this pioneering period. It was also during this period when writers began to experiment with the size (scale) of tags. Using the creative commons of their craft, writers began to create tags that were larger, with letters that were thicker, and outlines with additional colors. After writers began to use caps from other aerosol products, they learned that the width of the spray could be increased. This discovery, widely credited to SUPER KOOL 223, who used the cap from an oven cleaner can, led directly to giant signatures known as "masterpieces" (or "pieces," short for masterpiece), large-scale visual themes and/or statements, with bigger letters and bolder styles and ideas. Credit for the development of the first masterpieces is commonly given to SUPER KOOL 223 (of the Bronx) and WAP (of Brooklyn). Soon, pieces began to appear on the entire height of subway cars, these pieces were known as "top-to-bottoms;" RIFF 170 is credited for having revolutionized top-to-bottoms. During this period of intense

---

[8] History of Graffiti, Part I," @149th Street (http://www.at149st.com/history.html). There was a burgeoning graffiti movement growing on the streets of Brooklyn at this very same time, with FRIENDLY FREDDIE being one of the most recognizable Brooklyn writers at the time. Also see: Stephen Hager, *Hip Hop: The Illustrated History of Break Dancing, Rap Music, and Graffiti* (New York: St. Martin's Press, 1984), 13.

"sampling," style became the most important aspect of graffiti, as it was more prestigious for writers to create original lettering styles. Lesser writers who merely imitated others became known as "toys," and writers whose tags were *just* local and not "all city" (scene in all five boroughs) were described as DGAs: "Doesn't Get Around."[9]

With competition steadily driving the movement, forcing less talented writers out of the limelight, styles began to move away from the typical tag pieces. The Broadway style, introduced by TOPCAT 126 (who had moved from Philly to New York City), emerged. The Broadway style led to block letters and leaning letters. Then came the bubble letters, a style first developed by and credited to PHASE 2. It was the combination of PHASE 2's work and competition from other style masters that began what became known as the style wars. "Style wars" was the term used to describe the explosion of writers who took ideas from each other, improved upon them, and took them to a new level. During this period, pieces became incredibly more complex in style, especially in size, depth, and meaning. Finally, by 1974, works with scenery, illustrations, and cartoon characters, popularized by TRACY 168, CLIFF 159, BLADE ONE, started to appear.

It was also during this time when writers began gathering in loose-knit groups that mirrored small artistic professional associations. Meetings among writers were held at various "'writers' corners" around the city. The two most prominent of which were located in the Bronx and Manhattan: the writers' corner at a subway station at 149th Street and the Grand Concourse in the South Bronx; and the writer's corner at 188th and Audubon Avenue in upper Manhattan. Wherever writers gathered, they shared sketch ideas from their personal art books, compared notes on various lettering styles, and generally talked shop about their craft. Through their various writers meetings and gatherings and artistic protocols, graffiti writers, like b-boys, soon developed their own slang and fashion styles.

It is widely considered by most graffiti historians that by 1974, all of the graffiti standards (or graffiti's foundation) had been

---

[9] *Ibid*, 19-24.

established. That being said, the period between 1975-77 marks the time when the heaviest bombing in New York City took place, no doubt due in some part to the New York City's mid-1970s fiscal crises. During this time, "whole car" pieces became standard fair, and the "throw up" became the definitive form of bombing. The throw up, a style based on bubble lettering, is a piece (hastily rendered, usually just two letters) that consists of just a simple outline and a fill-in. Just like competition had driven writers in 1971 to put up as many tags as they could, competition for the most throw ups exploded throughout the city between 1975 and 77. Incidentally, during this time the number of graffiti crews increased dramatically.[10]

Between 1978 and 1981, there was a graffiti revival of sorts, brought on by the new style wars between major writing crews like UA, CIA (founded by style master DONDI), TDS, TCF, RTW, TMT, and more. But this period also marked the final wave of bombing before the New York City Transit Authority ratcheted up their efforts to end graffiti on trains. Though graffiti writing would continue on through the mid-1980s, by 1985 the New York City street graffiti culture would decline.[11]   However, due, in large part to the efforts of graffiti writer and sharp self-promoter Fab 5 Freedy, graffiti would find a new audience in the downtown New York City art scene.[12]

Finally, it must be noted that the New York City subway system played a tremendous role in the development of New York City's graffiti culture. Both in terms as a de facto art "canvas" and more importantly, as a line of communication and a unifying element for all of the different graffiti writers and separate graffiti developments (movements) throughout the five boroughs.[13]

---

[10] *Ibid.*

[11] There are many reasons for the decline of graffiti culture in the mid-1980s, notably the stepped-up anti-graffiti efforts of the Transit Authority, stiffer penalties for graffiti, drug usage, and the allure of hip hop/rap music as a "safer" and more profitable career path.

[12] Fab 5 Freddy's efforts in the downtown New York City art scene of the mid-1980s not only helped popularize graffiti in the mainstream, it also helped break rap music and hip hop to a wider (white) audience.

[13] Hager, 19. Graffiti culture is parallel to beatmaking culture, in that it is quite racially and ethnically inclusive. Although during the first pioneering graffiti period (1971-1974) many writers were Puerto Rican, it's a little-known fact that most of the first writers in

B-Boying ("Break Dancing") and DJ'ing

Dance has always played an integral part in the development of the African American (Black) music tradition. But the explosive new dance style that was taking hold in New York City in the early 1970s was quite different. "Going off," "burning," or the "good foot" (named after the James Brown song of the same name) were the names used to describe what would become "b-boying," later on widely known as "break dancing." "Going off" was a dance style that featured an erratic assortment of floor drops and spins and other James Brown-inspired leg movements. Dancers who "got wild" would wait for the "break," the part in the record where the song is stripped down to just the high energy of the rhythm section, just the drums, guitar or bass licks, maybe some additional syncopated percussive elements, no melody. Once they heard the break, they would get out on the dance floor and "go wild."[14]

At the same time dancers were "getting wild," Kool Herc was building a name as a DJ. And after seeing these dancers go wild whenever he played the breaks, Herc began calling them "break boys," which he shortened to "b-boys." In the dialogue between Kool Herc and the b-boys (and b-girls), it was the b-boys who perhaps had the most influence. B-boys pushed Herc just as much as he pushed them. But in addition to helping the b-boys further develop their art form, Herc also found that by using two turn tables, two copies of the same record, and a DJ mixer, he could not only keep the b-boys engaged, he could also keep the party going for everybody, *without* interruption.

Herc wasn't the first American DJ to use two turntables. Club DJs, especially New York City disco (early disco) DJs were already using two turntables before Herc. However, the club/disco DJs played one record at a time; that is, they let one record play all the way through before playing the next one. But it was Herc who first came up with the style of only playing the breaks continuously

---

the South Bronx were black.

[14] It's certainly worth observing that throughout the development of the b-boy dance form, dancers continued to draw their cue from a rich musical heritage that had long valued rhythm and breaks.

with two turntables.

Herc was directly influenced by a South Bronx DJ named John Brown. While still in high school, Herc (not yet Kool Herc) used to hang out at a small nightclub called the Plaza Tunnel. By his own admission, Herc spent time at the Plaza Tunnel soaking up the records (most early funk) that John Brown played, as well as the style of DJ'ing he was exhibiting.[15] It was this experience and interaction at the Plaza Tunnel that led directly to the style of DJ'ing that Herc showcased at the infamous Sedgwick party in 1973 and other subsequent parties.

As Herc, and other DJ's like Grandmaster Flash and Afrika Bambaataa, continued to pioneer the hip hop DJ style (Herc's style), specifically, the elongation of the break of early funk records (the "merry-go-round" technique), the b-boy culture continued to solidify and become more definitive. B-boys would create "ciphers," dance rings (circles) in which b-boys would enter one at a time and compete against each other. Now that the music had been extended, the energy level had gone up, and more intense competition sparked the creation of new moves. Early b-boys like the Nigger Twins (Kevin and Keith, who were only 12 years old when they attended their first Herc party), the Zulu Kings, and "Clark Kent" (of the Bronx) continuously borrowed moves from each other and used the *extended* break to experiment and come up with new moves. During this time, spins became more prominent and footwork grew more complex. Floor drops, where b-boys dropped to the ground and popped back up again *on beat*, became basic stuff for all b-boys worth their weight. Arm- and hand-use for body support developed quickly; freezes and leg shuffles became big; knee spins and butt spins emerged. And around this same time, out in Brooklyn another early funk-based dance style known as the "Brooklyn Uprock" or "Brooklyn Rock" (soon it would come to be known as "uprocking" in the South Bronx) was serving as the foundation for another pivotal dance movement. Each of these moves, and others based upon them, eventually became part of the definitive architecture of the b-boy dance style.

---

[15] Hager, 31.

And just as graffiti was developing into its own subculture with its own slang, fashion, and crews, b-boying was quickly morphing into its own subculture, complete with its own slang, fashion (at first jeans and sneakers, then sportswear, usually warm-up suits and sneakers), and crews. B-boying was also just like graffiti, in that it "was all about battling…Breakin' on somebody was the attitude you had to have if you called yourself a b-boy. You had to be ready to battle at the drop of a hat, whether you were on the street, in a park, or at a jam, and you had to be on your shit if you dared to compete."[16]

By 1977, many DJs had followed Kool Herc's lead, however, none more notable than the first two who appeared directly after him — Grandmaster Flash and Afrika Bambaataa, respectively. Although Herc was the first DJ to use turntables as instruments, it was Grandmaster Flash who took the art of hip hop DJing to the next level. While Herc had developed the style of elongating the break, he used the "needle-drop" technique. That is to say, he dropped the needle of the turntable on the groove of the record where he *thought* the part he wanted started. Flash moved past the needle-drop and developed techniques and methods for *blending* records, mixing them, and cutting the beats together all *on beat*. Rather than simply keep records playing continuously, Flash wanted to create a continuous groove, one that was made up of all the "reorganized pieces of songs" he'd found. He wanted to "keep the beat." That is, he wanted to figure out a way to start and stop records on the left and right turntables without listeners knowing where one record stopped and the next one started.[17]

Grandmaster Flash became the first DJ to actually *physically* put his hands on the vinyl while the turntable's platter was spinning, giving him a level of control previously unrealized by other DJs. Using his hands to wind the records back and forward, a technique he dubbed the "spin back," and keying in on the *marks* (pencil lines at first) that he placed on the labels of his records, Grandmaster Flash developed what he called the

---

[16] Grandmaster Flash and David Ritz, *The Adventures of Grandmaster Flash: My Life, My Beats* (New York: Broadway Books, 2008), 39.
[17] *Ibid*, 54-84.

"clock theory." Soon, he took the clock theory further and developed the "quik mix theory," which was a collective of his own techniques for quickly cutting back and forth between records *on beat*, making one musical passage flow seamlessly to the next. Flash's "quik mix theory" included a number of firsts, but it most notably included the "spin back," a method for quickly rewinding records, and the "punch phase," a method for *punching* a record forward, right on the break.

As Kool Herc was winding down his career, and while Grandmaster Flash was pioneering the use of turntables as instruments, Afrika Bambaataa was making a name for himself as a cultural unifier and DJ, one whose stash of records knew no bounds. Although the name "hip hop" is curiously credited to being first used by Lovebug Starski, it was Afrika Bambaataa (ca. 1975-76) who first (consciously) used "hip hop" specifically to describe the type of jams (parties) he was throwing. All of Bambaataa's jams were well-attended by graffiti writers, b-boys, DJs, and rappers alike. And thus, it was mostly because of Afrika Bambaataa that "hip hop" came to (informally at first) describe the collective culture (movement) that encompassed the four separate New York City underground street elements (i.e. art forms): graffiti writing, b-boying, DJ'ing, and rapping.

While a Grandmaster Flash music set was characterized by turntable wizardry and precision, an Afrika Bamabaataa set personified an eclectic musical mix. Although Bambaataa certainly played funk music, he also experimented with other forms of music, particularly late 1960s and early 70s rock.

Finally, even though Kool Herc, Grandmaster Flash, Afrika Bambaataa, and other pivotal DJs of the time ultimately developed distinct hip hop DJ performance styles (all based upon Herc's original innovation), it must be remembered that the parties that each threw between 1973 and 1978 were really more like events, wherein all four of the elements of hip hop culture were always well-represented.

The Late Years of B-Boying and the Birth of Break Dancing

After developing the b-boy style for more than five years, many blacks stopped by 1978. But it was at this time that more Puerto Ricans were just starting to get into b-boying. By 1979, b-boying, which had once been a movement almost exclusively practiced by blacks, had become a new movement that was now lead by Puerto Ricans. New crews like Rockwell Association, TDK, TBB, and the Rock Steady Crew (founded by Jimmy D and JoJo) emerged, taking over where the earliest b-boys (i.e. Zulu Kings, Profile, and The Nigger Twins) had left off. During this period, b-boying moved forward, then suddenly in 1980, it began to enter a new decline. That's when 14-year old Richie Colon stepped up and changed everything.[18]

Having grown up in the Bronx most of his life, Richie Colon moved with his family to Manhattan in 1980. Before he had moved to Manhattan, he had spent two years practicing the b-boy style in hopes of one day joining Rockwell Association. He had changed his name to Crazy Legs, and he was now ready to join the ranks of master b-boys. But Rockwell Association and Rock Steady Crew were no longer dancing as much as they had been in the previous two years. So Crazy Legs was forced to find his own crew. After getting permission from Jimmy D (co-founder of Rock Steady Crew), Crazy Legs started a Manhattan branch of Rock Steady Crew. It was Crazy Legs and this branch of Rock Steady Crew that would bring the most fame to the RSC name.

The early and mid-1980s brought the advent of the so-called "power moves," these were dance moves that emphasized more spinning action and gymnastics. From this period, dances like the infamous "windmill" (credited to Crazy Legs), and "1990s" (one-hand-stand spin) emerged. The early and mid-1980s also brought a level of media coverage of b-boying that had previously been unimaginable. This is when the Rock Steady Crew, along with another pivotal New York City b-boy crew, New York City Breakers, and

---

[18] Hager, 86-89. Also, information extracted from interviews with various 1979s Bronx and Brooklyn residents, specifically my close family friend, Canell Johnson.

movies like *Style Wars* (1982), *Wild Style* (1982), *Beat Street* (1984), *Breakin'* (1984), and *Breakin' 2: Electric Boogaloo* (1984), combined to spark a break dance craze all across America.

While b-boying was developing in the South Bronx and "Brooklyn uprocking" was happening in Brooklyn, (the latter dance form unifying into the b-boy movement), there was a parallel dance movement, "locking" and "popping," happening on the west coast. Like b-boying in the South Bronx, locking and popping were inspired by funk music as well. But it should be noted that early west coast funk, which too focused on the groove, was slightly different than east coast funk.

From out of this separate early 1970s "funk movement" in Los Angeles, California emerged Don Campbell, aka "Don Cambellock," originator of "locking" (ca. 1970-73). Locking, a dance somewhat based on the "funky chicken," another popular dance at the time, featured a locking motion of the joints of one's arms, and the bending of one's elbows. Soon after introducing locking, Cambellock formed a group called The Lockers. The Lockers were very influential in that they pioneered a number of new moves and other dances that made up the locking repertoire, including: "knee drops," "butt drops," the "stop n' go," "the fancies," "the lock," and "scooby doos." And, as with some of the later b-boys of New York City, some of the west coast lockers incorporated dives, drop downs, and other gymnastic moves.[19]

"Popping" was introduced in 1976. Originated by Sam "Boogaloo Sam" Soloman, one of the three founders of The Electronic Boogaloo Lockers, popping was a dance that featured the tick-like contraction movement of hands, arms, neck, chest, and legs, which gave off a mechanical or smooth robotic effect. There are conflicting stories as to how locking and popping made their way to the Bronx and the rest of New York City, but it is widely regarded that the dance was picked up (and initially misnamed

---

[19] Information extracted from interviews with various b-boys and dancers, including King Uprock, Mariella Gross, and Canell Johnson. Also see: Jorge "Popmaster Fabel" Pabon, "Physical Graffiti: The History of Hip Hop Dance," DaveyD.com. Further, see: episodes of television dance show *Soul Train* (ca. 1976), as well as other television shows of the same period, including: *Dick Van Dyke Variety Show*; and *The Carol Burnett Show*.

"electric boogie") by dancers in New York City, after groups like The Lockers and The Electronic Boogaloo Lockers appeared on 1970s television shows like *Soul Train, Saturday Night Live, The Dick Van Dyke Variety Show*, and the popular sitcom *What's Happening*.

By the mid-1980s, mainstream media had grouped together most of these dance forms, both from the east and west coasts, and dubbed it all "break dancing." Soon, break dancing became over-commercialized, and all of the separate art forms that comprised hip hop dance lost emphasis on their root structures and nuances. More specifically, the essence and spirit of b-boying culture faded and seemingly disappeared. (More than twenty years later, however, some elements of b-boy culture is thriving once again.)

Rapping (MC'ing)

Rapping's Pedigree

To truly understand the force that is rapping, one must accept the conceptual heritage and material artifacts and their authentic significations in history, origin and social intercourse, and orature.[20] The roots of the art of rapping go back much farther than most people recognize. In fact, rapping, a clear example of the broad black vernacular tradition, is a continuance of the African American "toasting" tradition, an oral tradition of lively verbal art that stretches back from the Reconstruction Era through the jazz age and the social movements of the late 1960s and on through today. A uniquely urban phenomenon, the African American toasting tradition — *not*

---

[20] For context and reference, see Wole Soyinka, "The Critic and Society: Barthes, Leftocracy and Other Mythologies," *Black Literature & Literary Theory* (New York and London: Methuen, 1984), 44. In his essay, Soyinka illuminates the problem that arises in academia when *critics* of African literary theory attempt to *teach it*. Specifically, Soyinka points out that because these critics of the African literary tradition "refuse to accept the conceptual heritage or even material artifacts and their authentic significations... as valid dialectical quantities" for any literary theory, the "roots" of African literary are mis-taught, and students are ultimately "imprisoned" by the subsequent mis-teachings. I find the same parallel in the ways in which the various elements of hip hop, specifically rapping and beatmaking, are taught. Because many contemporary teachers willfully refuse to accept the roots of rapping and beatmaking, new rappers and beatmakers are often imprisoned by mis-teachings, and are, therefore, prone to misrepresenting these two art forms.

to be confused with the Jamaican toasting tradition of the late 1960s and early 1970s[21] — is a dynamic poetic performance art, traditionally learned directly from or by studying other "toasters" and through intense verbal training. African American forms of "toasts," which often feature boasts, "trickster" tales, adventures, and social commentary, are typically laced with slang and profanity and center around some form of heroics or uplift made by a central black character who *beats the odds* (a tragic event, a villain, etc.) by using his wits and common skills. Often in toasts, the central character "top talks" (out talks) a clear opponent, often a dangerous and/ or tyrannical authority figure. Also, within this toasting tradition, versioning, improvisation, and using one's individual style is highly valued. Here, it's worth mentioning that while some women have participated in the African American toasting tradition, toasts were usually performed by black males. Finally, I should point out that before rapping emerged, the three most common forms of African American toasts were: (1) "signifyin' toasts;" (2) "radio DJ toasts;" and (3) "hustler toasts."

"Signifyin' toasts," which appeared in both print and music and often performed a capella, stem from the African American vernacular practice of "signifyin'(g). Signifyin' describes a verbal process of using the direct (denotative and figurative) meanings of words to say something *else* indirectly. Signifyin' is often used to parody or satirize a character, theme, subject, or event. More importantly, signifyin' emphasizes the connotative (secondary), context-bound significance of words or expressions in addition to their explicit or primary meanings, which is accessible only to those who share and/or well-understand the unique cultural values of a given speech community. Signifyin' involves the conscious use of specific language and/or slang and concepts specifically

---

[21] The Jamaican toasting tradition of the 1970s has wrongly been considered by some to have played a major role in the art of rapping in hip hop. But this can not be more further from the truth. Presmumably, because Kool Herc migrated from Jamaica, some historians and musicologists have incorrectly drawn parallels of the separate Jamaican toasting movement with the African American toasting tradition's clear influence on rapping and hip hop. Despite evidence that refutes the theory that Jamaican toasting influenced rapping, including Kool Herc's own testimony that it did not, this false historical account is still maintained by many today. But the truth is that the Jamaican toasting tradition played absolutely no role in the development of rapping or the hip hop style of music.

understood by a given speech community. In signifyin' toasts, performers tell "trickster tales" in which central characters use the aforementioned verbal strategy to cleverly tap the *direct* meanings of words while summoning *indirect* meanings, often for the purpose of obtaining "hidden" but intended outcomes.[22]

"Radio DJ toasts," which were pioneered in the 1950s by Philadelphia, PA radio disc jockey Douglas "Jocko" Henderson, of "JOCKO" & The Rocket Ship Show fame,[23] were quite different than signifyin' toasts. Unlike signifyin' toasts, radio DJ toasts were typically not too narrative in nature, and they were most often not characterized by a central character, but instead, simply a "hip," improvised telling of the moment. Radio DJ toasts were rapid, quick-witted radio "raps" (rhymes) or "skats," usually simple one- and two-liners filled with "hip" urban slang. Radio DJ toasts were impromptu and performed *throughout* radio shows, but particularly before and after records were played. DJs like Jocko would use toasts to help keep their shows moving or to boast about themselves, their radio shows, and/or the hit records they played. Often, Jocko would say things like, "Eee-tiddlee-dock, this is the Jock! Back on the scene with the record machine," or "Oo-papa-doo, how do you do?" "He ain't mean, he just wanna be seen;" "Mommy-Os and Daddy-Os;" "The Ace from outta space;" and similar toasts all exemplify the kinds of toasts black radio DJs performed and their limitless ability to extemporize hip rhyming slang. Black radio DJs borrowed from each other and used their toasts to build up their radio shows and to communicate in a more personal way with their listeners.

By the early 1970s, there were a number of black radio DJs who performed radio toasts, but the clear leader in 1970s New York City radio was Frankie Crocker. Frankie Crocker "the Chief Rocker", who was also the MC (Master of Ceremonies) at the

---

[22] Two of the most popular African American signifyin' toasts are "Shine and the Titanic," and "The Signifying Monkey." In "Shine and the Titanic," a black stoker named Shine uses his wit and common abilities to both escape the sinking of the Titanic and the threat of a hungry whale. In "The Signifying Monkey," the Signifying Monkey in the jungle cleverly dupes a Lion. See: Henry Louis Gates, Jr., *Black Literature and Literary Theory* (New York and London: Methuen, 1984), 288.

[23] Other important pioneering black radio DJs of the time who performed radio DJ toasts include Maurice "Hot Rod" Hulbert, Jr. and Rufus Thomas. It should further be noted that the radio DJ toast tradition was pioneered first on rhythm and blues radio stations.

Apollo during the mid- and late 1970s, said toasts like, "More dips in your hips, more glide in your stride;" and "If Frankie Crocker isn't on your radio, your radio isn't really on." Frankie Crocker, and later some New York City disco radio DJs, would have a role in the development of rapping in hip hop, as early rappers certainly borrowed from them.

"Hustler toasts," which reached prominence in black street-corner culture and black prison culture between the mid-1960s and early 1970s, shares more similarities with signifyin' toasts than radio DJ toasts. Hustler toasts are mostly narrative and carry a message; but that's where the similarities stop. While signifyin' toasts often emphasize the connotative and are indirect, hustler toasts usually emphasize the straight-forward (often confrontational) and are mostly direct. While signifyin' toasts are often *versions* of well-known toasts, hustler toasts are often the true accounts of the individuals who perform them. Finally, while signifyin' toasts are generally humorous and contain profanity in a passive context, humor (when it is used) in hustler toasts is often sinister, and profanity is used much more aggressively or matter-factly. Although all three common forms of African American toasts played a role in the development of rapping in hip hop, no form had more direct influence than the hustler toast. And the most important hustler toasts to hit the streets of the South Bronx was James Brown's version of "King Heroin," and the infamous Lightnin' Rod album, *Hustlers Convention*.

Released in 1973, and performed by Jalal Nuriddin, under the pseudonym, "Lightnin' Rod," *Hustlers Convention* became the single biggest inspiration for the early formulation of rapping in hip hop. Set to the music of Kool and The Gang, Bernard Purdie, Billy Preston, and Colonel Dupree, *Hustlers Convention* masterfully demonstrates the African American toasting and rapping traditions. The album contains a series of "rap songs" (prison-style toasts) that tell the story of two hustlers, Sport and Spoon, as they hustle their way through the ghetto one summer. Each rap spares no punches, as stories of drug use, dice and pool games, sexual episodes with random women, drug sales, and shoot-outs color the balance of the album. Told through the first-hand account of Sport, the story begins with Spoon coming home from jail. It ends with Sport going back to jail, where after "twelve years of time," he realizes that he was just a "nickel and dime hustler," and that the "real hustlers are those rippin' off billions from those millions who are programmed to think they can win."[24]

There can be no doubt that James Brown, and the album, *Hustlers Convention*, were the two biggest and most direct influences on the development of early rapping in hip hop; most (if not all) of the earliest hip hop/rap pioneers have maintained this. In fact, the first hip hop/rap music architect and pioneer, DJ Kool Herc, plainly said as much more than 25 years ago: "The inspiration for rap is James Brown and the album *Hustlers Convention*."[25]

Rapping in Hip Hop

Early on in the development of hip hop, rapping was very simple, and rappers (MCs as they were also known then), were primarily a sideshow to the DJ. The first hip hop toasts (raps) ever performed were by Kool Herc, who, inspired by James Brown and the album *Hustlers Convention*, would say impromptu toasts while DJ'ing. To be certain, the toasts Herc performed were not long or particularly narrative, but instead, they were simple expressions designed to keep the energy of the party going. He would say things like, "Yes, yes, y'all, it's the serious, serio-so joint*ski*," or "YES-YES, Y'ALL! TO-THE BEAT, Y'ALL." He would also say

---

[24] *Hustlers Convention*, (United Artists, 1973). At the time of the release of *Hustler's Convention*, Jalal Nuriddin was the leader of The Last Poets, a group of Harlem poets and musicians who earned acclaim through their searing social commentary and oft-described black nationalist sympathies. It's further worth noting that prior to becoming the leader of The Last Poets, Nuriddin was, in fact, incarcerated.

[25] Hager, 45-49. Famed early rapping pioneer Grandmaster Caz of the Cold Crush Brothers makes a similar unwavering claim: "I knew the entire *Hustler's Convention* by heart. That was rap..." See also, Toop, 53-58: "James Brown was the most direct connection between soulful testifying and Bronx poetry... His position as spokesman for black consciousness and minister of super-heavy funk might have been on the wane by the '70s, but for the b boys he was still Soul Brother Number One." Accounts by Herc, Caz, and other early hip hop architects contradict the romantic notion that rap comes from or is inspired by African griots. Some scholars maintain that rap is directly linked to the African griot tradition, but the immediate roots of rap say otherwise.

expressions that singled out the names of some of the party-goers, combining these shout-out-like expressions with rhymes and some of the well-known slang of the day: "As I scan the place, I see the very familiar face…of my mellow;" or "Wallace Dee in the house. Wallace Dee, freak for me." Soon, Herc added Jay Cee and Clark Kent (The Herculords) to the show, and the Herculords would rap the same type of toasts first performed by Herc. [26]

Interestingly enough, it was another DJ who pushed rapping in the direction that eventually lead to modern rapping. In an effort to keep pace with Kool Herc, Grandmaster Flash — borrowing from Herc — wrote a rhyme (sometime between 1974 and 75) that would prove even more influential than Herc's initial toasts. The rhyme went like this: "You dip, dive and socialize. We're trying to make you realize. That we are qualified to rectify that burning… desire…to boogie." Hardly the sort of lyrical dexterity that we sometimes recognize in today's rhymes, but what Flash's rhyme did was open up the possibilities for *how* rhymes could be written and performed.

Grandmaster Flash was not consciously trying to advance the art of rapping, he was just acting out of necessity. According to Flash, "vocal entertainment became necessary to keep the crowd under control."[27] Flash soon put together a group of rappers to be part of his DJ show. The group, The Furious Five, which was composed of rappers Cowboy (Keith Wiggins), Kid Creole (Nathaniel Glover), Eddie "Mr. Ness/Scorpio" Morris, Guy "Rahiem" Williams, and last but not least, Creole's younger brother, Melle Mel (Melvin Glover), would quickly become one of the most pivotal rap groups of all time, almost immediately sparking similar groups like the Cold Crush Brothers and The Treacherous Three.

Between 1975 and 1979,[28] rap styles were an assortment of

---

[26] Hager, 47. Also, Flash and Ritz, 102.

[27] *Ibid*, 47.

[28] There were a countless number of rappers who helped advance the art of rapping, but some of the most notable rappers of the period include: The Furious Five (Melle Mel, Cowboy, Rahiem, Mr. Ness, and Kid Creole), The Cold Crush Brothers (Grandmaster Caz, Whipper Whip, Dot-A-Rock, Easy A.D., DJ Charlie Chase, Kay Gee, DJ Tony Tone, J.D.L., and Mr. Tee), Double Trouble (Lil Rodney Cee and KK Rockwell), The Treacherous Three (Kool Moe Dee, Special K, and LA Sunshine), Funky Four Plus One More (Lil Rodney Cee, KK Rockwell, Sha Rock, Keith Keith, and Jazzy Jeff with

party rhymes, nursery rhymes, boasts, and comic book inspired joke rhymes. Rap routines, like the ones first performed by The Furious Five, became more elaborate and more entertaining in the late 1970s. The quintessential "rap routine" was perhaps most personified (and perfected) by The Cold Crush Brothers and The Fantastic Five. Just as with graffiti, b-boying, and DJ'ing, rapping became increasingly more competitive as rappers borrowed from one another and created new styles. Rap "battles" became a defining event of the time. It was also during this time that personal styles, like those from Grandmaster Caz, Kool Moe Dee (of the group the Treacherous Three), and Spoonie Gee, were rapidly developing.

By 1980, the art of rapping had begun to shift towards the style and structure we recognize today. Paramount to this broad directional shift in rapping was Kurtis Blow and Melle Mel. Kurtis Blow's big hit, in terms of sales, critical acclaim, and influence, was "The Breaks." Neither a party rhyme, a boast, or a joke rhyme, "The Breaks" was the first attempt at serious subject matter, albeit to a party-style backing track. Using an updated, hard-hitting version of the studio band sound of the time (inspired by the studio-band approach used for the Sugar Hill Gang's "Rapper's Delight), Kurtis Blow articulated a more direct and consistent flow, one that was more rhythmically balanced than any other rap previously recorded.

In 1982, barely two years after "The Breaks" and just months after the release of "Planet Rock," the breakaway hit by Afrika Bambaataa, Melle Mel, a former b-boy, pushed the art of rapping into another stratosphere when he and The Furious Five released "The Message." Building off of Kurtis Blow's pioneering efforts of serious subject matter, Melle Mel and producer Duke Bootee, leader of Sugar Hill Record's in-house studio band, created what was, in effect, the very first "reality rap" song. "The Message," which featured a grim, down-tempo rhythm track created by Duke Bootee, was a stark departure from the club rhymes and light (party) subject matter of the period. Reminiscent, both in tone and performance, to Lightnin' Rods' *Hustlers Convention*, "The Message" tells the stories of many typical figures living in the ghetto, and it ends with a youth

---

DJ Breakout), and Spoonie Gee.

going to jail, where, after being raped, he commits suicide. Equally impressive to the straight-forward subject matter of the song, was the structure of the rhyme itself. The meter that Melle Mel used was much more rhythmic in nature, and the bars that made up each stanza were rather conversational, certainly moreso than any rap that had been previously recorded. "The Message" marked the beginning of the rhyme style in which a rapper seemingly talks directly to individual listeners rather than addresses an audience, which had been the impetus for most rappers up to that point.

In 1983, just one year after Melle Mel laid down the foundation of modern rapping, Run-DMC released their first single, "It's Like That." Similar to "The Breaks" and "The Message," "It's Like That" was a rap re-telling of "the way it is" in the hood. However, what set "It's Like That" apart from those other earlier efforts is the fact that the rhymes were set to a sparse, drum programmed beat, a fact that seemingly inspired rappers Run and DMC to borrow and merge the rhyme styles of Kurtis Blow and Melle Mel, respectively.

In 1984, T La Rock broke on the rap scene and introduced the "complex lyrical rhyme style" with the single, "It's Yours," produced by a then unknown producer named Rick Rubin. Unlike the message-driven and crowd-moving rhymes of Kurtis Blow, Melle Mel, and Run-DMC, T La Rock's "It's Yours" was a celebration of lyricism. Backed by a sparse drum track (a sound that would come to personify the period), T La Rock put forth a lyrical arsenal that clearly separated his style from the less complex rhyme structures that preceded him. Rather than use the typical "A B A B" rhyme structure, T La Rock instituted a rhyme style that completely abandoned conventional rhyme structure, offering up stanzas in "A A A B" and "A A A B B" form. Eschewing simple rhyme patterns and easy metaphors, T La Rock introduced a new rhyme structure, one that was much more dense and layered than anything before. Until T La Rock, words were mostly used to set up the rhyme that came at the end of each line. T La Rock pioneered the rhyme style in which any word in the meter could be rhymed. In addition, the use of more multisyllabic words emerge at this point.

Between 1985 and 1988, there were six new rappers who

emerged and solidified the modern style of rapping: LL Cool J, KRS-One, Rakim, Slick Rick, Kool G Rap, and Big Daddy Kane.[29] With his debut album, *Radio* (1985), LL Cool J borrowed from the collective lyrical energies that proceeded him and furthered the tradition of *aggressive rapping*, an approach that was perhaps first pioneered by Grandmaster Caz. Incorporating the blastmaster skills of the Cold Crush Brothers, Kurtis Blow, Melle Mel, and Run-DMC, and utilizing the dexterity of T La Rock's rhyme structure and Silver Fox's phrasing, LL Cool J (only 15 or 16 years old at the time), put together a lyrical force that combined the complex rhyme style with the blastmaster approach.

With his first two singles in 1986, "Eric B. Is President" and "My Melody," Rakim (of Eric B. and Rakim fame) immediately secured his position among the most influential rappers (lyricists) of all time. Using a rhyme style perhaps inspired by T La Rock, Rakim pushed the boundaries and dimensions of the poetics of rap, in a way in which new structures could be explored. Coupling both complex and easy riddles with a dead serious rhyme flow and an uncanny knack for using breath control and delivery to accentuate each word in a rhyme, Rakim established a dense, multilayered rhyme scheme approach that helped revolutionize the complex lyrical rhyme style.

Not to be outdone, in that very same year Kool G Rap met Marley Marl (DJ and first modern beatmaker and made the single "It's a Demo." Although he was also most likely inspired by T La Rock and definitely influenced by Silver Fox, Kool G Rap shattered the previous complex lyrical rhyme style. With "It's A Demo," Kool G Rap further pushed the complex lyrical rhyme style. Taking full advantage of sample-based beats (then the dominant style of beat), which featured tight rhythms and repetition (repetition being the special fuel that powered the more skilled rap lyricists to shine with their own rhythmic flows and verbal dexterity), he aggressively attacked the basic poetic structure and exhausted simple

---

[29] After 1987, most "new" rhyme styles were really stylistic innovations that were based upon the canon of lyrical work produced prior to 1988. Rapper Silver Fox unfortunately recorded very little, but he must be credited for his influence over the lyrical style and techniques of LL Cool J and Kool G Rap.

meter. Kool G Rap doubled-, tripled-, and even quadrupled-up hyperactive rhyme couplets, judiciously stretching and chopping words and using slant rhymes more as a means for tempo control and stylistic intonation than for their implicit value. And like Rakim (perhaps even more so), Kool G Rap demonstrated an extensive understanding of breath control and its effect on delivery and flow. Powered by increasingly more aggressive and complex sample-based beats, Rakim and Kool G Rap helped establish the complex lyrical rhyme style architecture that later influenced many lyricists of the same cloth like Nas, O.C., AZ, Ghostface Killah, and Black Thought.

In 1987, the South Bronx crew Boogie Down Productions (BDP) dropped the seminal album *Criminal Minded*. An album distinguishable for many reasons, not the least of which being that it contained a song that sparked one of the most infamous beefs in hip hop/rap history,[30] *Criminal Minded* featured KRS-One using yet another new rhyme style. Drawing on his true experiences in the streets of the South Bronx and borrowing from Kurtis Blow and Melle Mel, KRS-One introduced a new style of "reality rap," one that was defiant, in your face, conversational, pulled back in pace, and educational; that is to say, educational in the same vein as Lightin Rod's *Hustlers Convention*. One year after *Criminal Minded*, KRS-One and BDP dropped *By Any Means Necessary*. Although the album still featured KRS-One's own brand of reality rap, it also presented a much more educational minded KRS-One. Here, I should mention that although KRS-One and Chuck D of Public Enemy laid down the foundation for so-called "conscious rap," both rappers were not considered as such at the time; they were merely thought of as great rappers with unique rhyme styles that were well-grounded in hip hop's rap tradition.

As far back as 1975, the storyteller rhyme style was in effect

---

[30] The album *Criminal Minded* (1987) included the songs "The Bridge Is Over" and "South Bronx," both diss records aimed at Marley Marl and M.C. Shan and the Queensbridge Housing Project (Long Island City, Queens, New York), where KRS-One apparently believed that Marley Marl said hip hop started. Truth is, Marley Marly never made such a claim. It would appear that KRS-One lobbied the first strike over what he felt was a slight. As the story goes he tried to give his demo to Marley Marl, but Marl didn't accept). Whatever the actual causes were, however, the songs personify the classic BDP/Queensbridge battle.

in hip hop. But prior to 1988, the form was used rather sparingly. However, that changed after the release of Slick Rick's *The Great Adventures of Slick Rick* (1988), an album that was completely dominated by the storyteller rhyme style. Unlike the storyteller rhyme style of the 1970s, Slick Rick's style, which borrows extensively from the South Bronx reality rap style, featured a narrative approach that was both broad and meticulously detailed. Moreover, Slick Rick's rhyme flow was easy and not overbearing, something entirely unassuming yet incredibly engaging. It should be recognized that the modern standard for the storyteller rhyme style was established with Slick Rick.

Finally, in the same year that Slick Rick made his debut, Brooklyn rapper and Juice Crew member Big Daddy Kane dropped his debut album *Long Live the Kane*. As far as rhyme *styles* go, Big Daddy Kane falls somewhere in between Rakim and Kool G Rap. However, Big Daddy Kane introduced a consciously "smooth" element to the art of rapping. Before Kane, rappers were not particularly concerned with the polish of their rhyme style, but instead the rawness of it. Kane, who could just as easily rip the complex lyrical rhyme style as he could the more straight-forward rhyme styles, introduced a new component to rhyme styles, something that I call the "showmanship delivery." The showmanship delivery refers to the delivery style in which a rapper delivers lines in such a way that they resonate much more clearly, and come off more profoundly (perhaps even more than they really are). Using the "showmanship delivery" and his mastery of rhythm and tempo, Big Daddy Kane carved out a rhyme style that on the one hand, mirrored the confidence of Grandmaster Caz and the mid-1970s MCs, and on the other hand, personified the structural dexterity of the newly created modern rhyme style.

To sum it all up, rapping itself was certainly nothing new. In fact, it was a continuum of the Black American oral tradition, specifically, the vernacular tradition of toasting in the United States. In particular, rapping was a blend of the signifyin', radio DJ, and hustler toasts of the African American toasting tradition. That being said, the art of rapping in hip hop did distinguish itself and present a new development in the black vernacular tradition. From borrowed simple toasts and nursery rhymes, boastful and light subject matter, complex lyrical structures and reality rap concepts, rapping developed into the newest, and one of the most powerful, vocal strategies of the twentieth century.

The Hip Hop Sensibility & Hip Hop Attitude

Having looked at the development of the four original elements (art forms) of hip hop, we can conclude that hip hop clearly has its own esthetic standards as well as its own aesthetic priorities. More importantly, it is my contention that together, these standards and priorities form what I call the **"hip hop sensibility."** To understand what the hip hop sensibility is and how it drives and informs creativity in hip hop, one must look at the five fundamental attributes (properties and traits) that personify it.

First, there is **the importance of style**; more specifically, there is a sharp focus and emphasis on individual style. Style identity was a critical factor in the development of the four original elements of hip hop. The early hip hop pioneers were completely consumed with forming and representing their *own* style. In fact, to the pioneers, originality was not based so much on some arbitrary "newness," but rather on the stylistic innovations of the creative commons that one was able to make.

Second, there is the transgressive philosophical approach to creativity. As is often the case in ghettos, and their subsequent street cultures, there exists a **culture of sampling.** That is, a culture which enables its residents (in this case, the residents of the South Bronx and other similarly hard-hit sections in New York City) to take and make use of pieces of culture from both within *and* outside of their own settings, particularly from mainstream American society. Immersed in this culture of sampling, hip hop pioneers learned how to convert those pieces of mainstream American culture in accordance to their own needs, principles, priorities, and values. In this culture of sampling, everything is fair game and open to transformation, reconceptualization, and recontextualization.

Music, music instruments, language, aerosol cans, fashion, automobiles: If it can be converted and flipped, it will be.

Thus, the early hip hop pioneers openly relied on their ability to convert traditional forms and elements of music, art, and fashion into a distinctly hip hop aesthetic. In this way, hip hop has always been a transformative, transgressive culture. For example, b-boys reconceptualizing karate moves and gymnastics, and converting popular black American dance moves like the "bus stop" or James Brown's "good foot" into an entirely new dance form, all of this while simultaneously turning sportswear into a new fashion: streetwear.[31]   And how about hip hop DJs using turntables as instruments, that is to say, in a way that transgressed their traditional use and designed boundaries?   Then there's the case of graffiti writers, who used aerosol paint cans to create a fresh new art form, which they applied on non-traditional "canvases." And finally, we see this culture of sampling at work when we look at how rappers (MCs) borrowed from toasters and radio DJs, and how they break up and extend the implicit and indirect meanings of words (even inventing some words), formalize slang, and reconstruct traditional poetic (rhyme) forms and meter.

Hip hop's transgressive nature is governed by what I like to call its "rules/freedom duality." The rules/freedom duality describes the sensibility that hip hop practitioners *consider* before they use something (i.e. a form, expression, element, etc.) outside of hip hop. This simply means that hip hop practitioners work with a sense of freedom to use tropes and elements from other traditions or cultures, provided they can convert these tropes and elements into the hip hop form.

Communal creativity[32] is the third attribute of the hip hop sensibility. All of the early hip hop pioneers participated in and mastered their art forms through the process of communal creativity. This is to say that every new style and method that was originated

---

[31] B-boys (and the b-boy culture) are most responsible for why sneakers are today *fashionable* in hip hop. Prior to b-boys, sneakers were something mostly worn for sporting events and children's play.

[32] The cultural tradition of communal creativity is further discussed in greater detail later in chapter 10.

entered directly into a well-known creative commons. From this creative commons, wherein canonical works, styles, methods, and techniques were developed, the architects of hip hop openly drew, as they were expected to, ideas and knowledge. In turn, they further created new styles, methods, and techniques that also went directly into the creative commons, codifying the hip hop tradition.

This communal creative pipeline was perhaps best personified by the practice of "versioning." **Versioning** can best be described as the stylistic reworking of established (popular) styles or works. Versioning was paramount to the overall creative process of all hip hop's earliest pioneers. When PHASE 2 introduced bubble letters, every graffiti writer thereafter developed their own *version* of the new style. And incidentally, it's important to point out that although PHASE 2 is credited with having introduced the style, it was not considered *his* style; instead, it was *one* established style that, once created, entered directly into the creative commons, and therefore, it belonged to all graffiti writers. Similarly, when Kool Herc began using two turntables and two copies of the same record, focusing exclusively on the "break," his style, method, and technique entered directly into the creative commons, which other DJs borrowed and developed into new styles, methods, and techniques.

Within hip hop's early communal creativity, syncretism played a major role. Syncretism, as I use it here, refers to the combination or fusion of the inflectional forms (slang), practices, principles, presuppositions, and/or ideologies of each of the original four elements (art forms) of hip hop. Cross-fertilization of the four elements of hip hop culture and cross-participation by the architects of hip hop in the four elements was not only extremely common, but expected. Most of the pioneers participated in at least two of the four elements, while many participated in *all* four of the elements.[33] In this way, each element influenced the other in a uniquely reciprocal manner. Thus, the incredibly high level of syncretism

---

[33] This means that the pioneers and original architects of hip hop were embedded with a deep overall understanding of the culture, in particular, how and why it coalesced into a movement. Today this understanding is basically mute. More and more people enter into beatmaking with little to no understanding of hip hop culture. This disadvantage threatens the preservation of hip hop culture and rap music, as a widespread lack of knowledge leads to a misrepresentation of hip hop.

that occurred between the four distinct (separate) elements of hip hop led to their unification and, ultimately, to the formulation of one common hip hop ideology and philosophy.

Finally, because of hip hop's early communal creativity, many of the architects of hip hop willfully entered into short and long-term apprenticeships. In hip hop's developmental years, there was an objective reverence for the masters of the art forms. As such, most (if not all) style masters took on apprentices, often as an obligation to the development of the art forms. And because they understood the importance of training and having the proper foundation (knowledge), many budding style masters actively and unshamefully sought to be apprentices.

Competition is the fourth attribute of the hip hop sensibility. The *competitive consciousness* of the architects of hip hop was second only to *style consciousness*. That is to say, the earliest hip hop pioneers saw competition not only as a necessary component of creativity, but also as a critical means to individual recognition.[34]   Through their commitment to regular, intense competition, the architects of hip hop were successfully able to police the overall level of originality and quality of each art form. It is also worth mentioning that the hip hop pioneers competed based on their knowledge and mastery of established styles as well as the styles and innovations that they were able to bring to the table. In other words, although competitors were revered for their ability to introduce something new and innovative, they were also judged by their knowledge and manifestation of the core tenets of the art forms that they represented. Finally, it's important to understand that through such vehement, quality-based competition, the architects of hip hop were able to maintain an incredibly strong sense of artistic integrity and pride. Moreover, they consciously established the process of intense individual practice as a critical right of passage.

The fifth attribute of the hip hop sensibility is the "hip hop attitude." The **hip hop attitude** could perhaps best be described as an anti-establishment, "me-against-the-world" sentiment that grew out of the harsh socio-economic backdrop of hip hop's beginnings.

---

[34] Flash and Ritz, 39.

The architects of hip hop took to heart the notion that *This is a tough world*, one in which, *Nobody gives you anything*; and therefore, *You gotta take chances, because you can't sit back and wait for things to happen. You gotta make it happen*! Within the DNA of the hip hop attitude is the ever important idea of survival, which means that there's no room for weakness. Thus, the hip hop attitude is in-your-face and often confrontational, a reflection of the harsh realities of the South Bronx Disaster.

Again, it's worth remembering how this attitude was, in large part, created. Hip hop culture represented a cultural and social change from the bottom-up. And among the many emotional and philosophical conditions that the South Bronx Disaster created, a heightened level of urgency and uncertainty about the future were two conditions that profoundly (and disproportionately) affected the South Bronx youth, hip hop's most earliest architects and pioneers. This urgency and uncertainty was predicated primarily upon one thing: daily survival. Therefore, it should really come as no surprise that hip hop/rap music, and the encompassing hip hop culture, has a distinct sense of urgency and chaotic certainty (controlled chaos) that is governed by a proactive, "Get yours!" attitude. Perhaps a fair analysis would deem this attitude pragmatic, given the socio-economic climate and urban renewal circumstances that flanked hip hop's earliest pioneers from every angle.[35]

√Check This Out – The Evolution from Hip Hop to "Rap Music"

By 1978, a noticeable change had emerged in hip hop culture. Though DJs were still the central figures (for the most part) at this point, rappers were now almost at par with them. Between 1976 and 1978, rappers had developed their performance showmanship and lyrical content so significantly that crowds were steadily coming to parties to see *them* almost as much as they were coming to see

---

[35] Hip hop/rap music is based foremost on its own *practical* aesthetic standards. Hip hop/rap music carries a straight-to-the-point musical philosophy; because of this, it often has little use for drawn out conceptions based on abstract knowledge.

(hear) DJs. Moreover, cassette tapes of "rap music," then the only means through which hip hop/rap was documented and distributed, were becoming ever more popular, delivering even more notoriety to rappers. Then, in 1979, one single event instituted a seismic shift in hip hop that would never be reversed.

"Rapper's Delight," released in 1979 by Sugar Hill Records, *six years* after hip hop music had been brewing in the South Bronx, was the first bonafide hit rap record on radio airwaves.[36] The story surrounding the song itself is as much legend as the milestones that it set and the doors it opened up. Sugar Hill Records owner, Sylvia Robinson, who lived in and operated her label (with her husband, Joe Robinson) out of Englewood, New Jersey, became interested in the commercial prospects of hip hop music, purportedly after noticing her children's affection for rap music. (By 1979, rap tapes were traveling throughout New York City and in some parts of New Jersey, where people there had family in New York, thus this story appears to be the most accurate). The Sugar Hill Gang, the rap *performers* of "Rapper's Delight," were actually not an original Bronx hip hop group of rappers at all. Instead, they were a make-shift "hip hop/rap" concoction, assembled by Sugar Hill Records label-head Sylvia Robinson.[37]

Despite the Bronx-style unauthenticity of "Rapper's Delight," the record went on to popularize rap music nationally, setting the stage for rappers to become just as iconic as soloists and lead singers from other music forms. Thus, of the four original elements that comprised early hip hop culture, rap music would become the most far reaching, most visible, most commercially viable one of them all. Rap music stepped out of the park jam and off of cassette

---

[36] "Rapper's Delight" was not the first rap song ever commercially recorded and released. That distinction belongs to Brooklyn's The Fatback Band, which released the single "You're My Candy Sweet," which had on the B side a rap called "King Tim III (Personality Jock)." Neither the Fatback Band's song or the Sugar Hill Gang's song was considered to be the *authentic* hip hop of the time, primarily because each song's musical track was performed by a band rather than a DJ.

[37] David Toop, *Rap Attack: African Jive To New York Hip Hop* (New York: Pluto Press, 1984), 71-81. Information also extracted from my interviews with Marley Marl and Minnesota. Although "Rapper's Delight" was the first rap record on the radio and first rap hit, it is widely considered to be one of the most non-authentic renditions of rap music ever offered.

tapes right into the recording studio and, subsequently, the music business. It went from a mainly live performance medium to a more fine-tuned recorded medium. Once this happened, rap music garnered a widespread acceptance from both the music industry and the mainstream media. In no time at all, the term "rap music," the music *of* hip hop, was shortened to "rap."

Soon, hip hop culture in general, and rap music in specific, was co-opted and commercialized by corporate American interests and influences. Once this occurred, many self-described hip hop purists and traditionalists began arbitrarily rejecting the "rap" classification, ignoring the fact that it was the architects of hip hop who first described the music as "rap", and instead began referring to the music synonymously with and exclusively as "hip hop." Perhaps this was a means to both reclaim the music as well as distinguish and signify a more truer, supposedly more traditional form of hip hop, a brand of hip hop that was seemingly more influenced by the love for the art-craft and less influenced by the spoils of commercialism. Whatever the real cause, this conscious move to not use the "rap" designation ironically opened up hip hop music to much more broader interpretations than it can fundamentally hold.

Finally, as rap music grew, inevitably the significance of the rapper increased, while the role of the DJ decreased. Thus, it was also inevitable that the beatmaker, the direct descendent of the DJ, would soon become the primary music provider for the rapper.

A Culture of Sampling Summary

Although hip hop is indeed a music-based culture, it should be understood that it grew from the coalescence and informal unification of four distinct art forms: graffiti writing, b-boying, DJ'ing, and rapping. Collectively, these art forms were brewed first in the streets of the South Bronx, then soon after in other areas throughout New York City. And prior to Afrika Bambaataa dubbing his parties "hip hop parties" (ca. 1975-76), each artistic expression represented its own subculture, complete with its own creative aesthetics and priorities, its own slang, and even its own fashion. And here, it's important to remember that most (if not all) early hip hop pioneers participated in at least two of the four elements.

Because of the heavy cross-participation in each of the four elements, there was much creative (especially stylistic), ideological, and philosophical overlap. And the hip hop sensibility, in particular the culture of sampling, was the common thread that underscored and linked the four original elements. Thus, by the time that the 1970s had drawn to a close, hip hop had been established as a New York City subculture, one complete with its own musical styles, dance, graphic art, fashion, slang, and underscoring philosophy. It would not be long, however, before this little known New York City subculture would explode around the rest of America. The catalyst of this explosion would not be hip hop DJs, who up until 1979 were the central figures in hip hop, but instead, rappers.

Hip hop was not an invention by one lone man. It was a movement and culture established and driven by a number of creative architects, all of which who freely borrowed from each other and made many conscious aesthetic decisions. And it must never be forgotten that there were a number of critical socio-economic and cultural factors that played a role in the development of the hip hop movement and the culture of sampling that continues to underscore it to this day.

Chapter 2

Looking for the Perfect Beat

The Birth and Rise
of the Beatmaking Tradition
of Hip Hop/Rap Music:
Eight Periods of Distinct
Development

DISCLAIMER:

The purpose of detailing the developments of the seven periods
of the beatmaking tradition is in no way to pass judgment on any
period, but rather to document each period as it occurred in the
past 40 years. In this chapter, there has been no attempt to present
one period as superior to another, but rather to show the actual
developments (or lack there of) within each period of beatmaking,
and how these developments may have effected hip hop/rap
music overall. Therefore, I encourage you to draw any additional
conclusions that can be reached about each period. Likewise, it is
my hope that the information presented in this chapter further
informs and helps beatmakers make those compositional choices
that are right for them.

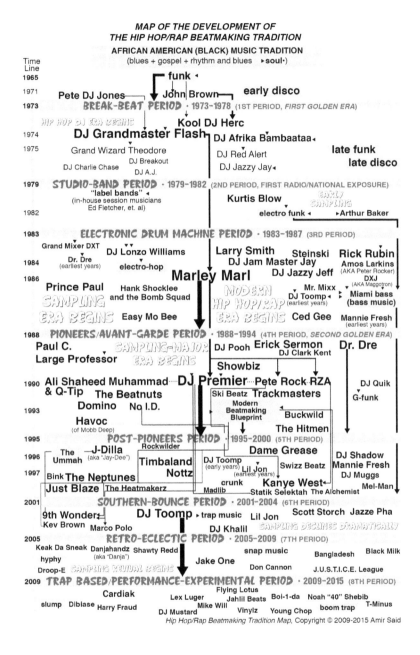

Figure 1 Map of the Development of the Beatmaking Tradition

To Herc, a DJ set was one continuous piece of music. My man was composing something. And if he was a composer, that went for me too. –Grandmaster Flash

Fuck the melody, forget the chorus, and leave the verses alone; we're talking about the pure rhythmic groove. –Grandmaster Flash

Beatmaking, or the compositional practice of "making beats," has been a part of the hip hop/rap music tradition right from the start. In addition to rockin' the crowd or providing music for people to party to, early DJs like Kool Herc, Grandmaster Flash, and Afrika Bambaataa considered what they were doing (the DJ "element" of hip hop) as a form of music composition, not just a method for spinning records. The DJs of hip hop's first era used the breaks and other fragments from records (mostly funk, some disco, and other genres that fit the hip hop style) to make new musical statements. But in the earliest years, beatmaking, as a stand alone element of hip hop, had yet to formulate into what we would come to commonly know it as today. Thus, what follows is an examination of the eight developmental periods of the beatmaking tradition, from 1973 to 2015.

Break-Beat Period, 1973-1978: The Hip Hop DJ Style, the Foundation of Sampling

The art of sampling in the hip hop/rap tradition evolved from live hip hop DJ sets, wherein the DJ (spontaneously) wove together a (blend) mix of record breaks, cuts, scratches, ruptures, and other sound effects.

Between 1973 and 1978, the first five years of what can be described as the hip hop movement, the job of making beats through the use of turntables was something done only by qualified DJs. But before I begin my discussion of the Break-Beat Period, it must again be noted that the use of a particular brand of funk records — that became the foundation for hip hop/rap music — was first performed

45

in 1970 by a lesser known South Bronx DJ named John Brown. John Brown was the DJ at a place called the Plaza Tunnel, a local South Bronx spot that was situated in the basement of the old Plaza Hotel, which once stood on 161st Street and the Grand Concourse. It was at the Plaza Tunnel where John Brown became the first (in the South Bronx) to play funk records (in a specific style) like "Give It Up or Turn It Loose" by James Brown and "Get Ready" by Rare Earth. It was also at the Plaza Tunnel where what would become known as the hip hop *style* of DJ'ing was first born in the mind of a teenager who went by the name Kool Herc.[38]

While still in high school, Herc (not yet Kool Herc) used to hang out at the Plaza Tunnel, soaking up John Brown's style of DJ'ing and the records he played. It was this experience and interaction at the Plaza Tunnel that had a direct influence on the style of DJ'ing Kool Herc first showcased at the infamous Sedgwick party in 1973. Herc's style of DJ'ing, which was influenced as much by dancers (whom he aptly dubbed "b-boys") as it was by John Brown, centered around the use of a mixer, two turntables, and two copies of the same record on two separate turntables. Herc would go back and forth between each record (mostly funk), only playing the "breaks," the raw rhythm section, stripped of melody, and underscored by the pulse and groove of the drums, bass guitar, and rhythm guitars. He would extend these breaks continuously, pumping up the action by b-boys on the dance floor. Thus, by cueing and extending a particular rhythmic break, Herc was the first person to use turntables as *instruments*, thereby setting the tone for a new group of non-traditional musicians. Incidentally, he was also the first DJ in hip hop to stress the importance of having the most unique records.

As Herc's new DJ style took the South Bronx by storm, other DJs soon followed, most notably, Grandmaster Flash, who appeared on the scene within a year of Herc's initial success, and Afrika Bambaataa, who first appeared sometime shortly after that. It was during this period between 1973 and 1978 that DJs emerged as the most powerful and most revered figures of the hip hop movement,

---

[38] Hager, 31.

which is why at the time, the average South Bronx teenager aspired to be a DJ, especially after attending a Jam given by either Herc, Flash, or Bambaataa.[39]

It was during the Break-Beat Period that the break-beat style or hip hop style of DJ'ing began to lay the foundation for the modern beatmaking tradition. First, Herc developed what he called the "merry-go-round" technique, a process of using two copies of the same record, one to play and one to cue up while the other was playing. Then Grandmaster Flash took the "merry-go-round" technique and developed new techniques as well as a new performance style of his own. Flash moved to *blending* records, mixing them, and "cutting the beats together in exact syncopation and planning out" his DJ sets "like a chess game." Flash wanted to create a continuous groove, one that was made up of all the "reorganized pieces of songs" he'd found. More specifically, he wanted to "keep the beat," that is, he wanted to figure out a way to start and stop records on the left and right turntables, without listeners knowing where one record stopped and the next one started.

In his pursuit to develop his own unique DJ style and to surpass Kool Herc once and for all, Grandmaster Flash became the first DJ to actually *physically* put his hands on the vinyl while the turntable's platter was spinning, giving him a level of control previously unrealized by other DJs. Up until that point, DJs, including Herc, were "needle dropping," that is, lifting up and placing the needle down on the record's groove. But, using his hands to wind the records back and forward, a technique he dubbed the "spin back," and keying in on the *marks* (pencil lines at first) that he placed on the labels of his records, Grandmaster Flash developed what he called the "clock theory." Soon, he took the clock theory further and developed the "quik mix theory," which was a collective of his own techniques for quickly cutting back and forth between records

---

[39] Of equal importance, it was during the Break-Beat Period wherein the first DJ/rapper (MC) crews were born. Groups like Grandmaster Flash and the Furious Five and the Cold Crush Brothers were among the many DJ/rapper (MC) collectives that typified the Break-Beat Period. Within the DJ/rapper (MC) crews, the DJ was the one solely responsible for providing the music that the rappers (MCs) rhymed to.

on beat, making one musical passage flow seamlessly to the next. As I mentioned in chapter 1, Flash's "quik mix theory" included a number of "firsts," but it most notably included the "spin back," a method for quickly rewinding records; and the "punch phase," a method for *punching* a record forward, right on the break.[40] In effect, Flash had developed a method for essentially "looping" the breaks and other segments of the same record. Thus, it was the pioneering developments of Grandmaster Flash that first hinted at the looping, cutting, and chopping techniques of the modern beatmaking tradition.

Grandmaster Flash must also be recognized for other innovations that laid the groundwork for the modern beatmaking tradition. In addition to being the first DJ to "rig" his mixer, specifically for the purpose of creating his own headphone input jack, Flash was the first DJ to use an electronic beat box, incorporating additional percussion sounds and effects with his regular DJ setup. And while Herc was the originator of the break-beat style, and Grandmaster Flash was the first true *technician* and the closest link to the modern beatmaker, it was Afrika Bambaataa (perhaps the undisputed record collection king at the time), who hinted at the future of sampling when he pioneered the "pause tape," a technique of using a cassette tape to record a segment of audio (from a record, the radio, TV show, etc.). Utilizing the pause button on the tape recorder, he would record the breaks (or desired segments) press pause, then record the same section again in effort to create what could best be described as a crude loop.

Summary of the Break-Beat Period

The Break-Beat Period represented the first group of beatmakers in hip hop/rap music. These DJs were all conscious of the fact that what they were doing was certainly not the norm, but something non-traditional and anti-establishment. In fact, in many ways

---

[40] *Ibid*, 34. Also, see Flash and Ritz, 54-84. During this same period, other DJ techniques emerged like the "scratch" (widely credited to Grand Wizard Theodore, once an apprentice to Grandmaster Flash), and the earliest form of "pause tape" sampling, done first by Afrika Bambaataa.

what the first beatmakers were doing was a rebuttal to a lot of the popular, slick and polished disco that was on the radio in the mid- to late 1970s. Furthermore, that all of the first beatmakers were DJs is not a fact that can be taken lightly. For six solid years, the DJ was the sole controller of the music of hip hop. More importantly, in this period, hip hop DJs became the first musicians to use turntables as instruments. In doing so, they became the most non-traditional musicians in America. Finally, it must be recognized that as a self-contained music-maker, who used non-traditional or non-conventional compositional practices, the hip hop DJ, in effect, sketched the blueprint for the model of the modern beatmaker.

Studio-Band Period, 1979-1982

Prior to the late 1970s and early 1980s, DJs were the main draw. They were the most powerful, most revered, and most imitated figures in hip hop. However, at the same time, rappers were a secondary thought; their main purpose being to introduce the DJ and to provide a level of crowd control.

But as lyrical content (subject matter) transformed and the mechanics and language of the art of rapping grew more complex, rappers moved to the forefront, replacing DJs as the center of attention in hip hop. At the same time this was happening, hip hop was going through its first experience with the music industry. Before 1979, there were no studio recorded hip hop/rap songs and/or hip hop/rap acts signed to a record label. Until then, hip hop/rap songs were mostly live DJ/rapper performances that were recorded on cassette tape and distributed "hand-to-hand" throughout New York City. However, after the first two official studio hip hop/rap recordings in 1979 ("King Tim III (Personality Jock)" by Brooklyn's The Fatback Band, and the monster hit "Rapper's Delight" by the Sugarhill Gang), studio recorded hip hop/rap music became a more regular occurrence.[41]

Beginning in 1979, DJs, who had once possessed a level of invincibility, saw their power decrease as the lane of fame and

---

[41] Toop, 82-89.

opportunities widened for rappers, who were now becoming more eager to cut a record in the studio. Further, independent labels, sensing a quick payday, were completely enamored with the idea of making rap records. Having seen the break away success of the Sugar Hill Records release, "Rapper's Delight," upstart self-described "rap" labels where bent on capturing the same lightining in the bottle that Sugar Hill Records had.

The most noticeable feature of the Studio-Band Period was the *replacement* of the hip hop DJ by the studio band (recording studio session musicians) as the sole music provider for rappers. During this period, indie rap labels actively sought out rappers and brought them into the recording studio, where the label's in-house studio bands (who were not at all a part of or even aware of the hip hop movement) worked up "cover versions" of the breaks and grooves from the very records that were most popular among the hip hop DJs of the time.[42] In effect, the indie rap labels had come up with a way to cheaply manufacture rap records. Moreover, the indie rap labels, most notably Sugar Hill Records and Enjoy Records, figured out how to use the wisdom and influence of the hip hop DJ without having to actually use or *pay* the hip hop DJ. Subsequently, it was during the Studio-Band Period that the DJ/rapper connection began to break down; and for the first time in hip hop's history, the DJ and rapper, once a unified force, were separated. It was also during the Studio-Band Period wherein rappers, who had by the late 1970s and early 1980s displaced the DJ as the most visible figures in hip hop, first began to realize that the DJ could not adequately serve as the sole music provider for studio recorded records, which were based on the recording studio environment and model, not the live party structure.

Around the same time that hip hop/rap music was finding its way into the studio, there were key advancements rapidly occurring in audio and recording technology. Drum machines and more

---

[42] It has often been reported that "Rapper's Delight," the first hit rap record, used a sample of the song "Good Times" by the group Chic. This is not correct. The truth is that the Sugar Hill Records in-house band played a cover version of the main riff (a "break" so to speak) of Chic's "Good Times." That was the rhythm track that the Sugar Hill Gang rapped to, not an actual sample of Chic's song.

affordable digital samplers were just beginning to hit the market, giving access to an enhanced music-making process to not only DJs, but also to a larger pool of would-be musicians who had missed out (or couldn't cut it) in the first DJ era. Thus, realizing that they no longer had to be *attached* to one specific DJ, that they were now essentially self-contained, independent contractors, and that the art of rapping was moving into new levels of complexity and reaching new artistic heights, rappers began to see themselves as any other recording artist who was eager to get into the studio and cut a record.[43] Therefore, the need for hip hop/rap DJ-inspired music — *without* necessarily the DJ — soon developed.

To be sure, there were other pivotal developments that occurred during the Studio-Band Period. By 1981, the studio-band method of music production for rappers had all but died out. After getting over the initial novelty of hearing rap on the radio for the first time, there was a huge pushback from those who recognized that the studio band "hip hop" was certainly not authentic hip hop/rap music. In fact, many participants of the hip hop movement began to outright reject the studio-band sound, as it did not represent the *essence* of hip hop.[44]   It was around this time that Kurtis Blow, Grandmaster Flash, and Afrika Bamabaataa (the latter two being among the first architects of hip hop/rap music), emerged as the new leaders and pioneers of the studio recorded rap song.

In 1980, Kurtis Blow, a former b-boy and DJ who went by the name Kool Kurt, tapped into his DJ roots and a lesser-used rap style and form — the message rap, yet another development in hip hop

---

[43] The distinct element of beatmaking (aside from the element of DJ'ing) that began to formulate into its own tradition, didn't emerge until the late 1970s and early 1980s. Beatmaking emerged as its own distinct element because of three main factors: (1) the displacement of the DJ as the central figure in hip hop/rap music by the rapper; (2) hip hop/rap's move into the recording studio and, subsequently, into the modern music industry; and (3) rapid parallel advancements in audio and recording technology. [44] It's worth pointing out that the initial success of "Rapper's Delight," Sylvia Robinson's Sugar Hill Records and the like was due more to the novelty of rap being heard on the radio for the first time after its birth six years earlier. However, the studio band-lead "hip hop" inevitably died within two years of its inception, as young hip hoppers who had grown up with the real thing reclaimed the movement, and brought back the hip hop DJ. This sentiment has been widely expressed and shared by many hip hop/rap pioneers of the time. In fact, the rejection of the studio band "hip hop" sound was directly mentioned by Marley Marl in my interview with him.

that had been overlooked by the recent emergence of the rap music sub-industry — and came up with the seminal hit "The Breaks."[45] Though Kurtis Blow and co-producer Larry Smith did indeed use a number of musicians for the making of "The Breaks," they did not merely do cover versions of the breaks of funk records that were popular with hip hop DJs. Instead, they used an original rhythm track that was inspired by both funk and Kurtis Blow's block party DJ'ing days. The other pioneering achievement of "The Breaks" could be heard in both the lyrics and rhyme style that Kurtis Blow employed. Before "The Breaks" in 1980, most raps were of the bragging and boasting style and form; Kurtis Blow changed all of that. Two years *before* "The Message" (Grandmaster Flash and the Furious Five) would shake up the standard lyrical form and style in the art of rap, Kurtis Blow had already perfected the "message rap" form and style.

In 1981, for the making of the landmark song, "The Adventures of Grandmaster Flash on the Wheels of Steel," Grandmaster Flash made a triumphant return to his DJ roots. Opting not for any assistance of a studio band, Flash instead chose to do what he had always done best: Serve as the sole controller of the music. Using *three* separate turntables and all of his best techniques — cutting, scratching, blending, punch phasing, and back spinning — Flash weaved together various records into one cohesive tapestry, demonstrating for the first time how, given the chance, the hip hop DJ could translate to the studio recording environment.

"The Adventures of Grandmaster Flash on the Wheels of Steel" was pivotal to the advent of the beatmaking tradition for two reasons. First, it established a model for how the hip hop DJ could in fact make it in the studio recording environment. Remember, by 1981, when Flash made "The Adventures of Grandmaster Flash on the Wheels of Steel," the hip hop DJ had been written off as a hip hop element that couldn't translate well in the studio recording environment. Moreover, it was thought at the time (mainly by the indie culture vultures and exploiters of rap) that the hip hop DJ

---

[45] Though "Rapper's Delight" was the first big rap hit record, "The Breaks" by Kurtis Blow was the first big rap hit record on a major label (Mercury Records).

was *naturally* a casualty of the progression of hip hop into the music industry and, subsequently, the mainstream. In fact, when Sugar Hills Records owner Sylvia Robinson signed Grandmaster Flash and the Furious Five to her label, she did so to capitalize off of and use Flash's *name*, but not any of Flash's ideas about music-making. In fact, "The Message," the biggest hit song credited to Grandmaster Flash and the Furious Five, wasn't written or produced by the members of the group, except for Melle Mel (Melvin Glover). "The Message" was acually the brainchild of Duke Bootee (Ed Fletcher), the leader of Sugar Hill Record's in-house studio band.

Second, the making of "The Adventures of Grandmaster Flash on the Wheels of Steel" established the model of the principle (lone) beatmaker in a studio setting. When Sylvia Robinson finally permitted Flash to go in the studio alone and record a hip hop/ rap album in the vein of the original (real) essence of hip hop, he took full advantage of the opportunity. Inside the studio, Flash combined his hip hop sensibility and unique DJ style with the recording technology of the time. It was his unique use of both his DJ skill-set and the recording studio tools that paved the way for the beatmaking tradition, as it would come to be known five years later. [46]

Much in the same way that Grandmaster Flash had returned to his roots, Afrika Bambaataa reached back to his DJ and "king of the record collection" roots to make a series of critical hit singles, between 1981 and 1983. "Jazzy Sensation" (1981), "Planet Rock" (1982), "Looking For The Perfect Beat" (1982), and "Renegades of Funk" (1983), all featured Afrika Bambaataa's hip hop DJ sensibility and examples of his forward-thinking usage of recording studio technology. Bambaataa used his understanding of cutting, mixing, and rupture, and combined it with the recording technology of the time. He used synthesizers and other gear. And in perhaps one of his truest pioneering moments, he reached into his extensive record collection and, with the help of co-producer/engineer Arthur Baker, he digitally sampled some of the most unlikely sound sources.

---

[46] Grandmaster Flash and "The Adventures of Grandmaster Flash on the Wheels of Steel" are credited for being the catalyst of the art of turntablism.

Bambaataa called his new infectious sound "electro funk," a homage to both the funk music (records) that had originally inspired hip hop and to the level of creativity that electronic instruments and equipment was able to uncork.

Summary of the Studio-Band Period

The Studio-Band Period represented a number of critical developments in the art of beatmaking. First, it is in this period that the DJ is first separated from the rapper.

Second, it is within this period that hip hop/rap music gets on the radio for the first time and, subsequently, gains a national audience outside of New York. Moreover, the Studio-Band Period marks the first time the distribution of hip hop/rap music first began to move from street-sold cassette tapes to store-sold records. In fact, one could say that the Studio-Band Period represents the first time that hip hop/rap was first snatched from its creators (rightful owners) and exploited commercially.

Third, within this period there was a decisive move away from the *actual* use of breaks from records as the primary (basic) material for making new music compositions. Although most of the in-house studio bands continued to draw inspiration from what hip hop DJs were spinning at parties, they never brought the DJ into the studio for input on the creation of their "rhythm tracks" for rappers.

Fourth, it is in this period that we first see the emergence of the lone, self-contained beatmaker (producer). Fifth, it is in this period where we first hear how a limited use of melody can be used in the rhythm and groove-orientated form of music that hip hop/rap is. Kurtis Blow's "The Breaks," co-produced by Larry Smith, features a recognizable melody line along with the central rhythm; "The Message," produced by Duke Bootee (Ed Fletcher), soon followed suit.

Finally, it is also within the Studio-Band Period where many hip hop/rap practitioners are becoming increasingly aware of hip hop/rap's ability to distinguish itself as a popular genre in the music industry; in fact, in this period, Kurtis Blow becomes the first hip hop/rap artist to ever sign with a major record label.

The Studio-Band Period does *not* represent the original hip hop movement. Many people wrongly consider this period to be the real roots of hip hop/rap music and the beatmaking tradition. This is inaccurate. The roots of hip hop/rap music took shape first in 1973 (perhaps even a year or two earlier) and consistently developed for six years *before* the Studio-Band Period began in 1979. Furthermore, aside from the isolated developments of Kurtis Blow, Grandmaster Flash, Afrika Bambaataa, and Duke Bootee, the beatmaking of the Studio-Band Period was, for the most part, simply a poor "knock-off" of the authentic hip hop style and sound of the early 1970s. Most of the music put forth by the first indie rap labels in this period was nothing more than ill-conceived, superficial renditions of the compositions that the hip hop DJs had been doing in the South Bronx since 1973. Moreover, it was a music that was not in deference to the hip hop sensibility or the underlying hip hop style and sound. Instead, it was a flash in the pan form of music that was designed more for making a splash on national radio than representing authentic hip hop/rap music or hip hop culture.

Finally, to appropriately analyze the Studio-Band Period, one must again remember that the hip hop/rap movement had been going on strong in the South Bronx for six years *before* label-head Sylvia Robinson came around and *manufactured* a make-shift "hip hop/rap" group, and took a non-authentic caricature of hip hop/rap straight to the airwaves. Oh, to be certain, "Rapper's Delight" by the Sugarhill Gang was the first single to take hip hop/rap to the mainstream, and it was the first single to popularize hip hop/rap music nationally. But it must never be forgotten that the Sylvia Robinson invention[47] (or experiment) was not considered real hip hop/rap by any of the hip hop/rap pioneers and architects of the time. This is why by 1982, the Studio-Band Period, which

---

[47] Despite the Studio-Band Period's penchant for a "less-than-true" approach to the South Bronx-born hip hop, it must be recognized that Sylvia Robinson and Sugar Hill Records, for better or worse, helped crack open the music industry's doors to hip hop/rap music. Moreover, Sylvia Robinson and Sugar Hill Records played an indispensable role in the early commercialization of hip hop/rap music.

was really more the result of a business innovation, rather than a musical development, was all washed out. Having no real pipeline to the streets (where hip hop was still emanating from) or to the new rap groups and crews that were rapidly emerging, the Sugar Hill-inspired outfits were all displaced, paving the way for a new development in the hip hop/rap music and beatmaking traditions.

Electronic Drum Machine Period, 1983-1987

In 1983, a number of events occurred within the beatmaking tradition, which was now steadily solidifying. Taking a cue from Afrika Bambaataa and his electro funk sound as well as other elements of the Bronx/New York style and sound, DJ Lonzo Williams (Alonzo Williams) formulated a sound he dubbed "electro hop." DJ Lonzo Williams is significant for two reasons. First, he is widely recognized as the first person to perform and create any form of hip hop on the West Coast (Los Angeles). Until Williams came on the scene, there was no hip hop in California. And though California indeed had its own funk and dance movements (most notably "locking"), these artistic expressions, which had some parallels to the funk inspired b-boying, were not quite the same thing. Thus, it was Williams who developed the first hip hop-based music style on the West Coast. Second, in 1984, DJ Lonzo Williams served as an early mentor to and group mate of a young Dr. Dre.

By the end of 1983, the studio-band "hip hop" was dead, and in the Bronx as well as all the other boroughs in New York City, there was a widespread resurgence of hip hop/rap DJs and park jams. At the time, "nobody wanted to see the bands anymore," says Marley Marl.[48] In fact, during this period there was a hip hop renaissance. B-boying, known as "break dancing" or "breakin'" by 1984, pushed forward like never before, due in large part to Crazy Legs (Richie

---

[48] From my interview with Marley.

Colón) and the Rock Steady Crew.[49] Also, graffiti writing, which had previously lost its "turf" battle with NYC subway administrators, began to see a new surge of expression all across the city, especially in the Bronx and Brooklyn. This larger hip hop renaissance coincided with further developments in audio and recording technology, specifically in the area of electronic music production instruments (EMPIs). But it was the new focus on rhyme form and style (within the hip hop renaissance, ca. 1983-1985) that was the most pivotal factor in the further development of the beatmaking tradition.

Rappers, standing on the shoulders of Melle Mel, Grandmaster Caz, and Kurtis Blow, began experimenting with more complex rhyme schemes. They were now increasingly pushing the boundaries of the rap form and style, offering up rhymes that were more poetically dense and even more rhythmically charged. Rising to the challenge of the more extensively developed rhyme form, DJs, who were now becoming more aware of their role as beatmakers (producers) and other recording professionals (typically studio engineers) began creating sparse, drum track-based compositions that were intended to highlight the lyricism and rhythm of the rappers. And the key to this new beatmaking sound was the electronic drum machine.

Among those at the forefront of the electronic drum beat sound were Larry Smith, DJ Jam Master Jay, and Rick Rubin. In 1983, Larry Smith crafted the two beats that would serve as the instrumental tracks for Run-DMC's first two records, "It's Like That" and "Sucker M.C.s." Following the success of Run-DMC's debut single, Larry Smith, joined by Jam Master Jay's assistance on occasion, would continue to make up hit tracks for Run-DMC. Rick Rubin's first officially acclaimed beat was the instrumental he provided for T La Rock's "It's Yours." But it was with Run-DMC (and later LL Cool J, and then later still The Beastie Boys), that Rick Rubin would distinguish himself as a pioneer in the beatmaking

---

[49] The Rock Steady Crew which first caught national acclaim did not feature Jimmy D and Jojo (the original founders) of the South Bronx RSC. Instead, the Rock Steady Crew that most people were familiar with in the mid-1980s was composed of a crew from upper manhattan that Crazy Legs had put together after he and his family moved from the South Bronx to Manhattan sometime around 1980. See: Hager, 81-90.

tradition. While he was clearly influenced by Larry Smith's earlier work with Run-DMC, Rick Rubin must be recognized for the individuality that he introduced into the beatmaking lexicon. Drawing on his rock music background, Rubin was the second beatmaker (producer) to successfully fuse together elements of rock with hip hop/rap music,[50] a feat that hinted at the potential range of the beatmaking tradition and pointed to inevitable appeal of hip hop/rap music in the mainstream.

In 1985, an event occurred that would establish forever the model of modern beatmaking. One day, while in Unique Recording Studios in New York City sampling sounds with Arthur Baker, Marley Marl (an intern at Unique at the time) made the revelation that changed the hip hop/rap and beatmaking traditions forever. Marley Marl remembers:

> My first step was I got my break-beats up. All the songs I used to hear them cuttin' up…I got my break-beats up. And then after that, I would go out into the park and have my crew rhyme over it. After that…I kind of discovered sampling by accident. That's how I got into looping… **I was getting another part of the record, and we didn't truncate it yet. The snare was there and the vocal. I was playing a beat that I made on the drum machine, and I heard the sampled snare playing with it. Then I realized… I was like, "Yo, I can take any kick and snare from ANY of my break-beat records on how rap should sound…**
> I don't know if I would call it hunting for a new sound. **I was trying to make rap sound accurate to what I was brought up on. That's basically it. I wasn't looking for a new sound… Maybe you could call it looking for a new sound. But I know the representation of what I was hearing [on the radio at that time] was NOT what I grew up on… hearing on these cassettes…and I just wanted to make it more like the rap that I heard before it hit records.** That was my whole premise of everything. [emphasis mine][51]

Soon after his initial sampling revelation, Marley Marl single-handedly took the beatmaking tradition to another level. Before Marley Marl, there was very little examples of *digital* sample-based

---

[50] Larry Smith was the first producer to fuse rock with hip hop/rap music.
[51] From my interview with Marley Marl. Complete interview in *The BeatTips Manual*.

compositions in hip hop/rap music, other than Bambaataa. Although DJs of the first beatmaking period were indeed "sampling," their use of breaks from records was more of a *virtual* form of sampling. Marley Marl was not only the first to realize the full potential of sampling technology and the implications that it held for beatmaking, he was also the first to grasp the complete picture of beatmaking. That is to say, he was the first person to recognize *beatmaking* as a distinct art form and collective musical process that drew on the foundation and understanding of DJ'ing, sampling skills, *and* traditional instrumentation.

With the combination of his DJ background and his recording studio knowledge, Marley Marl took to devouring his crates of records for drum sounds and all sorts of musical fragments and phrases. In the process, he developed a number of fundamental standards in the beatmaking tradition. First, he developed the modern practice of using unique drum sounds. Until Marley Marl, the drum sounds in beats were always of the generic, unmodified stock electronic drum machine variety. In pursuit of a more accurate, realistic, and customized sound, Marley Marl sampled actual drum sounds from the records he learned as both a kid and DJ. He followed this up by using his engineering knowledge to further color and customize these sounds, giving him a sound that was (at first) not easily duplicated.

Second, Marley Marl also established the modern method for all sample-based compositions. Marley Marl was the first beatmaker to recognize that *any* piece on a record, not just the break near the middle or end, could be converted to hip hop/rap form. Also, it was Marley Marl who first developed the techniques that would come to be commonly known as "chopping" and "layering." The truncation of sounds had been practiced before, but only with the stock sounds of electronic drum machines. Marley Marl took the concepts of truncation and tuning to a new level, instituting the practice of carving up *any* sound so that it worked correctly in the loop and fit into a desired rhythmic and sonic pattern.

It was also Marley Marl who first instituted the use of whole drum breaks as the primary drum track to a beat. He was the first

59

beatmaker to sample entire drum breaks and match them or "lock them up" — without any quantizing or timestretching — with a variety of different types of musical phrases and sound stabs.

Finally, Marley Marl perhaps even had both an indirect *and* direct role in the birth of the "Miami Bass" sound, also known as "bass music," one of the biggests sub-developments to emerge during the Electronic Drum Machine Period. Marley Marl recalls:

> I brought the bass to Miami… I was with my 808 drum machine… I used to be on tour with Shanté; this before Miami had bass! Me and Shanté was doing a show for Luke and Ghetto Style DJs, before he even had 2 Live Crew… This before they even started their sound! There was no 808s out there. What I did, I brought my 808 to a show, 'cause I used to play live beats while she rhymed. I went up there with my 808, and was [imitates sounds] BOOM… Everybody ran over to the booth like, "What is THAT?" Right away, people was like, "What is that?" I was like, "it's the 808." I brought the bass to Miami… At a Ghetto Style DJs show…bass didn't start hitting them until '85… In '84/'83, I brought the bass to Miami.[52]

It was during this same period that DJ Toomp first came on the scene. Toomp, who was admittedly very much influenced by Marley Marl, worked directly with Luke (of 2 Live Crew fame) right out of high school. After spending some time in Miami, Toomp returned to Atlanta, where by 1994/95, he had already played a role in the development of the "Atlanta-Miami Sound" or more appropriately the "Southern bounce" sound. It would be this sound (along with the New Orleans version of bass music) that would go on to serve as the foundation for all of the sounds that collectively defined the "Southern rap sound."

Finally, the Bomb Squad (Hank Shocklee, Eric "Vietnam" Sadler, Keith Shocklee, and Chuck D) must also be recognized for their contributions in the areas of sampling. The Bomb Squad were the first beatmakers to approach sampling not merely as a collage of sound, but rather an almost indiscriminate "wall of sound." The Bomb Squad also helped solidify the "booming" sonic impression that had been brewing in New York production, but had yet to

---

[52] *Ibid.*

completely materialize, prior to 1987.

Summary of the Electronic Drum Machine Period

The Electronic Drum Machine Period can be characterized by several key developments. First, this is the period in which individual drum sounds came alive. The drum sounds of this period were characterized (for the most part) by the preset (generic) drum sounds that were stock in the earliest drum machines. However, Marley Marl's use of drum *samples* from various records would change that. The Electronic Drum Machine Period can also be characterized as the period in which the matching of drum breaks to other supplied musical components occurs. Mechanic-like drum patterns and sparse sample-stabs typified the kinds of beats (rhythm tracks) that were made throughout this period. This is also the period in which the 808 sounds are prominently used for the first time. Finally, the Electronic Drum Machine Period represents the period in which the foundation for the modern art of sampling is established.[53]

Pioneers/Avant-Garde Period, 1988-1994

The Pioneers/Avant-Garde Period brought an explosion of new developments in the beatmaking tradition. First, this is the period in which the quintessential self-contained, lone beatmaker is typified; and it is during this period that for the first time beatmakers begin to gain recognition similar to that of rappers.

Next, this is the period in which the beatmaker virtually resurrects the role of the DJ as the sole controller of the music for the rapper. In fact, not only is DJ'ing seen as a rite of passage for many of

---

[53] Key or notable beatmakers and other figures who emerge in this period include: Larry Smith, Rick Rubin, DJ Lonzo Williams, Kurtis Mantronik (of Mantronix), Marley Marl, The Bomb Squad (Hank Shocklee, Eric "Vietnam" Sadler, Keith Shocklee, Gary G-Wiz, and Chuck D), DJ Toomp, Grand Mixer DXT, Prince Paul, EZ Mo Bee, Steinski, and Mannie Fresh. Key sub-traditons of hip hop/rap to emerge during this period: Electro-hop and Miami bass or bass music. Note: Miami bass stems directly from electro funk, electro-hop, and other elements of early/mid-1980s New York hip hop/rap music.
Key gear of the period: Roland TR 808, E-Mu SP, Technics Turntables.

the beatmakers (producers) of this period, the notion of "diggin' in the crates" and having a thorough record collection, the original essence and foundation of the first hip hop/rap DJs, becomes paramount.

It is also during this period that there is a celebration of hip hop/rap's underground heritage and sub-culture roots. More importantly, there is a return to and reaffirmation of the importance of the use of the break and riffs as source material. Also, during this period rhythm and groove once again more clearly stand out as the guiding compositional principle in beatmaking. And along with the experimentation of filtered bass lines, drum frameworks become more pronounced, as they are designed to create distinct rhythmic grooves that more often resemble the core drum arrangements and backbeats of early funk and disco records.

In this period, electronic music production instruments (EMPIs) become critical to a beatmaker's methods and techniques. In fact, there are three key EMPIs that stand out during this period: the Akai S950, the Akai MPC 60 (II), and the E-Mu SP 1200. It was in this period when updated sampling technology began to further point to the potential for a new direction in hip hop/rap music. During the Pioneers/Avant-Garde Period, pivotal strides in sample and arrangement strategies are made. Furthermore, the use of rare and obscure records for source material characterize the middle of this period.

Also, during the Pioneers/Avant-Garde Period, hip hop/rap music experiences a second art-based renaissance. By 1988, the modern hip hop/rap era was two years old, and hip hop/rap had shifted from a mostly dance-based music to an art-based one that celebrated beats as works of art in and of themselves, rather than mere tracks for rappers to rhyme over. This created the new *art/dance duality* that continues to underscore hip hop/rap to this day. Further, it was during the Pioneers/Avant-Garde Period that beatmaking began to distinguish itself as an art form of equal weight to DJ'ing and rapping. In other words, the beat was drawing even with the rhyme. This new development in beatmaking was best personified in fifteen noteworthy albums that were released between 1988 and

1994: *It Takes a Nation of Millions to Hold Us Back*; *In Control*; *Critical Beatdown*; *3 Feet High and Rising*; *Peoples Instinctive Travels and the Paths of Rhythm*; *Step In the Arena*; *The Low End Theory*; *Mecca and the Soul Brother*; *Breaking Atoms*; *Daily Operation*; *The Chronic*; *Enter The Wu-Tang (36 Chambers)*; *Midnight Marauders*; *Illmatic*; and *Ready to Die*.

Public Enemy's *It Takes a Nation of Millions to Hold Us Back* featured the Bomb Squad's signature poly-sample collage sound. Dense and staunchly rhythmic, sonically aggressive and fresh, the beats on *It Takes a Nation...* amounted to what could best be described as harmonic chaos. Cuts, ruptures, screeches, voices, breakbeats, and sound-stabs were all intricately blended together into lively, often unpredictable sound walls.

With *In Control* (1988), the first "producer album" that *featured* rappers, Marley Marl surpassed his own innovations and created trends that would become hip hop/rap standards; in the process, he raised the bar for all other beatmakers thereafter. One of the album's songs, "The Symphony," stands out for two reasons. First, it was the first beat to feature all of Marley Marl's innovations: It included Marley's talent for beat Juggling, mixing/blending, and cutting; it included both individual drum samples layered over a whole drum break; it included a chop of the front end measure of a soul classic; and it included a haunting 808 drum sound that created a powerful sonic impression. Together, "The Symphony" (now perhaps considered a simple arrangement) was innovative for its arrangement strategy and its overall sonic composite. The second reason that "The Symphony" stands out is because it was essentially the first "posse cut" that included multiple rappers (Masta Ace, Craig G., Kool G Rap, and Big Daddy Kane) who were *not* all in the same rap group but in the same crew.

1988 also gave us the Ultramagnetic M.C.'s album *Critical Beatdown*, which marked the first notable appearance of lesser known but influential beatmaker Paul C. Although not officially credited for the bulk of *Critical Beatdown*, it is widely understood that Paul C. was responsible for the sound of that album. Paul C. would go on to make beats for Eric B. & Rakim, and he was poised to do work for Biz Markie, Main Source, and others. However, in 1989, at the age of 24, he was murdered. Even though Paul C.'s production career was tragically cut short, he left an indelible legacy on the beatmaking tradition through his apprentice, Large Professor.

In 1989, De La Soul dropped *3 Feet High and Rising*, one of the most original, enigmatic and experimental albums in hip hop/rap history. Largely regarded as one of the most important albums in hip hop/rap history, it helped develop the alternative hip hop/rap subgenre, it introduced the proverbial rap skit, and it offered a serious crossover hit and the beatwork on this LP was outstanding. The production, which was decadently sample-based, featured a number of sample-based motifs: more deliberate uses of longer musical fragments; a more streamlined arrangement approach; emphasis on one primary sample and two or three secondary fragments; more original drum machine programming and less reliance on break beat frameworks as the main drum pattern. All of these sampling motifs would go on to become common characteristics of the beats made by all sample-based beatmakers. Finally, Prince Paul's drum programming work (e.g. "Potholes in My Lawn") and deliberate use of longer musical fragments foreshadowed the direction that the art of sampling would go in during this beatmaking period as well as the major sampling era overall.

In 1990, A Tribe Called Quest released its debut album, *Peoples Instinctive Travels and the Paths of Rhythm*. If Marley Marl hadn't yet made it clear how pivotal individual stylized sampled drum sounds could be to a beat's overall sound, A Tribe Called Quest emphatically hammered this point home with *Peoples Instinctive Travels...* It is on Tribe's debut that we first hear their signature crushing and smacking snare drum. And though this album did not have the musical dexterity of their second and third LPs, it was clear from the start that A Tribe Called Quest (Q-Tip) would prove to be very influential in the burgeoning beatmaking tradition.

1991 and 1992 would prove to be power years in the beatmaking tradition. First up, Gang Starr released its second album, *Step In The Arena*. This is the album that first hinted at that DJ Premier would be a mainstay in the top tier of beatmakers. Drawing from a wealth of knowledge shared by other beatmakers — Large Professor's knowledge of filtering and the importance of deep crates; Showbiz's knowledge of sampling, especially chopping; and Marley Marl's use of the break and distinct drums — DJ Premier crafted one of the most influential art-based, beat-driven albums in the history of hip hop/rap music. From the chop patterns and arrangements that he developed, to the virtual pioneering of the "scratch-hook" (a highly-regarded signature of songs that Premier produces), DJ Premier pushed the art of beatmaking into another atmosphere. And in 1992, Gang Starr released *Daily Operation*, an album in which DJ Premier, seemingly not content with his accomplishments a year earlier, further laid down the drumwork foundations that would soon lead to the distinct signature drum sound that he's still known for today.

One year after their 1991 debut EP, *All Souled Out*, Pete Rock and CL Smooth dropped their first full length LP, *Mecca and the Soul Brother*. With this album, Pete Rock both demonstrated his dedication to soul source material and established himself as a master drum programmer. Furthermore, just like DJ Premier, A Tribe Called Quest, Large Professor, and RZA, Pete Rock demonstrated his commitment to a signature drum arrangement and a compositional strategy that sought to balance out the original essence of the hip hop DJ with the commercial (mainstream) and technological realities of the mid-1990s. Finally, I should point out that Pete Rock set the bar for the art/dance duality of beatmaking with the beat for "They Reminisce Over You (T.R.O.Y.)."[54]

Just one month after *Mecca and the Soul Brother* was released, and several months after Gang Starr released *Step In The Arena*, Main Source (then Large Professor's group) released its first and only album, the classic, *Breaking Atoms*. Large Professor, who produced every beat save for one Pete Rock-assisted track "Vamos a Rapiar," helped further propel the art-first trend that began to underscore the beatmaking tradition sometime between 1988 and 1990. Large Professor's beatwork on *Breaking Atoms* was an

---

[54] "They Reminisce Over You (T.R.O.Y.)" was a seeringly emotional tribute to Pete Rock's and CL Smooth's deceased friend, Troy Dixon AKA Trouble T-Roy. Because of its message, style, and form, It is widely considered the best hip hop/rap song ever released.

explosive demonstration of "diggin' in the crates" (a phrase that would reemerge during this period) and carefully crafted sampling arrangements.

Two months after Main Source released the Large Professor-anchored *Breaking Atoms*, A Tribe Called Quest put out *The Low End Theory*. On this, their second go-round, Tribe was intent on maintaining their smooth, but hard-hitting drum-driven sound. In fact, the song "Check the Rhyme" was clearly built off the momentum that they had gained with songs like "Can I Kick It" and "Bonita Applebum" from their debut. But it should also be noted that Tribe were also obviously bent on showing a much rougher production sound. With cuts like "Scenario" (one of the best posse cuts of all time), "Buggin' Out," and "Verses From the Abstract," Tribe created a formula that blended their colorful bounce sound with an edgier (sometimes more funkier) drum arrangement strategy.

At the end of 1992, Dr. Dre released *The Chronic*. With *The Chronic*, Dr. Dre (who by this time had already made a name for himself with N.W.A.) launched his self-described "G-funk" sound. In addition to relying on rhythm and groove as his guiding compositional principle, Dr. Dre introduced a new (some might say ambitious) style, one that sought to use distinct melody lines to compliment fundamental hip hop/rap grooves. Admittedly inspired by P-funk (a sound developed by George Clinton and Parliament, who used late 1970s West Coast funk as their basis), Dr. Dre created a unique sound that represented the sum of his various musical experiences and ideas. Moreover, with his G-funk sound, Dr. Dre helped create the sound that would typify what would soon be known as the West Coast sound. Because *The Chronic* was released in December of 1992, it had a strong shelf life that lasted well throughout the balance of 1993; a fact that further established the West Coast Sound as the new national hip hop/rap sound of the time.

In 1993, A Tribe Called Quest released their third album, *Midnight Marauders*. In their third installment, Tribe delivered their most comprehensive album and ground-breaking beatmaking offering to date. With two albums and four years under their belt, Tribe put together an album that summoned both the best of their prior innovations and their obvious recording studio experience. Cuts like "Sucka Nigga," "Oh My God" (ft. Busta Rhymes), and "Steve Biko (Stir It Up)" display both Tribe's (Q-Tip) commitment to deeper crate diggin' and the new multi-layer chop scheme that they were using to compose their "gut-tough" rhythm tracks. Then with tracks like "Electric Relaxation," "Award Tour," and "Lyrics to Go," Tribe showed off a new artistic shine and polish of the beatmaking craft, much in the same way that Dr. Dre had demonstrated on *The Chronic*. What's more, on *Midnight Marauders*, Tribe profoundly delivered the new "listening pleasure" component to beats and rhymes that had come to personify the Pioneers/Avant-Garde Period.

Near the end of 1993, the force known as Wu-Tang Clan crashed the hip hop/rap scene with the release of their debut album, *Enter the Wu-Tang (36 Chambers)*. On an album recognized as much (if not more) for the individual Clan rappers who appeared on it as the beats it contained, RZA orchestrated a *designed chaos* of soul source material, 1970s karate-flick nuances, and the darkest, rawest underground sonic composite ever heard at that time, and perhaps thus far. As was the case with his beat pioneering peers, RZA constructed his own signature drum programming style and sound. At the heart of RZA's drum sound was his time-*correctless* approach to drum programming. RZA pioneered the technique of capturing the natural feel of drum programming and arrangement *without* relying heavily (if at all) on the time correct function. RZA's experimentation in this area allowed him to explore arrangement ideas that took full advantage of the concepts of rupture, rhythm, and groove, creating what has appropriately been described as the "Wu-Tang Sound" or simply the "Wu Sound." Finally, it's also worth mentioning that it was both RZA and DJ Clark Kent who first pioneered the use of sped-up soul samples, not Kanye West. And it should further be distinguished that RZA's use of sped-up soul samples was more in a complimentary or sound-wall role rather than a featured role, as was the case for Kanye West and many of those who followed.

By the middle of 1993, most of the nation's attention had been driven to the popularity of the West Coast sound, spearheaded by Dr. Dre and *The Chronic.* However, in 1994, with the release of two more classic hip hop/rap albums, *Illmatic* and *Ready To Die,* the overall focus in both the beatmaking and greater hip hop/rap communities abruptly shifted back to New York.

For *Illmatic* (1994), Nas assembled what has been commonly dubbed the first all-star team of hip hop producers. The beatwork for *Illmatic* was served up by Large Professor, DJ Premier, Pete Rock, Q-Tip (of A Tribe Called Quest), and DJ L.E.S, all of which were either approaching or at the beginning of their prime. Taken alone, the lyricism of *Illmatic* was a seminal event; but it was the beats of this album that both helped illuminate Nas' lyrics and make *Illmatic* not just one of the most memorable hip hop/rap albums of all time, but one of the most creative albums in the history of twentieth-century popular American music. Had Notorious B.I.G. not released his debut album that very same year, *Illmatic* would have no doubt been THE album of 1994 (still, for many it was).

Taking a page from Nas (in more ways than one), several months after the release of *Illmatic,* The Notorious B.I.G., aka "Biggie Smalls," released his debut album, *Ready To Die. Ready To Die,* which also featured somewhat of an all-star line up of beatmakers: Easy Mo Bee, Chucky Thompson, Poke, DJ Premier, and Lord Finesse. Though not as perhaps artistically *far-reaching* as the beatwork that permeated throughout *Illmatic, Ready To Die* did feature a sound strategy that was well-designed for radio and national appeal; even the lone DJ Premier produced track, "Unbelievable," featured an R Kelly assist via Premier's signature scratch-hook. But in no way was *Ready To Die* completely a jaunt just for the radio. The meat of the album did feature the sharp East Coast drum style that had recently been established, and the sonic composite of *Ready To Die* was dark and menacing.

Summary of the Pioneers/Avant-Garde Period

The Pioneers/Avant-Garde Period is best summarized, first and foremost, as the period in which beatmaking first became a nationally recognized art form, sub-culture, and distinct tradition *within* the broader hip hop/rap art form, culture, and tradition. In fact, it is during this period where the beatmaking tradition essentially explodes and becomes more codified, in terms of styles, methods, terminology,[55] and gear usage. This is also the period wherein beatmakers first become more recognized figures in their own right. Also, in many ways, the Pioneers/Avant-Garde Period represents the manifestation of the DJ in the beatmaker. During this period, there is a fundamental return to and reaffirmation of the importance of the use of the breaks from records and the rhythm and groove as the guiding principle in beatmaking. Furthermore, this period is also characterized by the extensive development of the techniques first established by Marley Marl. Finally, it should be recognized that the beatwork of the Pioneers/Avant-Garde Period (specifically the fifteen noteworthy albums singled out in this section) provided the blueprint for modern beatmaking and hip hop/rap production.

Among all the various developments that took place throughout the Pioneers/Avant-Garde Period, there are six critical developments worth pointing out. First, the art of sampling is explored and expanded way beyond marks previously imagined. In this period, sound-stabs and horn phrases become common place; and there is an extensive use of bass filtering. Second, the scratch-hook becomes a major staple of hip hop/rap songs. Third, Dr. Dre, introduces the first "orchestral-like," broad-based sound to hip hop music production. Fourth, the emphasis on *the mix* as an equally important production process is realized during this period. A Tribe Called Quest, DJ Premier, The RZA, and Dr. Dre stand out in this regard. Fifth, the modern New York sound or East Coast sound reaches

---

[55] Beatmaking (hip hop/rap production) vocabulary and lexicon, i.e. chopping, layering, flippin', filtering, etc., becomes more formal during this period. Also, it's worth noting that much of the vocabulary used in beatmaking actually comes from the engineering and recording terminology associated with the operation of a reel to reel tape machine.

its zenith, drawing even with the West Coast Sound, which had reached its own plateau earlier during the same period. Finally, it is during the Pioneers/Avant-Garde Period that beatmaking drum frameworks begin to emulate those of soul and funk records; this move further increased hip hop/rap music's use of common song structure.[56]

Here, it's important to point out that during the early/mid-1990s, beatmaking and hip hop/rap music began (necessarily) to fragment in a way similar to how jazz fragmented into big band, bebop, cool jazz, and later fusion. This fragmentation laid down the foundations for new styles of hip hop/rap music (styles that were based fundamentally off of the East Coast or West Coast sounds). It is also worth noting that during this period, beats were driven, in large part, by "the listening pleasure" aspect. In other words, much how Western classical music was a music meant for *listening* to and not *dancing* to, beatmaking and hip hop/rap became something that was lauded (recognized and appreciated) as much for its listening pleasure as it was for its dancing and partying function.

Post-Pioneers Period, 1995-2000

Fresh off all of the explosive strides that were made in the Pioneers/Avant-Garde Period, the Post-Pioneers Period begins in 1995 with the new, well-codified New York sound poised to reign supreme. Barely two short years into the period, Mobb Deep, Raekwon, and Jay-Z all release classic albums; each album staunchly reinforcing the New York sound and feel. But by the second half of this period, things would begin to change, and for great reason.

The latter half of the Post-Pioneers Period really represents a period of inevitable change in both the hip hop/rap and beatmaking traditions. The first noticeable change was the dramatic new interest in beatmaking. In 1997, the beatmaking tradition got its first big

---

[56] Key or notable beatmakers and other figures who emerge or appear in this period include: Marley Marl, DJ Toomp, DJ Premier, Erick Sermon, Prince Paul, Dr. Dre, Q-Tip (of A Tribe Called Quest), Buckwild, The Beatnuts, No I.D., Havoc, D.R. Period, DJ Quik, and The Hitmen. Key sub-traditons or styles of hip hop/rap to emerge during this period: G-funk and "hardcore" hip hop/rap.

surge of new interest, due in no small part to EMPI maker Akai. 1997 marked the year Akai introduced its MPC 2000, a monster of an EMPI that Akai aggressively marketed to the burgeoning hip hop/rap production world, making beatmaking instantly accessible to more people at one time than ever before. Thus, the new interest in beatmaking, coupled with the advent of the Akai MPC 2000 (an EMPI soon to become an important stable in late 1990s hip hop/rap production), the sheer number of beatmakers increased dramatically. By the last quarter of the 1990s, the beatmaking tradition is no longer a small, little-known-about sub-culture, it is a phenomenon that's gaining new steam in the United States and around the world.

The second noticeable change of the second half of the Post-Pioneers Period was that most of the new beatmakers in the late 1990s went straight into beatmaking, bypassing the DJ'ing phase, which was once considered a rite of passage in the previous two beatmaking periods. This was a major change because it assured that for the first time in hip hop/rap's history, there would be a generation of beatmakers that was dominated by those without DJ backgrounds, a critical link to the foundation of hip hop/rap music.

The third significant change that takes hold during the Post-Pioneers Period is the beginning of the end of the sampling-major era. After the *criminalization* of the art of sampling, brought on in large part by the landmark *Grand Upright v. Warner* case, the use of sampling as a primary compositional method in beatmaking begins to decline. Furthermore, because many new beatmakers either have a lack of interest in DJ'ing and/or access to it, the art of sampling slowly begins to lose ground as a core beatmaking method. Moreover, at the same time, there are increasing commercial (pop) influences that are pushing even some of the veteran beatmakers (producers) away from sampling into other compositional methods.

The move away from sampling led to the fourth significant change of this period: the increased usage of keyboard or synth styled beats that feature little to no sampling. Remember, at this time, hip hop/rap music is beginning to become more national than regional, and although it's not as national as it would become by the late 2000s, many new beatmakers are not necessarily deferring to the art of sampling, but rather being drawn to the appeal of two new creative sounds emanating from beatmakers like Timbaland and The Neptunes. Seemingly overnight, this very noticeable shift away from the art of sampling opens up an entirely new beatmaking lane.

Around this same time, hip hop/rap music is beginning to return to its party roots. With the appearance of the Puffy "shiny suits" and the "Get Jiggy" era, the party trend comes at the expense of art. However, it should be noted that even though sampling is indeed on the decline and the party scene is on the rise, beatmakers (producers) such as Timbaland, The Neptunes, and Dame Grease keep the notion of art at the forefront of their production styles and sounds. Finally, by the end of the Post-Pioneers Period, a pushback against the tone and mood of the national sound of hip hop/rap music emerges. This pushback is sparked in part by a sampling renaissance led by Just Blaze, J-Dilla, and Kanye West.

Summary of the Post-Pioneers Period

Beatmakers of the Post-Pioneers Period were the first group of beatmakers to directly benefit from the massive blueprint that was constructed by those of the Pioneers-Avant-Garde Period. Thus, it is no surprise that during the Post-Pioneers Period, there were a number of important strides made in the beatmaking tradition. During this period the synthetic-sounds-based style (commonly known as "keyboard beats") is born, a major developement, as it represents the first sound in beatmaking that primarily uses synthetic or so-called "live" sounds (instead of samples) while still attempting to remain true to some of the fundamental tenets of the overall hip hop/rap form and style. Also, during the Post-Pioneers Period, production duos/teams become an important new development, no doubt inspired by The Neptunes. Finally, it is during this period wherein the beatmaking culture begins to become one of the most racially/ethnically integrated sub-cultures in hip hop.[57]

The Southern Bounce Period, 2001-2004

The Southern Bounce Period marks the beginning of the dominance of the Southern rap sound in America. During this period, sampling is marginalized more than any other time in the history of beatmaking.[58] Also, although the basic form of rhythm and repetition are left in tact, it is during this period that the hip hop/rap compositional ethic and form undergo their most obviously pop/traditional music-influenced changes yet. During this period, the number of changes or "switch-ups" and "sweeps" in a typical beat increase within arrangements, and bridges, intros, and choruses become more pronounced and elaborate.

During this period there is also a diminishing interest in customized or signature drum sounds and drum frameworks. In fact, during this period the use of stock or preset drum sounds become commonplace, and drum patterns, based on the use of claps instead of snares, become rather prevalent. Furthermore, extra heavy syncopation, particularly of the stutter hi-hat, kick drum, and snare variety, coupled with the 808 boom and kick, become a standard (echoing drum patterns from the electro funk, electro-hop, and Miami bass sounds).

Next, while the Southern bounce sound was clearly on its way to becoming the national hip hop/rap sound, another renaissance, one based on the New York sound of the mid-1990s, begins to take shape. Beginning with Jay-Z's album *The Blueprint* (2001), Kanye West and Just Blaze established themselves as both sampling aficionados and commercial realists. Seemingly balancing the

---

[57] Key or notable beatmakers and other figures who emerge or appear in this period include: DJ Premier, Timbaland, Just Blaze, Kanye West, Dame Grease, The Neptunes, J-Dilla, Swizz Beatz, Lil' Jon, Mel-Man, Dr. Dre, Focus, Madlib, Mannie Fresh, DJ Shadow, Megahertz, Erick Sermon, Rockwilder, and DJ Toomp. Key gear of the period: Akai MPC 2000XL, Korg Triton, Korg Trinity, Roland Fantom, and Akai MPC 3000.

[58] In fact, this period marks the first time in the history of beatmaking that a number of hip hop/rap beatmakers began to make accusations that sampling isn't creative or original. Such sentiment is a direct assault on the fundamental roots of hip hop/rap music and the beatmaking tradition. Moreover, it demonstrates a lack of respect for and understanding of the richness of the beatmaking tradition in its entirety.

differences of artistic integrity and commercial viability, the pair go about developing a sample-based sound that is respectfully obscure, but not too terribly arcane or intricate that it pushes away non-fans of sampling. This new sound of theirs is even more conducive to additional live instrumentation. And around the same time that Just Blaze and Kanye West latch on to their new styles and sounds, Swizz Beatz finds his own style and sound, after perhaps having seen the advantages of beatmaking's compositional middle ground, and after seeing the successful direction of Just Blaze, Kanye West, and Dame Grease. But unlike Just Blaze and Kanye West, Swizz Beatz's sound is not based upon sampling, but instead, synthetic-based (live) sounds.

But even this push from Just Blaze, Kanye West, and Swizz Beatz can't stop the force that is the southern bounce at this time. And when it comes to the Southern bounce or trap music sound, there is perhaps no one beatmaker (producer) more responsible than DJ Toomp. A long-established veteran DJ and beatmaker (producer), DJ Toomp is widely considered to be the chief pioneer of the trap music sound, a sound that, along with snap music some years later, would come to personify much of what could be described as "the Sound of Atlanta."[59] It should also be noted that this is the period in which Lil Jon comes to major prominence, through the use of a three-chord signature synth sound.

Interestingly enough, the Southern Bounce Period also marks the beginning of the all software-based production setups. Even though the mighty Akai MPC 4000 is introduced during this period (2002) and the Roland Fantom series is still in its prime, new software applications like Proellerhead's Reason and Image-Lines Fruity Loops (now FL Studio) become the chosen production tools of many new beatmakers.

---

[59] While DJ Toomp is the originator of trap music, Shawty Redd is often given credit for helping to popularize the style and sound.

Summary of the Southern Bounce Period

The Southern Bounce Period signals the start of three important developments in the beatmaking tradition. First, it is during this period that a noticeably synth-heavy sound is established. As sampling is marginalized as a compositional method, many beatmakers take to using groups of synthetic or live sounds as the basis for their beats. There is debate as to why the synth-heavy sound gains ground during this period. On one hand, the sample clearance issue certainly pushed many veteran beatmakers away from sampling and dissuaded some newcomers from even considering the method. On the other hand, one could argue that the *trends of the time* influenced many beatmakers to move towards the "synth-heavy" sound. Still, it might be argued that as a disconnect from veteran beatmakers to new beatmakers broke down, so went the relationship of veterans passing on important knowledge and guidance to rookies. Subsequently, rookie beatmakers made do with the EMPIs and information that was available at the time. I suspect that all three factors (and several more, including the advent of ringtones as a new major source of revenue for music-makers) contributed to the rise of the "synth-heavy" sound and a lack of hip hop/rap quality standards.

Second, during the Southern Bounce Period there are some noticeable changes in composition methods and arrangement schemes. During this period, the increased use of melody begins to stand out. Furthermore, while rhythm and repetition still remain in tact (for the most part), the concept of linear progression starts to gain importance in the work of some notable beatmakers.[60] Again, it is during this period that the number of "changes" within an arrangement increase; and in many cases, other arrangement constructions (e.g., bridges and the like) become more pronounced and elaborate.

Finally, the Southern Bounce Period marks the start (perhaps

---

[60] Most of the new interest in melody and progession can be attributed to the commercial success of beatmakers like Scott Storch (once-regular producer with Dr. Dre and ex-keyboardist for The Roots) and to an increasing number of new beatmakers who enter into beatmaking with Western classical-trained music backgrounds.

not ironically) of a somewhat *populist* return to sampling. In the beginning of 2004, at the end of this period, Kanye West releases his debut album, *College Dropout*. Both a critic's choice and a commercial success, *College Dropout*, which features very pronounced and straight forward sample-based beats, (perhaps Kanye's deliberate alternative to Southern bounce), sparked a new "popular" interest in sampling.[61]

Retro-Eclectic Period, 2005-2009

The Retro-Eclectic Period is a period marked by an eclectic mix of both a return to some of the elements of beatmaking's earlier periods and the incorporation of a number of non-hip hop/rap compositional influences. Off the success of Kanye West in 2004, sampling gains a new audience, and a number of key sample-based beatmakers capitalize off of the seemingly sudden interest and appreciation for sampling. But whatever strides sampling has been able to gain (or regain) in the Retro-Eclectic Period, it is clear that one other development during the same time has also gained a foothold: non-hip hop/rap compositional influences.

The Retro-Eclectic Period marks a heightened use of non-hip hop/rap compositional influences. In the past, if and when melody was used in hip hop/rap, it was always used in a subordinate role. However, during the Retro-Eclectic Period, melody has taken on a more prominent role. Furthermore, in this period, the concept of linear progression or material growth is increasingly gaining interest by various beatmakers. This trend is particularly curious (if not alarming), as such concepts are actually *counterintuitive* to the hip hop/rap form and the fundamental tenets of its tradition. Still, J Dilla's album *Donuts* (2006) played a crucial role in igniting a resurgence in the art of sampling.

The Retro-Eclectic Period also represents the first beatmaking

---

[61] Key or notable beatmakers and other figures who emerge or appear in Southern Bounce period include: DJ Toomp, Lil Jon, Scott Storch, Jazze Pha, Just Blaze, Kanye West, Swizz Beatz, Timbaland, The Neptunes, J-Dilla, Mel-Man, Dr. Dre, Madlib, Mannie Fresh. Key sub-traditons to emerge during this period: trap music. Key gear of the period: Akai MPC 4000, Roland Fantom, Akai MPC 3000, Reason (by Propellerhead), Recycle (by Propellerhead), and Fruity Loops (by Image-Lines).

period where the majority of new beatmakers *start off* with software-based production setups. Prior to this period, the majority of new beatmakers entered into the tradition using hardware-based production setups. However, this trend began to change during the Southern Bounce Period. After beatmaker (producer) 9th Wonder garnered critical acclaim and commercial success working from a software-based production setup, many new beatmakers followed his path (it's worth noting that 9th Wonder now uses hardware, an Akai MPC 2500, as well). Moreover, software beatmaking tools became even more affordable, which made them much more accessible to the average person interested in beatmaking. Then add to that fact that software EMPIs are more mobile and in some cases, more flexible, than hardware EMPIs, and it was inevitable that software-based setups would increase in popularity.

Finally, one development that has continued on into the Retro-Eclectic Period is the general inclusiveness of the beatmaking tradition. Of all of the sub-elements and sub-cultures of hip hop, beatmaking, like graffiti, continues to be the most ethnically and racially inclusive. In fact, more ethnic groups and races are now involved in beatmaking (both professionals and hobbyists) than in any of the four original elements of hip hop combined.

Summary of the Retro-Eclectic Period

What makes the Retro-Eclectic Period particularly unique is the amount of cross-fertilzation of styles from the different previous beatmaking periods. During this period, there has been as much of a noticeable return to some of the compositional trends of the Electronic Drum Machine Period as there has been to some of the developments made during the Pioneers/Avant-Garde Period. But things have not all been nostalgic. In fact, in many ways, the Retro-Eclectic Period further confirms the Southern bounce sound (and its peripheral styles and sounds) as the national beatmaking sound. And while there has indeed been a return to extreme minimalism, there has also been even more development in the area of arrangement, particularly when it comes to the concept of linear progression or material growth. Moreover, during this period, there has been a widespread attempt by many beatmakers to *conform* the hip hop/rap compositional approach, style and form, to the styles and compositional approaches of other forms of popular music, rather than reaffirm hip hop/rap's own tradition. Finally, as these high levels of cross-fertilization persist during a time where audio and recording technology is all but making the beats for some beatmakers, the question remains: What role will beatmakers allow technology to play in their fundamental compositional processes?[62]

Trap Based/Performance-Experimental Period, 2009-2015

In many ways, the Trap Based/Performance-Experimental Period is a broad continuation of the Southern Bounce Period. In this period, trap based beats, that mostly build off of the trap music tropes and themes first popularized by DJ Toomp and later Shawty Redd, become the dominant sound. And within this trap based continuum, two approaches emerge: the minimalist approach and broad orchestral approach. The minimalist approach features sparsely made beats that mostly rely on 808 sounds and bare-bones drum frameworks. The broad orchestral approach features the familiar trap sound (808 drums and percussion, Synth tubas and other synth brass) along with some sampled elements and additional instrumentation, usually elements found in urban dance or mainstream pop trends that run parallel to this period.

Besides the utter dominance of trap, performance-experimentalism also marks this period. A growing number of beatmakers, notably Araab Muzik and Flying Lotus, take to live performance, demonstrating their beatmaking skills in front of audiences in real time. At the same time, there is a growing number of beat battles and producer showcases, wherein a new type of focus is given to beat instrumentals. Within this climate, an increasing

---

[62] Key beatmakers who stood out and/or emerged during this period include: J Dilla, Danjahandz, Don Cannon, Jake One, Black Milk, Keak Da Sneak, Droop-E, Young Chop, Vinylz. Key sub-traditons to emerge during this period: hyphy. Key gear of the period: Reason (by Propellerhead), Recycle (by Propellerhead), FL Studio (by Image-Lines, Akai MPC 1000, Akai MPC 4000, Akai MPC 3000, Akai MPC 2000XL.

number of beatmakers create beats that are intended for battles and showcases, rather than for use in traditional songs. Of course, the noticeable effect of this is that a growing number of beats are made purely for instrumental purposes and not intended for traditional rap songs. In other words, a number of beatmakers in this period take to making beats that have little to no room for vocals.

While the concept of linear progression or material growth continued to be a feature of this period, it should be noted that this concept takes on a deeper hip hop connection. In this regard, traditional sampling approaches remain, but increasingly beatmakers are using their sampling skills to repurpose stock sounds in software and hardware EMPIs, rather than relying on pre-recorded songs as primary source material. This has created a new kind of diggin in the "crates" experience for many beatmakers, where one is mining the vast sound libraries of EMPIs, which include a number of ever-growing sounds and vintage plug-ins. Right now, Marco Polo is the leading beatmaker (producer) in this vein. But I expect more beatmakers to take up the same charge in future beatmaking periods, especially given the sampling capabilities and sound libraries found in the likes of Native Instrument's Kontakt and Komplete series.

Software EMPIs like Ableton Live, Reason, and FL Studio, and the previously mentioned Kontakt and Komplete maintain a high profile in the Trap Based/Performance-Experimental Period, but hardware EMPIs remain as stalwarts, and hardware/software hybrid EMPIs like the Maschine by Native Instruments and the Akai MPC Renaissance emerge as popular go-to production units for many beatmakers in this period.

Finally, while trap dominates this period and performance-experimentalism carves out its own small niche, what appears on the horizon is yet another sampling revival. With the emergence and popularity of new rappers like Joey Bada$$, who conjures up memories of '90s style sample-based music, and Mac Miller's early success with '90s style sample-based beats, a number of new beatmakers have taken to the art of sampling and, for the most part, have rejected the trap based style and sound.

Summary of the Trap Based/Performance-Experimental Period[63]

This period does not stand out for its uniqueness. On the contrary, with so much trap parity and little distinction from one trap based hit song to the next, the Trap Based/Performance-Experimental Period stands out because of how much of this dominant sound echoes itself. Compare this to the Pioneers/Avant-Garde Period, a period that featured a collective sampling aesthetic as a whole, but nonetheless a period that held for a broader space of interpretation of the aesthetic itself. I believe that one important reason for this is due to the nature of a beatmaker working with different pre-recorded songs as source material. On the other hand, the core component (the engine really) of the trap sound is the 808 aesthetic, which because of its limited number of sounds and familiar programming, it naturally lends itself to duplication, including everything from arrangement scopes, drum frameworks, percussion structures, and general style and sound. Thus, trap based music benefits from and relies on familiarity: One knows the style, sound, and aesthetic; it's unmistakable. But the very thing that makes trap popular and easy to emulate right now is also the same thing that makes it susceptible to duplication and a surplus of beats that nearly all sound the same.

As for performance-experimental component of this period, I believe some conceptual strides may have been made. However, I do not believe that the live performance of beats alone will be a sustainable model for beatmakers in future beatmaking periods. And finally, as with the Retro-Eclectic Period before it, within the Trap Based/Performance-Experimental Period, there continues to be high levels of cross-fertilization. Yet, there has also been renewed

---

[63] Key beatmakers who stood out and/or emerged during this period include: Shawty Redd, Lex Luger, Bangladesh, Harry Fraud, S1 (Symbolic One), Flying Lotus, Boi-1da, Noah "40" Shebib, Mike Will, Jahlil Beats, J.U.S.T.I.C.E. League, DJ Mustard, T-Minus. Sub-traditions to emerge during this period: slump, boom trap. Key gear of the period: Maschine (by Native Instruments), Reason (by Propellerhead), Recycle (by Propellerhead), Kontakt and Komplete (by Native Instruments) FL Studio (by Image-Lines, Akai MPC 2500, Akai MPC 1000, Akai MPC 4000, Akai MPC 3000, Akai MPC 2000XL, Akai MPC Renaissance.

focus on minimalism in various pockets of the beatmaking tradition of hip hop/rap music.

Conclusion of the Eight Periods of the Beatmaking Tradition: Three Modern Production Sounds

There are three basic modern production sounds that have emanated from the first six beatmaking periods: (1) The East Coast rap sound, also known as the New York rap sound; (2) The West Coast rap sound; and (3) The Southern rap sound.

The traditional East Coast rap sound or New York rap sound is best characterized by the art of the dig and the chop. That is to say, the East Coast/New York rap sound features the unique truncation of random samples (usually from arcane records), obscure sounds, and heavy (often dark) drum sounds and heavy-hitting drum patterns. The East Coast/New York rap sound is also characterized by thick filtered bass lines and straight-forward 2- to 4-bar loops. Finally, it's worth mentioning that of the three basic production sounds, the traditional East Coast/New York rap sound remains the one sound most dedicated (or conducive) to the use of extensive or complex lyricism.

The West Coast rap sound is an amalgamation of late 1970s West Coast funk and some elements of the East Coast or New York rap sound. The West Coast rap sound is perhaps best characterized by a collage of heavy moog-like bass lines, live instrumentation, *and* sometimes samples. Also, in contrast to the heavy "chop-n-loop" sound of New York, the West Coast Sound is much more orchestral and laid back. It's more open-ended than the New York Sound, as it also features melody in a more prominent role than the East Coast/New York rap sound.

Finally, the Southern rap sound, which is based fundamentally on a Miami bass-Atlanta sound hybrid with early 1980s New York undertones, is characterized by stutter drums and of course heavy bass lines. The Southern rap sound carries two opposing styles: one style that is sparse with simple keyboard melodies; and another style that is conceptually, structurally, and texturally dense. The latter style includes more extensive melody motifs and chromatic harmony accompaniment. Both of these styles, however, still often feature 808 drum sounds and heavily syncopated snare, hi-hat, and kick patterns.

Given all of the collective developments that have occured throughout the eight periods of the beatmaking tradition, the art of sampling has survived. Because of hip hop/rap's mainstream rise, in some periods it would appear that sampling all but went away. Truth is, sampling has always flourished above and underground, despite the mainstream shift in hip hop/rap. And now, with a renewed interest in the art of sampling among new beatmakers and the beginning of the changing of the guard of beatmaking leaders, the art of sampling is poised to thrive at the forefront of hip hop/ rap music once again.

Part 2
Instruction
Aesthetics,
Compositional Analysis,
Performance,
and Philosophy of
the Art of Sampling

Chapter 3

An Overview of the Art of Sampling

This is why we sample. We're borrowing from music that was already here, and just like Rakim said, we converted into hip hop form. Hip hop can take anything and just make an ill beat. It's just about who's constructing it and understanding the science of it and understanding how to listen to it. –DJ Premier

What Is the Art of Sampling?
Consider the Context first, then the Meaning, Purpose, Value, and Conceptual Understanding

By the coldest, technical definition possible, sampling is simply the act of digitally recording a sound. However, in its most fundamental context in the hip hop/rap music tradition, sampling is the artistic process of extracting fragments of pre-recorded music from old recordings (usually vinyl records) for the use of making new beats (music). But still, even that's the simple definition. The complete and most accurate definition of sampling requires a much deeper examination.

To understand sampling, one must first comprehend hip hop DJ'ing, hip hop culture, and the hip hop sensibility. In chapter 2, I discussed how hip hop DJ'ing was born from the central use of record "breaks." The earliest hip hop DJs were the first to use turntables in ways that transcended their designed capabilities. Hip hop DJs cut, blended, and mixed the breaks of various records in an impromptu fashion that was a compositional style all its own.

In chapter 1, I pointed out that one prominent result of an isolated and fragmented culture is that its residents learn to make use of and salvage everything within and outside of their environment. I further discussed how the fragmentation caused by the South

Bronx Disaster had, in effect, led to a "culture of sampling," a culture which enabled the residents of the South Bronx (and other similarly hard-hit cities across the United States) to take and make use of pieces of culture from both within their own settings *and* from mainstream American society. Thus, the earliest architects of hip hop learned how to convert those pieces of mainstream American culture in accordance to their own needs, principles, priorities, and values.

Also in chapter 2, I discussed how the culture of sampling is an important part of the hip hop sensibility, and how the culture of sampling often manifests itself. I pointed out that in a culture of sampling, everything is fair game and open to transformation, transgression, and recontextualization (reconceptualization). In reality, this is not much different from how traditional musicians and artists utilize everything within culture for the source and inspiration of their creative activity. And thus, it is from this context and *perspective*, the culture of sampling context and perspective, that we must continue our discussion about what sampling is. But before delving deeper into the many things that sampling is, it's worth discussing why sample-based beatmakers sample in the first place.

Why Sample-Based Beatmakers Sample
The Connection, the Dig, the Find, and the Flip:
Being a Part of Hip Hop's Past Tradition and
the Value of the Sound and Process Itself

Every musician, every artist, working from within a specific tradition or medium makes the decision whether or not to stick to or scale the fundamental techniques and philosophies of that tradition or medium. In this way, sample-based beatmakers are no different. We make the choice to create beats in a way that helps us maintain a connection to the hip hop DJ style and allows us to use the backbone compositional technique of hip hop/rap music. Although the DJ's role in hip hop/rap music has been dramatically reduced from its heyday — when the DJ was the music's figurehead and chief composer — the essence of the hip hop DJ lives on

85

through sample-based beatmakers. And although recent electronic music production tools have helped to bring about new approaches and techniques for making beats, the fundamental process of diggin' for and finding new material to flip remains the same for most sample-based beatmakers.

But then there's also the sound of sampling itself. Sample-based beatmakers are drawn to the-one-of-kind sound and sonic quality that only older songs/sound recordings can provide. The preferred (but certainly non-exhaustive) music eras among most sample-based beatmakers falls between the years 1965 and 1975. For those of us who prefer to sample soul, funk, and rhythm & blues in particular, we like the feeling that that particular music gives off. We like our grooves and rhythms to cook with soul and feeling. And the sound of the late 1960s and mid-1970s represents a sonic quality that deeply appeals to us; not to mention the fact that these years represent exceptional achievement in popular music. Thus, the sound of these periods share one important common characteristic: an analog sound and feel that can't truly be duplicated today.

Besides the fact that current recording, engineering, and mastering trends lean heavy towards the digital side of things, the other reason why it's difficult to re-create the sound that so many sample-based beatmakers prefer is the fact that the talent pool of musicians, who could reference or approach an specific historical sound with all of the nuance and resonance of that era and moment in time, is limited. There are simply not that many musicians today who can play, convincingly, in the same manner or feel. Also, the number of recording engineers who might be able to recapture that particular sound is dwindling. And while some may feel that replays of recordings are a decent alternative (for the best example, think Dr. Dre's "Nothin' But a 'G' Thang"), the truth is that replays are rarely a real substitute for the aesthetic sound of older recordings. (That said, however, live-instrumentation sampling, which I discuss later in this study, is coming much closer to the aesthetic sound and feel of older recordings.)

Finally, sampling holds another connection for sample-based musicians: It answers the desire of those musicians who want to actively interact with history. Historical fiction writers are celebrated for their ability to engage with history. These authors (artists), in particular, have long referenced history, commented on it, and reworked it. In doing so, they have brought new or alternative histories that have entertained, informed, and provided fresh perspectives on the human condition, all while reminding us (more or less subtly) of the original history they've sampled. In a similar vein, sample-based beatmakers are celebrated for their ability to reference, comment on, and rework fragments of old songs and other sound recordings. By using pulses, snippets, sound-stabs, and phrases from old songs — many long forgotten or overlooked — sample-based beatmakers are able to engage with history in ways that remind us of the old and the importance of cultural heritage, while demonstrating how to combine the valuable old with the valuable new.

What is Sampling Really?

Sampling is a Special Kind of Derivative Art

Sampling is a special form of derivative art. Whether consciously or subconsciously, musicians borrow and incorporate sounds, rhythms, melodies, ideas, and musical frameworks from other artists all the time. Thus, the question: What is sampling? is also grounded in the notion of an artist's ability, necessity, and right to create art based on works that came before. Sampling, of course, is different than the meaning of creating a "derivative work" in terms of copyright law. For example, making an exact drawing from a photograph is what it means to make a derivative work in terms of copyright law. Simarly, a "remix" of a song, where the original is the core, is a derivative work of the original. However, in sampling, only a small piece of a song is used in the creation of an entirely new song. Therefore, the new song is not a derivative of the song it borrows from.[84]

Derivative art itself is a necessary and an inevitable process; it's also a tradition long-practiced in every major art form. In fact, all music, at its core, is virtually derivative, inasmuch as it's derived from ideas and works that have come before. The intellectual reuse of tropes and elements from pre-existing songs is nothing new in music, it has always been a major part of the creative process in music and the other arts. Every musician, every artist at some point within their creative process *borrows* in one way or another. Historically, musicians/recording artists have, in their pursuit to create new music, routinely "sampled" ideas, musical phrases, notes, or sounds from each other. There is no such thing as a musician or recording artist that does not intellectually, i.e. *virtually*, sample and draw influence and inspiration from other musicians and recording artists or practitioners of some similar artistic medium.

This process of intellectually (*virtually*) sampling other musicians/recording artists is widespread, overtly expected, and accepted as normal. In fact, in some musical cultures, it is often celebrated. What is new, however, is the *physical* use, i.e. *digital sampling*, of these elements in a fixed recorded form, which is also what sampling is. But here, we must be careful not to forget that there is no conceptual difference between the intellectual (virtual) copying and the physical (digital sampling) copying of someone's work. Both involve copying and intellectual transformation. Thus, "it is not accurate to say, as the *Bridgeport* court does, that when 'sounds are sampled they are taken directly from that fixed medium. It is a physical taking rather than an intellectual one.'"[85] An artist

---

[84] "Thus, 'sampling' could almost never create a derivative work. Section 101 defines a 'derivative work' as one 'based upon one or more preexisting works, such as a translation, musical arrangement, dramatization, fictionalization, motion picture version, sound recording, art reproduction, abridgment, condensation, or any other form in which a work may be recast, transformed, or adapted.' As should be evident from this definition..., one could not create a derivative work in this context unless the original work was used as the main theme of the new work." Quote from Jennifer R. R. Mueller, "All Mixed Up: Bridgeport Music v. Dimension Films and De Minimis Digital Sampling," *Indiana Law Journal*, Vol. 81, Issue 1, Article 22 (2006), 451. Further, in *Williams v. Broadus*, the court noted that "a work is not derivative simply because it borrows from a pre-existing work." *Marlon Williams v. Calvin Broadus* No. 99 Civ. 10957 (MBM), 2001 WL 984714 (S.D.N.Y. Aug. 27, 2001).
[85] Mueller, 450.

who samples a song doesn't literally "take" the sound out of the original recording, rather sampling technology creates a copy that is transferred to a computer hard drive. An actual physical taking of a vinyl record would mean that after sampling a vinyl record, the sampler would spit out a piece of the actual vinyl record, and the original vinyl record would be missing the piece that was physically taken.

Sampling is Sound Collage

Sampling is part of the broader tradition of sound collage, the art technique that involves combining portions of sounds from previous recordings, including songs. In sound collage, or better stated, musical collage, sound recordings are viewed and treated as sound sources. Thus, music collagists extract pieces and snippets, commonly regarded as "found sounds" from these sound sources to create musical montages, which represent wholly new songs.

The sampling tradition of hip hop/rap music fits within the borders of musical collage, as the aims of the musical collagist and the sample-based beatmaker are mostly mutual, both seek to create new music from the sound objects of other sound recordings. But the sampling tradition of hip hop/rap music has its own distinct priorities and parameters. And so, while every sample-based beatmaker is in fact a musical collagist, not every musical collagist is a sample-based beatmaker.

Sampling is a Technique, Method, and Compositional Style

Sampling, or rather sample-based beatmaking, is a music making technique that relies primarily on the use of samples of recorded sound for the creation of new music works. In its most common and fundamental case, these samples (snippets and segments) of riffs, melodies, or sound-stabs are sampled from vinyl records. But it should be noted that sampling is not limited to just old songs. For most sample-based beatmakers, any sound recording can be sampled and transformed.

Usually, beatmakers who employ the sample-based style try to remain close to the vein of the second Golden Era of beatmaking, ca. 1987-1995. In fact, the most noticeable characteristic of this compositional style is its timeless sound. Practitioners of this approach typically frown upon the mis-perceived laziness and the sometimes lack of commitment to the art of beatmaking that is often associated with the synthetic-sound compositional style, which in its most primitive form involves a rather low level of creative programming and arrangement. But that said, it should be noted that the sample-based style certainly does allow room for useful melody phrases, additional percussion, and the like.

Another important characteristic of the sample-based style is that it indirectly familiarizes beatmakers on many of the methods that were initiated and mastered by beatmakers from the first two Golden Eras of hip hop/rap music. Beatmakers who rely on the sample-based compositional style are often masters at complex and unique sound customization techniques as well as the advanced tier of other processes like chopping and looping (which I discuss in greater detail later in chapter 4). Because of this, many sample-based beatmakers have the advantage of being able to create a sound that is on the one hand, reminiscent to a past era, and on the other hand, inline with contemporary trends.

Sampling is Versioning

Sampling is also a natural extension of "versioning." Versioning can best be described as the reworking of popular melodies or familiar folk tunes, songs, catch phrases, and the like. The process of using intellectual (*virtual*) samples of other works as source material (and inspiration) or rather as the model for new works is nothing new, particularly in the African American (Black) music tradition.

Sampling is Fine Art

Within the beatmaking tradition, sampling is also a fine art. Some critics maintain that sampling is uncreative, limiting, or even worse, *lazy*. On the contrary, sampling is a real-time mix of all of one's musical understanding. That is to say, sampling forces beatmakers to identify multiple sounds, tones, and rhythms all at once, in one completed composition. Furthermore, what makes sampling a fine art is the fact that it is also what I like to call "a grid of discovery." It's substantial training, part intuition, part accident, and a whole lot of *diggin' in the crates*. In fact, beatmakers who use the sample-based compositional style are rewarded for their "discoveries," i.e. for what they find and flip.[86]

Sampling is Digitally Recording a Sound

As a technological concept, sampling is simply the act of digitally recording a sound, then rearranging and assembling that sound into a programmed sequence. Next, the idea is to turn this programmed sequence into a new composition. As an art form, however, the practice of sampling is rather intricate. Not only does it involve a creative understanding of how sounds, tones, and pitches work, it requires a uniquely meticulous method for editing and manipulating sounds. In this way, the art of sampling represents a number of important musical processes.

Sampling is Referential Music-Making

Sampling is also referential music-making. No music is truly independent and free of any references. All forms of music are referential, as all musicians create by referencing the elements, styles, themes, sounds, principles, and priorities of music created by others, either before or during their time. The art of sampling builds on this truth and sensibility, as it is a compositional process that uses — *references* — segments of recorded music and other sounds to create new music. And again, the fact is, *sampling*, in terms of referencing of ideas, has always gone on in music. Borrowing pieces, segments, or fragments of songs for the purpose of creating

---

[86] **Flippin'** (or to Flip) a sample is the process of manipulating and fashioning a sample into a beat. Often this sample is manipulated so much that it's impossible to identify its origin. Still, there are other cases where a sample can be flipped even while it contains its original identity.

new works is certainly not anything new in the world of music. For instance, jazz giant Charlie Parker is widely considered to be a genius for snatching (referencing) a little bit of Gershwin's "I Got Rhythm" and recontextualizing and reconceptualizing it into new musical works. Thus, are not all of the jazz greats throughout the 1930s, 40s, and 50s "geniuses," for snatching (referencing) pieces of many blues standards in the creative process of new musical works?[87]

Sampling is Musical Recycling

Sampling is also musical recycling, especially as it celebrates the very concept of musical recycling. Recycling is a major component of all contemporary music practices. But for hip hop/rap's earliest and recent pioneers and contemporary practitioners, the art of sampling is the *rightful* recycling of a common heritage. Sampling stems from the art of hip hop DJ'ing, which itself stems from a keen interest in the heritage of the African American (Black) music tradition, specifically the major sub-traditions of soul, funk, and disco. This "heritage music" is an embedded tradition (style, sound, and unique nuance) that can not be easily duplicated. The first hip hop DJs, who were acutely aware of and sensitive to this fact, took to recycling this music at a time when it was considered past its prime and no longer "usable" and/or "relevant." The art of sampling extends the tradition of the hip hop DJ, as it makes relevant use of a musical heritage that is considered unusable and/or no longer

---

[87] "I Got Rhythm" was a George Gershwin song composed for the 1930 Broadway musical, *Girl Crazy*. That a song from a Broadway musical was used for the basis of new jazz works demonstrates just how critical "sampling" and "versioning" was to the existence and development of the jazz tradition. Moreover, it personifies the importance of "sampling" and "versioning" in the African American (Black) music tradition. In fact, the use of pieces of songs for the creation of new music is certainly nothing new, especially in the African American (Black) music tradition. "These early pieces [of blues songs provided] a basic repertory of stock melodies that have been drawn upon innumerable times by jazz composers." Quote from Eileen Southern, *The Music of Black Americans: A History*, (New York: W.W. Norton & Company, 1971), 339. Here, it is also important to note that within Black (African-derived) musical cultures, "the past" has always served as common fertile ground and inspiration for creativity. Thus, the notion of musical recycling is certainly a valued principle in the African American (Black) music tradition.

relevant.[88] In this way, sampling, as musical recycling, speaks to part of the original purpose of U.S. copyright law: to promote the progress of useful arts.

What's a Sampler and How Does It Work?

Technically speaking, a **sampler** is any EMPI (Electronic Music Production Instrument) that can digitally record sound, usually through the use of external audio sources like turntables, CD players, cassettes, and microphones. Instead of having the ability to simply generate and manipulate tones (like a synthesizer), a sampler deals with the actual digital *recording* of sounds. Once sounds are recorded into a sampler, they can be altered in pitch, duration, or sequence, while the unique timbre (tonal qualities) of the sounds within the sample remain intact. The sampled sound(s) can then be "triggered" (played back) through the use of a MIDI instrument such as a keyboard/MIDI controller or drum machine.

A Sampler comes in two basic forms: hardware or software. Each essentially does the same thing, however, each offers different advantages and/or disadvantages, depending upon your intended use, gear preference, and comfort zone. Typically, most hardware samplers (not all) can only play samples of its own or similar audio file formats. On the other hand, software samplers, which are basically virtual hardware samplers, are usually not limited to any one particular file format. They can read and use just about any audio file format.

Here, it's worth mentioning how samplers *determine* the clarity of sound. Samplers use something called "audio bandwidth" to determine the clarity of a sound. The general formula states that: bandwidth of the sample signal is usually around half the sampling rate. So 16kHz is = 8kHz audio bandwidth. But clarity does indeed vary from sampler to sampler. The Akai S950, one of the samplers infamously linked to the development of the art of sampling in hip hop/rap music, samples at 12 bit. However, it's just as clear as

---

[88] Sampling is actually not only an extension of the hip hop DJ art form, it is an extension of the *competition* hip hop DJs maintained with one another to find the rarest and "meanest" records and breaks.

many of the 16 bit samplers that are currently available, but not as bright and clear as let's say a 24-bit sampler.

Finally, it's important to remember that samplers can be and are often used to sample practically any sound imaginable. They can be used to sample the smallest tones, like for instance, a closed hi-hat, or they can be used to sample large musical phrases, like drum loops, extended vocal passages, and even more. The important thing to remember is that the art of sampling is not limited to the use of recorded music as source material.

Fairlight, the First Sampler

Sampling has actually been a part of the music recording process for over 25 years (*technically, even longer!*). The first digital sampler, the Fairlight CMI (Computer Music Instrument), was released to the commercial market in 1979. Two Australian engineers, Kim Ryrie and Peter Vogel founded the Fairlight Company in 1975. Frustrated by the limitations of analog synthesizers, the pair wanted to design a digital synthesizer, or rather a digitally controlled analog synthesizer. In fact, they wanted to make a device that could create sound by modeling all of the parameters of a waveform in real time. Their initial quest failed, prompting them to take their efforts in a different direction. After enlisting the help of then Motorola consultant, Tony Furse, and after many revisions of their eventual prototype, the QASAR M8, Ryrie and Vogel developed the Fairlight CMI I.

Described as a computer-based digital sampling instrument, the Fairlight came equipped with two six-octave keyboards, an alphanumeric keyboard, and an interactive VDU where sounds could be edited or drawn on the screen using a lightpen. Among the many major contributions of the Fairlight, perhaps the two additions that stand out the most were: the first ever graphical pattern-based sequencer and the first user-interface arranged in a set of menu views, called pages. During the 1980s, the Fairlight Company introduced two new models, the Fairlight II and the Fairlight III. The last revision of the Series III, which replaced the cumbersome lightpen with a graphics tablet that was integrated into the alphanumeric keyboard, was made in 1991.

Because of its hefty price tag, the Fairlight was out of reach for pro-sumers and even many recording artists. Only the most affluent recording artists[89] and the most high-end recording studios could afford it. The original Series I sold for $30,000; the Fairlight Series II generally sold for around $25,000; and the Series III started at $40,000.00; customized with the many available options, it often exceeded $100,000.00.

But by the late 1980s, the unreachable suddenly became reachable. The advent of complex and affordable samplers from Ensoniq, E-Mu, and Akai ended the era of absurdly expensive digital sampling instruments.[90]

A Brief History of MIDI: The Technology that Makes Sampling Even More Flexible

By 1981, the "stability, playability, and polyphony" of synthesizers had evolved from the first musician-used electronic synthesizers of the mid- to late 1970s. However, the issue of combatibility had remained a problem for manufacturers Moog, Oberheim, Sequential Circuits, Korg, Roland, and Yamaha. Because of the multifarious nature of synthesizer design, each manufacturer had been defining pitch and timing data in their own way. Thus, unless all of a musician's synthesizers were of the same brand, they could not operate together through a single keyboard, there was no standard of compatibility. But the compatibility issue would soon be successfully addressed.

In 1981, having been concerned about the lack of compatibility between manufacturers, and likely encouraged by Herbie Hancock, the first person to customize different models of pre-MIDI synthesizers in order to connect them, Dave Smith and Chet Wood (both programmers and audio/design engineers at Sequential

---

[89] Stevie Wonder, Peter Gabriel, The Art of Noise, Tears For Fears, Howard Jones, and Thomas Dolby are among the many popular recording artists who were known to have used the Fairlight for some of their biggest hits.

[90] "Fairlight- The Whole Story," ANerd.com, http://www.anerd.com/fairlight/fairlightstory.htm.

Circuits) came up with a concept of an Universal Synthesizer Interface, for which they presented to the 1981 Audio Engineering Society (AES) Convention. The following year at the 1982 Winter NAMM[91] show, a meeting (organized by Dave Smith) took place between the leading American and Japanese synthesizer manufacturers where certain improvements were made. What resulted was what Dave Smith dubbed the Musical Instrument Digital Interface: "MIDI."[92]

MIDI is the electronic music industry standard communications protocol that enables electronic musical instruments such as synthesizers, keyboards, keyboard controllers, digital samplers, computers, and other electronic equipment to communicate, control, and synchronize with each other. MIDI allows computers, synthesizers, MIDI controllers, sound cards, samplers, and drum machines to "talk to one another," that is, control one another, and to exchange system data. MIDI does not transmit audio signals or media, it only transmits "event messages" like pitch and note velocity, and it renders control signals for parameters such as volume, vibrato and panning, cues, playing and recording, and clock signals to set the tempo. In other words, by allowing digital samplers to essentially be "played" over a variety of electronic musical instruments, in particular, drum machines, MIDI extended the flexibility of digital samplers and, in effect, gave beatmakers a tool that they could use for the performance aspect of their compositional goals.

The History and Evolution of Sampling in the Hip Hop/Rap and Beatmaking Traditions

Sampling, as we've come to know it today in the hip hop/rap tradition, finds its roots in the hip hop DJ'ing of the early and mid-1970s. As discussed in chapter 2, early hip hop DJs like Kool Herc, Grandmaster Flash, and Afrika Bambaataa normalized the

---

[91] National Association of Music Merchants.
[92] For an extensive history of MIDI and synthesizers, see "Tutorial: History of MIDI," MIDI Manufacturers Association, http://www.midi.org/aboutmidi/tut_history.php (accessed July 28, 2009).

practice of finding and repeating the breaks in a record. They used turntables to play only the breaks, mostly from funk records and other soul music forms, early disco, and even some late 1960s and early 1970s rock 'n' roll records. Thus, in effect, early hip hop DJs were "sampling" what to them were the *choicest*, most valuable parts of the records.

Pushing the boundaries of the turntables, pioneering hip hop/ rap DJs (most notably Grandmaster Flash) transformed turntables into *manual* sampling machines. And under the early guidance of recording engineer/producer Arthur Baker, Afrika Bambaataa began experimenting with synthesizers and early samplers. As hip hop/ rap music grew, both in terms of size and scope, this fact did not go unnoticed by major EMPI manufacturers like E-Mu, Ensoniq, Akai, Roland, and Yamaha. Thus, by the mid-1980s, there were five big EMPI corporations that were jockeying towards advancements in sampling technology.[93]

At this time, hip hop/rap DJ's, who had steadily been experimenting with all sorts of electronic sound-making devices and who had spawned an entirely new league of music-makers, were the perfect consumer group for the new samplers that the major EMPI manufacturers were marketing. For the first wave of hip hop/ rap DJs (beatmakers), turntables had been their chief instruments. But having seemingly pushed turntables to their limits, these DJs began to incorporate echo boxes, drum machines, synthesizers, and early sound modules into their music rigs, soon these music rigs morphed into what we now commonly call production setups.

Again, these new developments in the hip hop/rap DJ world prompted the big five EMPI companies to release a wave of EMPIs that would go on to become classic instruments in the beatmaking tradition. In 1985, Ensoniq introduced the Mirage, a digital sampling keyboard, the first sampler with keyboard control. In 1986, Akai released their S900, which was quickly updated to

---

[93] The primary focus on a high-end clientele and an inability to dramatically decrease manufacturing costs were the two factors that ultimately led to the Fairlight Company going out of business. It's worth noting that after Fairlight, sampler manufacturers increasingly reset their attention on common "consumer musicians" rather than high-end users. This was a clear indication of where they believed sampling and samplers was headed.

the celebrated S950, one of the most important EMPIs in the development of the beatmaking tradition. Later that same year, Roland introduced their own 12 bit, high-powered sampler: the S50. Then in 1988, two of the biggest sampling classics came to market: the SP 12 by E-Mu, which was soon succeeded by the SP 1200; and Akai's MPC 60, which was quickly succeeded by the much revered MPC 60 II, and later the MPC 3000.[94]

Advents like the E-Mu SP 1200, Akai S950, and the Akai MPC 60 II, ushered in an entirely new way of sampling and further extended the compositional process, who's foundation was laid down by early hip hop/rap DJs. Before the late 1980s, beatmaking was best characterized by sparsely arranged drums (particularly Roland's TR 808) and equally simple keyboard patterns. But by the late 1980s and early 1990s, the pioneers of sampling (notably Marley Marl, The Bomb Squad, Prince Paul, DJ Premier, Large Professor, Pete Rock, Dr. Dre, and The RZA), used the sample technology of their time to introduce a more dramatic, more aggressive way of making beats. These pioneers went beyond just sampling the break. Instead, they explored the entire record and sampled sound segments from practically everywhere. In turn, they would then *flip the samples*; that is to say, they would take these sampled sections and *chop* them, filter them, and fashion them into new musical compositions — compositions that were more challenging and creative than anything previously produced in the young history of beatmaking.

Through an aggressively creative style of trial and era, pioneering beatmakers, particularly those of the Pioneers/Avant-Garde Period (1988-1994), were able to establish the foundation for which all sample-based beatmakers now build upon. The primary sample-manipulation techniques that were fostered and developed by the aforementioned pioneers *still* serve as the basis for the sampling process that we now recognize in beatmaking today. Therefore, all beatmakers who sample are forever indebted to these pioneers.

---

[94] The original Akai MPC series was actually designed by Roger Linn, the inventor of the Linn Drum, an EMPI which many regard as the predecessor to the first Akai MPC.

The Impact of the Sampling Pioneers and the Response of EMPI Manufacturers

The new compositions created by the early sampling pioneers were drum-backed re-creations or savvy hip hop/rap conversions of the original recordings that they sampled. The processes that they formulated were critical to the overall development of the beatmaking tradition for a number of reasons, but perhaps the biggest one is the fact that it allowed a generation of impoverished blacks and Latinos, who had been deprived of instruction with traditional musical instruments, to be reconnected with the sounds, culture, and general heritage that they had been mostly stripped of. This connection, which brought about a renaissance for soul and R&B music of the late 1960s and 1970s, helped make beatmaking a legitimate alternative to traditional musical instruction and creation. And thus, today, beatmaking (hip hop/rap music production) is a musical discipline that is appealing to all sorts of people, from all races, ethnicities, and walks of life. Young kids who might dream of playing the saxophone or maybe the guitar when they grow up, still dream of playing those instruments; only now, many of them want to use an MPC, a sampling keyboard, FL Studio, or some other EMPI to do so.

The sampling process formulated during the end of the Electronic Drum Machine Period (1983-1987) and the Pioneers/Avant-Garde Period (1988-1994) also had a considerable impact on the technological advancements of the samplers and other EMPIs of today. Before 1995, no manufacturer offered an EMPI with the function name: "chop" or "chopping." Chopping was the jargon used by the pioneers (and other practitioners of the time) to describe the multi-part process of sampling, dissecting, separating, and rearranging of the desired pieces of the original sample. Before 1995, beatmakers had to manually chop up the original sample into sections. After 1995, however, manufacturers began offering EMPIs with "auto-chop functionality," chopping functions that *automatically* chopped up samples into regions and sections for you.

Finally, as the sound in hip hop/rap music production and other genres grew cleaner, brighter and generally more louder, the EMPI manufacturers once again targeted the hip hop/rap beatmaking audience when they began offering samplers with higher sampling bit rates. From 1985 to 1996, the only available sample bit rates were 8khz, 12khz, and 16khz. After 1996, the sample rate in samplers blew up to 24khz. The sampling terminology (mostly created and first echoed by hip hop/rap beatmakers) and the evolving sound design of the beatmaking pioneers prompted EMPI manufacturers to completely re-structure their design and marketing strategies. By the late 1990s, it was quite clear that hip hop/rap music was the king of all styles of electronic music production. Hence, two of the big EMPI manufacturers of the time, Akai and Roland, made sure that their product lines were *hip hop/rap production compliant*. And what was the result of the EMPI manufacturer's dramatic re-direction and commitment to hip hop/rap music production? The result was *more* intuitive samplers, complete with more standard sampling time, higher sample rates, more critical sampling techniques (like mute groups), and more dynamic processing effects.

So there are several questions that beg answering: Why did EMPI manufacturers continue to develop their sampling technology? And why did they continue to mass market their new sampling product lines? Did EMPI manufacturers anticipate a decline in the interest of sampling and, therefore, a decline in the use of samplers? Or did they anticipate (correctly) for the interest in sampling to grow and, subsequently, the demand for their samplers? Given their collective advancements in sampling and sequencing technology, then and now, it's clear that EMPI manufactures saw (and still continue to see) sampling as a valuable art form that's here to stay.

Chapter 4

The Mechanics of Sampling, Part 1:
The Sampling Equation

Sampling is not simply the reshaping and reuse of recorded text, but a method of textual production…that proceeds by listening for and incorporating discrete parts, rather than completed wholes, and constructing an aesthetically satisfying text out of them.
–Richard L. Schur

Hip hop can take anything and just make an ill beat. It's just about who's constructing it and understanding the science of it.
–DJ Premier

A tool is just a tool and the craftsman is responsible for how he uses it. However, craftsmen need to understand a tool's built-in biases and limitations in order to wield it well. —Jeff Sonderman

The Sampling Equation

The Sampling equation is a term that I use to describe the core set of processes that make up the compositional tract of the art of sampling. It also, not coincidentally, describes some of the fundamental factors that ultimately determine the success and effectiveness of the art of sampling. There are seven separate but interrelated components that make up the **sampling equation:** (1) the **philosophical approach**, (2) the **sampler's code**, (3) **"diggin' in the crates"** — source material/music, (4) **signal chain**, (5) **chopping/editing** and **sound manipulation**, (6) **triggering**, (7) **arrangement/programming** and **sequencing.**

The **philosophical approach** refers to the overall philosophy of sampling that a beatmaker holds; it also refers to the style of sampling that a beatmaker employs. The **sampler's code** represents the creative and ethical standards of sampling in the hip hop/rap music tradition. Each beatmaker's adherrence to this code goes a long way in determing the quality and originality of their beats. **Diggin' in the Crates — Source material/music** refers to what the sample actually is, where it comes from (e.g. a vinyl record, CD, mp3, cassette tape, .wav file, etc), and how it was found. **Signal chain** refers to how the source material/music is accessed. That is to say, through which capture media is the source material/music accessed, and through what audio connection is it achieved. In other words, the format of the source material/music, and where the source material/music goes *before* it's sampled. **Chopping/editing** refers to the "trim" techniques and the other editing processes that sample-based beatmakers use to transform samples through a series of cuts and trims — chops. **Triggering** refers to the means through which samples are triggered and played, for example, through the use of a drum pad on a drum machine, a key on a keyboard or MIDI controller, or key on a computer keyboard. **Arrangement/Programming** and **sequencing** refers to the process of programming/arranging samples into sequences and linking sequences together into fully arranged songs. In this chapter and the next, I will more thoroughly break down each component of the sampling equation.

The Philosophical Approach

In order to further explain what is meant by the philosophical approach, I thought it would be a good idea to share the approach that I (and many other sample-based beatmakers) use.

My philosohphical approach to sampling is this: I look at sampling as a grid of musical discovery with vast creative potential. Unlike a single note on a keyboard or soft-synth (software synthesizer), a sample of a pre-existing sound recording can give you more than just movement up or down the pitch scale. And aside from the various incidental nuances that samples provide when they're looped, samples often act as cementing agents. That is to say, samples, especially when serving as half of the rhythm section of a beat, *glue* the drums of the beat in a way that makes the whole composition move more organically rather than mechanically. Furthermore, the art of sampling can educate you on tones and textures, rhythm and timing, function and feeling, in ways that traditional musical processes can not. Whenever I sample a record, I always learn something new about composing and arranging music. More importantly, I gain a better understanding of how to insert a particular mood that I'm feeling into my music.

Whatever your philosophical approach to sampling is, you should always consider three factors when you take up the sample-based compositional style. First, you should always seek and fully expect to find something fresh and unique every time you sample something, even if it's just a sound-stab, like a new hi-hat or snare. Second, concern yourself with the mood and feeling of the source material/music that you want to sample. Regardless of what you're sampling, whether it's a complete-phrase or spare-part phrase, focus your attention on identifying the mood and feeling of what you're about to sample. Third, having identified the mood and feeling, shift your attention to trying to get an *audio snapshot* of where you want to go with what you've sampled, like how can you use, and in some cases reuse, what you've just sampled.

The approach that I just outlined is the one I employ, but I certainly encourage you to add your own unique thoughts to it, because it is extremely critical that you identify and incorporate your own approach to sampling. In doing so, you will carve out your own sampling identity, and in turn, you will also develop your own healthy approach to sampling, an approach that will undoubtedly spawn a variety of good side-effects. Furthermore, because sampling requires that you devote serious time to mining through source material (mostly vinyl records, CDs, MP3s, or .WAV files) for things to sample, having a clear-cut approach and expectation will dramatically increase your overall beatmaking efficiency. Finally, I should add that the proper sampling approach will train your musical ear, giving you a better indication on what kinds of samples that you're likely to *flip* (transform into something new) more successfully.

The Sampler's Code: The Ethics and Unwritten Rules of Sampling in the Hip Hop/Rap Tradition

The purpose of the sampler's code is to help sample-based beatmakers create the best art that they can. The sampler's code is not meant to be a restriction of art, but rather a guide and catalyst for creating the best art possible. There are a variety of unwritten ethical rules that govern the general beatmaking community, but no where are such rules more clearly defined and adhered to than in the sample-based beatmaking community. For most seasoned samplers, these rules, which are often learned directly or indirectly from other samplers, are well understood and timeless. Also, the ethical rules of sampling are an extension of the creative, stylistic, and competitive rules that governed over the four elements (main artistic expressions) of hip hop's earlier days. As such, these rules implicitly stress the importance of knowing the fundamentals of the art form as well as knowing the work and styles of the art form's most respected artists. Moreover, the ethical rules of sampling are inextricably connected to notions of originality and aesthetic value. What follows below is a list of the most recognized ethical rules of sampling.

Know the Art Form

Before anything else, a sample-based beatmaker should know the art and craft of sampling. This part of the sampler's code means that you should have a commitment to studying the art of sampling; for this is the first prerequesite for developing a skill and appreciation for sampling. Within this understanding, a serious sample-based beatmaker is expected to know: The history and heritage of sampling in hip hop/rap music; the styles and work of the art form's key practitioners; the aesthetic and technical characteristics of the art of sampling; and the practice of diggin' through source material. Also, knowing the art form of sampling in itself underscores the importance of preserving it.

Be Creative and Original

Second only to knowing the art form is the rule of being creative and original. Hip hop culture prioritizes originality in general, but in beatmaking, and sampling in specific, being creative and maintaining an original sound is especially important. For one thing, the most sought after source material in the sampling tradition of hip hop/rap music spans from the late 1960s to the mid-1970s. (As I discussed earlier, this is for the aesthetic value of records released in that time frame.) This means that sample-based beatmakers are often using the same kinds of source material and, in many cases, the same exact recordings or recordings from the same album. Necessarily, to be original, a sample-based beatmaker must commit to being creative by using his knowledge of the art form along with his own ingenuity and imagination. Further, being original can mean diggin' deeper for more rare and obscure source material. It can also mean transforming known source material in new ways that thoroughly demonstrate the sampler's level of creativity and originality.

Finally, the creativity and originality rule in sampling also adheres to the hip hop sensibility's competition dimension. Because sample-based beatmakers aim for creativity and originality, either through a unique blend of their skills or through the use of obscure recordings, they are upholding one of hip hop's driving forces: competition. In my interviews with DJ Premier, Buckwild, and 9th Wonder, each pointed out how, on many occasions, they were motivated and pushed by the beats of their peers to come up with even more dope beats of their own. Each described this as "healthy competition." This chain of respectful competition and motivation plays a major role in the sample-based beatmaking community, and being creative and original are important aspects of this competition.

No Biting Allowed

Biting, the overt (sometimes less overt), deliberate copying of another artist's work has never been respected in any of hip hop's four artistic expressions. As I discussed in Part I, style and originality has been prioritized in hip hop culture since its inception. As two of the most valued and celebrated traits in hip hop, individual style and originality also means that you don't bite! You don't copy someone's style and sound. Instead, you develop your own style and sound, and you always aim for originality. And while demonstrating clear influences of other sample-based beatmakers' works is certainly not a violation of the sampler's code, a total mimic of another sample-based beatmaker is a clear violation of the sampler's code.

Same Sample/Source Rule: Is Using the Same Sample (Record/Source Material) Ever O.K.?

It's generally understood that sampling the same record and using it in the same or substantially similar way is unethical, a clear violation of the sampler's code. However, there are three main exceptions. First, the use of a different section of the same record. Using a different section of the same record, especially in a creative and original way, does not violate the sampler's code. Second, it's totally acceptable to even use the same section (part) of the record as another sample-based beatmaker, so long as you flip it, i.e. substantially transform it through your own creativity and skills. Third, coincidental usage of the same source material does not violate the sampler's code. Many sample-based beatmakers of the early '90s held common cultural backgrounds, and therefore, they shared access to or awareness of much of the same vinyl records of the 1960s and 1970s. So *coincidental* uses of the same record, even the same part of the same record, have always been inevitable.

But either way, it doesn't matter how many people have used the same sample, because if you can flip it differently, then that's perfectly acceptable within the sample-based community. After all, what is using the same sample and flipping it really all about? Is it not a more transformative form of versioning? So the bottom line is this: Every sample can be flipped differently; it all depends on the ingenuity, imagination, creativity, and skill set of the particular beatmaker.

Using Break-Beat Records (Compilations) is the Norm

Using break-beat records (or compilations) is highly ethical, especially when it comes to drum sounds. Every beatmaker I've interviewed in the past ten years has mentioned their use of break-beat records (compilations), specifically noting the "Ultimate Breaks & Beats" series of compilations. I've seen "Ultimate Breaks & Beats" volumes in the studios of various beatmakers, including DJ Premier, Buckwild, True Master, and Marco Polo. When I first began making beats, the "Ultimate Breaks & Beats" were widely considered an invaluable piece of a sample-based beatmaker's arsenal. They were used regularly by beatmakers throughout New York City, Atlanta (DJ Toomp mentions his use of them in my interview with him), Miami, and LA. Thus, I suspect that most (if not all) sample-based beatmakers of the Pioneers/Avant Garde Period used so-called break-beat records (compilations) particularly for the creation of new drum sounds. Therefore, to avoid using break-beat records is certainly not the normal stance amongst most sample-based beatmakers, nor is it a purist declaration. In other words, opting not to use break-beat records (compilation) is simply a matter of personal choice, and it should not be looked at as being aesthetically superior or inferior.

Diggin' in The Crates – Source Material/ Music[95]

The Importance of Mining

Since the traditional art of sampling has been about retro-fitting long-abandoned recordings to fit the aesthetics of hip hop/rap, sample-based beatmakers are a special breed of "sound collectors." Sample-based beatmakers mine through used, long-forgotten (often poor-conditioned vinyl records)[96] for music elements of value. These elements of value are what beatmakers strip down, re-work, and refashion into new works of art. This is why sample-based beatmakers are only as good as their source material. And when it comes to record collections, it's never about quantity, it's *always* about quality and value.

Records (and other source material, i.e. any recorded sound or sound that can be recorded) are more valuable to a sample-based beatmaker than instruments are to traditional musicians. For sample-based beatmakers, records (or pre-existing music in any available media format) are the primary currency from which the heart of their beats are made, which is certainly not the case for traditional musicians in the West. For instance, a guitarist or pianist has the exact same tool to draw from every time they set out to create something new. They know that musical notes aren't going anywhere; middle C is always *middle C.* In other words, the *framework* which traditional musicians work from essentially remains the same. However, a sample-based beatmaker has to rely on a *new* tool every time out. I mean, one good album might have anywhere from 0 to 10 (perhaps more) good segments to sample. Thus, a sample-based beatmaker never really knows what they'll be

---

[95] There are two basic forms of sampling source material: arcane and familiar. Arcane source material refers to source material that is uknown or unrecognizable (to most) or obscure. Familiar source material refers to source material that is recognizable or easily identifiable. "Diggin' in the crates" is a term used to describe mining for source material (usually records). The term comes from the act of DJs storing their vinyl records in milk crates.

[96] In addition to vinyl records and CDs, sample-based beatmakers now also use MP3s and WAV files as well as streams.

able to get from a record until they *mine it*, i.e. listen attentively to it. Therefore, the ability to mine quality source material is paramount to a sample-based beatmaker. In this way, mining — ie. diggin' in the crates — is a fundamental part of the music process for sample-based beatmakers.

Diggin' in the Crates as Competition and a Means for Harnessing History

Much of sampling in the hip hop/rap music tradition is about besting other sampler's source material. Because of this, having a deep record collection or broad knowledge of records is something that is highly respected and regularly celebrated within the sample-based beatmaking tradition. In fact, in the hip hop/rap music tradition, sample-based beatmakers are often respected for their diggin' prowess (the size and scope of their record collection, their knowledge of records, and their historical music knowledge in general) just as much as they are for their beatmaking skills. Thus, in this way, diggin' in the crates is also about discovering and harnessing history.

This is why all serious diggers carefully study the credits and names on the albums that they sample from. Not only is it a widely held tradition that goes all the way back to Grandmaster Flash, the second of the first three founding hip hop DJs and the grandfather of modern beatmaking, it's one of the best ways to enhance your familiarity with the musicians and writers of a given era and genre.

Tips for Digging for New Records

Besides the obvious advantages to previewing records in record shops before you purchase them, I don't necessarily believe that this is the most effective way to shop for records. *Beats are made by the moment*, not by the minute, not by the hour, not by the day. Therefore, the inspiration you pick up (hear) from an intro or outro of a record, while in the record store, may not be the same thing when you get back to the lab. What I mean is, if something grabs you, you might be hard pressed to go back to that initial moment when you first heard it at the record shop. All too often it doesn't sound or feel the same. And thus, your approach shifts; how you initially envisioned flipping your source material completely changes. Therefore, my recommendation for record shop diggin' is this: Whenever you're in a record store diggin' for new vinyl, be quick with your decisions. When you pick out an album, if the name of the artist or the album cover catches your interest, just get the album. When I'm in a record store, I dig and leave. I come in with a preset mission and budget. Whatever strikes my interest, I simply put it off to the side. When I've reached my predetermined budget, I leave. When I get back to the lab, that's when I thoroughly check out what I've copped. This way, I can immediately capitalize on the moment, my first gut reaction. I've found lots of nice surprises, or better yet, I've discovered good musical "accidents" within the realm of my regular beatmaking mode and environment. But, of course, diggin' in shops goes on far less these days.

E-Diggin' vs. Record Diggin'

Before comparing "e-diggin"[97] to traditional vinyl record diggin', there are several contextual points that must be made. First, it must be remembered that hip hop/rap was the first music tradition to be entirely predicated upon the use of previously recorded music. This wasn't an accident, this was a conscious decision by the earliest hip hop/rap practitioners (chief among them, Kool Herc, Grandmaster Flash, and Afrika Bambaataa). Furthermore, the preferred recorded music came from vinyl records. And from the onset of the hip hop/rap music tradition, this wasn't merely some cost-effective necessity, this was the life-force of the entire tradition. Truth is, buying a keyboard — a one-time purchase — would have been much more cost-effective than regularly buying records. In fact, vinyl record diggin' is/was often an expensive proposition. During the earliest

---

[97] The general principles of sampling apply no matter what audio source you're sampling from. The only difference that may exist can be found in the amplification of the original audio source. No matter how you dig for source material, it's paramount that you not only listen to music in beatmaking-mode. That is, take time to listen to your finds while doing other things, not just making beats.

days of hip hop/rap, there weren't any second hand vinyl record stores, records were not yet displaced by CDs (and later streaming) as the main consumer media format. Therefore, all records were sold at full retail price.

Second, crate digging itself was/is considered as a part of the artistic process for those beatmakers who make sample-based beats through the use of vinyl records. Many beatmakers considered the ability to dig for quality source material a skill, something that required a unique music education and much music research experience.

Third, diggin' for records is not something that is old fashion or in danger of being displaced by technology. There's nothing old fashion or outdated about building your knowledge base. Technology serves at the command of the one who uses it. That is, technology is to be used in the manner that each individual deems that it can best be used. And it should be added that one's over-reliance on technology for technology's sake can have a negative effect on their creativity. The goal of technology is not simply to replace something, the goal of technology is to facilitate and make easier those fundamental things that we have always done. For instance, shooting a full length feature film with digital cameras is very cost-effective, yet nearly all feature length films are still shot with film. Shooting with film, as opposed to digital, is not considered an old fashion or outdated way of doing things in the movie business. On the contrary, it is an artistic choice, one that still holds tremendous value to filmmakers on both sides of the movie budget extremes.

Although technology has provided a new method for diggin' for source material, we must be careful not to conclude that this new method, e-diggin', should replace the existing method of diggin' for vinyl records. And consider these facts: (1) hundreds of thousands of vinyl records, containing jazz, rhythm and blues, rock, soul, and funk, were cut between 1969 and 1975; and (2) most hard core vinyl record collectors own on average just about 1,000-5,000 records — that's not even 5% of the possibilities. So while e-diggin', which is essentially technology in the form of a search engine, may help one find rare records, technology can not displace the vinyl record search method. Why? Because search technology depends upon *the data that it only has access to*; 100s of thousands of songs may never be uploaded to YouTube or shared elsewhere online. Thus, for sample-based beatmakers, the only access we will have to loads of songs released in the twentieth century will only be through vinyl records. That's actually one of the things that makes hip hop/rap so unique: It has always been based on the principle of *unique access*. And being unique, well, that should not ever go out of style.

Finally, it must be pointed out that diggin' for vinyl records doesn't necessarily determine whether you can be an effective beatmaker or not. In fact, it doesn't even give you an advantage (unless perhaps you really value vinyl and everything that surrounds it). You could have all the vinyl records in the world, but if you don't know how to effectively extract value from them, then you're only taking up space with otherwise useless source material.

As for the process of e-diggin' — diggin' for source material on the internet — it should not be seen as an inherently good or bad thing. Instead, it should be considered as a necessary component for many sample-based beatmakers. Fact is, vinyl records are simply not as accessible as they were many years ago. Therefore, diggin' for source material online has become the only reality for some beatmakers. Moreover, it's another legitimate means for finding/discovering new music, often quickly. This is why I strongly endorse e-diggin'. However, that being said, there are some key differences between e-diggin' and traditional record diggin' that are worth noting.

The primary difference between e-diggin' and record diggin' is that the source material found on the internet has a notable difference in sound quality. The sound of a vinyl record is more rich in character, and the nuances of the recording translate better from a vinyl record than an MP3 or .WAV file that has been "squashed" (overly compressed) and flattened.

The other difference between e-diggin' and record diggin' could be found in the processes themselves. Traditional record diggin' is a more extensive, physical pursuit, while e-diggin' is essentially the process of using an online search engine. Record diggin' permits you to actually hold a record, which allows you to get a feel for the artwork and perhaps the intentions of the artists behind the music, this adds another dimension of creative inspiration. More importantly, the physical record bares critical information such as relevant dates and the ever vital musician, production, or studio credits. Such information is generally not provided in the process of e-diggin', and therefore, the potential for a more extended musical education (which traditional record diggin' provides) is usually not afforded with the e-diggin' process.

√Check This Out – The Validity of E-Diggin and Why I Support It

As I stated before, e-diggin' is simply the process of diggin' for music (source material) on the internet. In and of itself, that should not be seen as an inherently bad or good thing. Instead, it should be considered as a necessary component for many sample-based beatmakers. There are, however, a number of beatmakers (some of them very notable) who view e-diggin' as some sort of bad or inferior process. Inasmuch as e-diggin is, fundamentally, a means to searching for and finding new music, I don't see how anyone can dislike it. In fact, it would appear to me that the basis of opposition towards e-diggin' lies in the fact that it does not correspond with the nature and unwritten protocol of diggin' for vinyl records. But let's be clear here: Diggin' for or possessing vinyl records doesn't necessarily determine whether or not someone is going to be a dope beatmaker. On the contrary, knowledge, skill, and creativity, above all, determines that.

Thus, the rants against e-diggin' itself are actually off base. I have been diggin', consciously, for records for nearly 20 years. As a result, I, like many music diggers, am a *de facto* collector of vinyl records. And not just any collector, perhaps you could say that I'm a preservationist preserving otherwise forgotten music. But I don't allow my slant as a collector/preservationist of vinyl records to cloud or otherwise interfere with my interest in searching for and discovering "new" music, particularly those recordings that I would never be able to find in the rapidly dwindling number of vinyl record stores.

Spending hours upon end in record shops, flea markets, yard sales, Salvation Army branches, record exchanges, used book stores, or the basements, attics, and storage spaces of friends and relatives (*all of which I have done*) does not equate to any superiority in the area of musicianship, nor does it necessarily make anyone more skilled at the art of sampling. Instead, it mostly equates to the desire for that particular process and experience. Furthermore, it is also simply a reflection of one's "collector's slant," because the reality is this: Most beat diggers with large vinyl record collections will most likely never sample even 25% of their total collection. There are many people (myself included) who have upwards of 2,000 or more vinyl records that they have never sampled. (I can assure you, out of my own 3,000+ vinyl record collection, I have yet to sample anything from 2,500 of those.) And if those who tout 10,000 and 20,000 vinyl records in their collections have really sampled even 15% of those records, then it stands to reason that there should have been a much larger number of classic sample-based beats in use over the past three decades.

Furthermore, as I stated earlier in this chapter, technology serves at the command of the one who uses it. So it matters less how I came to discover "new" music. As long as I discover it, I'm fortunate. After all, I can't flip something that I can't hear. And I can't hear something that I don't have access to. And whether I prefer to handle vinyl in my hands or stream a song on YouTube, I still can't ignore the fact that e-diggin' gives me much more access to "new" music than diggin' for vinyl records ever did or ever could. I also can't ignore the fact that the e-diggin' search process generates, on a whole, more suggestions for similar findings than any cross-credits referencing I've done reading the credits or liner notes of vinyl records that I've acquired.

Still, I certainly do recognize that there is a difference between diggin' for vinyl records and e-diggin'. There are some nuances that come with sampling a vinyl record. Perhaps most notably the sound quality of a vinyl record, or the sort of connection to a musical past that a vinyl record can offer, or the connection to the traditional method of sampling in the beatmaking tradition. But that being said, the notion that someone is lazy or somehow uncreative, or that someone is doing it (i.e. sampling) *wrong* just because they use source material (music) that they've found (discovered) online rather than a vinyl record that they've acquired from a record shop or another place where vinyl records are typically sold, is ridiculous and completely out of tune with the realities of the day.

In most cases these days, e-diggin' is the only choice for would-be sample-based beatmakers; it's the only way many people have access to valuable music of eras gone past. And accessibility to the music (source material) that is to be sampled has always been a key factor of the art of sampling. Thus, because sample-based beatmakers have always been distinguished not only by their skill but by what they actually sample, it should be understood that sample-based beatmakers are also often distinguished by the music (source material) that they actually have access to.

But because of the limited accessibility of vinyl records, the playing field for sampling has been largely uneven. For years, those who lived in or near hot-spot centers for vinyl records (major cities and towns that contain a healthy supply of vinyl record stores and the like) have had an advantage of access over those who did not live in those centers. But e-diggin' virtually makes an indefinite number of hot-spot centers available to anyone with a working internet connection. In this way, e-diggin' has scuttled the "advantage of access" that some samplers previously held. Through this new level of access to the same music most privileged by veteran vinyl diggers, e-diggin' has leveled the playing field for sample-based beatmakers. Moreover, because of the scarcity of vinyl record shops and the like, e-diggin' is providing a pivotal link to the sampling tradition — a link that many people might not otherwise be so fortunate to enjoy.

Finally, any capture method, whether it be through the vinyl diggin' or e-diggin' process, that adheres to the fundamental tenets of the art of sampling while also bringing to light the elements of valuable music from eras gone past, should be embraced, not spurned. Beyond that, we should remember that no one judges sample-based beats according to the original audio format of the music (source material) that was sampled. Besides, there's no way for anyone, other than the sampler who sampled the source material, to be absolutely certain what audio format was actually used. One can just as easily say that they sampled a piece of music from a vinyl record when, in fact, they sampled it from a source online. Who's to know either way?

But the truth of judgment remains: The basis for how we judge sample-based beats is pretty much the same for how we judge any style of beat: Our personal tastes; the level of quality of a beat; and the beat's cohesion with the lyricist, are all main factors that determine how we rate a beat. Therefore, if e-diggin' plays any role in the creation of a beat that suits our taste and measures up to our individual and collective perceptions of quality, then we have no choice but to support it.

Practicality of Diggin' in the Crates

Vinyl records are also valued for their practical nature. Scanning a record, searching for pieces, parts, and sections to sample, has always been as simple as moving a turntable's needle across the record as desired. The speed and accuracy at which you could locate (and relocate) different parts on a record gives sample-based beatmakers a certain level of immediacy and efficiency. For decades, no other medium could compare to the search speed that vinyl records allowed. Today, however, current production software programs like FL Studio and Pro Tools allow beatmakers to import entire songs (digital versions of course), which can than be quickly searched over with a click of a mouse. So with regards to search speed, other mediums have caught up with vinyl records to some degree. Still, search speed aside, there will always be a difference (sometimes slight, sometimes more pronounced) between the sound of a vinyl record and another format like a digital download or CD. And, of course, there's also the fact that each vinyl recording has its own subtle differences. Unlike a digital recording, no vinyl record sounds exactly the same because the wear and tear of each vinyl record is unique. In essence, static, hisses, warps, pops, and even scratches make each vinyl record a one of kind recording.

Setting the Record Straight About Vinyl Purism: Vinyl Records Are Not the Only Acceptable Medium to Sample

As I've discussed in this chapter, there is an aesthetic value to vinyl records that many sample-based beatmakers (all of the interviewees for this study and myself included) prioritize. Further, diggin in the crates, in the traditional sense, will always be linked first to vinyl records. Still, we must remember that the underlying idea and motivation behind diggin' isn't just about using one particular audio format or recorded medium, it's about the practice of mining/searching for new material to sample. In other words, diggin' in the crates, both as a traditional idea and practice of hip hop, extends beyond any one audio format or recorded medium even though vinyl records unquestionably represent the foundation of diggin'.

For example, as I discussed in chapter 2, in the early pioneering days (hip hop's first golden era), Afrika Bambaataa became the first to sample television commercials onto cassette tape and incorporate those samples into his DJ set. In doing so, Bambaataa made clear that diggin' for new source material wherever and however you could was the essence of diggin'. And that it was Bambaataa, one of the first three and most important hip hop DJs, who did this first means that diggin' for and sampling any material (that interests you) on any available audio format is just as traditional as diggin' for, sampling, and using vinyl.

√Check This Out – Should You Dig and Discard?

The question of "What to do with the music that you dig after you've sampled from it" is often asked. So here, I'll introduce a question and answer exchange that took place between a regular member of The BeatTips Community (TBC) and myself.

Question:

"I've been recording my records straight to Pro Tools, stopping it, if a song is done, grabbing what I like out of it, while looking at the waveform. And after I got what I want, I just delete the rest of the track. I think this approach may not be the best. How do you do it? Do you not record anything except the sample you want? When you sample from a record and you hear something you like, do you sample it immediately or do you wait for the song to end and then go back and grab it?"

Here was my answer in full:

I assume that you record a song straight into Pro Tools as a means for speeding up the musical process — that's understandable. But making music isn't a race against time. Sure, there are some things that can unnecessarily slow down the musical process. However, if you're going to sample, and you plan on being particularly skilled at it, then you're going to have to embrace the fact that it calls for a lot of patient listening to music.

I understand exactly what you (and others) are doing and why, but in exchange for saving some memory on your computer, you're actually decreasing your understanding of the essence of sampling. Thing is, by recording records straight into Pro Tools (or any DAW) with the conscious intent to essentially throw away what doesn't interest you, you're indirectly ignoring one of the most important components of the musical process: truly listening to music in a revolving capacity, over and over again through various periods. Recorded music is a reference that presents a timeless musical education. Why not take advantage of this reference?

Unfortunately, this is perhaps a consequence of e-diggin' or a rush towards a proficiency in sampling. Music is about having an emotional and physical connection. If you decrease that physical connection, you inevitably decrease the emotional aspect as well. Without an emotional connection to the music, you will always be limited to how well you can translate the essence and feeling from the music you sample. Sure, anyone can develop a "technical" proficiency in the science of sampling. But at the end of the day, that's all you're gonna get if there's no real emotional connection or reverence (or at least respectful admiration) for the source material that you sample.

There's nothing technically wrong with getting your music into Pro Tools. But I would recommend that you at least first record it on to a CD, then listen to it from the CD. When you have an idea of what you want to use, then sample (record) it into Pro Tools. This way, you still have the music in your personal collection for reference. For example, one thing that I do with the music that I'm able to find on YouTube and elsewhere, is that I play it through my Mackie analog mixer, then record it straight to CD. So not only do I have a complete reference of the song, I have it amplified and warm, as opposed to what it sounds like just coming through my computer audio outputs.

Finally, if you're picking at music like a vulture, discarding the parts of the song you're not interested in, like they hold (nor ever held) any other value other than to be sampled, then how can you truly understand the essence of sampling? It's no accident, nor is it coincidental that the overwhelming majority of music sampled falls between 1965 and 1975. There is a reason for that; there is something about the music itself that is being sampled. If you slice up a song, without any real regard for the song, how will you obtain any of the meaning or essence that the song yields? Furthermore, going forward, how will you be informed about what direction to take if you're destroying all of the clues?

Build Your Sampling Ear – How to Listen to Source Material, What to Listen For, and How to Find a "Good" Sample

A lot of people don't even know how to listen to records! –DJ Premier

There are two ways to approach listening to sample source material (music): **spot-listening** and **full-listening**. Both approaches require you to listen or survey the music that you intend to sample; however, the difference is in *how* you listen and survey the source music. Spot-listening is the process of randomly and rather quickly surveying a record. The idea here is to give quick-listens to areas of the record where you might expect the intros, breaks, bridges, and outros to be. For intros, you affix the turntable needle to the beginning of the record. Intros often have a "ready-made loop" that is free and clear without drums. This is why intros are very appealing to many sample-based beatmakers.

When I first started making beats, that's all I pretty much did. I probably spent three years like this. I would buy records and skim over them until something popped out. I would check over the beginnings of songs on an album, looking for ready-made loops. If I didn't find one, I would leave the record alone, thinking it held no value, without ever really listening to each song on the album thoroughly. I assumed that this was how most beatmakers did it. I reasoned, *'Who had time to actually listen to the complete songs on an entire album?'* But as purchasing records became more costly, I found myself going back to my crates for those records that I had once mislabeled as invaluable. The second, third, and even fourth time around that I listened to a record, I increased my patience and discipline until I was able to give each song on an album a full-listen.

In the process, I learned that spot-listening was most useful when working with records that I was already familiar with. For example, if I was looking for kicks and I remembered a drum intro or break from a particular song. In this case, it was helpful to target the areas of the song that I was already familiar with. But try to limit how much you spot-listen a record that you've never heard before. There's too much that you will undoubtedly miss. Hence, I recommend that when you have some records that you've never heard before, give each song a full-listen. Don't skim or skip ahead, and don't scrap the record just because you can't immediately find anything useful.

The Five Categories or Types of Samples: Complete-Phrases, Spare-Part Phrases, Section Pieces, Sound-Stabs, and Sound-Tones

All songs, regardless of the music genre, are made up of a combination of any number of varying musical phrases and smaller pieces of sound.[98] Thus, samples themselves can be broken down into five categories or types: **complete-phrases**, **spare-part-phrases**, **section-pieces**, **sound-stabs,** and **sound-tones**.

A **complete-phrase**, or full musical pattern, measuring one complete bar or more,[99] is like a short story. It has a clear beginning, a middle, and an end. As such, it's already conducive for a beat. In fact, think of complete-phrases as "ready-made-loops." Complete-phrases are very easy to identify, and therefore, they are easier to sample and loop, which makes them big targets for many sample-based beatmakers. Most sample-based beatmakers (new *and* advanced) often tend to listen for complete-phrases first and foremost. However, the more crafty sample-based beatmakers realize that the more rare the record that you're sampling from, the more rare the complete-phrases, and thus, the better the chance you have for achieving creativity and of avoiding the sample police.[100]

Spare-part-phrases are simply sections of larger complete-phrases. Sampling spare-part-phrases is more challenging because it requires serious patience and a knack for intuitive chopping.[101] The most interesting thing about spare-part phrases is how they stand alone like missing pieces of dialogue; as such, they help signal where the discussion may go. That is to say, each spare-part-phrase helps to determine how the entire beat will flow. Although it's much more difficult to identify and sample useful spare-part-phrases, the process is considerably more creatively rewarding.

---

[98] Here, I use "musical phrase" to describe any structured musical pattern that lasts for a measure of one bar or more.

[99] Usually, the complete-phrases that are sampled by beatmakers measure 2 to 4 bars. However, there are also some that measure just 1 bar, and there are some that measure up to as many as 8 to 16 bars. Samples of 4 bars or more are easily identifiable, and therefore, they usually present a sample-clearance headache.

[100] Sample Clearance is the process of securing permission to use samples (portions of a pre-existing recordings) within a new composition. Labels employ people to scan music for any sample that may have been used within the creation of a new hip hop/rap song. Therefore, beatmakers take heed: If you sample a very identifiable or well-known complete-phrase (typical of the *sped-up-chipmunk-sound* variety), beware of a potential sample clearance problem. It used to be that the artist would pay to clear the sample, now, many artists are sticking that tab with the beatmaker. Chapter 11 includes a thorough examination and critique of the sample clearance process.

[101] **Mental-Intuitive Chopping** is the ability to hear any musical phrase and formulate a chop-pattern or scheme in your head. It's similar to how film directors shoot footage according to the edits that they foresee inside their heads while they're shooting the film. In this way, these film directors are virtually editing the film in their heads.

With spare-part-phrase sampling, you sample the root notes/ sounds of a complete phrase (not the entire measure of the phrase) of a preexisting recording, then flip it, i.e. creatively transform it into something new and original. Here, the phrases or pieces that you sample won't be nearly as easy to identify as the original complete-phrase from which it came. Therefore, when you use spare-part-phrases, it's more likely that you will avoid any sample clearance woes. Another benefit of spare-part-phrase sampling is that it trains and develops your musical ear and overall understanding of rhythm arrangements and drum and loop programming.

It's worth noting that a number of classic beats, produced by many of the beatmaking pioneers, were actually recreations (random manipulations) of just one sample. In those cases, spare-part phrases were almost always used. The more experienced beatmakers are skilled at one-sample beats. They know how to chop, copy, or manipulate *one* sample to the point where the original sample is unrecognizable, even though the original mood and integrity is in some way still left in tact. In fact, the core track[102] of nearly all sample-based beats are composed of or based upon one primary sample. The main point with spare-part-phrase sampling is that it always prompts you to create beats using the shortest or simplest fragments of pre-recorded music and sounds.

Both complete-phrases and spare-part-phrases are comprised of smaller elements called **section-pieces**. Section-pieces are shortened or incomplete musical patterns. Because of their duration, they're often uneven, and therefore, they usually require something else to sustain them, for example an additional complete-phrase or spare-part-phrase. As with spare-part-phrases, section-pieces offer *source anonymity*. But it's substantially more difficult to identify the source record from which the section-pieces were sampled. Because section-pieces are widely uneven, heavy or light at the beginning of the phrase and heavy or light at the end of the phrase, they require a great deal of chopping. So as you would expect, beatmakers who hone their chopping skills with section-pieces become master

---

[102] The **core track** is the fundamental beat framework, it consists of the primary rhythm section and main theme of the beat.

choppers.

Sound-stabs are individual instrumental sounds, single hits, like a drum kick. Surveying records to sample is a meticulous process. A lot of times, you can feel prohibited from sampling something, either because the record doesn't have any interesting phrases or because the good (interesting) phrases are *trapped* (not free and clear from other unwanted sounds).[103] But the fact is, nearly all records can be salvaged for sound-stabs. Everything from short or long horn-hits to keyboard strikes and tambourine shakes make for excellent sound-stabs.

Sound-tones are sustained fragments of section-pieces. They work like sound-stabs, in that they are quick single hits. But sound-tones are slightly different from sound-stabs because they are often made up of multiple sounds, not just one single instrument. Since they are simply chipped off fragments of a larger section-piece, sound-tones are a big favorite among chop-masters like DJ Premier, Pete Rock, Kev Brown, Marco Polo, and 9th Wonder.[104]

Finally, I should point out that complete-phrases, spare-part-phrases, section-pieces, sound-stabs and sound-tones can all be used and blended together in a variety of ways, but the two primary types of **sample blends** are: **phrase-blends** and **stab-blends**. **Phrase-blends** are usually more about connecting one phrase or more to the front or back end of another phrase, whereas **stab-blends** are usually more about layering[105] one sound-stab with another.

Signal Chain

A **signal chain** is the connective audio route between two or more devices. When it comes to sampling, a proper signal chain plays a critical role in the *capturing* of the distinct nuances of a

---

[103] **Free and Clear**. When sampling sound-stabs and phrases, a sample is considered to be *Free and Clear* when there are no surrounding sounds, particularly drums or vocals, that prohibit it from being "isolated" and sampled clean and clearly.

[104] For a more thorough education on the sound-tone technique in practice, study DJ Premier and Pete Rock. Both of these beatmakers are chop-masters, and sound-tones often play a prominent role in their production.

[105] **Layering:** The process of combining two or more sounds into one. It is typically achieved by taking one sound and placing it on top of the other.

sample. Furthermore, a proper signal chain is paramount to the development of a beatmaker's own unique sound.

For instance, I run my turntable, CD player, cassette player, VHS, and DVD all through my Numark DJ mixer, which outputs an analog signal. From my deejay mixer, I send the master L/R outs to my Mackie analog mixing console. Then from there, I route two direct out channels (which carry the Numark's signal, from my Mackie), to the LINE input of my Akai S950 or my Akai MPC 4000. I use this signal chain so that I have more control over the E.Q.'s and amplification of the sounds and music prior to me sampling them. When you sample something, the idea is to arm (prepare) the best (perhaps loudest) possible audio signal, *without clipping*, that you can. To achieve this sort of amplification, it's best to use some kind of DJ mixer as the hub through which you run all of your audio sources to be sampled.

BeatTip – Naming Samples and Choosing Audio Bandwidth Settings

Before I sample anything, especially drum sounds, I come up with a short and descriptive name. If I do not readily have a name to associate with the sound, I simply use a "default" name. For instance, if it's a snare, and I can't relate anything to what it sounds like, I simply name it "snrx1" ("snr" for snare, and "x" for whatever number). If and when I use the snare again, I rename it more descriptively, then I store it with my library of drum sounds. (I avoid using elaborate names because it takes up too much time scrolling and assigning long names.) Bottom line: When it comes to naming samples, I try to keep it as simple and as relative as I can. Also, I should point out that I never name anything a "loop." Why? Because complete-phrases are not actually loops, they are breaks that are *programmed* to loop. (Because songs of the 1960s and 1970s were typically recorded using live musicians in the studio, most of those songs do not come with "loops," *per se*.)[106]

Further, whatever sampler you use, I recommend that you use a default audio bandwidth setting.[107]   More specifically, I do not recommend using dramatically different bandwidth settings for everything that you sample. Don't get me wrong, you won't really disrupt anything that you normally do when you use varying settings. It's just more time consuming, and it goes against customizing your sound. But if you do ultimately decide to use different audio bandwidth settings, I recommend that you at least make those the default settings for the types of sounds that you sample. For example, always use the same audio bandwidth setting for deep, hard kicks, or thick bass lines, etc. One benefit to having a default audio bandwidth setting is that it saves you a lot of valuable production time. Moreover, it enables you to sample new sounds more rapidly and efficiently. It also familiarizes you with what works, like how certain sounds might best be sampled and edited. Finally, another reason that I utilize a default bandwidth setting for nearly everything that I sample is because it allows me to customize and uniform my sound.

Chopping/Editing

> When, we chop, we do it in a way that even the artists who are really against how rappers use shit would appreciate how we put it into a different form, out of respect! All of that pours into the way that I make beats. That's what always keeps me fresh. —DJ Premier[108]

Samples are edited (altered), fundamentally, through one or two processes: "chopping" and/or "filtering." **Chopping** describes the process of dissecting, separating, and rearranging a sample

---

[106] When beatmakers say that they got a loop from a record, what they actually mean is that they sampled a complete phrase, usually 2 or 4 bars, and then looped it. This is why the notion of *looking for "loops"* in pre-recorded music is a misleading proposition...
[107] A higher Audio Bandwidth setting, or rather higher frequency response level, will make the sample sound brighter. The frequency response level is one of the things that separates the Akai S950 from the E-mu SP 1200. Although both units are 12-bit, the Akai S950 has a higher (range) frequency response level, therefore, sounds have a bigger, warmer overall sound. Many samplers today offer a choice of 24- or 16-bit.
[108] Excerpt from my interview with DJ Premier.

(and other sounds) for use in a beat. It's the process of removing or trimming unwanted sections from a sample. Typically, it involves trimming sections from the start and end of a sample. However, as your overall beatmaking skills develop, you will undoubtedly chop and manipulate various sections of a sample.

When you chop a sample, your main concern should center around an audio snapshot. Let me break it down. When you play a record, you know, move the needle around, what happens when you hear something that you like? You get a broad, quick "audio snapshot" of where you might be able to take that segment. So you sample it. Now that it's sampled, what's your prime objective? To simply tune it (trim it) down to the right start and end points? Not necessarily. Naturally, the first thing to do is to chop it to the exact segment that you heard. Sometimes this works out just like you imagined it, but most of the time it doesn't. So when you chop a sample, you should be prepared to end up with something that you didn't necessarily see clearly at first. Remember, when you hear something that you like for the first time, before you sample it, it's just a quick, broad audio snapshot; and thus, the photo, so to speak, is not entirely clear. It's only after you've sampled the segment, chopped it, and tried it *within* a drum framework that the picture starts to become more clear.

In this way, sampling is like sculpting. What I mean is that you always have to be prepared to shave off *more* than you initially intended. And on the other hand, you have to be ready to reapply, reshape, and reconfigure those seemingly unwanted shavings. The goal is to make the illest beat that you can; it's not about how many chops you can work in or how many modifications that you can apply to a sample. Chopping is about extracting the pieces that work best with your drums. It's not just about cutting and truncating something; it's really more about understanding what happens to a sample when a piece of it is removed or rearranged and reapplied. Thus, chopping prompts you to uncover the unintended sounds and feeling of the original sample. It let's you survey the texture of the initial sample, giving you a broader pallet from which to paint your beat portraits.

Chopping is also akin to improvisation, because it involves embellishing the source material/music, on the fly, with little to no musical direction at the onset of the beat. From one recording to the next, a sample-based beatmaker *improvises* how to transform what he samples.

Finally, there are two broad forms of chopping: basic and complex. **Basic chopping** describes a simple, minimal form of truncation of a sample/sound at its start and end points. The most notable form of chopping within the basic chopping form is loop chopping. **Loop-chopping** describes the basic chopping form that is used for chopping loops. **Complex chopping** describes the more extended form of chopping. It includes the processes of cutting sounds down to "tonal chops," that is, chopping samples/sounds down to individual notes for the purpose of being played (often in some chromatic manner), over drum pads or keys, or *drawn* into a beat sequence through the use of a mouse. Within the complex form of chopping, there are two sub-forms: **stab-chopping** and **phrase-chopping**. **Stab-chopping** describes the complex chopping form that is used for chopping sound-stabs, e.g., drum-hits, key-stabs, and tones. **Phrase-chopping** describes the complex chopping form used for chopping phrases.

BeatTip – Precision Chopping: Finger-Point Accuracy

Here's a good rule for precision chopping. In the sample edit mode of your sampler, tap (press) the play back button (or key on MIDI controller or key on a computer keyboard) repeatedly until the sound plays on the *hit* of your fingertip. If the sound is not falling on the hit of your fingertip, then you need to chop (cut) the **start point** of the sample some more until it does. If the **end point** carries over longer than you want it to, then you need to chop (cut) the end point of the sample until it stops where you want it to. The idea is to tap, not hold, the play-back button when you're first chopping the sample. If you hold the playback button too long, you will get an inaccurate starting point. After you establish the right starting point, then you can hold the play-back button down. This allows you to play back the sample in a way that permits you to capture the intended end point.

I should also point out that while chopping drum sounds is more straight forward than chopping any other type of sounds, when chopping phrases, you have to be much more careful. The reason is because the start and end points of phrases have the power to off-set any drum timing. That is, the precision chopping of phrases is critical for a different reason: phrases actually play *over* the drums. So, if the hit of the phrase is off a little, not hitting on that finger-point accuracy, it will make the entire drum program or looped sequence sound off.

√Check This Out – The Genius of Chopping Before "Auto Chop" Functionality

Technology has long raised questions about musicianship, musicality, creativity, and imagination. And now it would appear that it is reshaping what it means to have "skills" in beatmaking, especially in the area of chopping. Consider the auto-chop function on the Akai MPC (models 4000, 1000, 2500, and 5000). Where does the skill enter into the equation? Is it the source selection? Is it the setting of an automatic 16 to 32-piece, chronological chop, something previously only achieved through a beatmaker's careful selection, good ear, and meticulous manual chopping? I'm not sure where skill begins or ends when this now go-to functionality is used, but one thing's for certain: Auto chop, and it's ability to make some beatmakers appear to be doing much more than they actually are, has become more than just a tool for evenly chopping up samples, for some, it's become a creative crutch.

Even worse, some beatmakers are using auto chop as a means of copying the styles and sounds of some of the best known sample-based beatmakers. Auto chop functionality has virtually given birth to thousands of DJ Premier sound-alikes. But it's important to make the distinction that the core of DJ Premier's process and setup (he uses an Akai MPC 60 II and Akai S950 as well as a MPC

Renaissance) does not rely upon auto-chop functionality.   His sampling and chopping style is the product of a good ear and his unique manual chopping schemes, not auto chop functionality.

Though I'm an avid Akai MPC 4000 user, I'm reluctant to use one of its most popular features, the 32 region sample divide capability, aka "auto chop." Instead of sampling something and automatically dividing it into 32 regions, I prefer to sample something, duplicate it (two or three times, sometimes more, if necessary), then assign it to three or so separate drum pads on my MPC. In doing so, I find that I get a better feel for the many different ways in which the chops of one sample can be used.

But when it comes to auto chop functionality, I have mixed feelings. I was groomed on the Akai S950/MPC 60 II combo, and before that, I'd used the E-Mu SP 1200 along with my S950. Both setups only allowed me to chop samples manually, there was no 32 region sample divide, push-button architecture that would automatically chop up a sample for me. Because I knew that I'd have to manually chop samples, I found that I listened to source music more acutely. Specifically, I listened closely for possible start and end points of the streams of sounds on a given piece of music. As a result, I was able to develop a better feel for the ways in which sounds, particularly complete musical phrases, could be chopped up and re-arranged, in a manner that most favored my style, sound, and sensibilities. On the other hand, the use of auto chop hasn't prompted the same sort of experience. Instead, when I use auto chop, in some ways, I actually feel like I'm being less creative. The process of assigning multiple regions of a sample for it to be automatically divided into separate parts seems too easy (at times), or at least less demanding of your diggin' and chopping skills, specifically, how you hear chops in your head. Still, I'm not totally against using auto chop.

Auto Chop does have its advantages. For example, if you want to audition specific parts of a sample without having to manually chop each piece that you find interesting, then using auto chop is the way to go. Or let's say you want to quickly sketch out an arrangement idea using a full scale (12 chromatic pieces), of a sample. With auto chop, you can quickly slice up a sample, then program its parts with pitch adjustments. Of course, as I mentioned earlier, the same idea can be achieved without auto chop. But auto chop allows you to perform this process much faster, with more immediate separate chops per performed function. Because of its robust functionality, auto chop quickly opens up a new level of possibilities that could not otherwise be achieved without it. So when used thoughtfully and creatively, auto chop can certainly enhance your workflow.

But the workflow advantages aside, if you're not careful, auto chop can stifle the way in which you approach chopping all together. Auto chop can essentially reduce chopping to nothing more than a scheme of regions and numbers. Which is to say, it can take away a lot of the craftiness or ingenuity that you regularly find associated with manually chopping duplicated samples. Think about it: You load up a sample, assign the automatic splits, then voila!: 16 to 32 neatly sliced pieces of the same sample. Because of this, auto chop can prompt you to focus less on the ways in which a given sample can be chopped and more on the prospect of shoving a sample into the "auto chop box." This, in turn, can make you rely more on auto chop functionality and less on your own intuition and ingenuity or your familiarity with the given source material.

Sound Manipulation

Meticulous Transformation (and Disguising Samples)

The pursuit of creativity is one reason that many sample-based beatmakers engage in the meticulous transformation of samples. The other (practical) reason is to disguise samples. As such, there are a number of ways to both ensure creativity and disguise the source material that was used. And most transformation/disguise techniques fall into four main categories: chopping (which I've discussed earlier in this chapter), layering, distortion, and filtering, a more complex technique that I discuss in greater detail later in this chapter.

Layering Techniques

Layering, the process of taking one sound and placing it on top of the other, can be done with a number of sounds. Cuts and scratches, vinyl static, percussion and drum sounds, sound effects and more can all be layered over the top of a sample. Added together with any combination of other techniques like chopping, distortion, or filtering, a sample could be transformed or disguised beyond any recognition to its original source.

Distortion Techniques

Distortion, the process of modifying the sound, character, and texture of a sample in a way that makes it sound completely different than its original intent is another popular technique among sample-based beatmakers. When we sample something, we consider what the sound is, in its original state, and what it can become as being two entirely different things. For instance, a guitar riff can be chopped, layered to itself, distorted, and filtered and turned into a bass line. The sound of a shook key chain can be used as a tambourine; in fact, it can be layered with a snare to make a unique snare-tamb sound. A tom tom from a song can be sampled, pitched down, and converted into kick drum. The many different ways that a sample can be transformed and disguised through distortion are endless.

Note about all sound manipulation techniques: Each transformation/disguise technique contains any number of processes, including EQ'ing and other sound processing practices. So although there are four main categories of transformation/ disguise techniques, there is no limit on the number of ways you can transform or disguise a sample.

Making Samples Sound Thicker: Fattening up Samples

Two of the most common questions regarding the sound of samples are: 'How do you make a sample not sound *thin?*' and

'How do you add *umph* to a sample?' To answer these questions appropriately, you must first consider the sound source that you are using. Are you sampling from vinyl records? Are you sampling from a CD? Are you importing an .mp3 or .wav file? This matters a great deal because the potential modifications of a sample are only as good as the *sound* of the sample when you first sample it, the brighter the sample, the thinner it will sound, and therefore, the harder it will be to make it sound "warm." And *umph* is a separate issue that I discuss later in this section. But in both cases, the fundamental thing to understand is that the approach that you take in this matter is really determined by the sound and source that you *start* with. Typically, vinyl will always have a more thicker (warmer) sound than a CD. Likewise, a CD will always sound thicker than an .mp3 or .wav file. In fact, though .mp3 and .wav files may indeed be cleaner and brighter, they're thin to begin with. On any given recording, each of these formats produce an aural response that sounds as if 1/4 of the sonic quality has been shaved off (compressed) and flattened. Therefore, when you work with an .mp3 or .wav file, the first thing you might want to do is *re-sample* it into your own sampler. This way, you have more room to play with. Once you recapture the sound into an environment that you control (i.e. a sampler that you know), you can go about modifying the sample into a thicker sound.

With vinyl and CDs the process is a little different. Instead of *re-sampling* the sample from the vinyl or CD, just duplicate it (make an exact copy of the sample) then focus in on the lower tones and frequencies. The **duplicate and layer** method allows you to build up the sonic quality that you're aiming for. Many beatmakers will sample something and just let it be. Then after they throw in some drums and percussion, they believe that the sample is "thin." Most of the time, it's not even an issue of the sample being thin, it's just that the drums are texturally and sonically stronger than the sample. Thus, in a situation like this, I recommend that you "boost" (enhance the sonic impact) the sample with a lower frequency version (copy) of itself.

The other thing that you can do is program in low and low-mid sound-stabs. Here's what you do, check out the sample that you want to use, identify the parts in the sample that you hear thinness. Next, determine which sounds in the sample (instruments) are causing that thinness. The majority of the time the thin-spots will be either a guitar, bass, or keyboard. After you've determined the thin-spots in the sample, make and play sound-stabs that match the tone and timbre of the thin-spots. To get the sound-stabs to match the thin-spots, you'll have to modify either their velocity, sustain, attack, overall volume, or all of the above.

Incidentally, adding *umph* to a sample is very similar to what I just described. If all you want to do is add *umph* to a sample, you need not always duplicate and layer the sample. Instead, you can simply accentuate the sample with a combination of percussive elements and short (or medium) bass-stabs.

Filtering Samples

Filtering refers to the process of boosting or subtracting various EQ levels (i.e. bass, mid, and treble). Filtering is a sound coloring or enhancing technique that is often misused or grossly underestimated. Typically, when beatmakers are talking about filtering, what we're really talking about is tweaking the low and high frequencies of a given individual sound or sound phrase. The "low" being the *bottom*, for instance, the low frequency in bass lines, bass kicks, low-note piano and organ keys, stuff like that. Filtering is also about accentuating the hi and and mid instrument frequencies, like horns, strings, and hi-hats. The effects and enhancements that filtering can offer are tremendous. Creative filtering can *fatten up* (bring out) a weak bass line. At the same time, it can push down unwanted high and mid frequencies, or it can vitalize weaker high and mid frequencies. Furthermore, filtering can tuck or *hide* unwanted sounds (sometimes even vocals) deep inside the sample.

There's a couple of good filtering techniques that are commonly used. For your lows, the process is fairly straight forward, so long as your sampler has effective low and hi-pass filtering functions. Both of my samplers, the Akai S950 and the Akai MPC 4000, have filtering functions, yet each are very different. The Akai S950, a vintage sampler, has the simplest filtering function that I've ever used. Essentially, it has a filter value of 0 to 99, 0 being the lowest level and 99 being the highest level. Via the S950's menu dial, the value can be adjusted up or down until you reach the desired tone, feel, and texture. The Akai MPC 4000, on the other hand, contains a rather extensive filtering function that is comprised of a series of filtering *pages* that are designed to color the frequency of a sound in various ways. In order to filter samples on the Akai MPC 4000 (and many other contemporary samplers like software samplers and keyboard workstations with sample engines), you have to tweak both the low and hi-pass filters separately. But whether you use a vintage sampler or a contemporary one, in either case, the idea of filtering is universal: Bring down the lows to kill the high and mid frequencies and turn up the high frequencies for brightness. To achieve this with contemporary samplers, you have to increase the value of the low-pass filter and decrease the value of the hi-pass filter if you really want to fatten up low-end sounds. You also have to adjust the level of resonance, which essentially smoothens out the *scope* of the filtered bass line.

√Check This Out – My Process for Filtering Out Bass Lines On The Akai S950 or the Akai MPC 4000

Before I break down my process for filtering samples on the Akai S950, I should note that the technique which is used is, in theory, pretty much universal, and therefore, it can be applied to any hardware or software sampler. However, it must further be pointed out that the sound quality, feeling, and warmth will vary from EMPI to EMPI. So here's what I do, as well as the most notable masters of the Akai S950. *(Big respect to Peter Panic for teaching me this technique. And much respect to DJ Premier for confirming and thoroughly explaining it to me.)*

- In the EDIT PROGRAM mode, I locate the sample that

I want the bass filtered out on.

- Then I go to the Keygroup page (page 03).
- Where it says Copy (+), I initiate the (+) sign.
  This will copy the entire Keygroup, the sample, the filtering parameters, the assigned output channel, and all.
- Next, I locate the *new* Keygroup and assign it to a different channel, preferably the channel/output on my mixing console that is next to the channel/output of the high part of the sample. (Note: I use all eight individual outputs of my Akai S950, and each are assigned to their own channel on my mixing console.) Then I set the filter on the new Keygroup to 0.
- Now, when I strike the assigned pad on my MPC, I will actually trigger *two* sounds simultaneously. Thus, I'll have both a mid to hi sound of the sample and a low sound of the exact same sample.
- Therefore, on my mixing console, I simply mix the low part with a little more bottom, being mindful to keep it warm. On the other hand, I mix the mid to hi part with some hi, a little more mid, and nearly no low at all. And thus the proper blend will effectively filter out *(bring up)* the bass.

Today, while many beatmakers use some form of a mixing console, most do not use a S950 sampler. So essentially what I just described above is the practice of duplicating a sample, then treating it as left and right stereo sound, the left being the low, the right being the hi. So the idea is just to copy the sample, and EQ the duplicate in a manner that contrasts the original. To achieve this using a Hi-Pass/Low-Pass filter combo, make sure you *ground* the Low-Pass filter, that is to say, boost up the low. At the same time, you want to pull back on the Hi-Pass filter until you decrease the distorting *rumble* of the bass sound.

Pro Tools (or any DAW), really makes this process easier and even more effective. Regardless of whatever sampler you're using, if you have access to any DAW, then all you need to do is duplicate the audio track for which you want to filter. From there, just EQ the duplicated track until the bottom is out in front where you want it.

Filtering Out Bass Lines On The MPC 4000

My process for filtering out bass lines on the Akai MPC 4000 is different, but it's *easier* in it's own right and much faster than my process with the Akai S950. Here's how I do it. In the Program mode, I go to Edit page, then to the Filter page. It should be noted that within the Akai MPC 4000, there are 35 different types of filter modes (options). When I want to filter a sample to sound *comparable* to the sound that the Akai S950 generates, I use the "Lo<>Hi" filtering option. There, I set the default cutoff frequency somewhere between 15-23, and I set the Resonance value somewhere between 10-17. Keep in mind, increased resonance increases presence and "thickness" of the bass, but it also induces *rumbling* (distortion) the higher you go up the value dial.

Chapter 5

The Mechanics of Sampling, Part 2:
Composition and Arrangement in the Art of Sampling

Composition, Arrangement, Programming, and Sequencing

To really understand the concept of sampling, you must understand how arrangement works, more specifically, how to weave samples (fragments of recorded music) into a montage of sound. There's two ways you can look at arrangement. You can look at it as the order and measure (length) of sounds and sequences within a song (composition), or you can look at it as the pattern in which sounds correspond sequentially within any song (composition). The length (measured in bars or seconds) and sound of a sample determines the way in which the backing drum pattern is going to be arranged. Until the backing drum pattern is established, which gives you the core track (the basic rhythm track), the arrangement of the composition can not be completed. Understanding how standard drum patterns work with varying sample arrangements (e.g. 2-bar loop beginning on the downbeat), allows you to map out how you will be able to manipulate your samples. This is critical because it teaches you how to break samples into multiple sections, i.e. the intro, verse, chorus, and bridge.

Before discussing sampling and arrangement/programming and sequencing in detail, it is necessary to first look at composition, arrangement, and programming as it is understood in the beatmaking tradition. In its simplest understanding, composition, as it is in the beatmaking tradition, refers to the process of creating and coming up with sounds (ingredients) and the ideas for using them. The compositional process in beatmaking has no need for, is not predicated upon, nor does it necessarily rely on a *written* composition, as is the case in the Western classical music tradition.[109]   Instead, composition in beatmaking involves the process of developing components and pieces of music that in turn, are combined, arranged, and built into separate *blocks* of music that are then joined together to form one whole musical work. It is through this creation of separate music blocks, sequenced together using hardware and/or software sequencers, that the character of composition in beatmaking is most realized. In the beatmaking tradition, the overall aim and essence of the compositional process is to come up with a "break," the musical anomaly that the earliest hip hop DJ pioneers found on records, and then cut, mixed, and blended together into new compositions. In this vein, beatmakers are doing the job of the earliest hip hop DJ pioneers, and also the job previously reserved for traditional musicians and composers.

Here, I should further note that in beatmaking, this break that I speak of is usually made up of 2- or 4-bars. This is particularly important to know, as it helps in determining how and where *changes* (motifs) can be applied in the music work. For instance, a 2-bar break doubled up is 4-bars. So the typical spot that an effective change can be inserted is somewhere near the middle or end of the 4th bar. Likewise, 4-bars doubled up is 8 total bars, and therefore, the typical spot that an effective change can be inserted is somewhere near the middle or end of the 8th bar. (Of course, a change can be inserted anywhere in an arrangement, as long it serves your intended purpose.)

Programming

In the beatmaking tradition, the compositional process is closely linked to the programming process. In fact, in beatmaking, the term

---

[109] For a detailed comparison of some of the fundamental characteristics of the beatmaking and hip hop/rap music traditions and the Western classical music tradition, see the "Music Theory and Culture Part" of *The BeatTips Manual.*

"programming" can at times refer to several different processes all at once, it just depends on the context. Programming can refer to the technical organization of the compositional components; it can refer to the *technical* organization of the arrangement components; or it can simply refer to the process of inputting technical instructions into EMPIs, like the values for certain functions and the like. Drum programming, which is actually *drum composing*, specifically refers to the program (compositional) approaches beatmakers take to create their drum frameworks (drum patterns and overall designs). I like to divide drum programming (composing) into three different categories: simple, steady, or complex drum programming. **Simple drum programming** describes the composing approach that renders a bare minimum drum framework — drum patterns and designs that essentially stay the same throughout all sequences of a song. **Steady drum programming** describes the composing approach that renders a drum framework that contains a *steady* back beat and also slight changes on alternating bars, perhaps an extra kick here or there, maybe an open hi-hat. **Complex drum programming** is a bit more involved; it describes the composing approach that renders a drum framework that contains more deliberate pattern changes on alternating bars. Complex drum programming may include two or more kicks, snares, and hats, and double or triple drums. Break downs, custom drum rolls, drum fills, and "stutters" are also common characteristics of complex drum programming. Likewise, a more involved percussion scheme, like the inclusion of a timpani, chimes, bongos, and such are also great examples of complex drum programming.

Finally, if composition, in general, is the process of developing components and pieces that form music blocks, and if programming is best described as either the *technical* organization of the compositional components or the process of inputting technical instructions to EMPIs, then arrangement is the process of *creatively* organizing the components, pieces, and subsequent music blocks into a conscious thematic order. In simpler terms, arrangement, as it's understood in beatmaking, refers to the approach that beatmakers take when *arranging the elements* of their beats. This involves the use of different techniques in basic structure, for example, 2-bar, 4-bar, 8-bar, and 16-bar schemes. It also involves the use of different techniques within arrangement themes and within the sectional structures that make up songs, i.e., simple, steady, or complex transitional developments, and the schemes that make up the verse, intro, hook (chorus), and the build-up (bridge) sections. In the following section, I break down how the composition, programming, and arrangement processes manifest themselves in the three main compositional styles of beatmaking.

Parts, Components, and Elements; and Progressive and Repetitive Arrangement Schemes

All beats are made up of separate music parts. Each part contains a variety of music components; and each component is comprised of a number of different music elements. For example, a drum framework is a music part, and the particular patterns of each drum sound within a part is a music component, and the individual drum-hits (sounds) within a music component would then refer to the music elements. This formula can be used for phrases of strings, keys, and the like. In other words, **arrangement** is literally the creative organization of the separate music parts, components, and elements.

In beatmaking, arrangement can also be split into two broad schemes or rather structured varieties: **repetitive** and **progressive**. **Repetitive arrangement** is essentially the organization of music parts in a manner that consistently repeats a primary musical theme.[110] In the repetitive arrangement scheme, the onus is placed on remaining (in some way) close to the essence of the hip hop/rap DJ's musical processes, the earliest compositional roots of the hip hop/rap music tradition. This is to say, the repetitive arrangement scheme is a structure that seeks to represent the processes in which DJs cut or blended the breaks from records together into new compositions. Examples of repetitive arrangement schemes include

---

[110] Virtually all forms of mid/late-twentieth-century American popular music features some sort of a repetitive arrangement scheme.

sample-based beats like those that rely on one lengthy sampled music phrase, or those beats that take multiple chopped samples and fashion them into one cohesive music part. Further examples of the repetitive arrangement scheme include synthetic-sounds-based beats that rally around the use of prominent and oft repeated phrases. A sample-based song that really demonstrates the repetitive arrangement scheme quite well is Nas' "Memory Lane (Sittin' in da Park)," produced by DJ Premier. And a synthetic-sounds-based song that demonstrates the repetitive arrangement scheme quite well is Red Café's (feat. Fabolous) "Bling Blaow," produced by Reefa.

Progressive arrangement is essentially the organization of music parts into several (or more) progressively different musical themes. In progressive arrangement, the onus is placed on structuring a succession of music parts that unfold through a song in linear — rather than cyclical — progression. But even in the progressive arrangement scheme, repetition is still a key factor. However, unlike the repetitive arrangement scheme, the progressive arrangement scheme is not necessarily predicated upon the repeating of or consistent returning to one or two specific themes. Instead, the emphasis is placed more on developing multiple themes and, at times, more complex music components.

The progressive arrangement scheme can often be effective, especially when it's used in deference to the hip hop/rap music tradition. For one thing, a progressive arrangement scheme can shake up any monotony that may exist from generic drumwork or a typical loop of a very lengthy sample. Also, because a progressive arrangement can go a long way in establishing unique contrasts in a beat, it's very useful when you're trying to convey a sense of urgency within a song. Furthermore, a progressive arrangement can also be an excellent structural scheme for story-themed songs, because the changes within the music components and parts work like chapter accompaniments; moreover, the changes can provide more acute depth and *distinguished* meaning for each of the rapper's verses. A very good example of a progressive arrangement scheme (albeit a simple one) is 50 Cent's "If I Can't," produced by Dr. Dre and Mike Elizondo.[111]

Special Note About Some Beatmakers Moving Towards the Progressive Arrangement Scheme

I'm compelled to note that today there's a sizeable number of beatmakers who are increasingly moving towards the progressive arrangement scheme as their base arrangement method. There are several reasons for this development. First, there's a lack of knowledge of the roots of the beatmaking tradition among new beatmakers. So there are a number of beatmakers who are simply unfamiliar with the roots and fundamentals of the hip hop/rap music tradition. Furthermore, many new beatmakers are unaware of the fundamental aesthetics, tropes, nuances, principles, and priorities of hip hop culture itself and both the hip hop/rap music and beatmaking traditions. Thus, many of these beatmakers tend to take their musical cues from the music forms and traditions that they know. But more alarming than that is the fact that there are some beatmakers (mostly new ones) who project a total disregard for the roots (and even the recent history) of the beatmaking and hip hop/rap music traditions. So in both cases, these beatmakers are prompted to incorporate (in wholesale fashion) the aesthetics, tropes, nuances, principles, and priorities of *other* music traditions that are not in-line or consistent with the beatmaking and hip hop/rap music traditions. Incidentally, this is one reason why there's been a recent uptick in the number of beatmakers who have deliberately tried to fuse the "trained musician" nuance into beatmaking. Specifically, there's been a more concentrated, *forced* effort to apply advanced concepts of music theory to beatmaking.

The second reason that a sizeable number of beatmakers are increasingly turning to the progressive arrangement scheme deals with the lure of the pop music scene. Right now, pop music

---

[111] For all that the progressive arrangement scheme can offer, if there is any knock that can be made about the progressive arrangement scheme it's this: The more progressive an arrangement gets, the further the beat actually moves away from the hip hop/rap music tradition. And the more it steps *away* from the hip hop/rap music tradition, the closer it moves towards other music traditions or other forms of electronic music. In other words, it becomes *less* hip hop/rap.

seemingly presents itself as the "safe" music genre for the fledgling music industry to endorse, therefore, many beatmakers are largely buying into this. But the fact is, professional beatmakers have to deal with both the artistic and business realities of beatmaking. So I'm not quick to cast judgement on any beatmakers who have made, or are considering making, this journey. But even though trends can indeed offer short runs of opportunity, individuality and distinguishable creativity is what consistently offers the best sustainable opportunities and career longevity.

Finally, the move of a number of beatmakers towards a more progressive arrangement scheme has also been brought on by an identity crises, one perhaps caused by either a deep inferiority complex or a self-hate of their own music tradition. For years, the hip hop/rap music tradition operated in the shadows of mainstream neglect, but as the American mainstream made room for and, subsequently, co-opted key areas of the hip hop/rap music scene, many beatmakers found themselves in cultural and financial spaces that had been previously inaccessible to beatmakers, DJs, and rappers. Thus, for the first time in hip hop/rap's history, many beatmakers are forfeiting the pursuit of dope beats and are instead becoming much more preoccupied with how they measure up as "music producers" with those from other mainstream (more traditional) music forms. Hence, these beatmakers have come to view more elaborate arrangement schemes as a sort of conduit *out* of hip hop/rap music and into modern-pop and dance music. Many of the beatmakers within this group seemingly despise being labeled as "beatmakers" or "hip hop producers." They instead want to be known only as "music producers," free of the hip hop/ rap tag. This despite the fact that beatmaking and hip hop/rap music has been and is paramount to their ability to even compete in a narrow-minded and otherwise non-inclusive music industry.

Special Note About Sequencing

Before I go on with a more detailed discussion of the composing, programming, and arrangement processes in beatmaking, here, it's necessary to discuss the nomenclature that is associated with the term "sequencing." In beatmaking, the term "sequencing" actually refers to two separate things. One meaning of sequencing deals with the obvious: the sequencing (linking) of multiple EMPIs. It's the linking up of equipment through MIDI. Once linked up, sound generators (samplers, modules, etc.) redistribute their sounds through the main linking device, or better yet, the "master sequencer" within one's setup. In this meaning of the word, sequencing refers to the way that the pieces of your gear communicate with each other; each piece has its own say, but it is the master sequencer that has the *final* say. Therefore, the goal is to use a master sequencer that *talks* well with all of the gear in your setup. EMPIs use the same language to communicate with each other, via MIDI, but getting multiple pieces of gear to link in the manner that suits your workflow best is an entirely different dialect. For instance, the Akai S950 can be triggered by any Akai MPC as well as any keyboard workstation or controller; but *how* each unit *links* with the Akai S950 (or any other stand alone sampler for that matter) will vary.

The other (perhaps more prominent) meaning of sequencing deals with beat structure; that is to say, the actual process of *programming* the structure and arrangement of a beat. Thus, under this meaning of sequencing, a "sequence" is the arranged and recorded program data within any measure. And simply put, a beat is composed of multiple sequences linked together.[112]

Finally, I should point out that though beatmakers vary in the amount of equipment that they may utilize to create beats, nearly all beatmakers strive to sequence everything through one sequencer. This is one of the reasons MIDI is important. It allows the sequences created in other EMPIs to be streamlined and *sequenced* (recorded) into one master sequencer. This is yet another example that demonstrates how a beatmaker is, in effect, the composer, the arranger, programmer, *and* the musician all at once.

---

[112]The use of the term "sequencing" in this manner was popularized primarily by beatmakers of the Pioneers/Avant-Garde Period of beatmaking, ca. 1988-1995.

Group Map Assignments Extended: Triggering Non-Drum Sounds Through Drum Machines, Keyboards, and MIDI Controllers

Before discussing beat structure, it's important to first examine triggering sounds in more detail. "Triggering" sounds is simply the process of playing a pre-programmed sound, via a drum machine's pads or the keys from a keyboard or MIDI controller or computer keyboard keys. Whether you sample your own sounds, use preset sounds, or a combination of both, the way in which you trigger those sounds is critical to your workflow and personal beatmaking style. In order to successfully trigger your sounds, they must first be placed in the most effective position; and by effective position I mean that your sounds have to be assigned to the pads or keys that work best for you and your compositional style. With regards to drum machine pads, it's important to note that the manufacturers of these machines (most notably Akai, E-Mu, and Roland) give each individual pad a name, e.g. PERC, HIHAT, etc. However, you do not have to assign the drum sound to the pad name that denotes the sound that you want to assign. For instance, you don't have to assign a percussion sound to a pad marked PERC; you can assign any sound to any drum pad. In fact, you should ultimately develop your own preference for which pads you want to use to trigger your sounds. But no matter how you do decide to assign your individual sounds, I strongly recommend that you assign your sounds into Group Map Assignments.

A **Group Map Assigningment**, hereafter referred to as GMA, is a way of organizing sound categories into groups and then assigning sounds to drum pads or keyboard/MIDI controller keys, according to those groups. For example, "main drums" can be a group, "bass sounds" can be a group, "main samples" is a group, "percussion" is a group, etc. Organizing your triggering method into a series of GMAs will streamline how and where your sounds are placed and triggered; subsequently, it will improve the efficiency of your workflow.

Determining Where to Assign Your Sounds

If you use an Akai MPC of some sort, the Roland MV 80, the E-Mu SP 1200, or any other Drum Machine/Sequencer that uses a similar 16-drum pad design to sequence your music and gear, then you will be familiar with the snapshot below. Here's an example of how I map out particular sounds across the 16 pads of a given drum bank. I should note that all of my GMAs are also organized according to the different "banks" within my Akai MPC 4000. For example, the image below is a screenshot of my GMA for bank A, my "main composition bank." My main composition bank contains an assortment of separate sound categories. However, I use subsequent banks for GMAs of the same sound category, for example, I use bank C as my "percussion bank," it's where I assign my regularly used percussion sounds.

Figure 2 16-Pads of Main Composition Bank

Assigning Bass Sounds, Samples and Other Non-Drum Music

If it could be said that hip hop/rap music gets its identity from the drums, then it perhaps might be said that it gets its character from the bass. Therefore, when it comes to assigning bass sounds, I recommend that you assign them one row below your main drums. Keeping your bass sounds close to your main drums, in this case one row below, is very helpful for when you're trying out new drum ideas (and beat ideas in general), because it helps you facilitate the arrangement of those ideas quite effectively. Here, I should note that although playing the bass on drum pads is certainly quite different from playing your typical electronic bass guitar, the idea essentially comes down to the same thing: pitch progression. For samples, the notion of the rhythm section should be considered. And in keeping with the scope of the rhythm section in a band, I recommend assigning primary samples to the top row of four pads, just right above the drums. Finally, having assigned your main drums, bass sounds, and samples to the first top three of four rows or drum pads, I recommend assigning synth-stabs or percussion to the bottom row of pads.

√Check This Out – Inside My Process of Triggering the Akai S950 Sampler With the Akai MPC 4000's Sequencer

All digital samplers conform to the standards of MIDI, and therefore, they contain functions that are critical to effectively (and successfully) permitting the process of triggering the samples and sounds that it holds. In order for the samples of my Akai S950 to be triggered properly by my Akai MPC 4000, they must first be placed properly. Sample placement is simply the process of mapping samples out across the drum pads of a Drum Machine/Sequencer or across the keys of a keyboard or a keyboard controller. Samplers have different names for how you approach this, a vintage sampler like the Akai S950 uses "Keygroups" to facilitate this process. In order to playback samples from the S950 using the MPC 4000, I must first assign each sample (that I want to play/trigger) to a Keygroup inside of the S950. The way a Keygroup works within the S950 is that it denotes the pitch value at which each sample can be played back; in the case of the S950, the Keygroups contain 73 possible pitch value settings from which I must assign each sample to.

So here's my process. First, I set the pitch for Keygroup 1 to the exact same default pitch in which I sample all of my sounds. In REC mode, the mode in which all sampling is done on the S950, there's a page where you can set the "pitch of the sound being recorded" (sampled). I use the pitch value "C 60," the default setting of the Akai S950. Next, I move over chromatically, one pitch value (note) higher, as I assign new samples to new Keygroups. Thus, in my Keygroup settings, "Keygroup 1" is set at the pitch of "C 60," "Keygroup 2" is set at "C 61," Keygroup 3 is set at "C3# 61," and so on and so forth, all the way up to "G8 127," the highest pitch value possible of any pitch level within the S950. Keep in mind, however, whenever I need to trigger the same sample at different pitch values (note values), I either copy the Keygroup and assign the copied Keygroup to a different output of the S950 or I assign the sample to multiple Keygroups; for example, "Sample 1" assigned to "Keygroup 1," lowest key (pitch) "C 60," highest key "G8 127." If I were to assign "Keygroup 1" to the lowest key value of "C 60," highest key value "C 60," then "Sample 1" would only play at that pitch value from only one drum pad. However, by assigning the sample to varying lowest key and highest key values, the sample can be triggered at every pitch value (note) in between the programmed lowest key and highest key values.

So regardless of what sampler and sequencer combination you are using, you can easily apply the triggering methods and principles that I just outlined. It's not as complex as it might seem at first, but it can become difficult and very time consuming if you try to operate without a default Keygroup system of your own. This is why I advise mapping out the simplest Keygroup setting that you possibly can.

Beat Structure: The Basic Components – the Sequence and the Loop

A beat is composed of a series of sequences. A sequence is a program of chronologically arranged events (steps) within a measure of at least one bar. A "loop," the cornerstone time structure of beatmaking, is the perpetual repetition of the same sequence or series of sequences. For instance, a 1-bar loop means that the sequence plays for one bar, and when it reaches its end, it returns (loops) to the beginning of the sequence and plays again. Likewise, a 2-bar loop means that the sequence or series of sequences plays for two bars, and when it reaches its end, it returns to the beginning of the first sequence and plays again.

The Main Ingredients of a Successful Loop

The success or effectiveness of a loop depends on four things: (1) the chop (truncation) of the sound; (2) the pitch of the sound; (3) the tempo of the sequence; and (4) the drum framework (pattern and design of the drum arrangement). The chop or truncation refers to how the main sound phrase(s), whether samples and/or synthetic sounds, are chopped. This is to say, how *precise* the chops (cuts and truncation) are or how *purposefully off* they are; another way of seeing it is how long or short the main sound phrases are.

The pitch, in this case, refers to the pitch (speed) of the main sound phrases. Often the difference between a banger and a whack beat is the pitch of the primary sound phrase. Should you speed the sound up, slow it down, or leave it at the default pitch that you sampled it in? The tendency for most beatmakers these days is to speed the sound up. But remember, for every pitch value you go up or down, you affect how the sound will loop in a sequence as well as how it will sound over the drum framework and, ultimately, how the entire beat will flow.

The tempo of the sequence is just that, it refers to the tempo, the BPM (Beats Per Minute) value of a sequence, series of sequences, or song. Tempo determines the speed of the sequence and, subsequently, the beat. Hip hop/rap music usually falls within the

88 to 117 BPM tempo range, with 93-97 BPMs perhaps being the median. A deeper examination of tempo reveals that it does more than just determine the speed of the beat; the tempo also determines what I call "the turnover rate" of the loop. The turnover rate is the interval, the time and space, between the ending and beginning again of a sequence. The interval determines what I refer to as the "loop point," the audibly dead point right before the loop *turns over* to the next sequence. The slower the interval, the easier it is to hear the dead space, i.e. the loop point. Likewise, the faster the interval and, subsequently, the faster the tempo, the harder it is to hear or recognize the dead space, which means the loop point is seamless, no glitches. Unless you want to feature the dead point or a space-glitch as a component of the beat that you're making, you should generally increase or decrease the tempo until the loop point is seamless and indiscernible. Finally, I should note that whenever you're deciding on which tempo to use, always remember this: The right tempo can snap or slide the beat into place; the wrong tempo can drag the beat or crack it out of place, making the drum framework sound awkward.

Here, it's important to point out that "drum framework" refers to the pattern and design of the drum arrangement. When designing a drum framework, keep in mind that drum designs that are too *active* always disrupt the loop, if not the entire beat for that matter. On the other hand, drums that lack the right kind or level of activity (accents and overall structure) can really *drag* or *drain* the flow of the loop. The right drum framework is critical in beatmaking because the role of the drums is paramount in hip hop/rap music. This is because in the hip hop/rap music tradition, the drums are often called upon to maintain various responsibilities simultaneously. In all cases, the drums have to *steady* the beat, you know, keep it running smoothly. And in most cases, the drums also have to *knock* (present a distinct sonic impact) without overpowering the other musical elements within the beat. And still, in some other cases, the drums have to be balanced and subtle; that is, instead of taking a leading role, they take a supporting role.

Beat Structure: Creating and Programming Sequences

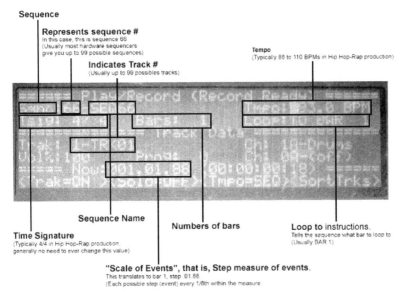

Figure 3 LCD of Main Screen, Akai MPC 60 II

As I mentioned earlier in this chapter, a beat is composed of a series of sequences. A sequence is a program of chronological musical events (steps) within a measure of at least one bar. An "event" or "step" within a sequence is simply the point at which any programmed musical *action* takes place. The event serves to represent when and where a piece of specific musical *action* (instruction) takes place within a sequence. An event can be anything. It can be as simple as a kick-stab, it can be a sample of any length, it doesn't matter. A "track" is also significant to our discussion here. A "track" is an individual channel (file) in which an event(s) is recorded in/on. Most sequencers allow up to 99 separate tracks within a sequence. Hence, all of your sounds (events) can be tracked within the same sequence, and on separate individual tracks. So you can have your kick on track 1, your snare on track 2, your hi-hat on track 3, your bass on track 4, and so on and so forth.

There are really two basic ways to create a brand new sequence, and, subsequently, create and build a brand new beat. You can either start with the drums, or you can start with the non-drum music material. What I mean by the *non-drum music material* is samples, bass lines, melodic lines of synthetic-sounds, etc. Many beatmakers can start a beat either way, so it's really not an issue of which way is better or worse; how each beatmaker begins a new beat ultimately depends on him, his mood, his resources, and his level of commitment to creativity.

You can start beats off by creating drums from scratch (that is, an entirely new drum design and pattern), or you can use your own default (preset) patterns that you've created previously and stored away. But if you're going to bang out a new drum pattern from scratch, please realize that the new pattern most likely will not be dramatically different from any other program you've created or will ever create. This is because (1) Many drum patterns share the same fundamental foundations; and (2) there are standard *drum pattern clichés* in beatmaking that all beatmakers consciously and subconsciously know. Thus, it is from these standard drum clichés that all beatmakers pretty much create new drum designs and patterns.

The other option for starting new beats is to go with the non-drum music material, i.e. samples, bass lines, melodic synth lines, and the like. The idea here is to get the music into a sequence as soon as possible. Take for example a simple sample, one bar in length. After I've assigned the sample to the pad that I will be triggering it from, I use the sample to create a new sequence in the sequencer of my Akai MPC 4000. The simplest way to do this is to record (place) the sample on the first step of bar 1 within the sequence. I can just go to step edit, then place the sample in. Next, I set a generic tempo, something like 93 BPM, then I play the sequence. As the sequence plays, I pay attention to how it loops. If there is a long pause (interval) between the ending of the sample and when the sequence loops over, then I know that the tempo is too slow. Likewise, if the sequence loops before the sample plays out *to the predetermined length that I've chosen*, then I know that the tempo is too fast. (Remember, when you're looping something, you want to make the loop point seamless, and unnoticeable). Once the sample is turning over (looping) to my liking, without any glitches, then I can go in and add drums, percussion, bass lines, keys, and whatever else. And once I know the tempo of how the sample should loop, I can also go to some of my preset (premade) drum patterns and put the sample in over the top of one of them.

Beat Structure: Song Form

All beatmakers are commissioned with the same seemingly impossible task: **make a loop not sound like it's _looped!_** Huh? Crazy, right? But the truth is, that's pretty much what it's about: Repetition without sounding monotonous. In this light, beatmakers are masters of the _misdirect!_ That is to say, we have to know how to misdirect the listener away from the monotony of the loop. But let's not forget that within the hip hop/rap music tradition, progression is based on and advanced by the concept of the loop, i.e. intentional repetition. Even though a typical hip hop/rap song may have any number of progressions, the power of the loop is what dominates the song. Other music traditions like jazz and rock 'n' roll are not as emboldened to the loop concept as much as the hip hop/rap tradition. Instead, in those music traditions, even though repetition plays an important role in the overall form, there is a premium on adding and advancing as many new changes in the arrangement as effectively possible, so as to progress towards some sort of thematic climax. It should be noted, however, that in the rock 'n' roll tradition, songs return to the core melody (or loop, if you will), but the changes are often so varied that it can not be considered loop-based in the same manner that hip hop/rap music is.[113] Hip hop/rap music is more about returning, that is to say, _returning to the core riff(s)/core groove and rhythm_, returning to the main loop(s). And because the hip hop/rap music tradition is based on cyclical progression (repetition) rather than linear progression (material growth), the arrangement of the musical elements is much more clear cut but _deceptively_ simple.

---

[113] There are certain forms of rock music that definitely lend favor to the loop-based medium of hip hop/rap music. For example, listen to 1970s power rock, especially Led Zeppelin; 1970s punk, especially The Clash; 1980s ska and pop blends, especially The English Beat and The Police.

The So-Called "Rules" of Song Form (Actually, In Beatmaking, We Like to See These "Rules" as Standards That Can Be Broken Whenever Necessary)

As with all twentieth-century American popular music, the song structure of hip hop/rap music subscribes to a general system of well-defined musical **sections**. In beatmaking, a typical song is composed of two to five different types of well-defined (arranged) sections. Each section is comprised of a series of sequences that are linked together through a program; that is to say, once all sequences are linked together they are converted into *song mode*. The two most important sections are the **verse** and the **hook** (chorus). The verse section refers to the *primary* section of the song; it's the instrumental section where the main rap verses (main vocals) will ride over, as such it is the section that will be heard the most. The main purpose of the verse section is to *establish and work the point* of the song. It's like the starting pitcher in baseball, it's job is to keep the winning momentum just long enough for the hook, the *closer*, to come in and ensure the victory (success).

The **hook** is the *secondary* section of the song; it's the instrumental section where the hook vocals will ride over. Even though the hook is secondary in terms of the real-time duration of a song, the hook is actually the **marquee** section: it's usually the section of the song that carries the most exclamation. This is why I like to call the hook section the "pay-off section." Even though it doesn't play nearly as long as the verse section, it's often the section that stands out the most because it carries the hook vocals, the most memorable part of any song. The main purpose of the hook section is to *reinforce and punctuate the main theme*, the main point of the song.

The other three types of musical sections that make up a song in beatmaking are the **intro**, the **build-up** (the bridge) and the **outro**. The **intro**, or what I sometimes like to call the "teaser section," is the lead-in section of a song. It's role is to establish the mood and to engage listeners, by giving a sneak preview of the caliber of music that's about to proceed; thus, in an arrangement, the intro is placed before the first verse section. The purpose of the intro is to draw you in, engage you, make you want to hear what's about to come next. An intro is also used for the initial ad lib vocals. I like to separate intros into two categories: either straight-ahead or counter. A straight-ahead intro is one that is made up of some of the same musical components (sequences/sounds) within the rest of the beat. This can mean the drum framework by itself, it can mean the melody and the hi-hat ridin', etc. On the other hand, a counter intro doesn't contain any of the components from the other sections of the beat, instead it contains components (sequences/sounds) that will not be heard again in the rest of the beat; i.e. it is independent of the rest of the beat.

The **bridge** (or "build-up") is a contrast or catalyst *change*. It's the section that *mediates* the verse and the hook. It's like the setup man in baseball, it relieves the starting pitcher, while at the same time, it sets up (*builds up* to) for the return of verse or the hook. The bridge usually occurs during the third main 8-bar phrase, and it is unique, in that it has the power to do two things to a beat: (1) it can serve as an interesting intermission or break within the song; and (2) it can serve as a crescendo or the last rising instrumental *statement*, signaling a climax or finale of a verse. The bridge is often just an octave or pitch change of the verse melody or rhythm. And just like the intro, it can be counter; it can be an independent section that contains entirely new components (i.e. sequences, sounds).

The **outro** section ties up the entire song. It's the section that advances the final thoughts of the beatmaker. It's the final touch, the finishing signature of the beatmaker. It also serves as that extra instrumental time (usually without vocals) that DJs appreciate for record blends. The outro, just like the intro and bridge, can be straight-ahead or counter. Typically, the outro is an understated (stripped-down) version of the main verse section, but it can also be completely independent, containing components that are entirely unique.

Here, it's important to note that when you're arranging and organizing sequences, remember to be flexible with the final structure, because until the beat is actually complete, every created sequence and subsequent section can be *rearranged*. This is why it's critical to know the different types of arranged sections, how they work, and their fundamental purposes. Indeed, when you're making a new beat, the entire arrangement is subject to change: The verse section can be reorganized to become the hook (chorus) section and vice versa; the intro section can become the verse; so on and so forth. Embracing this reality gives you more freedom to take intuitive chances when you're building those sequences that will ultimately be linked together into the current sections of the beat.

From Sequence to Section

By default, the first sequence that you begin with is your **core sequence**. From out of this sequence, you will most likely build the sequences that become the verse section. Most beatmakers do not start off making the hook (chorus) first. The hook (chorus) is usually just the verse section, sprinkled with just enough minor changes to distinguish it as the hook (chorus). This is why it's those changes and modifications that you're able to make to that initial core sequence that enables you to really get creative with the beat.

Earlier in this section, I broke down how sequences are often created, starting with either drums or non-drum music material. Here, I'll discuss more in-depth how beats are made, more *technically* speaking that is. The technical aspect of how beats are made can be described as: the composition of rhythm-based musical elements, followed by the process of recording these musical elements into sequences, followed by the process of linking these sequences together in preprogrammed arrangements.

And how are sequences linked together? The most common way that sequences are linked together is through the process of duplication, copying one complete sequence and attaching it to itself or to another sequence. You can copy and link as many sequences as you want to. In fact, you can even make a beat from just a 1-bar sequence. All you have to do is convert that 1-bar loop into a song; just copy the sequence to itself until you have the appropriate number of bars equal to the length that you want the song to be. This is the exact concept of duplication. Once you've established a **core sequence**, the idea is to copy the sequence to itself so that you can increase the length. A 1-bar core sequence copied to itself becomes a 2-bar core sequence; a 2-bar core sequence copied to itself becomes a 4-bar core sequence.[114] The advantage of duplication is that all events, especially the drum framework, remain in tact, even though the length of the measure has been increased. The more bars within your core sequence means the more opportunities to program in changes. Conversely, the shorter the number of bars within your core sequence, the less opportunities you have to insert changes. Remember, one bar *turns over* faster than two, and so on. Therefore, keep in mind that 1-bar loops also have the potential to restrict your programming and increase the probability of a simple loop; so it can increase the chance of the entire beat sounding stale or mundane.

Again, hip hop/rap music is not dependent upon linear progression, but instead, *cyclical* progression, i.e. repetition. Still, some beats that include a number of changes often come off *more pleasing* to a listening public conditioned to favor a more pop sound. On the other hand, rappers with great lyrical skills know how to incorporate their own verbal changes; to be certain, they can perform nicely off of any track. But all advanced rap lyricists favor tracks with more *stability*. That is to say, they tend to favor less noticeable changes, because the loop and repetition allows them to take advantage of a solid, continuous groove. Beats with too many changes often restrict a highly skilled rapper's verbal talents, forcing them to "dumb-down" their lyrical flow and subject matter. Therefore, one general "rule" you might want to consider for yourself is this: for highly *lyrical* rappers, keep the changes in your beat to a minimum. For all other rappers, it's O.K. to add more changes; in fact, the more changes in beat, the more easily their lyrical *deficiencies* are masked.

---

[114] Most hip hop/rap songs are based on 2- or 4-bar loops.

BeatTip – The Genius Of 1-Bar Core Sequences

Even though 1-bar sequences can be restrictive, as beats in and of themselves, establishing a 1-bar core sequence is one of the most fundamental ways to start a new beat. Point is, when I strike up a new core sequence, I already know beforehand that I will be duplicating the sequence, either way it goes. So it's important for me to establish a basic core sequence that has a tight (very effective) drum framework. Once I have a 1-bar sequence looping nicely, I copy it to itself, giving me two bars of a real tight drum framework. From out of these two bars, now I can take the beat anywhere. I can further build the verse section (the primary 2-bar sequences that I initially created from the 1-bar core sequence). I can build the hook (chorus), intro, the bridge, or outro sections, for example. After I've auditioned several changes, I make another copy of that 2-bar sequence, then I leave the initial 2-bar sequence off to the side as my default idea to return to, if I go too far off the range. Next, I move on, using the copy to sketch out any new ideas.

Song Structure

The bar structure of a typical hip hop/rap song (with three verses) breaks down like this:

- 8-bar intro
- 16-bar verse
- 8-bar hook (chorus)
- 16-bar verse
- 8-bar hook (chorus)
- 16-bar verse
- 8-bar hook (chorus)

Notice how the basis of this song structure is made up of 8-bar increments. From the song structure above, we can't automatically tell how different one section is from the next, but by seeing the mathematical relationship of the exact number of bars used for each section, we can perhaps infer that some sequences were duplicated to create others. Here's another example of a possible song structure:

- 8-bar intro
- 16-bar verse
- 8-bar chorus
- 8-bar verse
- 8-bar bridge
- 8-bar chorus
- 12-bar verse
- 8-bar outro

By making some common modifications to the previous song structure example, you're able to add more variety to the basic beat. In the second song structure example, notice the changes that I have inserted. One of the most difficult concepts for both new and advanced beatmakers to understand is the relationship between the measure of a sequence and timing. Think of the measure of a sequence as being a time-line of clearly defined, highly detailed events that once programmed, automatically repeat when the end of the time line (i.e. the total number of bars) is reached.

BeatTip – Section Contrast

A section contrast is the term that I use to describe an arrangement scheme in which two or more sections in a beat that are not predicated upon one another (based on most of the same elements) are moving in a similar direction and feel. One of the best things about a section contrast is the fact that, when done right, they appropriately add the value of variety as well as a strong sense of tension and release. This in turn makes both the chorus (hook) and verse sections of the song much more climatic, which ultimately keeps the interest of the listener. In sampling, these types of contrasts are often created using different chopped sections of the same sample.

BeatTip – Knowing the Right Tempo and Bar Structure for Samples

Most twentieth-century American popular music typically uses 4/4 time signature, which means there are 4 beats per measure (four beats per bar). It doesn't matter if there is any percussion to be heard, because any four-count will give you one complete bar in this time signature. Furthermore, beatmakers usually build beats using either 2-, 4-, 8-, 12-, or 16-bar sequences (basically, some multiple of 2). However, *which* numbered bar structure depends on the length of the sample(s) being used. One way to determine the right tempo and bar-count for a sample(s) is to simply determine the length (duration) of the sample(s). What you do is, listen to the sample, and run off a 4-bar count by snapping your fingers as if they were a metronome. If the sample(s) is a short phrase or riff, snap faster, if it's a longer complete phrase, snap slower.

An even easier way to determine the right tempo and bar-count for a sample(s) is just to record the sample(s) into a sequence and set the tempo to something like 89 or 92 BPM. Next, press play and let the sequence progress all the way through. Adjust the tempo as needed so that you can hear the complete sample(s) from beginning to end, without the end of it being cut off before it loops. After having played it completely through, when it loops back, without any exaggerated interval, then you've got the right tempo.

Sampling and Arrangement

The Three Forms of Sampling

When it comes to the various forms of sampling, there are both quantitative and qualitative considerations. Thus, the art of sampling can be broken down into three general forms: (1) **simple** or **"piggy-back" sampling**; (2) **break-beat or "mix" sampling**; and (3) **intricate sampling**. **Simple** (imitative) or **"piggy-back" sampling** is the form of sampling in which a substantial portion of a pre-existing recording is sampled and then "imitated" with little to no significant transformation of the sample used. Typically, this form of sampling involves looping a 4- or 8-bar break (from familiar or arcane sources), and combining it with a backing drum framework that "mimics" the drum pattern of the sampled work as close as possible. Usually, the "piggy-back" form of sampling utilizes known material (popular songs), wherein beatmakers use *sufficient familiarity* so that the listener may recognize the quotation (appropriated work) and may, in turn, pay more attention to the new material as a consequence of that familiarity. Finally, within the spectrum of piggy-back sampling is the simple *cut-and-paste* kind of sampling. Cut-and-paste sampling involves simply using a segement of a recording (usually the most prominent, most recognizable portion of another song) without transforming it in any real material way. Nonetheless, some cut-and-paste beats make for great songs, for example, Diddy's "I'll Be Missing You." Although it's a clear case of cut-and-paste sampling, the song is still recognized as a hit appreciated by many beatmakers.

Break-beat or mix sampling is the form of sampling in which breaks or patches of recorded works are woven together in a fashion more akin to a DJ blending and matching multiple segments of records. In this form of sampling, the sampled work can be both minimal and substantial, familiar or arcane. In this form of sampling, drum breaks are typically used as opposed to original drum programming. However, in some cases, beatmakers who utilize this form of sampling will add additional (usually very little) drumming.

Finally, **intricate sampling** is the most sophisticated (complex) form of sampling. It involves the deconstruction of the sampled work in an intricate manner, followed by a unique arrangement of the now substantially transformed sample. Using the intricate sampling form, beatmakers seek to convert both familiar *and* arcane sources into an entirely new medium, while staying within the aesthetic parameters of hip hop/rap music. A great example of the "intricate" sampling form can be heard in Nas' "Nas Is Like," produced by DJ Premier.

It should be noted that each of the three forms of sampling

involve either a use of *wholecloth, major,* or *partial* sampled elements. It should be further noted that each of the three forms of sampling are also distinguished by the degree of the transformative nature of the source material used.

BeatTip – Transformation, Reconceptualization, and Recontextualization

Much of sampling is about utilizing fragments of old songs (and other pre-existing recordings), altering and creatively rearranging them, then turning the altered and arranged elements into a new song. Of course the types of fragments chosen, as well as the preferred arrangement schemes and drum programming abilities of a given sample-based beatmaker, is what separates one sample-based beatmaker from another.

All samples and forms of sampling are not created equal. That said, however, those sample-based beatmakers who follow the sampler's code, especially with regards to creativity, always aim to do one main thing with the scraps of music that they sample: *Transform it!* And this transformation is most often achieved through reconceptualizing and recontextualizing the source material that they use. Some examples of reconceptualization and recontextuallization include things like: sampling musical phrases that originally served as brief intros on old records, then chopping them up, changing their pitch, contour, and sonic quality, rearranging them and using them for *any* song section (verse, chorus, bridge, even an extended intro). Another example involves using the tail- or front-end of a riff, duplicating it, and combining the twin sounds into one elongated sound that can be used for everything from a bass line to melody. In any case, the fundamental idea is to aim for creative transformation of samples by coming up with different ways to reconceptualize and recontextualize chosen source material.

I should further add that in this pursuit of transformation, transparency is not important for most sample-based beatmakers.

In fact, a distinguishing mark of dope sample-based beats is the intentional obscuring of the source material. Still, there are some instances where transparency is preferred, like when a beatmaker wants it to be known that he flipped a classic or well-known song. However, most sample-based beatmakers staunchly prefer not to be transparent with their source material.

Using Your Chopped or Filtered Samples to Make Beats

After you've collected and chopped your sample(s), you basically have two different ways to incorporate them into a beat. You can "paper clip" (blend and fasten) your samples to a preset drum beat that you've already created, or you can build a new drum beat from scratch, one that is based around the arrangement of your sample(s).

Minor paper-clipping is the process of taking a sample, usually a 2- or 4-bar complete phrase and *matching* a backing drum beat to it, or vice versa. It usually involves sampling a complete-phrase, i.e. a ready-made loop or a similarly long musical phrase. Essentially, it's just clipping one finished piece of music, i.e. a sample, to another finished piece (or pieces) of music, like a drum pattern. For example, let's say you have a preset drum beat playing on your MPC, keyboard workstation, or software sequencer. With the drum beat sequence in record mode, you simply trigger the sample right in over the drum beat. With the primary sample successfully recorded into the sequence, the sample (complete-phrase, etc.), along with the drum beat, now becomes the rhythm section, and as such, it serves as the **core track**[115] from which the entire beat's design (arrangement) will be orchestrated.

Major paper-clipping, or what I like to call **"B 'n' P-building,"** employs the same process. But in this case, you're using smaller samples (segments that have been put through the complex chopping process), and as such, it's somewhat more involved. Unlike minor paper-clippin', which tends to be characterized by complete-phrases and ready-made loops, major paper-clippin' is best characterized

---

[115] The **core track, composed of the core riffs and groove,** is the main framework for which the entire beat is based upon. The core track is the initial foundation of rhythm and groove and perhaps a simple melody. It provides the basis, the "core," of the beat.

by its use of "bits and pieces" (smaller segments of sounds). Major paper-clippin' requires a beatmaker to meticulously fashion both a backbeat *and* an air-tight rhythm while using non-ready-made loop samples to do so. Thus, B 'n' P-Building requires a beatmaker to have very creative chopping skills.

Building Arrangements Using Primary Samples and Derivative Samples

A sample or song that serves as the source material for which other samples are then derived from, is called the **primary sample**. A sample that's made *(chopped)* from a primary sample or any other sample already used in a beat is a **derivative sample**. One common purpose of **derivative samples** is to provide a change or progression to the sample from which it was derived. When sample-based beatmakers sample something from a record and build a new beat around it, we tend to return to that same record for the *changes* that we want to incorporate into the same beat (we also often look for separate recordings for changes.) Likewise, when we have a sizable complete-phrase, spare-part phrase, or a section-piece, it's somewhat intuitive to chop up the phrase even more, especially for the purpose of finding suitable changes that are likely to fit texturally and sonically with the core track that we've already established.

Building Arrangements Using Primary Samples Along with Derivative Samples

Whether you build your sample-based beat around your drums or build your drums around your samples, a very effective way of carving out tight compositions is by using arrangements that incorporate the use of primary samples *and* derivative samples. As I discussed earlier, you can make some quality beats with just one sample by itself. But one-sample beats are typically non-progressive in nature because they rely more upon a central, repetitive loop theme. So, if you're going to use samples and you would like to make more progressive arrangements, then you essentially have two choices: (1) incorporate several or more different samples from a number of different records; or (2) incorporate multiple samples from the same record. (This involves the process described above.) My recommendation is to aim for the derivative approach.

After you create your drum framework and you have the primary sample laid down, here's a couple of ways that you can work in the derivative samples. First, allow the primary sample to play for 4 bars, then program in one of your derivative samples, beginning on the 5th bar. Since the newly added derivative sample changes the sequence (program), it is considered a *change*; in fact, I call this "sample-change 1." When you only have one change, one very effective way to arrange your beats is on the "4" or the "8." That is, for every 4 or 8 bars, you work in "sample-change 1." If your "sample-change 1" is only 1 bar, double it up to 2 bars before you loop back to the primary sample. If your "sample-change 1" is 2 bars, you can either loop back to the primary sample, or you can double it up to 4 bars before you loop back to the primary sample.

If you intend to make an even more progressive arrangement, using only samples and very minimal synthetic-sounds, then you can add other derivative samples. Naturally, I call the next derivative sample added "sample-change 2," and the next, "sample-change 3," and so on. Multiple sample changes gives you a great deal of flexibility when you're building arrangements. For instance, you can bring one of them in right after the first sample change ends, landing the new change on every 7th and 9th bar that proceeds the primary sample. This technique enables you to *build out* the texture of the beat, using samples in a carefully crafted arrangement pattern. Furthermore, it allows you to build better sound collages for your drum programs.

Here's what the formula could look like, using primary samples and derivative samples:

- 8-bar intro = 4 bars of "sample-change 1" + 4 bars of "sample-change 2"
- 16-bar verse = 4 bars of primary sample + 2 bars of "sample-change 1" + 8 bars of primary sample + 2 bars of "sample-change 3"
- 8-bar hook = (This is where you can get really out there.

Mix up the drum program, rotate in two changes, while keeping the primary sample moving steady. Or you can drop the primary sample all together, and play the changes off of the new drum program.)

- 16-bar verse = 4 bars of primary sample + 4 bars of "sample-change 3" (or "sample-change 4" if you have it) + 6 bars of primary sample + 2 bars of "sample-change 1." (This is the middle of the song, so you can really push the envelope.)
- 8-bar hook = Keep steady.
- 16-bar verse = 4 bars of primary sample + 2 bars of "sample-change 2" + 2 bars of "sample-change 1" + 8 bars of primary sample.
- 8-bar hook (chorus) = Keep steady.
- 8-bar outro = 4 bars of "sample-change 1" + 4 bars of "sample-change 3."

Summary of the Mechanics of Sampling

If anything, the examination in the previous two chapters should dispel the notion that the art of sampling is simple, easy, or void of its own compositional system. Within the mechanics of sampling, there are many different dimensions. Collectively, these dimensions underscore the *science* of the art of sampling. This science, better stated as *the Sampling Equation*, encompasses a unique system that includes philosophical, technical, and compositional spectrums as well as a code of ethics. Thus, to truly understand (and appreciate) the mechanics and compositional tract of the art of sampling in the hip hop/rap music tradition, one must first understand this robust equation.

Chapter 6

Drums and Sampling

Without dope drums, you can't have a dope beat. –Marley Marl

Drums are the most important part of a beat. –DJ Premier

I spend a lot of time making sure that my drums are right.
–DJ Toomp

Drums are the cornerstone of a beat. Regardless of whatever non-drum arrangement a beatmaker creates, it is always the drums that serve as the foundation, the glue by which all other elements within a beat stick together. Therefore, it is typically the drums that garner the most attention from beatmakers. In this chapter, I will examine drums in all of their beatmaking glory. From the basics of drum sounds to the various structures that drum programs formulate, I will explore both the aesthetic and functional roles that drums play within the beatmaking process.

The Basics: Drum Sound Categories

In beatmaking, drum sounds are divided into four primary categories: kicks, snares, hats, and cymbals. For each type (category) of drum sound there are multiple variants. For example, from among the kick variety there are standard bass kicks, "booms," and "808s." A standard bass kick is your garden variety bass drum, a boom is a more amped-up bass kick sound, and an 808 (named from the famed Roland TR 808 drum machine) can be described as a super-powered boom with an additional sustain and broader resonance.

Within the snare drum variety there are standard snares, snare toms, woodblocks, and rim shots. It's important to note that in beatmaking, snare sounds (and kicks and hi-hats) can be anything that *represents* the role of a snare, not necessarily a typical snare sound (more on that later, when I discuss the role of drum sounds and programming).

Among the hat variety of drum sounds there are hi-, open-, and closed-hats (or mid-hats). **Hi-hat** refers to the sound of standard hi-hat cymbals in their default position, not tightly closed but resting close to one another. Think of a drum set in which one hi-hat cymbal rests on top of the other, held loosely together by the hi-hat foot pedal. Thus, in beatmaking, the sound made when these two cymbals are held loosely together and struck is what is meant by a typical hi-hat. Likewise, **open-hat** refers to the sound of standard hi-hat cymbals in the their maximum open position. **Closed-hats** refers to the sound of standard hi-hat cymbals in their closed position, i.e. held tightly together.

Within the cymbals variety there are "rides" and "crashes." **Rides** refers to the ride cymbal sound of a standard drum set, **crashes** refers to the gong-like cymbal sound that is created when two cymbals are *crashed* into each other. Here, I should also point out that there are a number of secondary percussive sounds that beatmakers use to compliment primary drum sounds. These secondary percussive sounds include shekeres, triangles, blocks, tympanies, sleigh bells, tambourines, and castanets.

Drum Sound Representation, Not Always Actual

In beatmaking, drum sounds do not always necessarily correspond with the actual category of sound that it represents. For instance, snares are not always actual snare-drum sounds. Instead, the term "snare" is used loosely in beatmaking to describe *any* sound that is *used, played, and programmed* where the snare drum sound typically would land within a drum pattern. In other words, in beatmaking, the term "snare" serves to represent *any* sound that acts like, or carries the purpose and associated dynamics of, a snare drum. Hence, snares in beatmaking can be anything from the captured sounds of a hammer hitting a chair, to a drum stick smacking the top of a shoe box (both things I've done before). It should be noted that this same representational/actual duality of drums in beatmaking applies to all drum sounds as well as bass sounds. For instance, a kick can be any sound that represents the sound and impact that simulates any variation of the sound that a bass drum typically makes. So for example, a kick can be something as creative as a sample of a boot kicking a shoe box stuffed with t-shirts (I've made a kick from that very sound). Likewise, a bass sound doesn't necessarily have to come from a bass guitar or the bass patch of a keyboard/synthesizer; a bass sound can be made from the low-end filtering of an organ patch or something similar.

How Many Drum Sounds Are Enough?
Core Set (limited) Drum Sounds vs. Unlimited Set of Drum Sounds, and Customizing and Sampling Your Own Drums

The number of drum sounds that a beatmaker should have is highly debatable. There are some who believe that you can never have enough sounds. On the other hand, there are those who believe that you should have simply a core set of drum sounds. So what is the right amount of drum sounds? Truth is, that's up to each individual beatmaker. However, when deciding upon how many drum sounds to carry, either a core (limited) set or an unlimited set, there are a number of things worth considering.

To begin with, you must recognize how the *sound* of drums are perceived and valued in the first place. In beatmaking, as well as in traditional drumming, the value of drums is predicated more upon *tonal* possibilities rather than simply *quantitative* possibilities. That is to say, it's not the sheer number of available drum sounds that are really important, but rather it is the various kinds of tones (unique sounds) that drum sounds can produce.

Traditional drummers can employ several different techniques to produce different tones. For example, they can tighten or loosen the skin heads on their drums, or they can modify their playing style to manipulate the velocity, attack, and sustain of a drum strike; each technique has the potential to render a unique tone. Likewise, through effects processors and the like, beatmakers can also modify their drum sounds. And just as with traditional drummers, beatmakers in their playing/programming can also manipulate the velocity, attack, and sustain of the drum sounds that they deploy. Here, it's worth noting that traditional drummers often do more with less. Celebrated drummers like Clyde Stubblefield, John "Jabo" Starks (both most famous for playing with James Brown), Bernard Perry, John Bonham, and Neil Peart did not have an arsenal of snare sounds, yet they were able to carve out very distinct sound signatures. This is because the style, approach, and modification that a particular drummer uses is paramount to their ability to tap the various tonal possibilities of a given drum sound. Because beatmaking is a form of electronic music production, there will inevitably be a larger selection of drum sounds to chose from. However, that being said, this does not change the fundamental value of drum sounds. The tonal possibilities of drum sounds still trumps the sheer number of drum sounds.

But those who advocate for having an unlimited set of drum sounds have their arguments as well. Some maintain that an unlimited amount of drum sounds leads to a better drum sound library, which in turn makes for more creativity. But if the purpose of a drum sound library is for amassing both a set of standard and customized drum sounds so that one can create and develop their own unique sound, then an *infinite* number of drum sounds actually undermines this purpose and contradicts the creation of one's own unique sound. After all, a unique overall drum style and sound requires familiarity; and familiarity depends upon a beatmaker's ability to repeatedly use a core set of drums in new (creative) ways. *All great drummers have their own style and sound.*

There are some beatmakers who purport to use entirely new drum sounds every time that they make a new beat. So it would seem that an unlimited amount of drum sounds presents a beatmaker with an unlimited amount of options. But here's the question that begs to be asked: Is such an approach actually practical or even worth it in the long run? An infinite number of drum sounds doesn't necessarily translate into an infinite amount of quality. For instance, let's say you have a set of 500 separate snares. If you were to critically survey each snare, how many of those snares would truly sound distinct and unique? In fact, how many times would a certain tone be replicated? Furthermore, how many would actually be *usable*? What I'm getting at is that out of a given set of 500 snares, it's not at all unreasonable for one to expect to find many that are quite similar. Finally, there's also the management and real-time use issue of deferring to an unlimited set of drum sounds. Scrolling through thousands of drums sounds just takes something away from the creative process. For one thing, it's time consuming; but more importantly, it disrupts a beatmaker's workflow, which in turn hampers the creative process.

√Check This Out – Core Drum Sounds and Unique Style

Another point I want to make is that a core (limited) set of drum sounds tends to breed a sort of familiarity and personal style and sound, whereas an unlimited set of drum sounds tends to breed an over-reliance on variety for variety's sake as well as a degree of uncertainty and indecision, which typically leads to bad choices.

At one point in time, I probably had more than 5,000 drum sounds. I had nearly all of the MIDI Mark drum kits, the Kid Nepro drum kits, Sample Kings drum kits, various drum sound CDs, the E-Mu SP 1200 full drum sound library, the Akai S950 full drum sound library, and, of course, sampled drum sounds from over 14 volumes of the Ultimate Breakbeat Records series. I even had drum sound libraries that were comprised of sounds that I recorded and had mixed at Unique Recording Studios and D&D Studios. Needless to say, I once had a large drum-sound library. Then I got real about what I was doing and what I *wanted* to do: Ultimately, I simply wanted to make meaningful, dope beats. But paying too much attention to building up an infinite drum-sound library was actually destracting me from this ultimate goal. Once I made that revelation, I vigorously started purging my drum sound library. I tossed out every drum sound that I wasn't using. After that, I did another purge; this time I tossed out all drum sounds that I considered to be just *okay*. I went on to do even more purges, separating the nice drum sounds from the good drum sounds, followed by a separation of the dope drum sounds from the nice ones. When all was said and done, what I was left with were those drum sounds that I thought were dope and those sounds that worked best within the style and sound of beats that I wanted to create.

I understand that some beatmakers thrive on having an unlimited set of options at their disposal. Some beatmakers simply like the notion of having unlimited choices. But what often happens in these cases is that you find beatmakers who are force-feeding their beats, using new drum sounds simply because they have them, not for their distinct tonal value or unique character or because they actually work well within their style of beats. For many beatmakers like myself, it's not about spending unnecessary time searching for an arbitrary perfect snare; it's about locating a snare from your library that you know well, and making that snare sound fit right with the theme of the beat at hand.

As I've already discussed, drum sounds can really be divided into four main categories, with additional sub-categories. For instance, you have heavy kicks and standard kicks; then there's standard snares and "irregular" snares; next there's hi-hats, closed-hats, and open-hats; and after that there's cymbals: rides and crashes and the like; and finally, there's the secondary percussion sounds: tambourines, rims, bells, timpani, and the like. Of all of the aforementioned kinds of drum sounds, I carry about three to five drum sounds of each variety. And *if* and when I find that I can't make any of those sounds work with a new beat that I'm making, then that means that the new beat is whack, simple and plain. Here's the bottom line for me: I know my personal drum sound library very well. In fact, I know my drum sounds far better than I know my gear, and almost as well as my favorite records. But when I had 5,000 drum sounds, there was no way that I could realistically ever know all of those sounds. Therefore, I prefer the feeling of knowing that my drum kit, if you will, is set and ready to go whenever I have a new idea.

Drum Sound Customization and Building a Drum Sound Library

Because the drums are such a prominent feature of the hip hop/rap music tradition, and because beatmaking is set in a pre-recorded-based medium as well as live performance-based medium, beatmaking relies, to a great extent, on extensive sound modification of individual drum sounds. But when it comes to drum sounds, the truth is, there are only but so many standard sounds that you can have: a typical bass kick, 808 kick, boom kick, mid-pitch snare, truncated snare, shekere, hi-hat, open-hat, closed-hat, ride, and crash. Thus, an appropriate number of standard drum sounds (within your choice of sound) should comprise of your base set of drum sounds. And once you've added the appropriate standards (within your choice of sound) to your drum sound library, the balance of a unique drum sound library is usually made up of customized drum sounds. For many beatmakers, the most effective drum customization comes from the manipulation and modification of drum sounds that are already in their base drum sound library. Hence, here, it is worth examining some of the methods for customizing drum sounds.

There are several somewhat simple ways to effectively customize drum sounds. The easiest way to customize a drum sound is through truncation or the chopping and shortening of sound. Next, you can manipulate the velocity (volume and release) of a drum sound, and you can also manipulate the pitch of drum sounds. There are also a number of complex methods for customizing drum sounds. There are those processes that involve the EQ'ing (sound coloring and leveling) of drum sounds. EQ'ing drum sounds essentially involves turning up or down the low, mid, or high frequencies of a given drum sound. Then there are those methods that incorporate the use of external or software effects processors; these methods include things like adding compression, chorus, or reverb to a drum sound. Methods like these are considered to be more complex, because they demand a greater amount of experience and understanding of sound frequencies, effects processors, and, of course, beatmaking itself.

BeatTip – Methods for Customizing Drum Sounds

Here are my primary methods for customizing drum sounds. First, it begins with a beat. After I track (record) a new beat into Pro Tools, I pick a drum sound, usually a kick or snare, then I sample it and rename it as a variation of the original. Because Pro Tools allows me to solo (isolate) individual tracks, I solo the drum sound that I want to modify, next I play the track, then I sample (duplicate) the drum sound and rename it as a variation of the original sound. For example, if the original drum sound was "snare 1," I name the variation "snare 1 x." If I want to thicken up a drum sound, I duplicate it a couple of times, then I play the track and sample all three sounds together as if they were one drum sound. For added effect, I may EQ each of the sounds separately or modify their pitch somewhat, before I sample them.

Another way that I customize drum sounds is similar, but it involves first using my Akai MPC 4000 and my Akai S950. First, I create a basic drum track, or I use a drum track from a previous beat that I made. Next, I take the drum hit or stab that I want to customize and I layer it on top of itself by programming the event in the sequence of the beat. But instead of layering the same hits exactly on top of each other, that is, at the exact same step (event) in the sequence, I offset each hit about one or two events (steps) in the front or behind the original hit. It is then this new "fattened," more resonant sounding hit that I then record into Pro Tools. Here, I should note that all of my EMPIs are routed through a Mackie 32 channel analog board (mixing console). So the signal that is ultimately recorded is further *beefed* up (amplified) before it lands in Pro Tools. Once inside Pro Tools, the process can get even more complex, as I might do additional EQ'ing or slap some reverb or other effect on the drum hit. Finally, when I'm happy with the result, I sample that sound back into my Akai MPC 4000 or my Akai S950. Again, it's important to point out that the signal routes through my analog mixing console *before* it hits my Akai MPC 4000 and/or my Akai S950. Once this is done, what I end up with is a new drum sound that is unique and modified to my desired tonal and sonic spec.

The establishment of one's own sound is mostly about sonic preferences (preferred frequencies), arrangement scopes, types of sounds and tonal preference, individual approach and technique, and, of course, an underlying style. Therefore, in this overall scope, drum sounds should be routinely interchanged and reused. This is one of the fundamental things that beatmaking is about: just flippin' (alterating) familiar sounds, techniques, and styles in ways that gives a beatmaker his own unique style and sound.

Assigning Your Main (Primary) Drum Sounds

Assigning drum sounds to pads (or keys) is every beatmaker's personal choice. Each person's musical inclination and eye/hand coordination directly influences the ways in which they assign sounds to a drum machine's pads. And though there are no real wrong or right ways for assigning drum sounds to pads (indeed, I have a peculiar way of assigning my main drum sounds, which I demonstrate in the figure below), I do believe, however, that some pad assignments are more practical than others. In the following section, I will describe one of the most simple and practical ways that you can assign your main (primary) drum sounds over a standard 16-pad bank of a drum machine.

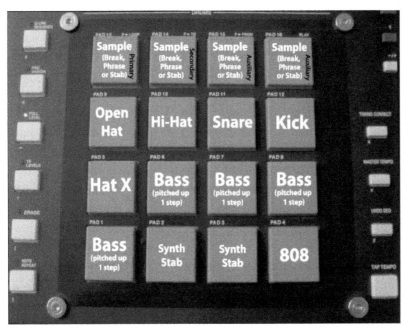

Figure 4 Front 16 Drum Pads—Primary and Secondary Drum Sound Assignment

For your main drums (kick, snare, hat), I recommend that you assign them to the top first-three pads or the bottom first-three pads. There are two practical reasons for this. First, drums are the backbone of a beat, and therefore, they get used more than any other element within a beat. Hence, it helps to have your drums mapped out and assigned in a position that compliments their overall importance. Another reason why it's practical to assign your primary drums to the top first-three pads or the bottom first-three pads is because drums are generally tracked (recorded) into DAWs in the same order: *kick, snare, hat*.

After you've assigned your main kick, move over one pad and assign your main snare. What's the logic behind this? Well, when you're trying to create drum patterns from scratch, it helps to have the snare as close to the kick pad as possible. Is this a rule? No. I've seen some beatmakers who have their snares assigned directly underneath their main kicks. When I started making beats, I tried each of these ways, and what I found was that it was easier and more effective for me to slide *horizontally* from kick to snare than *vertically* from kick to snare. Moreover, I found that I could make faster pattern progressions. That is to say, with the snare placed one pad over (horizontally) from the kick, I was able to jab my middle finger to the snare pad faster. This improved my drum timing, my overall timing, and my arrangement capabilities.

Having assigned your main snare, I recommend assigning the main hat (or ride) to the next pad over from the snare. You have to be careful with hats because at their best, they're actually very subtle, but at their worst, they can sound obnoxiously bad. Hence, the importance of hats and their role will vary from beat to beat. Even still, you should give hats (and cymbals) the same positional respect as the kick and snare. Again, pattern development plays a key role. So here's why hats deserve the same positional respect. Most beatmakers build the main drum framework by starting with the kick and the snare. Then, having successfully created a pattern, they then add the hat in over the top of the drum and snare, creating a basic drum sequence. After the individual kick, snare, and hat patterns are programmed and looped, the overall collective pattern becomes the main drum framework. And when a beatmaker plays back the drum framework (drum sequence), it is the hat that often gives you the most accurate indication of whether or not the pitch of the framework is right for the beat at hand.

I also like to keep the hat within the first three pads for another reason: timing. That is to say, I often use a hat in the same way that most beatmakers use the metronome tone. When I create beats, most of the time I actually don't even use the metronome tone; I know the tempos that I like to work within, usually 88-99 BPM; therefore, I have a good indication of where things are supposed to land in the measure of the sequence. When the metronome tone is audible, it disrupts my flow and concentration. So if I ever have a timing issue, I simply make a quick 1-bar loop of hi-hat hits. Since I know that a standard hi-hat pattern (1, 2, 3, 4, on up to 8) lands on basically every 6th step or event within a 4/4 measure, a simple 1-bar loop of hi-hats helps me get the timing right. After that, I adjust that bar to the desired tempo, using the hat pattern as a guide. From there, I play the kick drum and snare in real time over the top of the hi-hat.

For the next pad over from your main hi-hat, I recommend that you reserve this pad for your open-hat or even a second hat sound. In fact, the additional hat on this pad can really be anything from an open-hat, to a ride, to sleigh bells, or a tambourine. These second hats can be either used as layers, or they can be used more sparingly, like every other bar or every fourth bar, etc., for accentuation and emphasis.

The point I hope to make clear about drum sound assignments is that it's practical to assign your main drum sounds on neighboring pads (or keys). Having your main kick on the third pad, top row; your main snare on the fourth pad of a middle row; and your main hat on the first pad, bottom row doesn't seem very practical for programming your main drum sequences. Such an assignment, which would require your hand position and fingers to move much faster than perhaps necessary. And this factor can increase the probability that your timing will be off, or at least, it will make it difficult for you to achieve the timing that you want. However, on the other hand, if you assign your sounds in relative, pre-determined mapped out groups, especially your main drums, you undoubtedly will gain a number of advantages.

Group Map Assignments (GMA)

The most obvious advantages of Group Map Assignments (GMA), is the proximity that it allows, and ultimately, how practical it is. Presumably, the closer the pads (sounds) that you want to trigger — in conjunction — are to one another, the easier it will be for you to move from one pad (sound) to another. Instead of making distant pad-strikes that force you to go from row 4, then back to row 1, you can simply assign the sounds of an entire *group* to either row 1 or row 4. The idea here is to narrow down your GMAs to three or four pads per group. For drums, this is easy. Kick, snare, hat are already a natural group, so it's practical to keep them that way. And you can add any other drum-related sound to this group to make it a 4-pad group, thereby taking up one entire row of pads. Simple, plain, easy, organized, and above all, practical.

179

Perhaps the biggest advantage of a GMA is rhythm organization. That is, by mapping your sounds out into groups, you are in essence turning your sequencer/drum machine into a *de-facto* rhythm section: the drummer, or rather the drum GMA is on one row; the guitar GMA is on another row; and the piano/strings GMA is on another row.

Finally, here it's important to note that the kind of music production I've been discussing is fundamentally electronic. However, my perspective is that as the beatmaker (composer/ programmer/producer) you alone actually make up the rhythm section. In fact, a beatmaker's musical understanding is just as relevant as a traditional musician's understanding. The only difference between beatmakers and traditional musicians is that most beatmakers do not necessarily choose to play "traditional" musical instruments. Instead, we most often use EMPIs (themselves non-traditional instruments) to play, program, and sequence sounds, both in traditional and non-traditional ways.

The Significance Of Timing Correct

To beatmakers, timing correct is simply a steady hand and a mistake-proof measure for programming sequences. Timing correct automatically "corrects" time to the preset value that you choose. Here's how it works. Let's say you want to record a musical sequence. First, you set a time correct value; beatmakers typically set this value to 1/16th Note or 1/16th TRPLT. Next, you put your sequencer into record mode and compose a pattern. While in your sequencer's record mode, you play sounds (either internally or triggered from an external EMPI) in a pattern of your liking. Each "event-strike"[116] that you program lands anywhere within the measure that you choose. What happens with timing correct is that it *corrects* the placement of the event-strikes that you program. That is, it automatically shifts (moves) your actual event-strike performance (placement) to the *nearest* step in the measure that

---

[116] Every event that you program within a sequence is what I call an **event-strike**. For example, tapping a drum pad is an event strike, playing a key on a keyboard is an event-strike.

your timing correct value is set to. This means that a timing correct value of 1/16th will shift your event-strike over to the nearest 1/16th step in the measure. So for example, within a 1-bar measure in 4/4 time, if you play (program) a snare on the standard 2, then play it again on the 4, timing correct automatically places the hit two beats later, on the exact same 1/16th step of where you programmed the first snare. In other words, timing correct not only corrects your timing, for all intents and purposes, it essentially *perfects* your timing. This is why I refer to it as a mistake-proof measure for programming sequences.

Even though on the surface timing correct perfects the timing of the events in a sequence that you program, timing correct doesn't always help. In fact, in many cases, timing correct actually makes your timing *too* perfect and unnatural. For example, have you ever tapped in (played) a drum pattern on your drum machine or sequencer and it didn't play back *exactly* how you played it? Well, that's because the timing correct value "corrected" your timing. Remember, timing correct is a big-brother style function that automatically corrects your playing within a sequence.

But timing correct is indeed very helpful when it comes to creating a standard repetitive event-strike such as a typical hi-hat pattern, which lands on every 6th event (step) within a measure. In a case like this, you can set the timing correct value to 1/8th, then casually tap out a standard hi-hat pattern without worrying if your timing is right, because the timing correct function will automatically move each hi-hat event-strike to the nearest 1/8th. However, as helpful as this may be, it's important to remember that timing correct does not distinguish between what events that you do or do not want to apply corrective measures to. Though you may want to employ timing correct to ensure that your hi-hat strikes are landing exactly 6 events apart, keep in mind that whatever timing correct value that you have set will also correct every event-strike that you initiate, which means that you can very well use multiple timing correct values for different parts of the same sequence.

Choosing the Right Timing Correct Setting (Value) Depends on the Goal of the Drum Pattern

Timing correct is just that: It's a corrective measure for your timing. Therefore, how you set your timing correct values should be determined by how good (or bad) your general sense of timing is. If your timing is excellent, that is, your drum event-strikes are comparable to the playing of a traditional drummer, meaning you strike *on time*, with little to no mistakes, then you really don't even need to have the timing correct function on. But if your timing is fairly decent and you want to put in some swing, then you're probably better off setting the timing correct note value to either the default 1/16th NOTE or perhaps even 1/32 TRPLT. (If you're using an Akai MPC, you also want to make sure that the shuffle % is set to: 50, and set the Shift timing to: LATER.) If your timing is poor, then you almost certainly want to use the timing correct note value of 1/16th Note or 1/16th TRPLT. And note: the reason many well-known beatmakers set the timing correct to 1/16th and/ or 1/16th TRPLT is not because their timing is poor, but instead because their timing is so good, they know how to manipulate the corrective nuances of the timing correct function to their advantage. But when using the standard 1/16th NOTE value, you should be aware that if your timing isn't that good, and if you're not particularly skilled at note correction and the like, you run the risk of recording drum pattern sequences that sound stuck, robotic, or slow-dragging with an off-beat feel.

Generally speaking though, I recommend setting the timing correct to either 1/32 TRPLT (especially for vintage hardware sequencers like the Akai MPC 60 II or the E-Mu SP 1200), 1/16, or 1/16TRPLT, and leaving it as your default for all of your basic drum patterns. For instance, let's say that you have an arrangement of non-drum sounds looping nicely, and you've just added the main kick and snare to the sequence, and everything's really starting to come together. All you need now to complete the drum pattern is the main hi-hat. Why stop the loop, change the timing correct, restart the loop, then play the hi-hat with the corrective *protection?*

If you've got the loop going well and the main kick and snare are already in place, then just play the hi-hat right over the top of the existing pattern, in real-time. In this way, you're forced to trust your own timing rather than merely rely on the time correct function. I also recommended that you get accustomed to programming your event-strikes exactly how your fingers play them in the sequence, mistakes and all. This way, you'll build up your timing strengths and neutralize your timing weaknesses. Finally, though it may be a good idea to keep a default timing correct value for your main drum sounds and patterns, there are occasions where changing the timing correct value makes sense. For instance, depending upon the rhythmic nature of the event that you want to initiate and drum pattern that you want to achieve (especially in the area of additional syncopation like stutter hi-hat, kick, or snare patterns), choosing the most effective timing correct value is essential.

BeatTip – Timing Correct with the "Note Repeat" Function

Timing correct is a steady hand, but when used creatively with a sequencer's note repeat function, it becomes a stutter and roll sound maker. One of the most popular sound aesthetics in beatmaking is the stutter-drum hit sound (rapid, successive syncopation). This sound aesthetic first appeared in New York in the early/mid-1980s, around the time the Roland TR 808 drum machine started to get its first heavy use in hip hop/rap music. Since then, the stutter drum-hit sound has become a major cornerstone of the Southern bounce sound. There are many methods and techniques for achieving this aesthetic, but if you use an Akai MPC or something similar like a Roland MV or even a software program like FL Studio, the easiest method involves simply adjusting the timing correct value, turning on the note repeat function, and recording the drum-hit (kick, snare, and/or hat) to spec. For example, in order to achieve the stutter-hat effect, simply set the timing correct value to $1/8^{th}$ or $1/16^{th}$ or $1/16^{th}$ TRPLT, depending on the space and dynamics of the syncopation that you want to achieve.

Drum Programming (Composing)

The Two Basic Forms of Drum Programming: Break-Beat Blend and Hit-Stab Drum Programming

In beatmaking, there are two basic forms of drum programming: break-beat blend drum programming and hit-stab drum programming. **Break-beat blend programming**, which is characterized by the use of wholesale sampled sections of the break from records, most often funk soul, disco, and rock tunes of the late 1960s and the early/mid 1970s, was first popularized by Grandmaster Flash in the early 1980s. It was then further extended by Marley Marl, DJ Premier, and the like in the late 1980s and early/mid-1990s.[117] **Hit-stab drum programming**, which is characterized by the use of unique, individual one-hit drum stabs and hits (particularly kicks, snares, and hi-hats) that are played (programmed) in traditional drummer-like fashion, was initiated and first popularized by Marley Marl in the mid-1980s. Today, some beatmakers still employ the break-beat blend drum programming form, but since the mid-1990s, the hit-stab form has served as the unofficial default drum programming for all beatmakers.

Basic Concepts of Traditional Drum Programming and Arrangement

The most basic drum structure and arrangement within 4/4 time (the default time signature of nearly all hip hop/rap beats) breaks down like this: kick (bass drum) lands on the "1" and "3" (1st and 3rd beats); snare lands on the "2" and the "4;" and the hi-hat on

---

[117] In my interview with Marley Marl, he details how he came up with this form of drum programming. Although Marley Marl is rightfully credited with laying down the foundation for hit-stab drum programming, it must be noted that the form was further developed and extended during the Pioneers/Avant-Garde Period (1988-1994) by the likes of DJ Premier, Large Professor, Dr. Dre, Pete Rock, and The RZA. It's also worth noting that the hit-stab drum programming form was again further developed and extended during the Post-Pioneers Period (1995-2000) by the likes of DJ Toomp, Just Blaze, Kanye West, Timbaland, and The Neptunes.

every half beat. Regarding the placement of the hi-hat, it's worth noting that unlike electronic drum machines and sequencers, live drummers can not play the hi-hat uninterrupted throughout any given drum pattern while they're playing other pieces of a drum set (e.g. snare, toms, and cymbals) because it is not humanly possible. So there are times within any given pattern where the steady hi-hat sound naturally *drops out*. A live drummer has human limitations, an electronic drum machine or sequencer does not, because it plays whatever arrangement you program it to play, for as long as you program it to play.

Drum Patterns and How Drums Land in a Pattern/ Program

How the main kick, snare, and hi-hat lands

Generally speaking, kicks can either hit *flush* or *off*. A **flush-kick**, hereafter represented by the symbol **"fK"** on the drum pattern diagrams presented in this section, is the main kick sound. "Flush" refers to a prominent kick sound that lands on a whole or half-beat within a measure (a bar of music). The flush-kick is one of the most pronounced and sonically important elements within any sequence or any beat. In fact, it's the lone kick sound that anchors the beat. The **off-kick**, hereafter represented by the symbol **"oK"** on the drum pattern diagrams in this section, is the kick sound that is the least prominent kick sound. "Off" refers to the less prominent kick sound that lands on quarter and eighth beats within a measure. The off-kick's main purpose is to set up or accentuate the flush-kick.

The flush-kick can be doubled (paired), stranded, stretched, or stuttered. The off-kick can be *pinched-in* before or *wrapped* around the flush-kick. The terms doubled/paired, stranded, stretched, pinched-in, and wrapped all refer to specific event placements or steps in a sequence, the how and where the events take place. More often than not, the off-kick is pinched-in 2 events (steps) before a flush-kick. When pinching-in the off-kick, it's sometimes a good idea to decrease its velocity, especially when you're working with multi-sound samples. When you're creating new drum patterns

185

and programs, the velocity level is usually (by default) at its full value for all of the drum sounds. So one way to make your drums sound more real and more natural and perhaps more like a live drummer is to manipulate the velocity levels of some of the specific drum events within a beat's sequences. Since the flush-kick is more prominent than the off-kick, usually you don't want to tweak its velocity levels too much. However, decreasing the velocity level (volume and impact of the hit) of the off-kick often proves to be more effective. Remember, the role of the off-kick is to set up, accentuate, and generally play off of the lead role of the flush-kick. Therefore, decreasing the velocity of off-kicks helps you establish a more real drum texture.

Like kicks, snares either hit flush or off. A flush-snare, hereafter represented by the symbol **"fS"** on the drum pattern diagrams in this section, is the main snare sound. It's the sound that is commonly known to land on the *2 and the 4*, the second and fourth beats of a bar. The flush-snare is the snare sound that is the most prominent and audible within any sequence or beat. It's the main snare sound that, in effect, *times* the beat. Imagine, if you will, the metronome playing throughout a beat. On every second and fourth metronome tone the flush snare would hit, hence, the meaning of the 2 *and the 4*. The off-snare, hereafter represented by the symbol **"oS"** on the drum diagrams in this section, is the snare sound that is the least prominent snare sound within any sequence. Like the off-kick, the off-snare's main purpose is to set up, accentuate, and generally play off the lead role of the flush snare.

Hi-hats, hereafter represented by the symbol **"H"** on the drum pattern diagrams below, are generally flush. About 10 years ago, hi-hats played a more primary, default-like role in drum patterns. But since 2002 or so, they have increasingly been used in a more secondary percussive or featured role. Some beatmakers are even experimenting with leaving out hi-hats altogether (Indeed, I sometimes make beats with no hi-hat hits at all). Still, basic 4/4 time seems to beg for some sort of hi-hat construction. Thus, it's important to know when and where hi-hats land in a typical drum pattern.

BeatTip – Shared Fundamental Foundations of Drum Patterns

No matter what new drum pattern you create from scratch, the reality is that the new pattern most likely will not be dramatically different from any other drum pattern or program that you've already created or will ever create The simple fact is, *all drum patterns share some kind of fundamental foundation.* Moreover, there are a number of standard *drum pattern clichés* in beatmaking; and it is from these standard drum clichés that all new drum patterns emerge. In the diagrams that I've included in this section, I have catalogued what I find to be the three most commonly used drum patterns in beatmaking, and I demonstrate just how these patterns break down within a sequence, specifically the ways in which flush-kicks, off-kicks, flush-snares, off-snares, and flush-hi-hats land in fundamental beatmaking drum patterns.

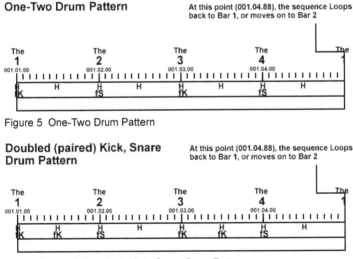

Figure 5 One-Two Drum Pattern

Figure 6 Doubled (paired) Kick, Snare Drum Pattern

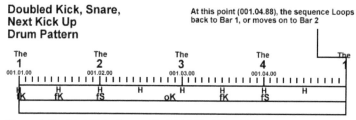

Figure 7 Doubled Kick, Snare, Next Kick Up Drum Pattern

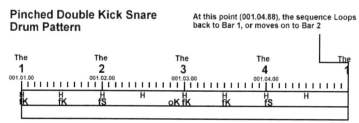

Figure 8 Pinched Double Kick Snare Drum Pattern

From these four diagrams, we can make numerous observations about drum patterns and the ways in which drum sounds tend to and can potentially land in drum patterns that are created in 4/4 time. First, we can see that **a sequence is actually a chronological time line of events,** *a grid of programmed action*. The sequencer grid of each of the diagrams contains measured parameters for which all events must be programmed, played in real time or placed in with your sequencer's STEP EDIT mode.

Second, we can see how each drum hit (event) plays off of the other. Looking at Figure 5, "One-Two Drum Pattern," we can see how the flush-snare (fS) plays off of the flush-kick (fK). The flush-kick within the bar occurs on the 001.01.00 step and the 001.03.00 step, twenty-four steps apart from itself. The flush-snare falls between each kick, exactly twelve steps apart from each kick and twenty-four steps apart from itself. This is what I describe as a **long spatial distance**, as opposed to Figure 7, where the flush-kick and flush-snare carry a **short spatial distance**. Understanding the spatial distance between the kick and the snare helps determine how the drum pattern can be further built up or stripped down. Furthermore, knowing the spatial distances between flush-kicks and flush-snares within typical drum patterns also allows you to identify whether you're working with a simple or complex drum pattern. One of the biggest mistakes that many beatmakers often make is that they mismatch or try to force simple or complex drum patterns to work with the wrong non-drum sounds and arrangements. But the reality is, most drum patterns should *never* be overly complex to begin with. Finally, we must remember that the drums are critical to keeping the time steady and holding the rhythm together. Therefore, a solid drum framework can't be too haywire or overly active, as this disrupts and undermines the entire flow and feel of the beat.

Understanding Spacial Differences Between Flush Drum Sounds

Knowing the spatial differences between the flush-snares and flush-kicks of typical drum patterns is key. Knowledge of spatial difference yields a better understanding of and feel for where the main drum hit events *should* occur within a sequence. In turn, this undoubtedly increases your sense of timing and feeling for rhythm, and thus decreases your reliance on quantizing, time stretching, and other synthetic (machine-/software-based) timing correction measures. Further, I should note that though knowledge of spatial difference is important for all beatmakers, it is particularly important for those beatmakers who primarily use software-based production setups, especially those software practitioners who prefer to "draw" in their hits.

Identifying Simple and Complex Drum Patterns

So how can we determine if a drum pattern is simple or complex? For instance, how do we know that the "One-Two Drum Pattern" is a simple pattern and not a complex one? We can identify the "One-Two Drum Pattern" as a simple drum pattern because there are only four total drum-hit events (not including the eight hi-hat events) that occur within one bar. Likewise, how do we know that Figure 7, the "Pinched Double Kick, Snare Drum Pattern" is a complex drum pattern? We can identify the "Pinched

Double Kick, Snare" as a complex drum pattern because it contains eight total drum-hit events (not including the eight standard hi-hat events) within one bar. Generally speaking, the higher the number of drum-hit events within a measure, in this case one bar, the more complex the drum pattern will be. Finally, I should point out that the recognition of simple and complex drum patterns is essential, because not only does it save you time when creating drum patterns, it also broadens your understanding of the ways in which drum sounds can work together as well as the multiple directions drum patterns can potentially take. This is all the more important when you're creating beats that feature complete-phrase samples, because they largely dictate what kinds of drum patterns are likely to fit. Moreover, this understanding, in turn, increases your ability to program in rhythmic samples, melody lines, and other non-drum sounds in a much more creative and efficient manner.

Knowing Drum-Hit Event Placements

Another reason why it's helpful to know the event placements of basic drum patterns is because it helps cue in your loop methods. By understanding the most fundamental drum patterns, you increase your looping skills. Furthermore, there is a practical reason for learning the basic drum patterns: corrective editing. When you're building sequences, you tend to quickly get caught up in the creative moment. Good ideas cook in your mind rather quickly, right? So what happens when a drum sound seems to be off-beat and awkward? Well, by knowing where the hits *should* occur, you can isolate the section in the sequence in which the event is in question and check it out, then quickly correct (or remove) it if necessary. For instance, let's use the "Doubled Kick, Snare Drum." If the event, in this case the flush-kick, starts on the first step of the sequence, then any flush-kick placement not exactly on (or very near to) the 6th, 24th, or the 30th step will sound awkward. However, if your isolation of the events reveals that all the flush-kicks are landing where they're supposed to, then you know that it's something else that's generating the awkward sound. This is key because it helps you to troubleshoot your sequences and loops much more efficiently.

Understanding Drum Syncopation

In my discussion of how drum hits land in a drum pattern, specifically the concept of "flush" and "off" drum-hits, I've focused primarily on "flush-hits." Here, I want to focus on "off" drum-hits, in particular, the meaning of syncopation. In all components of music, not just drumming, syncopation refers to the way in which musical events deviate (unexpectedly) from the established succession of regularly spaced strong and weak beats in a measure. In other words, syncopation could be the result of *stress* (action, e.g. a drum-hit event) on a normally unstressed beat or *unstress* (no action, e.g. no drum-hit event) on a normally stressed beat. So if a part of the measure that is normally stressed is unstressed, then rhythm is syncopated. Likewise, if a part of the measure that is normally unstressed is stressed, then the rhythm is syncopated. By looking at any of the four drum pattern diagrams discussed earlier in this chapter, you can imagine how and where syncopation might occur within any given drum pattern.[118]

Building Your Drum Frameworks with Your Samples

As I mentioned before, building drum patterns from scratch is pretty much rhetorical. What I mean is, no matter how *differently* you arrange your drum pattern, it will always be some variation of a drum pattern that you've already created or heard before. Even if you interchange the pattern with new drum sounds, the reality is that the patterns stay relatively the same. Hip hop/rap music, like jazz, blues, and rock 'n' roll, builds upon its clichés. Therefore, rarely will you ever hear a drum pattern that you've never heard *some variation* of before (this is especially true of trap music). When you're building a drum pattern from scratch, based around a primary sample, your goal should be to compliment that sample, not disrupt

---

[118] Syncopation is a fundamental component of the African American (Black) music tradition and the styles that stem from it, including the blues, jazz, rhythm and blues, rock 'n' roll, soul, funk, and, of course, hip hop/rap. And it's worth noting that syncopation is used in many different musical styles and pretty much all contemporary music.

it or distract attention away from it. In other words, when you use samples, let the samples stand out. The drums that you blend in should hold everything down. When you have a sample looping, in readying yourself to play in a drum pattern, keep your focus on building a drum framework that lets the sample *breathe* properly. Don't overpower the sample with drums that cloud or distort the sample. Drums can still bang without having to sacrifice the sound and feeling of the main sample. In fact, drums bang the most when the blend between the sample and the drum pattern is straightforward and not too busy or overly loud. Indeed, when it comes to creating a drum framework with your sample(s), a proper balance of well-grounded power and subtleness is the key.

How Drum Sounds Are Often Used in Drum Frameworks and Sequences: Kicks, Snares, Hats, and Cymbals Working Together

Drum sounds work together in various ways, and therefore, understanding the ways in which the different categories of drum sounds work together in drum frameworks (programs/sequences) is critical to a beatmaker's ability to insert quality and effectiveness to the overall arrangement of a beat. Below I have outlined a set of parameters for how each different sound category can most effectively be used in drum frameworks.

Kicks

Kicks are the *sonic glue* that hold both the drum framework together and the pulse of the entire beat itself. Therefore, knowing which types of kicks cause which effects within a drum framework and overall beat is important. For instance, *hard* kicks (heavier frequence and sonic impact) are best used with low bass-filtered driven or synthetic-sounds-based beats that aren't too active. Harder kicks are also very effective with beats that feature simple melodies and minimal changes. On the other hand, *soft* or *medium* kicks work best with more extensive compositional arrangements and sample-based beats that feature more complex (highly creative) uses of samples. Softer kicks are also very effective for beats in which the frequency levels range from mostly mid to high. They also work well in sample-based beats that are dominated by texturally thick complete-phrase samples.

Snares and Claps: Pitch-Shifts

In the beatmaking tradition, there is more experimentation with drum phrasing than in other twentieth-century American popular music traditions. One key way that unique drum phrasing is achieved in beatmaking is through the use of what I like to call snare "pitch-shifts." Pitch-shifts simply refer to alternating pitch values of the same or multiple drum-hits. In the case of snare pitch-shifts, the process of alternating the pitch value of the main snare within a drum sequence not only adds in a subtle but very effective change, it also gives a *push and pull* effect to the various sections within the song structure. This is why snare pitch-shifts work very well within the verse section of a song: they add change without unnecessary distraction, i.e. something subtle that lyricists can use as an additional timing mechanism for their rhyme flow. Snare pitch-shifts are also helpful for keeping solid time in sample-based beats that utilize longer complete-phrase samples. Snare pitch-shifts also work well in the hook section because they offer the level of variety that can further set a hook apart from the other sections of a beat/song.

The Genius of the "2" and the "4"

Understanding the *"2 and the 4"* means realizing that once the kick and the hi-hat are laid down, rhythm actually already exists. This is why snares do not necessarily have to be loud or mega-compressed to be effective. With 4/4 time, our minds are already pre-conditioned to hearing *something* land on the "2 and the 4." This is precisely why low velocity claps often work well with high powered kicks. Incidentally, this is why the Atlanta "snap sound" works. At first glance, the snap sound seems redundantly simple; I mean, musically, the sound appears to be devoid of any real *feeling*. However, the snap sound does actually take advantage of the genius of the "2 and the 4." Rather than emphasizing a heavy or unique snare, the snap sound focuses on building the track with a standard *snap fill* on the "2 and the 4." By restricting the feature component of the snare and stripping down other musical elements, beatmakers who create the snap sound can then build the track with more percussive collages, 808s, and other bass sounds. And although the snap sound is something primarily meant for synthetic-sounds-based beats (no samples featured), its philosophy does have its roots in the process of intuitive chopping.

Alternating Snares, Clap-Hits and Chopped Chimes, Velocity Modification, and Delayed-Snares

Another effective programming technique for snares involves the use of alternating the main snare drum-hit with clap-hits, chopped chimes, or other percussive-stabs or -hits. Instead of using the same snare-hit throughout the song, you can program in a clap-hit and alternate it with the main snare-hit. You can let the clap-hit play through for the first 8 bars, then come in hard with the main snare or any other alternating pattern you can come up with. Furthermore, you can cut up some chimes and layer them over the top of the snare- or clap-hit. And whether you apply this technique throughout the entire beat/song or just in certain sections, it is tremendously effective because it helps to build ambiance, and it offers a lot of personal nuance to your drum frameworks and overall sound and style.

Modifying the velocity, the attack and volume level or impact-level of each snare- or clap-hit, is a great way to naturally create swing. If you listen to traditional live drummers, you will notice that because of the "human factor," it is impossible for them to ever hit the same drum with the exact same velocity twice. This means that everytime they strike a drum, there is a slightly different attack, sometimes harder, sometimes lighter. In beatmaking, to achieve or rather *retain* this nuance and naturalness, you can simply turn off the velocity function within the EMPI(s) that you use to craft your drum frameworks, or you can record your drum programs with the velocity level at its full value, then afterwards go in and manually adjust (program) the velocity changes on specific drum-hits.

Finally, the use of "delayed-snares" is also another effective snare technique. Delayed-snares describes specific snare-hits that are purposely placed *off-time* within a drum pattern. Delayed-snares can be used to mask awkward pauses and gaps or minor glitches and other unwanted but unremovable blemishes within a beat. Also, delayed-snares can be used to create unique effects in the drum framework. For example, delaying the lead snare-hit for a bridge or a break-down. Furthermore, used correctly, delayed-snares can also conceal the short-comings of a less-than-perfect loop.

Hats

The use of different types of hi-hats can also serve multiple roles within the drum framework and the overall beat. Standard hi-hats (semi-closed), which are high in pitch, work to "push" the flow of the beat. Generally, standard hi-hats have a high pitch. Open-hi-hats are much slower pitched than standard hi-hats, and so they can work to drag the pace or *temper* the rhythm of the beat. Closed-hi-hats, which are typically faster in pitch than both standard hi-hats and open hi-hats, work like a clear-cut metronome. Sometimes their tightness can make a beat sound too mechanically clean and unnatural. Here, it should be noted that each type of hi-hat can add shuffle and swing to a drum framework. However, that being said, achieving this effect does depend on the actual pitch and tone of the hat being used. Finally, here are some general "rules" regarding hats:

- Standard closed hi-hats help with a tighter sense of time, while semi-closed hi-hats are best if you want to *shuffle* the time along.
- Rather than using external processors, e.g. reverb, etc., hats and rides are also great for achieving additional warmth and clarity through unique arrangement and pronouncement techniques.
- The use of alternating hi-hats and hi-hat patterns is a

good thing when you want to change the flow of the hook section in a song.

- Hats give tracks extra depth; and hats work like the second hand on a clock.
- Unique hat arrangements can shade (mask) the loop points in a beat.

Cymbals and Bells

Cymbals play an important role in certain drum frameworks. For example, rides work well for ambiance; they also help balance out the impact of rumbling (bass heavy, muddy, or distorted) kicks. Bells work well as "treble managers," that is, they're good at meshing with or handling the high peaks of samples or synthetic-sounds phrases. They're also useful at offsetting the flatness of low-filtered bass-driven beats. Cymbals can also substitute for the role of hi-hat patterns. This substitution carries an array of effects. For certain drum patterns, it can make a drum framework sound jazzier. Then again with other drum patterns, it can make the drum framework sound aggressive and very *hungry*, even haunting. Finally, cymbals can be very effective when they're layered over kicks at specific moments within each section of the beat/song.

Uncovering and Taking Advantage of the Open and Hidden Spaces

Every drum pattern has *open* or *hidden* spaces. The open spaces of a drum pattern refer to those spots in the pattern where you can imagine (hear) a non-drum sound being placed (recorded) over the top. For example, take a look at the diagram below:

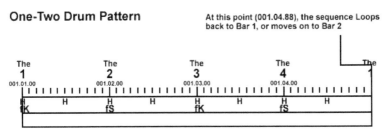

Figure 9 One-Two Drum Pattern

Imagine your favorite kick and snare in this pattern. Because of the spacing dynamics of this pattern, you will notice the *pause* that naturally stands out after each kick and before each snare. These spaces are *open* because they're empty, and therefore, they naturally stand out and seemingly invite a non-drum sound to be inserted.

On the other hand, hidden spaces are camouflaged by the drum pattern itself. That is, the hidden spaces are flush with the drum sounds. Look at the same diagram, imagine adding in a sample or bass line beginning on top of the kick, as opposed to between the kick and the snare. The results will be dramatically different for two reasons. First, keep in mind that the way in which a sequence *loops* is primarily determined by the particular placement of events within that given sequence. So for instance, if you insert a sample or bass line in the open space of the drum pattern, then realize that it will overlap in a way that might not coincide with how the sequence loops. However, if you insert a sample or bass line in the hidden space, that is, on top of one of the flush kicks or flush snares, it will likely mesh better with how the sequence loops even if it overlaps.

The second reason the result of the beat will be different when you insert non-drum music in hidden spaces is because these spaces determine the degree to which the drums ultimately stand out or fade back. Remember, though drums play a central role in a beat, they can serve this role in two different capacities: either in a featured capacity or as accompaniment capacity. Take for instance Jay-Z's song "Girls, Girls, Girls," produced by Just Blaze. In this song, Just Blaze uses the drums to *accompany* the samples; that is to say, the drum framework just works to keep the beat *steady*. Now consider Gang Starr's "Same Team, No Games," produced by DJ Premier.

In the latter song, Premier uses the drums in a *featured* capacity, that is to say, the drum framework is really the main component that drives the beat.

BeatTip – Matching/Fitting Drum Sounds and Patterns with Samples

One of the toughest skills to develop in sampling is knowing how to match drum sounds and patterns to primary samples. So here, I want to discuss those things that lead to having a better understanding of this area of sample-based beatmaking.

Probably the most important factor in matching drum sounds and patterns with samples is knowing your own drum sounds. As I discussed earlier in this chapter, knowing your drum-sound library, particularly your core set of sounds, is a critical part of effective beatmaking. And when it comes to matching drum sounds and patterns with samples, i.e. primary samples, knowing your sounds becomes even more important, as they provide the initial clues for the types of sounds that should go well with the samples that you're working with. Along with knowing your drum sounds, you should know the most effective combinations of your sounds. In particular, you should know which kick, snare, and hi-hat sounds fit and move best together.

Now, provided you know your drum sounds and *go-to* drum-sound combinations, you should have already developed a certain drum style. If you haven't, focus on doing so, as it will trim loads of time when it comes to creating new patterns to fit with the samples you choose. With your own drum style, whether it be heavy syncopation, a subtle accompaniment approach, or an out-front knocking style, whenever you work with the primary sample(s), you'll already have a decent idea of what will likely work, both in terms of sonic and rhythmic blending.

But even with a command of your core drum sounds and combinations and your own style and approach to drum programming, matching the drum sounds and patterns to samples can still be challenging. So here are a number of factors to consider when trying to match any drums to samples. First, consider what kind of sample-based beat you're working on. Are you creating a beat in which you want the drums to knock or hang back? If you want the drums to knock, that is, punch (bang) out in front of the sample, then you'll likely want to go with a sharp, distinct snare and a booming kick. If you're aiming for a subtle sounding beat, then you'll probably want your drums to just accompany the main sample. In this case, a tucked snare that matches the feel and sonic quality of the sample will be a great place to start, and of course, you'll want to go with a less boomy kick and a brushing hi-hat sound.

You also want to consider the type and sound of the main sample itself. Is the main sample loud and punchy? Is it smooth and jazzy? Is it soulful and funky? Are there gaps in the sample? Is one end of the sample louder than the other? Moreover, the main sample that you use clues you in to how complex or stripped down the drum pattern will need to be. It should also be understood that each kind of sample will warrant some audition of different drum sounds and combinations, but with a good grasp of the main sample itself, your audition period will take less time. Plus, if the sample comes from a record with drums, you might be able to use those drum sounds of yours that are similar. But this does not always work. In fact, sample-based beats are often carved out by using drum sounds that sound nothing like the drums of the primary sample that was used.

Here, I should point out that the concept of matching drums to samples is often misunderstood because many people mistakenly take the word "matching" to only mean a blending of sonic quality and pitch. This is why I believe that the more appropriate word to use is *fitting* drums and patterns to samples because that is more often the fundamental aim. Certainly, blending sound qualities is important, but the rhythms created and sustained with the drums takes precedent. Drums either dictate or support the character of the beat, and in all cases, they should never sound out of place. This is why I recommend having a default drum sound combination that you can regularly use to start up a new drum pattern. Once you've established the rhythmic pattern that fits with and feels right with the main sample, you can see about swapping out the kick, snare, or hi-hat. Plus, once the drum rhythm is set, the sound of the drums can always be further tweaked and blended through EQ fixes, velocity changes, layering, and other modification techniques.

Finally, one other important suggestion that I have is that you start with a snare as a barometer for any drum sounds and patterns that you ultimately go with. This is because no matter what sound or pattern that you create, the snare tends to always sit with the kick and hi-hat even when tucked in the mix. So using the snare helps you not only find your drum sound sonic compass, so to speak, it also clues you in to what type of syncopation or additional percussion will be most effective.

√Check This Out – The Human Touch: A Note About Playing EMPIs Like Various Traditional Musical Instruments

I see the drum pads on my Akai MPC 4000 drum machine/ sampler/sequencer the same way a guitarist sees the strings on his guitar; or the same way a keyboardist sees the keys on his keyboard; or the same way a drummer sees the skinheads on his drums. I don't merely *program* my MPC, I *play* it. This is the same way that most seasoned sample-based beatmakers feel. As Rsonist, one half of the production duo The Heatmakerz (Dipset) puts it: "the MPC is an instrument! Regardless… If I put 10 sounds in 10 pads and I gotta arrange it into a melody, I can do that! I don't know like… this is a C chord, or whatever it is. But at the end of the day, I know what's on key, what's off key, what's right, what's wrong…"[119] Indeed, beatmakers are not simply a bunch of clever electronic music production "programmers." Nearly all of us are performance artists much in the same vein of traditional musicians. However, what distinguishes beatmakers from traditional musicians is the fact that, by and large, we are not limited to just *one* instrument in

---

[119] From author interview with Rsonist.

the same way that one-instrument-capable traditional musicians are. On the contrary, for every beat, nearly all beatmakers are responsible for playing (or providing) the drums, the string, and/ or wind instruments. So EMPIs (like the Akai MPC) represent for us a *multi-instrument*. An instrument that, in effect, allows us to play and tap into the essence of *any* instrument that we want. One moment a beatmaker can be crafting the drums; the next moment he can be laying down bass lines; and still the next moment he can be *flipping* a sample or banging out a melodic keyboard phrase. It's important to note that this is one of the most liberating aspects of the beatmaking tradition. Because of this aspect, beatmakers have the potential to be much more versatile music producers than the average traditional musician. And EMPIs such as the MPC or FL Studio double as musical instruments and production hubs that virtually give beatmakers endless instrumental and musical possibilities.[120]

BeatTip – Default Workflow Systems: Default Drum Programs and Sequence Templates

To streamline your creative output, I recommend creating what I call **default workflow systems**. A default workflow system can be any stored beatmaking template, like a default drum sequence (pattern). It can also be a default method, style, and/or technique that you utilize in your personal beatmaking process, like a set approach to sampling, or a set approach to sequencing, etc. The main theme of a default workflow system is *recycling*; that is,

---

[120] Because EMPIs are both instruments and computers, beatmakers who use software-based setups should be careful to remember the "human touch," because you can easily become more *programmer* than musician if you focus more on computing and less on composing. One area to safeguard against this is to use an EMPI with pads (for example a MIDI controller with pads) for triggering sounds; this gives off the feeling of playing something rather than *programming* something. Note: One major characteristic of the African American (Black) music tradition and all of the music traditions that stem from it, most notably rhythm and blues, rock 'n' roll, soul, and funk, is that <u>all</u> instruments, particularly the bass guitar, are played in a percussive manner. Thus, playing samples and other sounds on drum pads harkens back to and pays homage to that tradition.

you want to consistently reuse and infuse those components and characteristics of your beatmaking that you find to be effective. The ultimate purpose of this being that it will (1) help you create new beats much more efficiently; and (2) it will help you develop your own unique style and sound.

A default drum sequence template (pattern) is any pre-made/pre-used/previously programmed drum sequence that you use to create new drum patterns. Default drum sequence templates can be extracted from beats that you've *already* made, attempted to make, or are currently making. Once you've created a beat, you can always scrap the non-drum music material and keep the drums. This left over drum pattern, what I call a **drum shell**, can then be saved and used again. This is extremely helpful to your beatmaking process because it provides you with an arsenal of drum sequences that you can tap quickly for ideas everytime you begin to create a new beat. By using default workflow systems you will not only improve your overall beatmaking efficiency, you will also streamline your entire beatmaking output. Hence, every new beat that you make is potentially a template for future beats. This does not mean that you do not ever make any new drum sequences, etc. from scratch. On the contrary, the idea of a default drum sequence (pattern) is to help you generate new ideas by incorporating some of your most successful old ones.

Finally, when it comes to drum shells, I recommend that you always keep at least fifteen drum shells (default drum patterns/sequence templates/programs) stored and ready for action. The more drum shells that you have, the more quickly you'll learn to process your ideas. Also, to help increase workflow efficiency, I recommend that you create default sequence templates that include alternating hi-hat patterns. I have 75 default drum sequences, ranging from 1-, 2-, 4-, 8-, and 16-bar sequences. This allows me to work much more efficiently. Moreover, it permits me to quickly extract my ideas and turn them into new music. Consider this: When a live drummer in a band creates a drum scheme for a new song, he recalls on patterns that he's played before in the past, then he makes alterations and adjustments as the song changes and develops. There's no big deal about making a new drum pattern from scratch, because 70%-90% of it will be something that you've already created and programmed before.

Chapter 7

Sampling Techniques
Extended Sampling Techniques, Notes, Tips, and Analysis

Sample Blending, Multi-Sampling, Spot-Note Sampling, and Shading Samples

There are four commonly used sampling techniques or methods that go a long way in shaping a beatmaker's sampling abilities: **sample blending**, **multi-sampling**, **spot-note sampling**, and **shading samples**. Like it sounds, **sample blending** is simply the process of blending samples together. There are a couple of ways to go about this. You can *splice* multiple samples, for example splicing a snare and tambourine so that the snare strikes, followed by the sound of the tambourine. You can also do manual blends (similar to layering)[121] where you actually play in (*program*) the samples to play together or in chronological variations.

Here, it's worth mentioning that front and end sample-fades, created through the use of the Attack and Sustain functions of a sampler, help make the sample blends even more effective. A front sample-fade refers to how a sample begins after it's been chopped. That is to say, how much of the very beginning of the sample is audible? Does it come in hard, heavy, or flush? Does it slide in? Does it blend in? An end sample-fade refers to how a sample ends after it's been chopped. That is to say, how long does a sample *sustain* itself after it reaches its end? Decreasing the sustain of a sample gives the effect of a fade. Thus, the right decrease of sustain at the beginning of a sample and the right decrease of attack at

---

[121] I use the term **layering** here to describe the process of combining two or more sounds into one. This is typically achieved by taking one sound and placing it on top of the other.

the beginning of another sample allows two (or more) samples to blend together more effectively, sounding as if they were just one sample. Sample-blends composed of sound-stabs are an excellent example of how front sample-fades and end sample-fades can be used. For an example of a great sound-stab sample blend, listen to "The Owners" (Gang Starr) produced by DJ Premier. That song has a bass-stab underneath a baritone horn-stab.

Sample blends can be complete-phrases and sound-stabs that are fused together by your sampler's splicing function. They can also be two spare-part-phrases played together with sound-tones and other pieces of sound. Chopping samples and then blending the "new" samples (the remains minus the cuts) together into one cohesive measure of music is one of the most creative ways of developing your own production style and sound.

Multi-sampling is the process of sampling the same sound (phrase, instrument, stab, etc.), multiple times, each at a different pitch. This neutralizes the awkwardness of short semitones. Here, the idea is to then assign the samples to the same limited area of drum pads or keys. Once assigned, you can play the various "versions" of the same sample.

Spot-note sampling refers to the process of sampling pieces of a musical phrase that *can* be sampled, while replaying the minor tones of the phrase that can not be sampled. For instance, the notes of a phrase that can not be sampled clean (i.e. clear and free from the surrounding sounds in the portion to be sampled) because vocals are running over them. Using the spot-note sampling method, you can sample the part of the phrase that *can* be sampled clean, then you play the "spot-notes." This can be done using a keyboard, synth, VST, or sound module to play the spot-notes *as close as sonically possible*. For example, if it's a bass phrase that's cut off by vocals, drums, etc., simply replay (emulate) the spot notes, the bass parts that you're not able to sample.

Finally, the process of layering samples with matching or non-matching notes, tones, frequencies, percussion, voices, etc. is what I like to call **shading samples.** It's a valuable sample editing technique that can be used to *disguise* a sample without having to forfeit the feeling and mood of the sample being disguised. Shading a sample can also be used to accentuate or punctuate the depth, texture, and feeling of a sample.

BeatTip – Adding Bass Fill-Ins

From the time beatmakers first began aggressively sampling vinyl records, the most sought after record samples have been extracted from records that were recorded and manufactured during the 1970s. Things are no different today. Soul, funk, R&B, and rock 'n' roll music of the 1970s still offers the most sought after source material for beatmakers to flip. Aside from the organic rhythms of that era, rhythms that were typically underscored by funky drums and smooth bass lines, the other appeal of the music of the 1970s is the way in which it was recorded.

Though the recording and mixing techniques of the 1970s may seem quirky compared to today's common industry recording practices, the reality is that they produced perhaps the warmest, most organic music ever recorded. Certainly, this fact has not been lost on many beatmakers. Plus, more often than not, it's the *sound* and its accompanying *feeling* that beatmakers are after. But while that '70s sound shines, typically when it comes to overall warmth and feeling, it often doesn't suit the sonic demands of today's audible standards. More specifically, it lacks the level of bass amplification that's usually associated with hip hop/rap music. Therefore, in order to maintain the warmth of a sample, while at the same time satisfy that deep bass sound that hip hop/rap music warrants, beatmakers often attach bass fill-ins or accents to their samples.

A **bass fill-in** is any bass phrase, tone, or sound that is deliberately blended into a beat. Bass fill-ins are usually added to beats in which the primary-sample, the main sample that the entire beat is built around, is devoid of a *fat* enough bass line (or bass part). For example, let's say you sample a guitar lick that dissolves into a crazy organ sound. You loop that sample — maybe one bar, maybe two bars — then add in a backing drum beat. Now, the framework might be good as it is. But remember, this is hip hop/

rap music: It's a bottom heavy genre. So most of the time, you're going to need some sort of bass element, e.g. 808 kick drum or a bass line. Hence, you throw in a bass fill-in right on top of the gaps, the parts in the loop where the sound is *thin*, where the musical events are diminished and lower in sound.

Typically, beatmakers use the bass sounds from their keyboards and sound modules as bass fill-ins. But this is a very tricky process, because when you attempt to combine synthetic-bass sounds that adhere to today's audio standards with samples that adhere to the audio standards of more than a quarter century ago, the sonic nuances of the sample can be diminished, if not outright destroyed. If the bass fill-in is too thick and dominant, it will disrupt, if not totally consume the warmth of the framework sample. Remember, the wrong bass sound or the wrong pitch and texture of the bass sound can result in the entire beat sounding uneven and overpowered by an awkward bass element. To guard against this, tweak the resonance of the bass fill-in that you've added. This will smoothen it out and warm up its ambiance.

BeatTip – Bumpin' the Sample

There are times when you come up against a sample that has *something* good or promising, but you can't figure out exactly what that is. Then there are times you come across samples that you know are very recognizable. Situations like these may call for what I've dubbed "bumpin' the sample." **Bumpin'-the-sample** describes the process of neutralizing the main sonic elements of a sample, then using the newly modified sample together with your own enhancement: your own "bump." To bump a sample, first, "remove" the bass frequency of the sample. Technically, you can't really *remove* the bass if it's actually within the sample. However, you can neutralize it (make it inaudible) by burying its sonic quality to an indistinguishable level. To do this, you have to filter down, i.e. flatten, the bass. Once you've *neutralized* the bass, add in your own bass line (bass parts/framework), either from a set of sampled bass tones or synthetic bass sounds from a synthesizer or sound module or software VST. This bass line (bass part) can be any pattern. In fact, when you bump the sample, I recommend taking your bass line (bass part) in a new direction. After you've added your own bass line (bass part), pull back the treble of the sample. Again, here, you want to employ some filtering techniques, but you don't want to remove the treble entirely, you just want to pull it back just enough to let it breathe some so that you keep some of the color and character of the sample that you're bumpin'. This is also effective because it enables you to beef up the sample further with your own treble sounds, accents, or percussion parts. Moreover, you can play new high pitched keyboard parts or high sample chops right of over the top.

The Evolution of Sampling Techniques: Sampling Live Instrumentation and other First Generation Sounds

Sampling live instrumentation is an extension of sampling records. The major difference being that you're sampling "live" instruments. Whether you're a trained musician or a keyboard "finger-stabber," you can still come up with your own effective riffs and other things to sample. In hip hop/rap music, it doesn't take much for something to bang, provided you know how to flip it. There are a wealth of hip hop/rap songs that carry only one or two chord piano (or guitar) licks. Point is, once you have the drums, and the drum programming down the way that you like, there's no limit to the ways in which you can sample live instrumentation.

Here's where studying music comes into play. It becomes osmosis, because the more you study and listen to music, the more you will subconsciously and consciously pick up things. Music, like all forms of art, is predicated upon a number of fundamental themes and clichés. For example, look at note progression on a piano. The right side has the *highs*, higher pitched notes; the left side has the lows, the bass, the lower pitched notes; and the middle has the *mids*. Thus, the further to the right that you progress on the keyboard, the higher the notes will be. Conversely, the farther left that you progress on the keyboard, the lower the notes will be. Get it? Right high, left low.

Granted, this example of note progression is a crude one, to say the least. So I'm not stating that someone *without* piano lessons or a strong understanding of traditional music theory has the same chance of mastering the keyboard as someone who takes a regular regiment of lessons. I'm a realist. But hip hop/rap music is a fast medium. Beatmakers who opt for taking music lessons, more power to them; that's a good thing. But the fact is, at the end of the day, those beatmakers will still be competing for production work with other beatmakers who have *no* formal training at all. Beatmakers who have been fortunate enough to have music lessons will always run the chance of being passed over by beatmakers without formal training. Sounds funny? Hear me out.

Take this scenario: Let's say two people decide that they want to go into the beat trade at the same time. Beatmaker X gets a keyboard and an MPC, and he signs up for piano lessons. Beatmaker Z gets the same keyboard and the same MPC, but he takes no piano lessons. One year later, both beatmakers submit their beats to the same rapper. Who's beats do you think that the rapper is going to pick? If you said beatmaker X, then you missed the point; and if you said beatmaker Z, then you missed the point. That's because the point is this: The rapper could care less if you took lessons, or if you know how to play the piano or any instrument for that matter. The rapper most likely doesn't care how the beat was created. The only thing that trumps process and method in hip hop/rap music is *the overall result of the final product*. Simple and plain. In this regard, it always comes down to one concern: Does it sound *good* to whom you want it to sound good?

Let me further clarify what I'm saying. Can instrument lessons help you improve your live instrumentation skills? Of course they can. In fact, incorporating the ability to play a traditional instrument, especially the piano, will definitely add to your entire beatmaking skill set. But remember this: There will always be beatmakers who bang out beats on the keyboard *without* any formal musical training or without any prerequisite requirement for beat completion other than *does it sound good.*

Some of the dominant sounds in hip hop/rap music (at the time of this publication), do not require that beatmakers actually *know* how to play Western classical music, let alone rudiment chord structures. And what about someone like Scott Storch or Pharrell Williams, you might ask? Well, Scott Storch is *Scott Storch* and Pharrell *is Pharrell.* They're both traditionally trained musicians; and if I had to guess, I'd say they had more than a few music lessons as well as some kind of consistent study in traditional music theory. However, whether they did or did not, doesn't matter. Their music is polished and controlled. He's a skilled keyboardist; he's obviously not just a finger-stabber. He doesn't simply "hit" the keyboard, he *plays* it. And it's evident that he's been playing the keys for *years.*

So in the broader picture, *anyone* can come up with their own live instrumentation to sample. It certainly helps to know how to play, but it doesn't hurt if you don't. Either way, sampling live instrumentation is about sampling the sound-stabs and riffs that you (or your hired musicians) play. The method adheres to the aforementioned process of sampling. But where sampling live instrumentation differs is in the texture and feel. Old songs offer second-generation sounds to be sampled, "second generation" in that they have been played within the context of a recorded song and mixed in accordance with the recoridg and mixing standards of their time. On the other hand, live instrumentation sounds are "first generation" sounds, i.e. they are *live* sounds. Hence, the management of these sounds obviously give you more control. But this control comes with several obstacles.

In order for first-generation sounds (like those that emanate from keyboards, VSTs, sound modules, guitars, drums, etc.) to hold their full sonic value, they must be routed or mic'd appropriately. This is the first obstacle that you face when trying to sample live instrumentation. If you do not have an elaborate assortment of microphones, you can still route instruments in a way that will enable you to sample them directly into your DAW (software recording system). Essentially, you just record what you want to sample onto a track, as if you were tracking a sound from a beat. This is actually another instance where having a mixing console comes in handy. The signal chain: *instrument to mixing console, mixing console to sampler*, gives you a greater flexibility over the sound of the original source instrument than the signal chain: *instrument to mic, mic to sampler*. Here, even the smallest mixing consoles (for example, an 8-channel model) gives you an edge, because a mixing console offers you tremendous amplification and sound coloring capabilities. Moreover, it gives you the opportunity to further color the sound of the original instrument source.

Combining Samples and Synths

Samples — sampled "breaks," various tones, and sounds, etc. — are typically made up of a collage of sounds. As such, the concept of matching synth sounds to the same "key" (pitch) of samples isn't as definite as some would like to believe. In fact, it's a bit misleading. Combining synth sounds with samples (i.e. samples of pre-existing recordings) is not necessary, but it is certainly useful in some situations. Either way, if you do decide to do a synth-sample blend, remember this: When blending a synth sound with a sample, keep in mind that you are trying to match the synth to the sample, not the other way around. That being said, here are some other important factors to consider when matching, blending, or combining samples and synths.

The Matter of Atonality and Sampling

There are many reasons why the art of sampling can not be understood (fundamentally) under the auspices of traditional music-making practices. But perhaps the most outstanding and often ignored reason is the fact that sampling has no partiality to traditional musical tonality. That is, in the sampling process, samples of recorded source material are modified and arranged without deference to the tones of the chromatic scale. In sampling, there is no deference (or reference) to key or a tonal center. On the contrary, sample-based beatmakers are concerned with three things: (1) whether or not a sample *sounds and feels good*; (2) does the sample(s) fit with the drum framework (program); and (3) does the sample(s) and drum framework together ascribe to the aesthetics, priorities, and principles of hip hop/rap music. Sample-based beatmakers are not necessarily concerned with adhering to music theory or concepts and principles of traditional musical tonality.

Here, it's worth noting that many traditionally trained musician-beatmakers often fail at sampling, precisely because they attempt to approach sampling through the guise of traditional music practices. As such, they attempt to apply the rules of music theory to a compositional process that has no deferential regard for music theory at all. If there is anything that must be understood about sampling it's the fact that sampling seeks, technically and theoretically, to simply use whatever works. If it uses any principles or concepts of music theory, it's not out of deference, but out of prudence.

What Does Tone, Matching, Blending, and Combining Mean?

In beatmkaing, there are a lot of terms that may carry several meanings; and without individual clarification, use of these terms can create some confusion. Hence, here, it's important to discuss the terms "tone," "match (matching)" "combine (combining)," and "blend (blending)."

When beatmakers speak of "tone," there's two meanings or concepts that we can actually be describing. There's "tone," as in sound, and then there's "tone" as in *feel*. Sound and feel are two entirely different concepts. "Tone," in regards to sound, refers to notes, timbre, sustain, etc. "Tone," in regards to feel, refers to variations of mood, like soulful, happy, sad, etc.

When beatmakers speak of "matching" something, there's two meanings or concepts that we can actually be employing. There's "matching," as in *matching the sound*, and there's "matching," as in *matching the feel or mood*. Matching sound and matching feel are two entirely different concepts, and each usually requires a different approach. In beatmaking, "matching" is commonly used to describe the process of working with sounds in the same pitch (key). However, as I've just made clear, it is not the only description, nor is it any more or less important than the other description of "matching." It all depends on the beatmaker and beatwork in question.

When beatmakers speak of "blending" something, there's two meanings or concepts that we can actually be employing. There's "blending," as in mixing or layering two or more sounds of the same pitch (key) together, and there's "blending," as in complimenting or accentuating two or more sounds that are not necessarily in the same pitch (key). Blending sounds of the same pitch (key) is an entirely different concept than blending sounds that are *not* of the same pitch (key). Therefore, each usually requires a different approach.

Finally, when beatmakers speak of "combining" something, we're not necessarily speaking about *blending* something. In fact, we're usually talking about *adding* two or more things (sounds or feelings) together, which is different from *blending* something together into one new sound. For instance, you can combine or add a 808 kick drum and basic kick drum to a drum pattern, that doesn't mean that you're *blending* those two sounds together as one.

Arrangement Scope

The arrangement scope of your beat/song is another important factor to consider when you're combining synths with samples. What's the scope of your verse and hook (chorus) sections? How different is your verse section from your hook section? What about the framework of your sequences? That is, what bar-framework is your verse section based on? Is it a 2-bar, 4-bar, or 8-bar loop? What about the sample scheme that you're using? Are you using just one main sample that is heavily chopped? Are you using multiple samples that are woven together? Are you using a relatively unmodified break of one or more bars? Each one of these factors will help determine what sort of synth combination is likely to work with your samples.

When I use a combo of synths and samples, *I never try to play a synth in the same key as the sample(s) I'm using.* To understand why, you need to know when and why I use synth sounds in sample-based beats. Whenever I add in synth sounds to a sample-based beat, I usually do so for one or two reasons: (1) to boost or "beef" up the sample, sort of like stacking synth sounds; or (2) to accentuate or emphasize a moment or element of the sample(s) I'm using. Therefore, when I'm making a sample-based beat, I'm not concerned with simply reinterpreting a sampled break with synth sounds of the same pitch. Why? Because then the focus would be more on the synth sounds, and that would essentially make it more of a synthetic-sounds-based beat.

Also, I should point out that in most sample-based beats, the primary sample itself contains multiple instruments. Therefore, if you want to match the sound of the synth to the sound of the sample, then sure, you can try to play the synth in the same overall pitch (key) of the sample. But for me, if I'm aiming to match the sound of the sample, it becomes an issue of manipulating the pitch (higher or lower) of the particular synth sounds that I'm using. More specifically, it's an issue of manipulating the pitch of the synth sounds higher or lower than the pitch of the primary sample and the sample scheme that I'm using.

On the other hand, if it's a matter of matching the *feel* of a sample, then I take a different approach. For instance, if I'm working with a low-pitched sample (something with a bass tone), I usually try to offset its sound with some level of brightness. In cases like these, I'll add in some synth sounds. This contrast makes for a unique, unforced change or accent. Here, one thing I want to point out is that matching the synth closely to the "feel" (not necessarily the key) of the sample typically works better for the overall impact of the sample-based beat. Keep in mind that synth sounds (which are first generational) have a completely different sonic quality than samples from pre-existing recordings (i.e. old songs, vinyl records, etc.). Therefore, whenever the synth sound is made to match the key of the sample, what typically happens is that the synth sound winds up *competing with*, if not outright dominating, the sample. In turn, this transforms a sample-based beat into a synthetic-sounds-based beat.

Now, here's how I combine samples and synths. Either I play

a phrase(s) straight up (from my Roland Fantom Keyboard) and record it through MIDI into a sequence on my Akai MPC 4000, or I play a phrase(s), sample it, then assign the phrase(s) to one drum pad or more. More often than not, I do the latter, because sampling the synth phrase(s) allows me more flexibility over the tone and timbre of the synth sound. And once I've sampled the synth sound, I can filter it, compress it, add reverb, whatever it takes to match the feeling (not the pitch) of the sample and the overall beat. For those times where I sample the synth sound, I run my Fantom through my Akai S950 sampler or my MPC 4000, depending on the feel and sound of the main sample. If I want more clarity and a bit more brightness, I sample the synth phrase(s) with my MPC 4000. If I want a warmer, perhaps "thicker" sound, I sample the synth phrase(s) through my S950. One more thing. In cases where I'm using synth sounds for slight emphasis or accents and changes, I focus in on the softest (deadest) part of the sample, then I add in the synth sounds. And sometimes when I have a sample cut off right at the loop point of a sequence, I'll throw some light (soft) stacked synth sounds right at the point of where the end of the sample drops out.

√Check This Out – Playing Synths in the Same Key of Sample?

A member of the BeatTips Community (forums) once asked me the following:

> I'm kind of confused. You're supposed to make everything in the same key and in tune. If you don't play in the same key as the sample, your beat is going to sound out of tune. So you're saying you play whatever notes on top of the sample?

Here's my answer in full:

Whoever said that you *have* to play synth/keys in the same key as the sample? That's not a rule. First and foremost, when attempting to combine synths/keys with samples, always remember the subtle nuances that samples have and that synths/keys do not. Again, samples are second -generation sounds, meaning that they are digital copies of pre-recorded composites of music (sound). On the other hand, synths/keys are first-generation sounds, in that they are generated from *sound generators*, etc; they are not digital copies of pre-recorded composites of sound. For me, this fact alone tells you that matching up synths/keys with samples most likely will never be achieved using the "exact same key." Sure, in some cases it *might* get the job done. However, if you really want to "match" synths/keys with samples more effectively — and by match, I mean timbre, color, weight, and feel — then more than likely off-tuning the synths/keys from the sample will be your best plan of action. The thing is, samples present a sonic quality that can simply never be matched *exactly* by first-generation sounds. And more often than not, when beatmakers attempt to force an "exact-key" synth-match with a sample (where the exact pitch is actually indiscernible), the sonic dynamics change. This in turn prompts a raise of the volume level of either the sample or the synth. In such a case, the original feel and nuance of the overall beat changes dramatically.

Here, I also want to point out that whether you combine synths with samples or not, always remember: Each beat is a slave to the style that you made it in. That is, if it's a sample-based beat, the synths that you add in should support the sample-based framework, not dominate it. And if it's a synthetic-sounds-based beat, then the samples that you add in should serve to support or accentuate the synthetic sounds. Thus, before you make additions and subtractions to a beat, it's important to always give deference to the style, sound, and scope of the beat you're making. Moreover, make sure you consider the rhythm quality and structure before you modify the major sonic (sound dynamics) qualities of the beat.

Having considered the "style-deference" aspect, whenever I use keys/synths I don't view it as playing any notes *over the top*. Never. If I played keys over the top of the sample, I'd essentially kill the sample's power. So instead, I view it as supporting the sample or playing keys to compliment the sample. Here, again, I must point out that hip hop/rap is much more about rhythm than melody. In beatmaking, since keys/synths are often better used for developing melody as opposed to rhythm, and since samples are mostly used for establishing rhythm and groove, you have to be careful how and when you combine them with samples. Plus, combining synths with samples is not merely a matter of playing notes over the top. However, many beatmakers confuse "playing synths over the top" with simply making a sample fuller or thicker. But the fullness and thickness of a sample is not a melody or rhythm issue, it's a sonic issue. Yet many beatmakers make the assumption that playing synths over the top will make the sample sound better. Wrong. It will completely kill the sample at worst, or it will neutralize the sample's true impact, nuance, and sonic quality at best.

So there's two things I want to make clear about this. First, if you want to increase the fullness or thickness of a sample through the use of synths, then I recommend that you sample the synths, chop them down into tones, then use the chopped synth tones to beef up the weaker points of the sample. Second, consider the length of the primary sample that you're using. For instance, if you're working with a 4-bar sequence, how long does the primary sample play for? If it doesn't play for the full 4 bars, you can add in synths on the "free" bars or "free" spots, i.e. the bars and spots where the sample is silent. In cases like these, you can play in (add in) synth patterns in whatever key that you like, as long as it sounds good to you. In fact, playing in a different key often works best here, because it will give your beat more balance and an increased dynamic quality.

BeatTip – Quality Parameters: Use the Right Ingredients, But Don't Overcook the Beat

Beatmaking is not only a rich art, it's also a musical science. That being said, some beatmakers get too carried away with the "science" part. (You wouldn't believe all of the different stories that I've heard that describe incredible levels of over-producing.) The science of beatmaking is a robust one, because it contains technical, logical, and creative spheres. The following section is about the creative science of beatmaking and, more specifically, the science of arrangement and how it effects the quality of a beat.

No matter how we all differ with our initial approach to getting a new beat started, we all set out trying to find relatively the same thing: a base (primary) rhythm framework that has the right drums and the right overall sound. Now, having achieved this framework, through a number of creative applied sciences that are mostly unique to beatmaking, a familiar dilemma sets in: What to add next?

Within the beatmaking lexicon, these "add-ons" are commonly known as "changes" or "switch-ups." For those more familiar with music theory, a change or switch-up in beatmaking parlance is actually most comparable to a motif or motive and an embellishment or ornament. In beatmaking, changes are typically worked in somewhere on 4th, 8th, 12th, or 16th bar, with a significant switch-up thrown in somewhere at the mid-point of the beat. But here's the thing: A beat does not require a significant change, and certainly not a major switch-up, in order for it to sound dope.

Consider this, let's say that you sample a 4-bar measure of any given soul or funk record from the 1970s. Now, depending on *where* on the record that you sample the measure from, you want to remember that contained in just that one sample, there can actually be a wide assortment of individual sounds; and combined together, those sounds form a wall-of-sound. Think about it: There could be the bass drum, the snare drum, a ride, a cymbal, a hi-hat, an open hi-hat, bass guitar, rhythm guitar, lead guitar, electronic keyboard/ piano, tambourine, timbales, horns, and the like. This is the typical sound-wall found in most complete phrases. And since drums are the most fundamental component of hip hop/rap beat structure, beatmakers are naturally drawn to those parts of the record that have the least amount of collective sounds. Remember, this part in a song is known as the "break." However, though I recognize what a traditional break is (the section where all of the music drops out, save the rhythm section, namely the drums and bass), I consider *any* fragmented musical phrase to be a break. In fact, fundamentally speaking, I believe that the quest for the perfect beat is really the quest for the perfect break. That being said, after this ultimate break, if you will, is achieved, many of us do something very detrimental to the beat itself: We over-produce it, by adding in unnecessary or counter-productive changes and switch-ups.

Creating beats is meticulous and very cathartic, so usually, the way we feel about a beat we've just made has a lot to do with what actually went into the making of it. For beatmakers, *process* matters a great deal. We value the unique processes, practices, and methodologies of our craft in a way that often borders on obsession. And as I mentioned earlier, we take great pride in our particular brand of musical science. Because of this, we're always surveying a beat, thinking about how can we make it better. This (sometimes unhealthy) preoccupation with perfection can sabotage many of the beats that we make. Somewhere in between a beatmaker carving out that ultimate break and officially calling a beat complete is where this preoccupation with perfection tends to go way out of whack. Thus, the best way to avoid over-producing a beat is to acknowledge that it can happen. Indeed, being mindful of quality means being tuned into only what the beat before you *needs*.

BeatTip – Sampling and Improvisation: Sample Vamping and Understanding the Relationship Between Impromptu and Scripted Elements of Beatmaking

The ways in which each beatmaker scopes out or plots a new beat may vary, but for the most part, we all improvise until something strikes us. And when it does, that's when we get busy! Thus, I've always maintained that one of the biggest keys to high quality beatmaking is understanding the relationship between the improvisation and prepared, i.e. scripted, elements of beatmaking.

Each beatmaker's own unique understanding of this relationship is one of the main factors that determines not only the processes and methods that each chooses, but also the frame of workflow and, ultimately, the dimension of creativity that each can access. Although the relationship between the improvisation and prepared (scripted) aspects of beatmaking shares a number of common characteristics in both sample-based and synthetic-sounds-based (e.g. keyboard beat/live instrumentation) styles, there are certain realities and key differences in how this relationship manifests itself in both compositional styles.

For beatmakers working from the sample-based compositional style, improvisation is actually not a choice but a necessity. Sampling is as much about one's penchant for rare musical discovery as it is about one's ability to transform — i.e. reconceptualize, recontextualize, and transgress — that discovery. This means that sample-based beatmakers must rely on their ability to adjust to and *improvise* off of whatever the source material presents to them. So in this way, sample-based beatmakers are limited by the source material that they discover. However, on the other hand, sample-based beatmakers are also liberated by the relative unpredictability of that very same source material. And one of the biggest keys to unlocking this unpredictability is improvisation.

Although the most often preferred source material of sample-based beatmakers comes from songs recorded between the late 1960s and mid-1970s, there is the strong sense among sample-based beatmakers of reacting and connecting with the "known unknown." That is to say, that even though sample-based beatmakers who favor this specific source material may know, *per se*, what sort of sounds, textures, and musical constructions to expect, they do not actually know how these elements will coalesce and manifest themselves on a given recording. Which means that their improvisational skills are put to test each time they work with new source material.

But while sampling offers a unique sense of "knowing the unknown," the same type of connection does not exist in the synthetic-sounds-based compositional style. For beatmakers working from the synthetic-sounds-based style, improvisation is also a necessity, but not to the same degree as it is in the sample-based style. In both compositional styles of beatmaking, improvisation is used as a creative process that compliments the elements that a beatmaker already knows. And herein lies the major difference in the way in which improvisation works in both styles.

In the synthetic-sounds-based style, improvisation takes on a different context, especially for traditionally trained musicians, because of the nature of the "known" elements is based on raw notes rather than samples. In other words, a preexisting knowledge of notes, in terms of tonal quality and mood conveyance as well as chords, common chord progressions, and the like, presents traditionally trained musicians with prepared (scripted) material from which to improvise upon.

But isn't the source material (pre-existing recordings) that sample-based beatmakers use also prepared material? Well, yes, it is prepared inasmuch as it has already been arranged and recorded. But to a sample-based beatmaker, what the source material (e.g. a vinyl record) holds can only be determined by the beatmaker's willingness to actually listen to the source material. From there, a beatmaker improvises using pieces of the source material's framework along with other sounds from his sound libraries. This form of sample vamping is similar to the process of traditional musicians vamping until they find the core groove or foundation for a song. I should also point out, however, that the prospects of such improvisation, i.e. **sample vamping**, is also governed by each beatmaker's arrangement and programming skills.

By contrast, non-sample-based beatmakers, particularly those who possess a decent knowledge of note architecture (music theory), aren't necessarily locked into the process of having to mine source material for the basis of their beats. Where musicians who sample are required, by the very nature of the sample-based compositional style itself, to actually listen to any recording that they would potentially like to sample, non-sampling musicians do not have to adhere to a similar obligation. For instance, non-sample-based beatmakers are not, necessarily, required to listen to what a chord in the key of A or D sounds like every time they want to compose something in the key of A or D. Presumably, they already know what an A or D note sounds like. It's already known to them; much like a sampler's stored sounds are known to them. Therefore, in beatmaking, this connection exists as a prepared element from which they can repeatedly draw upon and improvise, albeit within some of the rules of music theory.

Thus, an understanding of the relationship between impromptu and scripted elements of beatmaking will open up the ways in which improvisation can be utilized in the sample-based compositional style as well as the synthetic-sounds-compositional styles. Furthermore, having a firm understanding of this relationship improves your creativity, workflow, efficiency, and overall quality, as it helps you to build a keener grasp of what works and what doesn't within your particular style and sound.

√Check This Out – It's Never Just a Loop: The Main Decisions Made Before, During, and After a Sample is Looped

What Should You Sample?

What to sample is usually the first decision to be made. And of course, this decision depends on everything from one's mood to motive (purpose), to their style and sound preference, to their imagination and individual work ethic. For the purpose of this discussion of sampling, creating a loop, and building a beat, I will breakdown a beat that I made using a portion of the song "Heartbreak Hotel" by The Jacksons.

I chose "Heartbreak Hotel" for a number of reasons. First, it's a well-known hit, one with a great groove, by a popular group; certainly it's a song easy enough for readers to locate online. Many people are familiar with the record, so coming up with a beat and song that borrows a piece of such a hit, while still creating something "new" and appealing, is a bit of a challenge. Second, I wanted to choose a vinyl record that could readily be found in used record shops or at online vinyl record stores or in a relative's basement or attic. Third, "Heartbreak Hotel" has been sampled before, and I wanted to demonstrate the versioning tradition that runs deep in hip hop/rap music's roots by offering up *my* version. Fourth, because "Heartbreak Hotel" has a dominant drum pattern; and as such, I wanted to show how even a sample with drums can be tailored to your style and sound. Also, any seasoned beatmaker knows the type of obstacles drums in a sample can present. Finally, I chose "Heartbreak Hotel" because I'm a big fan of The Jacksons, and this is as good as any reason to thoroughly listen to one of my favorite songs by them.

What Section or Part Should You Sample?

Having settled on the song, what section of the song should I sample? The beginning? The middle? Near the end? Either way, it's gotta be a part of the record where the groove is "open" (well, as much as possible with a record like this). So that being said, it comes down to either the intro, the lead-up, or the bridge. I ruled out the bridge, simply because I heard something before with that part, and the strings intro isn't the part of the song that most people are familiar with.

So I go for the "2nd intro," or what I'm calling the "lead up," as in lead up to the first verse. But exactly where in the lead up? There's approximately 35 seconds between the beginning of the lead up and where Michael Jackson's first verse vocals begin. Within that 35 seconds, there are slight embellishments on the basic groove of the song, not to mention, at one point in this lead up, we hear one of Michael's signature vocal exclamations. No one wants that in there, right? Wrong. *I* do. I think it's dope, so I decided that no matter what, it had to be in the phrase that I would sample. Note: If I was using "Heartbreak Hotel" as source material for a beat for another rapper, I'm not sure what section I would've used. But since I'm rapping on this beat, I know which part of the song will suit my style, delivery, and flow.

So, How Do You Sample It?

Now that I've chosen the section of the record that I want to use, I have to decide how to sample it. There's no one way how to sample a record. Some beatmakers sample in stereo, some in mono. Some sample wet, i.e. with effects, while others sample dry, no effects. Some sample in 24 bit, 16 bit, even 12 bit.

For starters, I always sample in mono. Next, I usually sample

223

wet. I almost never sample any audio without its signal first flowing through my Numark DJ mixer (aside from the EQs on my mixer, a DJ mixer makes me feel linked to the earliest roots of the beatmaking tradition). My DJ mixer routes into my Mackie mixing console, where I do further EQ'ing, like "beefing up" the sample (making a sound heavier or warmer). Then I run the signal from the DJ Mixer's output on the Mackie into either my Akai MPC 4000 or my Akai S950. For the sample below, I sampled a portion of "Heartbreak Hotel" into my Akai S950.

What about the pitch question?

Do you sample the audio leaving the pitch as is, or do you turn it up or down? This decision, like others in the creative process of sampling, mostly depends on the ultimate beat/song that you envision. For my "Heartbreak Hotel Remix," I turned the pitch up a bit before I sampled it, then I fine-tuned it as I arranged my drums; and note: NO timestretch function was used in the making of this beat/song.

What About Chopping?

Of course, how to chop something is one of the big decisions in the sampling process. But the more complete a phrase is, the less difficult it is to loop, right? Not always. In fact, depending on what's actually in the phrase, getting it to loop "correctly" (according to your own rhythmic standards), it can be rather difficult finding and fine tuning the best start and end points. Here, let's remember that all of these aforementioned creative decisions have been made before the drum arrangement enters the picture. Of course, as those above decisions are being made, you should already be thinking about the ways in which to arrange the drums.

Which Way to Go with the Drums?

Even if you skip most of the aforementioned processes, you must still come up with a suitable drum framework. To pull this off, it takes a decent arsenal of drum sounds, a knack for choosing the right ones, and the ability to arrange those drum sounds into a drum pattern that works effectively with the so-called "loop" sample.

With audio that already has drums in it, you can fall back and let the drums in the sample do the work, only adding in light touches of your own drum sounds. Or you can also add your own drums to completely "mask" (cover up) the drums in the sample. You can also match your drums with the drums in the sample; but this can be very difficult, especially if you don't posses the right kind of drum sounds.

With a song like "Heartbreak Hotel," who could blame someone for going easy on the drums, that is to say, doing not much at all. Well, I never sample anything without a base idea of how I'm going to arrange the drums. Moreover, depending upon the extent of the groove (i.e. the feel and the level of kick and snare drums) that I've sampled and the ultimate groove that I'm going for, I will usually not only mask and match the drums, I'll flank everything with my own signature percussion. And this is exactly what I did with my "Heartbreak Hotel Remix" song.

Finally, I should note that the construction of the sample(s) is only part of the equation. Also, never forget the matter of the overall sound design. Here, I'm referring to the "color" of the sample that's achieved through sound modification techniques like filtering and EQ'ing, etc.

To hear my complete "Heartbreak Hotel Remix" song, go to: http:// www.beattips.com/beattips/2012/08/its-never-just-a-loop.html

When to Chop and When to Loop?

While context and feeling are critically important, so is one's individual philosophy on sampling. Nothing will determine when, why, and how you chop or loop more than your philosophy on sampling. Depending where your knowledge, understanding, and preference is situated on the overall spectrum of hip hop/rap music, you could be more or less devoted to the "break,"really the core compositional element of hip hop/rap music in its traditional form.

When you're devoted to the break, everything that you do in a sample-based beat (even a non-sample-based beat) is going to defer to the development of a central break (or loop) that everything else is based on. And in that case, if you find a record with what I prefer to call a "ready-made loop," then, you typically use it, without messing its feel and sound up with useless, unnecessary chops. Conversely, if you find a song with musical phrases that appeals to you — in terms of feel, tone, and timbre — but is not in a "ready-made loop," then you typically turn to chopping to develop a break that contains chops and arrangements that you make to fit as a loop.

Coming from this philosophy (or approach), the context and feeling of the parts of a song that you want to sample make you immediately think about Where's the break in this? What will allow for the tightest, most grooving break. Here's what's quite important to understand. The word "loop" draws its meaning from two things. First, "loop" or "looping" comes from the engineering world, where reel to reel tape was "chopped" (cut), rearranged, and often "looped" (repeated) for drum fills, dubs, etc. Second, the break was made to repeat by hip hop's earliest DJs using methods like the "needle drop" and more popularly the "spin back." So what hip hop's earliest DJs were doing was spinning back certain parts of a record, typically the break, and repeating, i.e. *looping*, those parts. This is where the evolution of what looping something means in hip hop/rap music.

Special note: Remember, it was considered a hip hop DJ skill to be able to find new records and unleash unheard breaks and other interesting parts on records. And while DJs would spin back (repeat/loop) these parts, they would let them play; they would not cut 'em unnecessarily.

Given that historical context, as hip hop/rap music and beatmaking grew, it attracted more people. Naturally, people bring with them their own biases and preferences about and knowledge of music and the musical process. So while some may adhere to a philosophical approach to sampling that fundamentally defers to the break, others still may defer to a philosophy that minimizes the importance of the break, and instead places emphasis on more changes or linear progression within an arrangement. Perfectly fine. But it's worth noting that the latter philosophical approach tends to lead to more chopping (often unnecessary levels), particularly because it grants more control to someone who's devoted to developing more extensive arrangements. And this is completely understandable, especially if you're less influenced by the historical place the break holds in the hip hop/rap music tradition, and more influenced by arrangement schemes that prioritize chord progression, melody, and the like. Furthermore, the philosophical approach that's further away from the idea of the break gives one the feeling and satisfaction that they're doing more than "just" looping something that they sampled. But I never like to think of anything as just a loop. Finding a record with a dope part, looping it perfectly and matching it with dope drums is a skill of its own.

Again, where you stand on the overall spectrum, the knowledge of and deference (or not) to the break, is the thing that's going to signal to you what to do every time you hear a new record. The more committed you are to the break, the less you're likely to think about evasive chopping or rigid ideas about when/where to chop, as you'll want what you're hearing on the record to be left in tact as much as possible, while still giving it a new context: a hip hop/rap context. Conversely, the less focused you are on the break, philosophically speaking, the more interested you'll likely be in breaking up — chopping up — the sounds that you hear, as it will be less important to you to keep what you heard on the record more in tact. Of course, in this case, these chopped-up samples become individual sound tones that can be melded in any number of ways. Special note: Undoubtedly, as you develop as a sample-based beatmaker, your musical sensibilities will, at times and for certain beats, lead you to move around the philosophical spectrum I described here.

Finally, it's worth looking at the career arcs of RZA, DJ Premier, Pete Rock, and J Dilla for guidance with this question. RZA's style and sound was predicated more on the break approach. Yet as his music career grew, he expanded his approach; but he never gave up his core approach: He can still bang out those classic Wu joints whenever he wants. Premier's style, which uses a chop-style that he first developed (and has now often been poorly copied), is also predicated on the break approach. In Premier's catalog of beats, you can hear many "straight loops," as well as many creatively chopped works. Pete Rock, while predicated on the break approach, used more chops as his career progressed. And Dilla, who mastered a number of different styles and sounds, became more minimalist and predicated upon the break approach towards the end of his career.

BeatTips Standards and Best Practices of the Sampling Tradition of Hip Hop/Rap Music

There are no written rules of creativity. All sample-based beatmakers can make beats in whatever manner that they choose. Nevertheless, in the sampling tradition of hip hop/rap music, a set of **standards and best practices** have evolved over the years. Although these standards and best practices have been informally shared (understood) among many beatmakers, they have never been formally organized or uniformly promoted until now. Thus, what follows here is a discussion of these standards and best practices.

Standards and Best Practices – Transformation
High Transformation, Reconceptualization, and Recontextualization

Creative, well-conceived chop arrangement schemes, no-matter how many or how little chops are made and used, constitutes standards and best practices. Chop arrangement schemes that effectively enhance the overall arrangement of a beat constitutes standards and best practices. Excessive chop arrangement schemes that sound overly forced, particularly cases where the multiple *triggering* sounds can be heard in the arrangement, fall below the threshold for standards and best practices. Chop arrangement schemes that serves no musical purpose (rhythm, melody, harmony) or sonic purpose (layering, sound design) also fall below the threshold for standards and best practices.

Chopping that relies more on the beatmaker's own ear and creative sense of arrangement and less on auto-chop functionality constitutes standards and best practices. Chopping that relies *solely* on auto-chop functionality, rather than the beatmaker's ear and arrangement skills, falls below the threshold for standards and best practices.

Although transformation may be subjective, when considering how transformative a beat is or isn't, ask yourself these three questions: Is the way in which the sample(s) is(are) used conceptually different from its source? Is the way in which the sample(s) is(are) used a change in context from the original? How much does the sample(s) used sound substantially similar to the sound recording from which it came?

Standards and Best Practices – Amounts Used
Sound-Hits, Sound-Stabs, Parts, Phrases, and Low Number of Bars

Sampling less and doing more with it constitutes standards and best practices. Sound-hits and stabs, which are both de minimis (insignificant) usages by default, are well within standards and best practices. Short music phrases and parts there of (e.g. riffs, drum fills, drum rolls, parts of melodies), used in contexts different from their source, constitutes standards and best practices. The lower the number of bars sampled and used, for example, 1 to 4 consecutive bars (the best practice), the deeper the sampling and use fall within the parameters of standards and best practices. However, a higher number of bars sampled and used does not automatically disqualify the sampling and use from standards and best practices. For example, 5 to 8 consecutive bars sampled and used constitute standards and best practices when substantial transformation takes place or when the sample is used in a substantially different

229

context. The sampling and use of 9 to 16 consecutive bars may possibly fall within the parameters of standards and best practices, provided transformation is high and the new context of the sample is different. Sampling 17 consecutive bars or more is generally below standards and best practices, unless theres a deeply transformative vocal element, let's say, like vocals written and performed to a song that was only an instrumental in its original form. (Think of a film score instrumental.)

What's important to remember when considering amounts is that the less that is sampled and used, the more highly regarded the instance of sampling. Further, creative transformation, reconceptualization, or recontextualization must always be a central aim of a sample-based beatmaker. No matter the amount used, the level of creative transformation, reconceptualization, and recontextualization determines whether an instance of sampling qualifies as standards and best practices or not. Finally, I advise against sampling the whole "heart" (main melody, etc.) of any well-known song. But if you do sample some or all of the heart, be sure to increase the level of transformation, reconceptualization, or recontextualization.

Standards and Best Practices — Significance of Sample(s) Used
Using the Heart of a Recording or Parts Less Significant

The sampling and use of less significant parts of a sound recording fall well within the parameters of standards and best practices. Sampling the whole or parts of the heart (the main theme) of a sound recording constitutes standards and best practices only when the use of the sample is highly transformative, or when the sample is sufficiently reconceptualized or recontextualized.

Standards and Best Practices — Original Drum Work or Drum Breaks in New Contexts?
Original Drum Patterns and Transformative Uses of Drum Break Samples

Drums are a cornerstone in the beatmaking tradition, thus original drum patterns created using individual drum sounds, especially a beatmaker's own customized drum sounds, constitutes standards and best practices. The use of drum breaks, either from break-beat compilations and other songs, instead of or in addition to individual drum sounds also constitute standards and best practices, especially when drum breaks are used in new contexts.

Standards and Best Practices — In the Matter of Loops
Obscurity, Familiarity, and Transformation

Typically, transformation always falls deeper within the standards and best practices. However, *ready-made* loops should be considered by a different transformation metric. For example, obscure ready-made loops (e.g. a couple of bars of a sample from a lesser known soul recording) with less transformation to the original sample but added original drum work qualifies as standards and best practices. However, ready-made loop samples of very familiar songs (i.e. well-known hit songs) are less likely to meet the standards and best practices threshold. However, ready-made loops of such familiar songs that effectively transform the context of the use may fall within standards and best practices.

Live-Instrumentation Sampling Revolution

For years, live-instrumentation sampling was all about coming up with passable re-plays of samples from records. Of course, the problem with this approach was that it was widely understood that re-plays could never match the sound and feel of the original sample. But in recent years (2012-2014) there has been a live-instrumentation sampling revolution.

The biggest development in this space has to do with the basic philosophical approach to sampling live instrumentation. Previously, the trend was to use live-band instrumentation as is, i.e. as the substitute for a beat. (Here, the stellar live-band hip hop group The Roots comes to mind.) But the tactic of using a live band as is — or, more specifically, the method of trying to merely replicate the sound and nuance of particular samples from old records — is giving way to a different scheme, one where brand new live instrumentation, not re-plays of old works, is created for the sole purpose of being sampled. Pioneers of this new wave of live-instrumentation sampling include most notably Adrian Younge, DJ Premier, and Marco Polo.

In this new paradigm of live-instrumentation sampling, the aim is not to do re-plays that closely match actual samples of records from the 1960s and 1970s, but rather to use the sound, feel, and nuances of these eras of music as a guide and reference for creating new music (instrumentation) to sample. In effect, this new approach to live-instrumentation and sampling is dispelling, to some degree, the long-held notion that replays can never be a passable substitute for the original's sound and feel.

Adrian Younge, who was once a sample-based beatmaker before successfully embarking on a mission to learn to play multiple traditional instruments, has been scoring films since 2009; and in 2013, he produced Twelve Reasons to Die, a concept album that saw Ghostface Killah rapping over Younge's instrumentation. While his style and sound — unabashedly soulful and psychedelic — mirrors the sonics and vibe of the 1960s and 1970s, it's the arrangement of his compositions that mostly stand out.

Younge's arrangements lend themselves to sampling primarily because of the rhythm and melody structures that he uses, along with the drum (backing beats) that he creates. Because he has a sample-based beatmaker's sensibility (he's actually an MPC alumni), and because he aims to make music reminiscent to something that sample greats like DJ Premier, RZA, or J Dilla would want to sample, his music often features wide open soulful grooves, funky drum breaks, and warm sound phrases and stabs. In 2014, Younge teamed up with DJ Premier and Royce da 5'9 for the PRhyme project. A fantastic project for the music alone, the PRhyme album represents a major breakthrough in the live-instrumentation sampling space, as all of the beats were made by Premier using samples of songs from Younge's catalogue. That the beats on the PRhyme album sound like they were sampled from older records is a major achievement for both Younge and DJ Premier. For Younge, it's validation that his music does indeed hold up to the eras of music that inspire him. For Premier, not only does it further cement him as one of the grand pioneers of beatmaking, it marks him as one of the chief architects of this new form of sample-based music.

While Adrian Younge has been steadily forging his sample-ready live-instrumentation sound, and while DJ Premier has been developing a new but familiar approach to modern source material (he's added the MPC Renaissance to his production setup presumably to aide with this new method of sampling), Marco Polo has been pioneering a similar style and sound of his own. A long-time sample-based beatmaker (producer) who once only swore by vinyl records, Marco has emerged as the chief architect of the sample-based method that features instrumentation made using sound packs, .i.e. stand alone sound libraries.

Sound packs full of samples and soul, funk, jazz, and rock inspired grooves have been around for years. And for the most part, sound packs have always tended to sound cheezy and nothing like the sound eras they purported to emulate. But the quality of modern sound packs have improved greatly. Keying in on the improvements of sound and sample packs like Native Instruments Kontakt and Komplete, Marco has developed a method for creating new instrumentation — entirely within the box — that he then samples and flips (with his MPC) as he would with any record or other source material.

Certainly, self-sampling has long been a tactic practiced among sample-based beatmakers like Pete Rock, DJ Premier, J Dilla, Jake Uno; but it's normally been an auxilary method of theirs, rather than a featured component of their styles. For Marco, this new method has become his main style. And what's most impressive about what he's doing is that, while he hasn't stopped using the traditional method of sampling records, the difference in sound and feel between his new method and the traditional method of sampling records is slim and often unnoticeable. In fact, when he produced the intro music for the Brooklyn Nets professional basketball team, many thought that the music — a rather intricate, hard-hitting and soulful affair — was a sample. It wasn't. Well, not exactly. It wasn't a sample in the traditional sense of an old record, but rather multiple samples of Marco's own live instrumentation made using sound libraries. When I interviewed Marco in mid-December, 2014, he shared with me his thoughts on live-instrumentation and sampling as well as his personal approach, philosophy, and process. I have included an extended excerpt of that discussion below.

> First of all, I did something with Adrian [Younge] on my last album, on Newport Authority II. He asked me to do a remix off the Delfonics album he did. And I flipped the beat, and then Tragedy rapped on it and Lil' Fame. So shouts to Adrian, he's incredible at what he does. My whole thing— I incorporate that type of sampling. I use Komplete to compose my own music, and to me it's all a learning process 'cause I do know this: You can over analyze the approach of like, "Yo, let me get a band and we'll make it sound like records," and I've heard people do that and fail miserably. And on paper, it's like, "Yo, it's all live instruments. And live drums…" You think like, "Yo, this is dope." Or it should be dope. But a lot of times, to me it's not! It's not! There's something missing. Something's missing. I don't care technically what you did. Yes, you have a Fender through the amp that they used in the '60s and through this board, and like… But that doesn't mean shit if it doesn't sound right and give you that feeling, you-know-what-I'm-sayin'.
>
> I don't get excited when someone's like, "Yo, I'm going into the studio with a live band…" I've heard people say that, then I heard [the music] and it failed my expectations. After all of these years of breaking things down, to me I just keep it really simple: Is it dope, or is it not dope? That's how it should be. But I think people get like, caught up in the whole pitch of, "Yo, but he used this band…" A lot of times, these newer bands that recreate that sound are extremely dope, but what I think needs to happen is producers need to take that shit — like they did records — put it in the damn

sampler and add their drums to where it knocks. 'Cause a lot of these live drummers are playing funky breaks all day and it sounds incredible how it's recorded, but the knock is not there. And as far as I know, when I came up with hip hop, shit knocked. Drums were the driving force.

The shit that I do these days is I sample myself essentially. I accumulate a lot of music — live instrumentation like you say. I'll buy sound libraries, like a soulful guitar pack with people playing riffs in different chords. Here's people playing keys and chords. Here's some horns. I take that shit like I do with vinyl, I put it into Komplete or Kontakt or my MPC, and I FUCK IT UP with compression, and take these luscious, highly recorded, 42-bit shit— I don't care about all that. I want it to sound dusty. So I put it in here [MPC, Komplete, or Kontakt] and I mess with it, then I add my own shit on top of it. As long as you got a wave file, you're good. You can put it into many programs. Absolutely. You're limitless with things. I was making music with some musicians and something wasn't happening. It wasn't working. And I was like, "Yo, we're making these ill things in the studio," then I'm like, "Yo, this is going to be a crazy beat." Then I sit down to make it and it was WHACK! [laughs]

[But] You have to have an ear. Absolutely it comes from the influence of the music I get off my vinyl, 'cause I know how shit's supposed to sound. I'm trying to make shit sound like if I went to a record store, and it sounds dirty, and I put amps on shit. And the reason I'm doing that is because I know that's what they did back then. But I don't have those same tools, so I gotta attack it from different ways. And whatever I can achieve that sound with, I'm going to use it. It all starts from me buying music and records, that's the foundation of all this shit. And that's why I'm able to achieve beats that don't have samples in them because I've studied what they do sound like, and I'm still learning about it. So, if I didn't start by diggin', you know, you can't just— You gotta understand.

[And now] It's unlimited the options that I have now. Now, I'm able to time stretch on new levels; I'm able to pitch down [in new ways]; I take a bunch of shit and individually tweak it. I have effects — I never got the effects board in my MPC, mostly because I heard it was whack. And the effects, to be able to pre-process and put reverbs on drums; dumb shit that people probably have and are like, "Why didn't you have that all this time?" "'Cause I didn't!" Now, I can take melodies and extend them. And you know when you hear a record and you're like, "Aw, man, the first bar of that is crazy, then it gets super whack on bar 2." Now I can be like, let me replay it and play what I want to be there. Or have someone do it. And then records really become inspiration because a lot of times I try to replay something that I hear on record, but I'm not a classically trained musician, so it'll just end up becoming my own thing anyways. An original idea inspired by something that just goes in a whole other direction.

Before Preem did what he did with PRhyme — which, by the way, he resisted doing it at first. Before he did it, there was this sort of slant, people in the shadows like, "I don't really want to fuck with that." But now, there's a before and after. Now that HE did it — that DJ Premier did it — it opens it up. It's still the same process. It's still sampling and flipping something.

The great thing about it is, it definitely opens doors to have my music to be submitted for licensing. And a lot of opportunities are instantly gone, because not saying that I did or I didn't, but if you have a lot of music where you haven't cleared the samples you're using, you can't use that shit past putting it out. You can't pitch it to movies and video games and T.V. shows. I was able to make money with this new approach. So I'm very for it. When you make music as a career, you have to think about shit like that. It's been very helpful. But it's not the main thing that drives me. It's just a great option to have, knowing that I have the freedom to do that now. But I'm just saying, there's all these types of new approaches that's crazy. Especially when producers that are making and composing their music, because they know exactly what producers (beatmakers) want to hear when they're looking for samples. So you have all these new avenues of music, where the live instrumentation and doing shit like that is positive. It all comes down to money, bro. The fucking people are just scared to sample and shit. And it fucking hurts the music, straight up, because to this day, like, if I pick my top 10 records, none of them shits is sample free. [laughs] Top 50! NONE of them shits are sample free. I know Dr. Dre definitely played some shit over, but even still, it was like playing over a sample. Name five amazing, classic [hip hop/rap] records, that don't have samples in them. Could you? I don't know. Maybe if I thought for a couple of hours. But I don't think so. And as much as shit progresses, it just goes back to the beginning. Is it fucking dope, or is it not dope?[122]

---

[122] Excerpt from my interview with producer (beatmaker) Marco Polo.

A Bridge of Musicianship: What the Live-Instrumentation Sampling Revolution Means for the Future

There are a number of things that we can take away from the live-instrumentation sampling revolution; all things that give us a good idea about the future of sample-based music.

First, the role of traditional source material from the '60s and '70s has taken on a new significance. Since the inception of the sample-based tradition of hip hop/rap music, such source material was sampled. Looking ahead, however, such source material will also more directly serve as a reference guide for the creation of compositions that are made for sampling. This means that listening to and studying the music of the '60s & '70s will become even more critical. Further, this will undoubtedly place a greater premium on diggin' in the crates; and it will likely familiarize new (younger) beatmakers with a wealth of music they would otherwise have missed. Certainly, this residual effect will bode well for the future of hip hop/rap music.

Second, the live-instrumentation revolution will extend the shelf-life of all sample-based beatmakers. With a fresh and truly infinite supply of copyright-free source material in the form of made-to-sample live instrumentation, sample-based beatmakers will more aggressively pursuit production and collaborative opportunities that were all but withheld from them due to sample-clearance concerns. Sampling wasn't in threat of dying, but now it has an entirely new frontier. One that's equally unlimited as the source material. Furthermore, if more traditionally trained musicians take this approach seriously and study (and master) the art of sampling as I suspect, this will be an area of music making where traditionally trained musicians can potentially excel, maybe even match the talents of most traditional sample-based beatmakers. This will be an important space in the future.

Third, the live-instrumentation will come to distinguish the 9th major beatmaking period. As a kind of Studio-Band Period and Pioneers/Avant-Garde Period hybrid in essence, the Live-Instrumentation Sampling Period will mark the time that live-instrumentation first exploded on the scene, prompting a level of interest in sample-based beatmaking not seen since the major sampling era.

Finally, while the live-instrumentation sampling revolution is a good thing overall, as a result of its very nature, it may have one adverse effect: a widespread move away from the actual use of the source material used to inspire the made-to-sample compositions. I do not believe that live-instrumentation sampling will ever completely overtake the traditional form of sampling; however, if it reaches the point to where some deem it the superior sampling method, I believe some critical sampling nuances will be lost.

Chapter 8

Misconceptions, Criticisms, and the Value of Sampling

Cultural Histories and Musical Orientations that Inform Our Opinions of Sampling, and Why Sampling is a Useful Art

The Influence of Race, Cultural Background, and Music Training on Perceptions of the Art of Sampling

Most blacks born in the United States between the late 1950s and early 1980s were brought up in a vast cultural space wherein important black identity tropes — embedded in music, dance, food, and language — were familiar to all. Aside from a few minor differences here or there, a black kid born in the 1970s in New York City would recognize the same fundamental elements at a party, barbecue, picnic, family reunion, or similar social gathering that his contemporaries born in Chicago, Raleigh, Los Angeles, Philadelphia, Detroit, and Atlanta (just to name a few American cities with large black populations) would have. And even with some hometown stylistic differences, the food would be familiar to him or her; the dance moves would be familiar to him or her; the language and laughter would be familiar to him or her; and the music would, of course, be familiar to him or her, because it was all part of popular Black American culture at that time — one shared cultural space and meaning.

This shared Black American cultural space, with its well-understood social cues, meanings, and reminders of identity, persisted as blacks grew older. For instance, it was not uncommon for the so-called "music of our parents" to be played by the DJ at the teenage parties that we went to. When I was 13, one of my favorite songs that I heard, at least once, at every house party thrown by someone black was Deniece Williams' "Free," a song recorded and released years before I was even born. What I distinctly remember about "Free" is how much my mother, father, grandmother, extended family (young and old), friends, and I *all* enjoyed it. I never questioned why that was, I just understood the connection with this song and plenty others that shared the same vocal and rhythmic aesthetics. It was this shared Black American cultural space — one with its own concepts of art and originality, creative nuances and priorities, and metrics of excellence — that was the preeminent cultural history of the first hip hop DJs, as well as the most influential sample-based beatmakers of the Pioneers/ Avant-Garde and Post-Pioneers beatmaking periods.

Thus, for most black American sample-based beatmakers who were born between the late 1950s and early 1980s, sampling holds a number of significant cultural meanings and connections. The act of exploring cultural heritage; or the practice of adding to this cultural heritage and creating a continuum of said cultural heritage; or the activity of reliving a shared cultural memory; or the act of proclaiming a shared black cultural feeling and voice.

By contrast, most whites born in the United States between the late 1950s and early 1980s did not grow up or participate within the Black American cultural space of twentieth-century America, even though many did indeed listen to and were ultimately influenced by Black American music. As such, it should be expected that most of their social experiences and cultural memories regarding food, language, dance, and music tracked differently as well. And while there were perhaps a number of parallels in specific areas, generally the experiences were different.

For example, in addition to the many house parties thrown by blacks that I went to in the late 1980s as a teenager, I also went to a number of white parties as well. But the scenes couldn't have been more different. The music at the black parties that I went to during this time was strictly soul, funk, R&B, hip hop/rap, and Caribbean. The music at the white house parties that I attended during the same period were dominated by rock: '80s pop, new wave, some British ska; sometimes a little reggae, and sometimes a little rap.

Further, DJs were at every black house party that I went to in 1980s as well. And everybody danced at these parties; it was expected. In fact, there were always impromptu dance-routine showcases and dance battles going on at these parties. There was never an official DJ at *any* of the white house parties that I went to (both in the inner city and suburbs). And there was absolutely no dancing — i.e. no serious, or non-drunk dancing — at these parties either.

One other big distinction was booze. Drinking was never an integral part of any of the teenage black house parties that I went to. (Typically, these parties were birthday or graduation celebrations, which meant that there were usually a parent around.) There may have been a group of kids that would drink outside before they came into the party or after; that was about it. But the teenage white house parties that I went to were normally the inspiration of parents *gone for the weekend*. These parties always included drinking. In fact, drinking, not music, was typically the center of attraction of every house party that I went to that was hosted by white teenagers.

But just as there are exceptions to almost any pattern, I'm sure there were a number of whites raised up on the same music as Black Americans. For instance, in my interviews with Marco Polo and Paul Cantor, both white and beatmakers (the latter also a music writer), each related stories to me about the jazz, R&B, and soul that their fathers introduced to them. Furthermore, I'm certain that there were some teenage house parties thrown by whites that included dancing along with some of the same music typically heard at black house parties of the time (hey, everybody loved

Michael Jackson's *Thriller* album). I'm also convinced that some of these parties even had official DJs. However, I consider these to be exceptions, not the norm.

The description of my experiences as a teenager at house parties thrown by whites in the mid- and late 1980s are consistent with the stories and experiences that were shared with me by *all* of my white friends and colleagues who lived in different parts of the America during that time.[123] Thus, while *my* initial view of sampling could be seen as a celebration of a music tradition that I was reared on and a support and appreciation for the continuum of this music tradition, this wasn't the initial view of any of my white friends or the white musicians that I spoke with on and off record. Their initial views of sampling, both good and bad, included considerations based on their specific cultural backgrounds, not the aforementioned shared Black American cultural space.

So by this discussion do I mean to show that blacks are more likely to have a favorable view of the art of sampling than whites? No. Of course not. But what I do mean to show is that an individual's given cultural background and racial identity (born into or chosen) does indeed influence his or her view of the art of sampling. I believe it would be absurd to think otherwise.

As the hip hop/rap and beatmaking traditions expanded in the United States, so did cultural diversity among its regular practitioners. Within the hip hop/rap community, especially the sub-community of beatmaking, the interconnections between blacks and whites increased, resulting in broad, tight-knit multicultural networks where many cues, meanings, social and creative priorities of Black American culture were picked up and passed on by whites. For many whites, this cultural exchange was encouraging, as they were able to successfully tap into the same canon of Black American creativity that their black contemporaries were able to. But for some whites, particularly those well-grounded in their own personal cultural memories, which prioritized different aesthetic and creative principles as well as different interpretations of originality and

---

[123] Having interviewed more than one hundred of my peers in music, art, and literature, who lived in various cities across America during the mid- to late 1980s, I found that my experiences were in line with there's, with no excecptions.

metrics of excellence, this cultural exchange was less motivating.

Over the years I've found that those raised within or more familiar with the Black American cultural space that I briefly described earlier are less hostile towards the art of sampling. On the other hand, in various conversations that I've had on and off the record with white recording engineers, musicians, other creative professionals, and acquaintances, I've found them to be quite hostile against sampling as an art form. This is certainly not to say that there aren't any blacks who look lowly upon sampling (there are plenty), or that there aren't any whites who look very favorably upon sampling (there are plenty). After all, the general point of view of sampling is not a race issue, as much as it is a *class* issue among musicians. However, the race and cultural background factors can't be ignored if we're interested in discussing the misconceptions and negative perceptions of the art of sampling in an honest manner.

Finally, it must be mentioned that although hip hop/rap music is squarely a part of mainstream American culture, with participants representing a number of different races and ethnic groups, it is still largely a black music form driven predominantly by blacks. As such, this perception often carries with it a racial bias against hip hop/rap music by a many critics of the art of sampling.

Music Training

In addition to race and cultural background (identity), one's music training also plays a role in how they're likely to perceive the art of sampling. By and large, I've found that formally trained musicians approach the art of sampling with their embedded biases (when it comes to music, we all have our biases formally trained or not). But some formally trained musicians, particularly those who care to learn about sampling, immediately appreciate sampling for what it is: a new, exciting musical process that still utilizes many of the basic principles of music theory. Still, other formally trained musicians, even some who venture to learn a little about sampling, typically see the art of sampling as a non-art, or a musical process unfit for *real* musicians. While this sentiment can be irritating, it's understandable. Everyone's opinion and perception about art, anything in culture really, is the product of their individual perspective, which is born out of their personal cultural history and their subsequent experiences. So one can see why a formally trained musician who is unfamiliar with the art of sampling – that is to say, its compositional intricacies, history, and place in popular culture — could have a negative perception of the art of sampling. This doesn't mean that all trained musicians have a negative view of the art of sampling. Acclaimed beatmaker (producer) and professor 9th Wonder, who I interviewed extensively, related to me that he was in a band and studied music theory throughout grammar and high school. Yet he also made it clear that when he discovered sampling as a music technique, he was hooked:

> I played clarinet, I played the saxophone. My band teacher was just throwing instruments at me, "Try this. Try this," because I was playing stuff by ear. And by the time I got into marching band, I was playing drums. So you know, doing that in the daytime...From 1986 to 1993 was my middle and high school years. You know the albums that came out during that time. So I'm playing — and my mom bought me a keyboard for every Christmas — I'm playing stuff, overtures at school, but I'm coming home [at night] listening to rap records, not really understanding that the music the cats was using in the background were samples, you know what I'm sayin'. I'm thinking everybody's playing it [Laughs]. But they're sampling people that played instruments...So I was trying to replay it on my keyboard....
>
> So I decided that I wanted to learn how to DJ...that made me really understand the importance of BPMs and how stuff speeds up and how some beats are faster and some beats are slower. You know stuff like that, and drum tracks. All that type of stuff. Knowing what songs go with what.... understand [how to do it]. You either had to grow up around it or you had to be there, one of the two. To be "authentic," you just can't wake up in the morning, man, and be like, "I wanna sample," without understanding the art of sampling. You just can't do it. You gotta— If you wanna sample, you gotta study.... You gotta understand all of that aesthetic first. Either you decide that this is something that you really wanna do.... And I had to learn what all of the samplers before me were doing before me, before I

decided what sound that I wanted to go for.[124]

9th Wonder is particularly interesting, because he did grow up in the Black American cultural space of twentieth-century America. Thus, in his case, we have an example of someone who was attracted to the aesthetic of sampling itself, and inclined to the cultural heritage and connection that it offers.

Criticisms and Misconceptions of the Art of Sampling

Critics of the art of sampling lack a serious understanding of what sampling really is. In fact, opponents of sampling know very little of its history or the unique processes that comprise it. (Which is another reason why the Instruction Part of this study is critical.) Thus, what follows in this section is a rebuttal of some of the most common criticisms lobbied against the art of sampling.

Is Sampling an Intellectual Appropriation or Just a Physical Taking?

When it comes to *sampling*, authors of literary works are treated differently than musicians who sample sound recordings. This is because when an literary author samples (*appropriates*) something, it's acceptable because the taking is considered by many to be an intellectual appropriation, not a physical appropriation. By contrast, when a musician digitally samples a sound recording, the taking is considered by some — thanks to *Bridgeport*[125] — to be a physical appropriation, not an intellectual appropriation. But to draw such a distinction is illogical. Literary works and sample-based beats are both, at all times, art processes that involve some level of creative borrowing from pre-existing works.

The main difference between works within these two forms lies

---

[124] Excerpt from my interview with 9th Wonder. Full interview in *The BeatTips Manual, 6th Edition.*

[125] Refers to the *Bridgeport* v. *No Limit* copyright infringement case wherein the Sixth Circuit unjustly stipulated that sampling constitutes a "physcial" taking. Chapter 12 features a detailed examination of *Bridgeport*.

in the level of appropriation. But the appropriation activity that occurs in either form is not any more intellectual or less physical. Moreover, creative borrowing is a necessary, an inevitable process that has long been practiced in literature and music. There is no such thing as a literary author or musician who has or does not intellectually sample and draw ideas, influence, or inspiration from other literary authors and musicians or practitioners of some other creative or informative medium.

Whether consciously or subconsciously, literary authors and musicians borrow and incorporate ideas from other literary authors and musicians all the time. And while musicians who sample may appropriate actual sounds from sound recordings, literary authors often appropriate *actual* words from various publications as well as sound recordings. Yet the sampling that literary authors engage in, which often exceeds the level of what the best sample-based beatmakers typically do, is still regarded as intellectual activity. Meanwhile, the sampling that sample-based musicians engage in is regarded as mere physical activity, something presumably absent of any intellectual fervor. But as I made clear in chapter 3, we must be careful not to forget that there is no conceptual difference between the intellectual copying and the physical (digital sampling) copying of someone's work. Both involve copying and intellectual transformation.

Still, literary authors have long been permitted (presumably under the protection of the fair use provision of the United States Copyright Act) to appropriate (sample) and incorporate passages from pre-existing literary works into their own works, with little to no requirement other than an open citation of the author and work that was appropriated. However, unlike the relatively easy path to appropriation for literary authors, the road for would-be samplers of sound recordings has been mostly contentious. In the obscure realm of sound recordings, even the most minute, inaudible sampling of a sound recording is contested. (In chapters 9 and 12 respectively, I discuss fair use and the main court cases responsible for shaping the notion that all sampling without permission is illegal).

√Check This Out–Reality Hunger: An Example of Validated Sampling (Intellectual Appropriation)

When it comes to literary works, permission is not needed by authors to sample lines or brief excerpts from the works of other authors. When the appropriation is recognizable, all that is required is a citation of the author and the work appropriated. This point of disparity has rarely been drafted into the greatly contentious sampling and copyright debate. But author David Shield's recent book, *Reality Hunger: A Manifesto* (2010), does expose the discriminatory view of sampling as a non-intellectual appropriation.

On the surface, *Reality Hunger* certainly isn't about the art of sampling within a beatmaking context. But it is, in large part, explicitly about the practice of borrowing (sampling) in any art form, particularly in the literary environment of fiction and non-fiction. But that isn't the big draw for me and other supporters of the art of sampling. What stands out to me, and I'm certain even the most rigid literary types, is *Reality Hunger's* peculiar twist: The book is made up entirely of appropriated passages from the pre-existing works of other authors.

In fact, *Reality Hunger* is comprised of more than 600 numbered (and indexed) paragraphs, each containing appropriations (samples) from other authors. What's more? The appropriations (samples) do not appear as quotes; and some appropriations (samples) are edited by Shields, while many are left as is, untransformed. Needless to say, for sample-based beatmakers, Shields' book, which one literary critic has hailed as a "rousing call to arms for all artists to reject the laws governing appropriation," is nothing short of a kill-shot at the prevailing interpretation of copyright law that is purportedly governing the art and practice of sampling sound recordings.

I can't say for certain if Shields had hip hop/rap music and its tradition of sampling in mind when he was writing *Reality Hunger*, but I'd like to think so. After all, the book is also explicitly about the future of fiction and non-fiction, specifically as it's situated somewhere between the puffed-up and outdated assumptions about fiction and non-fiction, the new ways in which art is now being created, and the effects that these new forms of creativity are having and will continue to have on literary works. But given the depth and aggressive charge of *Reality Hunger*, I can't help but believe that Shields consciously borrowed the bravado of a sample-based musician when he set about the task of lifting and surgically incorporating lines and passages from other authors into his own original work.

Here, I should note that *Reality Hunger* includes an extensive appendix, wherein the appropriated authors and their works are summarily cited. This indicates to me that the publishers did not before hand "clear" all the usages, or better stated, get the permission of the publishers and/or authors who own the copyrights to the works that Shields appropriated for *Reality Hunger*. Moreover, it further indicates that perhaps the publishers saw no legal reason, rightfully so, to have to seek such permission. And thus, it would appear that aside from giving perhaps more context, the appendix, which was added at the insistence of the publisher, serves one primary purpose: To protect the book from any copyright infringement challenges. Absolutely genius! Clearly, the publisher felt no need to contact the copyright owners of the appropriations used or to negotiate fees for the usages.

And what about the treatment of Shields for the way in which he created *Reality Hunger*? For the most part, the book has been well received. The New York Times proclaimed *Reality Hunger* to be "A mind-bending manifesto." Thus, even with clear and open appropriation, Shields' takings are, of course, considered to be strongly *intellectual*.

Is Sampling Creative and Original?

Actually, my question to the "creative" or "original" critique of sampling is: How can a practice that gave rise to a music tradition that has sustained itself for more than four decades not be original?

But to really get at this criticism, it is first necessary to take a look at those who typically make these sort of uninformed claims. For the most part, there are roughly six main groups who attack the creative sensibility and originality characteristics of sampling. First, there's the popular music press, which covers hip hop/rap music but knows little about the history and intricate elements of the art of sampling in the hip hop/rap music tradition. (Some hip hop/rap bloggers are knowledgeable about sampling, but surprisingly, most aren't.) Then there are those music industry "insiders" and lawyers who lack a sound understanding of the aesthetic preferences that comprise the hip hop/rap music tradition. Next, there are those musicians — who are entirely outside of the hip hop/rap tradition — who are ill-informed as to what the art of sampling actually is and the meticulous processes it entails. Then, ironically, there are some non sample-based beatmakers *within* the hip hop/rap tradition.[126]   And finally, there's also a broad crop of new generation beatmakers — a group that has arrived at a time when the most essential and celebrated characteristics of the hip hop/rap music tradition are being openly vilified, and when trap music is the most popular mainstream hip hop/rap sound.

The biggest misconception that each of the aforementioned groups hold about sampling is that there is no artistic skill involved in sampling, and that sampling is merely the "re-recording of a sound recording." Even worse, some commentators refer to sampling as "piracy." In his article, "A Pirate's Palette: The Dilemmas of Digital Sound Sampling and a Proposed Compulsory License Solution," Michael L. Baroni asserts that "samplers *pirate* and exploit the labor, talent, and uniqueness of another's musical expression, and may adversely effect potential markets for the sampled artist's sounds." But piracy describes the wholesale, verbatim copying and

---

[126] **Nearly all beatmakers who dismiss sampling as unoriginal, lazy, or uncreative** usually fall under three categories: (1) they do not posses any sampling skills; (2) they do not, nor have ever tried to, understand sampling, nor sincerely appreciate its fundamental role in the history of hip hop/rap music; and (3) they are more inspired by the potential financial gain of not using samples. Often, the third group of sample naysayers are actually envious of well-sampled productions. In fact, they even concede that their beatworks often lack the fullness and power of the works of their sampling adversaries. Thus, in order to suppress the competition from producers who feature sampling, they dismiss it.

distribution of copyrighted works. That's a big difference from what the art of sampling is. There is a "crucial difference between pirating or counterfeiting anothers[sic] work straight across in order to profit from the saleability[sic] of that single source, and the creative transformation of material from multiple sources into new, 'original' works."[127]

Another glowing misconception about sample-based beatmakers is that they seemingly expend little personal time or money developing their craft, and that they have no talent and/ or original artistic creativity. In "Pirate's Palette: The Dilemmas of Digital Sound Sampling and a Proposed Compulsory License Solution," Michael L. Baroni renders a dismissal of sample-based artists, claiming that "Producers who use samples reap huge benefits, both financially and through increased creative reputation, *at little or no personal expense of time, talent, money, or original artistic creativity.*"[128] This character assassination of sample-based recording artists is typical of critics of sampling, particularly those critics who have very little or no real understanding of the art of sampling or its value. I should add that what is also suspicious about Baroni's remarks is the fact that later in his article, he recognizes that sampling was born out of the hip hop tradition in the Bronx. With such an astute recognition, one wonders what motives lie behind Baroni's dismissal of sampling

Baroni's claims demonstrate just how little he actually understands about sampling, the sample clearance system, and the actual benefits associated with the art of sampling. First, sampling is an art form wherein much technical skill is required and tremendous thought and artistic skill are involved. As any one who's truly studied the art form will tell you, sampling is certainly not easy, and sample-based beatmakers, who often spend countless hours digging through records for "fragments" of sound, are not lazy. In fact, the art of sampling demands much of those who seek to develop a skill

---

[127] Michael L. Baroni, "A Pirate's Palette: The Dilemmas of Digital Sound Sampling and a Proposed Compulsory License Solution," *U. Miami Ent. & Sports L. Rev.*, no. 11 (1993-1994), 89. See "DO WE REALLY HAVE TO SUE THE RIAA????" http://www.negativland.com/archives/014riaa/, (Accessed March, 2012)..
[128] *Ibid*, 71-72, 83

for it. It requires loads of time, research, and a commitment to the study of pre-existing (usually decades-old) music.

Here, it's also worth noting that sampling is not about "recreating" the essence of an era, it's about the use of the "actual essence" of an era itself. No one will ever be able to truly duplicate, recreate, or replicate the "conditions" (the actual essence) of a particular era. Moreover, the individuals responsible for creating that sound can never be cloned. Therefore, the nuances (subtle, obscure, covert, and overt) can never be revived. Finally, many sample-based beatmakers feel an affinity for and a connection to a particular era in music and are, therefore, drawn to it. Moreover, the sound of this particular era (1970s) possesses the sound aesthetics (timbral, tonal, mix qualities) that have been valued in hip hop/rap music since its inception.

The simple take on sampling by critics like Baroni is that it's merely the digital recording of a sound, followed by the cutting and pasting of that sampled sound into a drum program. Well, if it were that simple, there would be far more beatmakers who've mastered it. Truth is, as with any art form, sampling is part knowledge and experience, part design, part intuition, part accident, and part constructive patience. The art of sampling prompts you to use all of your musical understanding, then it challenges you to reconfigure what you sample into a new composition. In fact, the art of sampling is so dynamic that when it is practiced to its fullest extent, the new composition can either reinforce the same mood and/or feeling of the original source material, or it can invoke an entirely new feeling, structure, and overall sound.

Finally, it must be understood that people don't sample because they're unoriginal or lazy. People sample because they like the aesthetic and enjoy the process, and because they like the idea of making something new out of something old, and because they like the idea of interacting with history. Hence, by its very nature, the art sampling is indeed creative.

For Most Critics of Sampling, Ignorance is Bliss: Observations About the Most Vocal Critics of Sampling

The people who often criticize the art of sampling the most are, not surprisingly, the ones who know the least about it. As I've noted previously in this chapter, critics of sampling attack it on three main fronts: creativity, originality, and piracy. Fundamentally, copying from other pre-existing works, in any art form, medium, or industry, is the bedrock of all creativity. In fact, creativity, originality and innovation are inseparable in this way. But most critics of sampling overlook this fact when it comes to the art of sampling. Why? Well, for one thing, the prejudices inherently built up from their cultural histories and musical orientations (some of which I explored earlier in this chapter) have a lot to do with it. But also, I find that most critics of sampling are incredibly ignorant of what the art of sampling truly is and what its mechanics entail. Unfortunately, many critics of sampling don't even see it as a music process. Instead, they see sampling as nothing more than a one-dimensional, cut-and-paste music-making gimmick that thrives on "stealing." By refusing to even consider sampling as a music process, many critics of the art form excuse themselves for not giving sampling a more serious exploration. So naturally, they fail to see just how multi-dimensional sampling is.

Also, most critics, and in many cases supporters, of sampling are not familiar with the works of sampling's most recognized practitioners. So they have a very limited scope of sampling's deeper creative nuances. More often than not, published reports that both criticize and support sampling point to The Beastie Boys or Public Enemy as beacons of the sampling tradition of hip hop/rap music, leaving out critical names that paint a clearer, more complete picture of the art of sampling.

In the various interviews (and off-record conversations) that I've had with music insiders, music lawyers, music writers, and college professors, none were well-acquainted with DJ Premier, Marley Marl, Pete Rock, or the RZA, and the important contributions that they made to the art of sampling; none had never heard of Large Professor, The Beatnuts, Buckwild, The Alchemist, and the like; and all cited The Beastie Boys, Puff Daddy (Diddy), De La Soul, and Biz Markie as "proof" of their understanding of sampling. Not coincidentally, The Beastie Boys, De La Soul, and Biz Markie were at the center of copyright infringement cases, and Puff Daddy's associated brand of sampling is considered by most sample-based beatmakers to be the most basic, non-complex variety of sampling there is.

Furthermore, I've found that most critics of sampling tend to ignore or conflate common, long recognized notions of creativity and originality when it comes to sampling. The most vocal critics perceive the type of borrowing that goes on in sampling as (presumably) only virtual, i.e. physical/digital, rather than intellectual. And they tend to describe sampling as an easy-button music-making scheme that requires little thought, time, or creative energy on the part of the sample-based musician. Therefore, for these critics, the art of sampling can never meet the common threshold of creativity and originality that is reserved for all other art forms, mediums, and industries.

But, I believe if more critics of sampling were simply more informed about the art of sampling, they would see things quite differently. To that end, I hope that this book goes a long way in helping to educate the most ardent critics of the art of sampling.

On Sampling and Thievery

Transformative justification aside, the art of sampling is often held in low regard, particularly by those unfamiliar with the art form. As I mentioned before, there are people who see sampling as one monolithic form of negative copying; an act that, by it's nature, is not only uncreative but morally questionable — an act of *theft*.

But the art of sampling is not morally questionable conduct. Sampling does not involve the activity of stealing information or committing fraud. Hence, the language of thievery that surrounds the art of sampling is misguided and excessive. And there are fewer accusations hailed against sampling that makes sample-based beatmakers irate than the slander of thievery. In my interviews with DJ Toomp and 9th Wonder, each were quite adamant in making it clear that sampling is not stealing:

> "'Thievery?' NO! ....what we do is recycle when we sample. Any producer who takes time to chop it, to where you be like, Oooh, that song don't go like that, you know what I mean. And that comes from DJ'ing, too. Like when I used to beat juggle, change beats around. That's when I started getting into sampling, like, Aw, man, it's the same thing....So when I sample, for me, I chop it up and get creative with it..you do something else and add more music to it, now THAT shows more creativity."[129]

> I say it's like when you go to the Louvre in Paris, and you walk down the hall and you see this big mural of somebody who took a whole bunch of *Time Life Book* magazines and made a big mural of *Time Life* Magazines of the years and call it a collage. What's the difference? They didn't contact every person from every book that they snatched a page out of and get permission. What's the difference? You know what I mean, I just don't understand that. And collages happen all of the time in art. Sampling IS art....We're just really trying to create a bridge. It's not about trying to "take" (steal) your record and just make a profit off of it. There is really an art form to this. All that we do — from chopping a record, taking a song that's 3/4 time and turning it into 4/4 time. All of that is art. And I wouldn't go [to Congress] by myself. I would take elders with me, and be like, "Look, you say that we're 'stealing,' these are the cats that I sample, these are the musicians that we use from time and time again."[130]

√Check This Out – Why Some Non-Sample-Based Beatmakers and Other Musicians Dislike Sampling as a Musical Process

I want to shed some light on that ridiculous accusation that

---

[129] Excerpt from my interview with DJ Toomp.
[130] Excerpt from my interview with 9th Wonder.

beatmakers who sample are "lazy," or worse, not *really* creative?" As I've previously discussed, sampling is a very meticulous, arduous, and often frustrating process that requires great amounts of creativity, patience, endurance, and ingenuity. Not only is sampling perhaps the most daunting beatmaking process that beatmakers face, it is the strongest link that we still have to the original hip hop DJ style, the original compositional process of hip hop/rap music.

That any opponent of the art of sampling would directly or indirectly claim that the sample-based style of production somehow denotes an air of laziness or lack of creativity is absurd. Moreover, a brief examination of such claims reveals several points that are rarely ever discussed candidly today. For instance, since the explosion of the hip hop/rap production medium began in the late 1990s and early 2000s, more and more new beatmakers have opted to work with keyboards, sound modules, and software applications (full of "stock sounds") rather than survey and flip pre-existing songs. Why is that? Is it because one process is superior to the other? No. It's up to each beatmaker to choose the compositional style that suits them best. I believe it comes down to one main reason: speed and access. Many beatmakers want to capitalize on the misguided notion that there's some awesome financial opportunity awaiting them for their production services. To that end, they are often very anxious to make "hot beats," so much so that they routinely employ whatever tool or electronic mechanisms which they believe will help them reach their goal the *fastest*. And because this particular elk of beatmakers typically lack a misunderstanding of the art of sampling or the patience and discipline required to mine for and sample records, they tend to want to write it off as some short-cut, second-rate production medium.

Thus, the negative view that some non-sample-based beatmakers hold towards the sample-based compositional style is rather unfortunate for two reasons: (1) Musical intuition is best built from listening to music, and a good music education — like the one that is naturally imbued to those beatmakers who regularly dig and sample — is highly critical to the development of one's musical intuition; (2) Many seasoned beatmakers (some well-known, some lesser known) have joined the frenzy towards live instrumentation. Though I acknowledge that sample-clearance has played a big role here, I still believe that the underpinning catalyst for this move is based on speed, accessibility, and a misguided belief that a payday awaits prospective beatmakers who don't sample.

Other compositional forms of beatmaking, such as the use of live instrumentation, keyboard, and soft-synth generated instrumental sounds, are further being legitimized not *primarily* because of their own merits but for two other distinct reasons: access and sample clearance concerns.

Instrumental sounds, especially of the sort that come with software applications, has made it more possible than ever for anyone to gain access to beatmaking and, therefore, instantly deem themselves a beatmaker. There is nothing inherently wrong with that at all. In fact, I embrace technology and the role that it has and is playing in bringing more quality beatmakers to the field. That being said, there is a substantial number of these new beatmakers who repulse at the thought of sampling, even though they have little to no actual experience with the art and science of sampling or what it has and will always mean to the hip hop/rap music tradition. Here, the simple notion of strength in numbers applies best. That is to say, the higher the concentration of new beatmakers who elect not to sample, the easier to push for the idea that sampling is a weaker or less legitimate music-making method. Again, this very notion reeks with absurdity, in lieu of the fact that sampling played a vital role in the development of the hip hop/rap music tradition.

Sampling is the Main Event, Not a Sideshow: Sampling Could Never Be Displaced, It's an Autonomous Art

Even while sampling is currently enjoying what some would describe as a reemergence or renaissance, there are still many people within the beatmaking and hip hop/rap music communities who hold a rather hostile view to the music process that helped fuel an entire music tradition. There are a number of reasons for this disdain for sampling among some beatmakers, and earlier in this chapter I addressed some of them in detail. At this point, I'd like to discuss one particular criticism and negative theme that is commonly lobbied against sampling: That sampling is an outdated, non-music process that was (is) doomed by evolution.

When beatmakers, of all people, criticize sampling like it's some 2-bit, non-music gimmick, they are really (knowingly or not) demonstrating a deep disrespect for what half of the essence of rap music is about. Ask some slightly less hostile, passive aggressive critics about sampling, and you're likely to hear that beatmaking has simply *evolved*, or something along those lines. The wanton disrespect for the music process that built rap irritates me, sure. But it's the "inevitable evolution" narrative that many have come to endorse that troubles me the most.

As a vocal performance medium, the durable nature and sheer flexibility of hip hop's rap vocal style lends itself to a number of different audio palettes and structures. From fists banging on lunch room tables, to human beat boxes, to live bands, rap's flexibility makes it possible for rappers to sound decent with virtually any sound backing them. And when it comes to audio backing, less we forget, rapping in hip hop culture — in its earliest incarnation and core manifestation — is about the marriage of the rap vocal style with pre-recorded music. That said, I have no problem with rhymes over non-sampled-based beats, trap beats, or any other kind of beats. (Although, I tend not to dig most rap/live band contraptions; The Roots being an exception.) But over the past decade, there's been a great deal of chirping (overwhelmingly by non-sample-based beatmakers) against sampling. As the theme goes, some maintain that sampling is an old, unoriginal crutch that was tossed on the side of the road as hip hop/rap music evolved.

But to situate the art of sampling as some sort of relic, pre-evolution music process grossly misses the point. Sample-based rap music is it's own main event; it's not a sideshow. Moreover, non-sampled-based rap music is not some natural, inevitable evolution to sampling. Nor is Non-sample-based rap music the rightful heir to sample-based rap music. Non-sample-based rap music is merely another music process, one with its own methods and metrics of

THE ART OF SAMPLING

quality. More still, non-sample-based rap music has not displaced sample-based music as the superior compositional style in the hip hop/rap music tradition. Both compositional styles have their own tract and distinct pedigrees within beatmaking. And while today there may be more people who opt for the non-sample-based style (synthetic-sounds-based style) than there was 20 years ago, we must be careful not to view this as one compositional style being superior to the other. There are a number of reasons and circumstances that led, and continue to lead, some people away from sampling. However, the notion that sampling lacks feeling, or that sampling isn't synonymous, both literally and symbolically, with rap music are not among these reasons. Further, no reasonable beatmaker, proficient in any style of beatmaking, disputes that sampling delivers an entirely different feel and sonic aesthetic that's hard to match without, well, sampling.

I should also mention that within the "inevitable evolution" narrative, lies a "pushing the envelope" sub-theme. "Pushing the envelope" is a common phrase used in all art forms that generally means expanding the limits of a given form, style, or tradition. With regards to sampling, "pushing the envelope" is used passive aggressively in rap music to mean the leaving off of sampling, or the graduating from sampling and stepping up to live instrumentation. Ridiculous. The sampling tradition of hip hop/rap music is its own art form in it's own space. It is an autonomous tradition. As such, it has its own standards, customs, and aesthetic qualities that need not adhere to any other contemporary music process. Thus, if someone from the sampling tradition of hip hop learns to play guitar or the piano, for instance, they are not *graduating* from sampling, they are simply adding to and improving an existing musical skill set and sensibility. So the only evolution all musicians ever really experience is the acquisition of skill. But the accumulation of new music skills can not render obsolete the music processes from which they came.

Are Samplers Musicians?

A "musician" is simply one who creates (makes) music. It's someone who is conscious of the notion of music as well as at least one type of music-making process. Whether one likes a particular music form, or prefers the methods used to make it, does not disqualify the creator of that form of music as a "musician."

With regards to sample-based musicians (i.e. beatmakers) and traditional musicians, well, traditional musicians don't exactly generate music from out of thin air. Instead, *they use instruments to grab* from the same bag of notes (sounds) that every other traditional musician does. In turn, they take theses notes (tones, sounds) and reconfigure them in ways that suit their creative ingenuity. Isn't that what sample-based beatmakers do? Oh, I forgot the big argument, you know the one that condemns sample-based beatmakers as *thieves* because they use pre-recorded music and sounds. But consider this: Musical notes are one of the most recognizable public domain sources, which technically means that every live musician borrows (samples) from the same well of musical notes.

I recognize the fact that sampling from a dormant assortment of public domain music notes is one thing, and sampling a pre-recorded performance is yet another. But is one form of sampling inherrently superior to the other? I mean, I've never heard an *entire song* sampled and looped in hip hop/rap. On the contrary, sample-based beatmakers use segments, fragments, chipped musical pieces and tones that usually measure between 1 to 4 seconds. Regardless of how much and/or what section beatmakers sample from, the *intent*, structure, and/or scope of their recreation is different than the intent of the artist(s) who originally created the composition that's being sampled. Isn't this what separates musicians from each other? Indeed, if all musicians have to rely on the same *bag of sounds*, if you will, then what are the primary variables that distinguish each musician? Is it not their intent, structure, and overall creative scope?

Furthermore, the idea that sample-based beatmakers simply press a button, and Presto!, a beat (song) is *automatically* created, is misguided. Like any other musician, sample-based beatmakers must arrange, identify tonal matches, cope with time changes, etc. While traditional musicians use guitars, horns, pianos, and the like as their instruments, sample-based beatmakers use samplers, sequencers, drum machines, and other EMPIs (and somtimes traditional guitars, horns, and pianos as well) as theirs. Today, both groups of musicians rely on electronic recording processors and equipment and modern software applications for minor or major tweaking. So even here the claim of superiority by traditional musicians and their supporters holds little weight.

For me, the foundation of creativity and/or originality, within any artistic medium, is predicated upon *arrangement*. Writers use words to tell stories and convey feelings and insights that have all been conveyed and told *before*. They use words that have been used over and over again (i.e. familiar or everyday words). So how do they avoid the exhaustion of these words and stories, while at the same time offer new insight and fresh (and old) feelings? It is through their unique arrangement of words and their meanings, that's how. Thus all musicians, like writers and any other artisans, distinguish themselves through the intent, scope and structure of their arrangement.

Why Sampling is So Threatening to Some

The art of sampling is threatening to some, particularly the institutional gatekeepers of mainstream culture, for a number of reasons. First, sampling reexamines and challenges traditional (mainstream and classical) ideas and presuppositions about the music-making process as well as concepts of composition and the use and reliance of technology. Moreover, sampling — and beatmaking in general — closes the gap between those who can create and those who can not, effectively increasing the number of producers in culture and commerce while reducing the number of consumer-only persons in society. Sampling also keeps a cultural and musical past, specifically a vast black American musical culture and heritage, relevant. Something that many modernists would otherwise prefer be left alone. Finally, sampling exposes the inequity of the twentieth-century corporate perversion of American copyright law. (A theme I explore more deeply in the Copyright

Part of this study.)

The Value of Sampling

Sampling has an emotional depth and richness that can not be duplicated or convincingly imitated. Beatmakers who use sampling as their primary compositional process do not do so *just* for the sound that sampling renders; though make no mistake, it is indeed a major factor in their decision. Instead, sample-based beatmakers also use sampling for the emotional effect and historical connection that it provides. In this way, sampling appeals to a fundamental part of the human condition.

Sampling is also good for absorbing the traditional music education process that accompanies DJ'ing, which was once a pivotal, seemingly mandatory step in becoming a beatmaker. The single biggest factor that made music group after group so successful throughout the twentieth century is the fact that musicians of those incredibly rich eras were able to witness and draw from one another. Thereby, they were able to continuously tap into a powerful collective musical ethos. With that ethos gone, the art of sampling is truly one of the only tools left that's capable of allowing modern musicians to tap into that very same ethos. Indeed, most of the "teachers" that represented that ethos are no longer alive. Furthermore, the number of possible teachers who can actually teach the perpetually growing youth about the styles, sounds, and cultures of the ethos of musical eras gone past have dramatically decreased. And thus, the act of passing down this widespread musical heritage is rapidly vanishing. Sampling directly addresses this void of "conventional" musical education, as it helps make up for the current lack of teachers who traditionally taught this kind of musical education.

The oral tradition that has passed down musical heritage for hundreds of years has all but evaporated. Though the art of sampling could never take the place of the rich oral tradition of passing musical heritage on to later generations, I do believe the art of sampling stands as one of the most viable means of continuing the tradition of passing on musical heritage. Further, the art of sampling is not simply a method or a process for making beats. As an educational aid, sampling teaches musicians a number of musical methods and approaches. For instance, I learned more about the dynamics of sounds through sampling than from any other music process I know.

And what of the historical preservation of twentieth-century American popular music, particularly African American (Black) music of the 1950s, 60s, and 70s? How many institutions (aside from a handful of elite academic institutions) or popular (non-scholarly) publications are in place that realistically and regularly attempt to preserve the vast canon of Black music and the most critical principles, tropes, and structures of the African American (Black) music tradition? Without such instruments to help preserve key components of the African American (Black) music tradition (a tradition, less we forget, that was incredibly vital to most, if not all, popular American musics), the link to a vastly significant musical heritage and culture will be neutralized, and twenty-first century music forms will be further at risk for diluted creativity. In this way, the art of sampling works as a defense against diluted creativity because it keeps important, meaningful music from the past in the public square of the present.

This is not to say that the art of sampling is the absolute solution to stopping the erasure of the *link* to an important cultural and musical past. I simply maintain that it is one valuable tool that contributes to the broader solution. More specifically, in the hip hop/rap music tradition, sampling bridges a gap between a musical heritage that once nourished a people and a new musical heritage that is becoming more and more foreign to the tradition from which it came.

Part 3
COPYRIGHT LAW

Chapter 9

An Overview of Copyright Law

Historical Clarity on Copyright Law and Policy in the United States

Since the advent of Western music, musicians have freely borrowed themes and ideas from other musicians. –Judge Thomas A. Higgins

If the United States adhered strongly to the principle of authorial reward as the sole function of copyright law, every rock-and-roll [sic] musician would owe money to Mississippi Delta blues musicians. –Siva Vaidhyanathan

What is Copyright Law?

Before examining United States copyright law and policy and how it pertains to the art of sampling, here, some words of background are necessary for those without prior knowledge of the basic framework of copyright law. Copyright refers to the bundle of secured exclusive legal rights associated with a creative expression, a creative "work," of an author. The rights granted to the author of a creative expression include: the right to perform, copy and/or reproduce the work; the right to authorize others to copy and/or reproduce the work; the right to make derivative works from the work; and the right to publish, sell, or distribute the matter and form of the work. There are eight categories of subject matter (also known as categories of copyrighted material) that the Copyright Act grants protection to, these include: literary works; musical works, including any accompanying words; dramatic works, including any accompanying music; pantomimes and choreographic works; pictorial, graphic, and sculptural works; motion pictures and other audiovisual works; sound recordings; and architectural works.[131] According to the Copyright Act of 1976, a work is protected in all media and for all possible derivative uses as soon as it is fixed in a tangible medium of expression. This means, for instance, that as soon as a recording artist records a song into a DAW or to CD, the work carries the protection of copyright law. Registration of the work with the Copyright Office of the Library of Congress is not necessary, unless one plans to distribute the work and wishes to receive formal copyright protection.

Foundations, Principles, and Scope of United States Copyright Law

When the delegates of the Constitutional Convention met between the early summer and fall of 1787, their main focus was to address the problems in governing a recently independent United States, which had been operating under the Articles of Confederation. However, a chief concern that arose within the discussions was the issue of copyright.

The leaders at the Constitutional Convention had recognized that the non-rights and non-liberties of the English Empire in the eighteenth century had, in effect, created an "empire" of creative works. Specifically, they saw that the total control over books by the British Crown and the Stationers' Company[132] had limited public discourse and stifled criticism (of royal and parliamentary policy).

"In 1710, the Parliament of Great Britain passed the Statute of Anne, which 'was designed to destroy the booksellers' monopoly of the book trade and to prevent its recurrence.'" The framers, who insisted that copyright clearly protect distinct expressions of ideas for a limited time, while allowing others to freely use, criticize, and refer to *the ideas that lay beneath* the text, would rely on the

---

[131] 17 U.S.C. § 102(a). 17 U.S.C. § 102(b): In no case does copyright protection for an original work of authorship extend to any idea, procedure, process, system, method of operation, concept, principle, or discovery, regardless of the form in which it is described, explained, illustrated, or embodied in such work. Copyright and *"copywrite"* are not the same thing. To "copywrite" simply means to write advertising or publicity copy (text).
[132] For a detailed description of the Stationers' Company, see Lyman Ray Patterson, *Copyright in Historical Perspective*, (Nashville: Vanderbilt University Press 1968).

statute of Anne in the creation of copyright in the United States Constitution:

> Our Founders codified this perspective in the Constitution in Article I, Section 8, Clause 8. Law professors Joseph Singer[7] and Tom W. Bell explain that the Framers relied on the Statute of Anne when drafting this clause, which reads, "The Congress shall have Power... to promote the Progress of Science... by securing for limited times to authors... the exclusive right to their respective writings." The Copyright Clause was intended "to be the engine of free expression."[8] This clause is the only clause in Article 1, Section 8, which outlines specific congressional powers, that conditions the enumerated power on a particular purpose.... Congress directly transferred the principles from the Statute of Anne into the copyright law of the United States in 1783, first through a recommendation to the states to enact similar copyright laws, and then in 1790, with the passage of the first federal copyright statute. They tried to strike the careful balance of not too much or too little copyright protection.[133]

In this way, the framers maintained that "copyright was to be a balance between the interests of the producer and the interests of the society of consumers, voters, and readers."[134] Thus, having thoroughly debated what copyright would look like in the United States, Congress "directly transferred the principles from the Statute of Anne into the copyright law of the United States in 1783, first through a recommendation to the states to enact similar copyright laws, and then in 1790, with the passage of the first federal copyright statute." Aiming to strike a careful balance of not too much or too little copyright protection, "the 1790 Copyright law had a fourteen-year term of copyright upon registration, and an optional fourteen-year renewal if the author was still alive. In critical distinction to copyright law of today, it was a system where

---

[133] Derek Khana, "The Problems with Natural-Law Copyright" http://www.cato-unbound. org/2013/01/31/derek-khanna/problems-natural-law-copyright, (accessed May, 2015)
[134] Siva Vaidhyanathan, *Copyrights and Copywrongs: The Rise of Intellectual Property and How It Threatens Creativity*, (New York: New York University Press, 2003), 28. For critical context of the "American Revolutionary" psyche that resulted in the United States independence from Great Britain and the creation of the United States Constitution, see Bernard Bailyn, *The Ideological Origins of the American Revolution*, Enlarged Edition (Harvard University Press: Cambridge, 1990), 230-231.

the copyright owner had to opt-in to receive copyright."[135]

Natural-Law Copyright

The argument of natural-law copyright, i.e. that copyright is a natural right — a human right — caused debate among the framers. However, this settled and reaffirmed more than 200 years ago. Thus, "the limited copyright system in our Constitution was not the default conception of what copyright as a concept was – rather it reflected a conscious rejection of the ideology of indefinite copyright." Furthermore, in the Supreme Court's first case on copyright — in 1834 — it rejected the doctrine of a common law copyright in published works, and affirmed that copyright was a right *created* by Congress — that "Congress, by the act of 1790, instead of sanctioning an existing perpetual right in an author in his works, *created* the right *secured for a limited time* by the provisions of that law."[136] Despite this fact, there are some today who argue that copyright is a natural right.

Idea vs. Expression

Another important principle of United States copyright law was the idea-expression dichotomy or idea-expression divide. To the framers, a specific creative expression necessarily divulges ideas that can and should be freely used by the public. That is to say, the framers understood that after a creative expression is divulged or shared with the public, *the ideas that lie beneath that specific creative expression* could not belong to any one person, because ideas are not susceptible to the notion of exclusive property. However, the framers also recognized the need to protect specific (distinct) expressions of ideas. But they believed that the protection of distinct expressions of ideas should not be so rigid and restrictive as to stifle the creativity of new distinct expressions of ideas. In other words, a balance needed to be reached between the limited protection of specific

---

[135] Khana.
[136] *Wheaton v. Peters*, 33 U.S. (8 Pet.) 591, 593 (1834) (emphasis mine).

expressions of ideas of authors/producers of creative expressions and the right of the public to freely use the ideas that lie beneath specific expressions.

To achieve the balance between the interests of the producer and the interests of the public, i.e. to strike a balance between protecting original works and stifling further creativity, the framers of the constitution, led by James Madison and Thomas Jefferson, made the incentive to create new works the core principle of American copyright law. This means that the purpose of copyright law is to serve as a *policy* that balances the interests of *existing* authors and publishers with readers and *future* authors. The framers understood the fact that creativity, consciously and subconsciously, depends on the use, consideration, supplementation, and criticism of previous works. They argued that authors should enjoy a monopoly, i.e. exclusive control over access and use, on their works "just long enough to provide incentive for them and others to create new works," but that upon the expiration of this *limited* monopoly, the work created should live afterward in the public domain, as *common property* of the reading public. In other words, the framers established copyright law as a deal in which authors and publishers would get a "limited monopoly" *for a short period of time*, and then thereafter the public would get access to those protected works and free use of the facts, data, and ideas within them.[137] Thus, U.S. Constitution, Article I, Section 8, Clause 8 states:

> The Congress shall have power to **To promote the Progress of Science and useful Arts, by securing for limited Times** to Authors and Inventors the exclusive Right to their respective Writings and Discoveries. [emphasis mine][138]

Although the framers believed in the rights of independent publishers, many, like Thomas Jefferson, were suspicious of concentrations of power and "artificial monopolies." Moreover, the

---

[137] Ibid, 20.
[138] U.S. Const. art. I, § 8, cl. 8. See also 17 U.S.C. § 102 (1976). The term "writings" is construed broadly and, according to the Copyright Act of 1976, it defines "works of authorship" that include: literary works, musical works, dramatic works, pictoral works, graphic sculptural works, architectural works, and audiovisual works.

framers were fearful of giving indefinite copyright protection to the most powerful publishers, because they believed that it would lead to no incentive for individual citizens (commoners) to create and distribute new works. This would mean a stifling of new creative works, creating an atmosphere that was akin to the "empire of creative works" of eighteenth-century Great Britain. Therefore, the intent of copyright law is to stimulate, motivate, and influence the creation of *new* creative works. In this way, the framers linked copyright law to the "greater good" of American society. That is, Jefferson, Madison, and others believed that the health and growth of the union depended in large part on its cititzen's ability to create and *innovate* within the spheres of the arts and sciences.

Thus, the framers felt that a reward (a limited monopoly) for creativity and innovation in the arts and sciences should be just long enough to encourage new works and innovations. Hence, the American Copyright Act of 1790, the first federal copyright act to be instituted in the United States, granted authors copyright protection for a term of 14 years, with the right to renew for one additional 14-year term should the copyright holder still be alive. After 1831 the term of copyright protection was increased to 28 years, with the right to renew for another 14 years.[139]

Key Twentieth-Century Developments In United States Copyright Law and Policy

If U.S. copyright law and policy in the eighteenth and nineteenth centuries had been about striking and maintaining a balance between authors, publishers, and the public — i.e. honoring the interests of *existing* producers and the interests of the society of readers, consumers and *future* producers — then copyright law and policy in the twentieth century was about the erosion of this balance, the broadening of the once limited trade monopoly for authors (producers), the *corporatization* of the fundamental

---

[139] It's worth noting that Thomas Jefferson objected to a limited monopoly for authors. He fought for an 8-year term of copyright protection for authors; and to him, even that was too long.

principles of American copyright, and the centralization of creative power in America.

Counter-Intuitive Copyright Term Extensions and the Corporatization of United States Copyright Law and Policy

Among the many developments of U.S. copyright law and policy in the twentieth century, two of the most pivotal and detrimental changes that occurred were the extensions of the monopoly that authors have over the works that they create, and the development of the corporation as the author/producer. The Copyright Act of 1790 granted authors copyright protection for just 14 years, and the right to renew for *one* additional 14-year term should the copyright holder still be alive. *You had to opt in for the additional 14 years.* In 1831, the term increased to 28 years, with the right to renew for another 14 years. And from 1909 through 1978, the term was 28 years, renewable for 28 more. Then, after the 1976 copyright revision, the term spiked to "the life of the author" *plus* 50 years. And in 1998, under the Copyright Extension Act — commonly known as the Sony Bono Act — Congress extended the term again, this time to the life of the author plus 70 years, 20 more years than before. Interestingly, works of corporate authorship were extended to 95 years after publication or 120 years after creation, whichever is shorter.

The extension of copyright protection to a term of the *life* of the author *plus* 70 years raises a number of questions. First, if the U.S. Constitution provides that "The Congress shall have power To promote the Progress of Science and useful Arts, by **securing for limited** Times to Authors and Inventors the exclusive Right to their respective Writings and Discoveries," how can the life of the author *plus* 70 years possibly be considered as a "limited time?" (Certainly, this is a radically different system from what the framers intended.)

The *life of the author plus* term in itself is so out of touch with the original term of copyright protection and the fundamental purpose of copyright law that one can only assume that such an extension was made, at the behest of American corporations, precisely to achieve what the framers of the Constitution feared: a central force of monopolists who hold complete control over the creation, use, and access to ideas and expressions. Moreover, these counter-intuitive copyright term extensions dramatically increase the time that it takes for works to make their way to the public domain.

Finally, how does a monopoly of the life of an author plus 70 years provide incentive for other Americans to create? It doesn't, because every potential author (creator) must come to grips with the fact that they will either have to sell their specific creative expression to the established monopolist (this usually means successful corporations) or compete with them. Though a minority of creators do indeed opt to compete with the established monopolists, such a competition is rigged in favor of the monopolists from the start. Moreover, should new creators become successful, they are immediately susceptible to joining the ranks of the established monopolists in their field. Thus, the cycle continues, and very little of the creative works produced make their way into the public domain.

"Property Talk" and the Property Model for Copyright Law and Policy

The framers of the Constitution understood well that "creative ideas and expressions" were not "property" as the general public understands property. From the earliest discussions about what copyright law should be, the framers were acutely aware of the dangers of arguing for copyright as "property." In fact, the property model for copyright was explicitly dismissed by Jefferson and others who recognized that such "property talk" would eventually expand to encompass *idea protection*, not just *expression protection*. Should an expansion of such magnitude occur, the idea-expression dichotomy, a crucial principle of copyright law, would be compromised, and the centralization of creative ideas would eventually take hold, giving monopolists (copyright owners) power to strengthen their control over the flow of ideas and the use of expressions. Simply put, the framers were fearful of duplicating the complete and ominous control over creativity, ideas, and freedom of expression that Great Britain held in the eighteenth-century.[140]

"Intellectual Property" and the Corporatization of Copyright Law and Policy

Despite the fact that copyright law was never intended to be a restrictive "property right," the twentieth-century brought about a dramatic reversal of one of the most fundamental principles of copyright law and policy. The phrase "intellectual property," which had been used before, started to make its way into common American business parlance around 1967. Soon after that, the American Patent Law Association and the American Bar Association Section on Patent, Trademark, and Copyright Law changed their names to incorporate "Intellectual Property." To understand copyright law and policy as it is currently perceived, one must first understand how it fits into intellectual property in general.

There are three main spheres or branches of intellectual property law in the United States: patent, trademark, and copyright law. Patents cover inventions and processes, not words, texts, or phrases. A patent for an invention is the grant of a "property right" to the inventor, issued by the United States Patent and Trademark Office. A patent is granted to an inventor of a new and useful process, machine, article of manufacture, or composition of matter, or any new and useful improvement thereof. *The term of protection of a patent is 20 years.* But unlike copyright, a patent protects the ideas, as well as the specific invention itself, so that a similar invention that operates along the same lines as the protected invention would be considered an infringement.[141]

A trademark "is a word, name, symbol, or device that is used in trade with goods to indicate the source of the goods and to distinguish them from the goods of others." A trademark allows a company or person to enjoy "goodwill" in the marketplace. A trademark can be a logo, design, sound, container shape, or even a

---

[140] Lyman Ray Patterson, *Copyright in Historical Perspective,* (Nashville: Vanderbilt University Press 1968), 192-200; Vaidhyanathan, 11, 23-24, 28.

[141] U.S.P.T.O. See: http://www.uspto.gov/web/offices/pac/doc/general/index.html#ptsc.

smell that points to the product's origin. Trademarks are associated or "linked" to particular brands or products in a way that offer a sense of predictability or perceived quality assurance to consumers. For instance, whenever you by a new Mac computer or another product made by tech giant Apple, the Apple logo (name) on the a product indicates specific design and functionality characteristics as well as performance expectations that are unique to the Apple brand.

Copyright is the protection granted to the authors (producers) of "original works of authorship" including literary, dramatic, musical, artistic, and certain other intellectual works, both published and unpublished. The grant of a limited monopoly to authors (producers) is supposed to provide a balance between the interests of existing authors, publishers, readers and *future* authors. Originality is an important part of copyright because it implies that the author or artist created the work through his or her own skill, labor, and judgment. But bear in mind: the bar for "originality" is low for a work to qualify for copyright.

By the mid-1970s, the notion of intellectual property had completely overtaken the original context of copyright law, and placed it in a context of "property talk." In effect, this reversed one of the most critical and fundamental components of U.S. copyright law. Just like *the life of the author plus 70 years* protection term extension, the reversal of the context of American copyright law helped to further solidify the greatest fears of Jefferson and other framers. As with the most notable copyright protection term increase of the twentieth century, the use of the property model for copyright helped strengthen the power of the monopolists (i.e. corporate copyright owners) to control the flow of ideas and the use of expressions. As a result, the centralization of creative ideas in America are now greatly unbalanced, and they have moved steadily under the umbrella of a small network of powerful producers and further away from the the public.[142]

Sound Recording Amendment of 1971

The first two decades of the twentieth century saw the invention of phonographs and recording machines. But it wasn't until 1971 that phonorecords or sound recordings would receive formal copyright protection. At that time, there was a growing problem of record piracy — illegal duplication, reproduction, and redistribution of entire records. Between the late 1960s and early 1970s, one-third of all records and tapes sold in the United States were illegal duplicates. Thus, Congress was pressed to react:

> While it is difficult to establish the exact volume or dollar value of current piracy activity, it is estimated by reliable trade sources that the annual volume of such piracy is now in excess of $100 million. It has been estimated that legitimate prerecorded tape sales have an annual value of approximately $300 million .... **The problem of record piracy has not been dealt with...We are persuaded that the problem is an immediate and urgent one, and that legislation to deal with it is needed now. The seriousness of the situation with respect to record piracy...is unique.... The committee agrees that it is necessary, without delay, to establish Federal legislation prohibiting unauthorized manufacturers from reproduction and distribution of recorded performances.** [emphasis mine][143]

Congress dealt with the growing problem of record piracy

---

[142] *Ibid*, 11-12. Vaidhyanathan maintains that "from the middle of the nineteenth century," there have been "those who have pushed to enlarge and deepen copyright protection" and "have invoked the need to protect authors from 'theft.'" It's worth noting that the notion of protecting authors from "theft" was never part of the original notions of U.S. copyright law and policy. The notion of protecting authors from "theft" came later, as larger publishers and corporations grew in power and influence. Furthermore, Vaidhyanathan points out that "since 1909, courts and corporations have exploited public concern for rewarding established authors by steadily limiting the rights of readers, consumers, and emerging artists." He further cites copyright historian Lyman Ray Patterson's articulation that "copyright has in the twentieth century really been about the rights of publishers first, authors second, and the public a distant third."

[143] *The House Report on the Sound Recording Amendment* of 1971, September 22, 1971 — Committed to the Committee of the Whole House on the State of the Union, H.R. Rep. No. 92-487, at 10 (1971), reprinted in 1971 U.S.C.C.A.N. 1566, 1572. (Hereinafter H.R. Rep. No. 92-487) In the House Committee's report, it is clear that the legislation was aimed at "*manufacturers* engaged in the unauthorized reproduction of records and tapes," not individuals who now use the art of sampling as a compositional method.

by amending the 1909 copyright law. The Sound Recording Amendment of 1971, which became effective on February 15, 1972, and was later made a permanent part of the Copyright Act in 1974, specifically granted a limited copyright to sound recordings.[144]

That the Sound Recording Amendment of 1971 was the reaction of Congress to curb rampant and out of control *record piracy* in the United States tells us much. First, it is clear that record piracy had been a problem for quite some time, but Congress had failed to act sooner. Second, Congress acted in 1971, at least eight years before the art of sampling became common and before the first digital sampler was even invented. This means that Congress was driven foremost by the need to stem the growing record piracy problem in the United States. And clearly, when Congress amended the copyright code in 1971, they did not intend to stop the art of sampling, a practice which, in its physical (digital) form, had not yet become commonplace.[145]

Despite the facts surrounding the Sound Recording Amendment of 1971, various legal commentators and opponents of sampling (and hip hop in general) have maintained that sampling is a case of "piracy." Of course, this notion is absurd. The art of sampling is certainly not piracy. In 1971, Congress had no way of knowing that hip hop/rap music would emerge and/or that the art of sampling would be a fundamental part of its development. How could Congress draft copyright code specifically intended to counter and restrict an art form and practice that did not exist yet?

Still, by using a curiously *loose* and non-intended definition of the term "piracy," some legal commentators are able to mislabel and misrepresent sampling as piracy. The detailed examination in Part two of this study demonstrates not only how much of a complex art from sampling is, but also how it is never piracy. The art of sampling requires any number of steps, the third or fourth (after digging for, listening to, and studying a piece of music)

---

[144] Sound Recording Amendment of 1971, P.L. 92-140, § 1 (a), 85 Stat. 391 (amending 17 U.S.C. (1970) (current version at 17 U.S.C. 114(b) [Supp. II 1978]). 2.10[A], at 2-145, 2-146. Also see: Paul S. Wallace, Jr., "Copyright Law: Legalizing Home Taping of Audio and Video Recording," Issue Brief number IB82075, updated 05/31/84, *The Library of Congress Congressional Research Service Major Issues System*, 07/08/82.

[145] H.R. Rep. No. 92-487, at 10 (1971), reprinted in 1971 U.S.C.C.A.N. 1566, 1572.

being the *physical* recording (digital sampling) of a sound. The term "recording," by broad definition, implies "duplication" and/or "copying." The Sound Recording Amendment of 1971 expressly prohibits "duplication of sound recordings;" furthermore, it grants authors the exclusive right to "make copies," and to authorize others to make "copies," and to "republish" those "copies."

Here, there are a number of points that have to be made. First, Congress did not distinguish between a whole sound recording and isolated pieces of it, there was no need to do so. In fact, we know that the language within the Sound Recording Amendment of 1971 used to describe sound recordings was understood to mean "whole sound recordings." There is no uncercentainy here; the *clear intent* of the amendment was to reign in record piracy. Moreover, it's not certain that Congress would have not made this distinction had the art of sampling been in common practice at the time the Amendment of 1971 was enacted. Second, the copying, republication, and distribution of *entire* records are the main conditions that properly define piracy. Third, in proving copyright infringement, the copyright holder must prove that the sample is an illegal appropriation (illegal duplication; not all forms of copying are illegal, as I discuss in the Fair Use chapter of this study). Of course, Sampling is not the process of wholesale duplication and redistribution.

In the process of *digital* sampling, the third or fourth step in the art of sampling, sounds are copied. Herein lies the illogical legal loophole — based on willfully misinterpreted nomenclature — that some legal experts rest their claims of piracy on. But the meaning and level of duplication in the context of the art of sampling must not be confused with the meaning of "duplication" in the context of *record piracy*, as Congress clearly defined it in 1971. A sample-based beatmaker does not make copies of *whole* sound recordings and then redistribute them; he or she does not copy a whole song (a complete fixed expression) then "republishes" or "redistributes" it. Thus, by the most common, practical, and legal definition of piracy, the art of sampling is certainly not piracy. Yet the opponents of the art of sampling aim to use the loosest, most impractical, and most thinly technical definition of piracy to link it to sampling. They are able to make this long, impractical leap from the art of sampling back to "record piracy," simply because of a shrewd game of technical and cultural semantics. Thus, these legal experts, who, incidentally are mostly the ones who have framed the public debate about sampling and its copyright implications, maintain that sampling has always been prohibited under U.S. copyright law.

Summary of Key Twentieth-Century Developments in United States Copyright Law and Policy

Overall, the story of copyright development in the twentieth century has been about the gradual but significant shift in U.S. copyright ideology; an ideology that is most characterized by the notion of copyright as property. This shift in ideology has resulted in the erosion of the purpose of copyright: To encourage members of society to "create" and innovate in the Sciences and Arts. The use of the property model for copyright, which both Madison and Jefferson warned against, helped strengthen the power of the monopolists (corporate copyright owners) to control the flow of ideas and the use of expressions. And as a result, the centralization of creative ideas in America are incredibly unbalanced. Moreover, the *right to create* has, in effect, moved steadily under the umbrella of the producer and further away from the consumer (the society). Therefore, because of the aforementioned twentieth-century developments in U.S. copyright law, what we now have is a copyright system that "protects the producers and taxes consumers," and further "rewards works already created and limits works yet to be created."[146]

Chapter 10

Fair Use
Communal Creativity and Understanding the Fair Use Doctrine

[i]n truth, in literature, in science and in art, there are, and can be, few, if any, things, which in an abstract sense, are strictly new and original throughout. Every book in literature, science and art, borrows, and must necessarily borrow, and use much which was well known and used before. –United States Supreme Court Justice Joseph Story

Nothing is original. Steal from anywhere that resonates with inspiration or fuels your imagination. Devour old films, new films, music, books, paintings, photographs, poems, dreams, random conversations, architecture, bridges, street signs, trees, clouds, bodies of water, light and shadows. Select only things to steal from that speak directly to your soul. If you do this, your work (and theft) will be authentic. Authenticity is invaluable; originality is nonexistent. And don't bother concealing your thievery – celebrate it if you feel like it. In any case, always remember what Jean-Luc Godard said: "It's not where you take things from – it's where you take them to." –Jim Jarmusch

African American originality departs significantly from dominant notions of creativity. –Richard L. Schur

Communal Creativity and the Concept of Originality in the African American (Black) Music Tradition

Originality, which is not often a definable aspect of a work, has always been a fundamental principle of copyright, as it implies that the author or artist created the work through his or her own skill, labor, and judgment. But that being said, how is originality actually defined, and more importantly, *who* gets to define it? When most commentators discuss copyright law, they typically overlook or ignore notions of originality and collective creativity as they have been understood in American culture — especially the African American (Black) music tradition — for more than 200 years. This is unfortunate because such notions of originality and collective creativity are at the forefront of what fair use is supposed to be: a recognition and protection of communal creativity.

To properly examine notions of originality within the African American (Black) music tradition, one must first understand the role of communal creativity. In the African American (Black) music tradition, the concept of music as community (common) property is absolutely critical. From field songs to the advent of the blues tradition, the foundation for nearly all forms of twentieth-century American popular music, the idea of borrowing other people's music, making it one's own, and creating new musical expressions on top of it — through the processes of versioning, improvisation, and the like — is paramount to the African American (Black) music tradition. Further, the African American (Black) concept of communal creativity is actually more in line with the philosophy and ideology of Madison and Jefferson than has previously be credited.

Musicians and singers in a culture that prioritizes communal creativity draw freely from the culture and creative environment that surrounds them. They inhale common musical themes, styles, and attitudes, and then rework and transform what they've taken in, all in accordance with their own style, sound, and other creative influences.

In the African American (Black) music tradition, once musical expressions and ideas are divulged to the community, they flow into a common well, where the most pivotal and popular musical practices, priorities, aesthetics, elements, styles, and expressions form a musical canon, or what I like to call "the mix." And it is the mix — the grand communal musical canon, this well of tradition — that all musicians (artists) are encouraged and certainly expected to draw new streams of musical expressions and texts from. And the mix (i.e. the communal musical canon) is not treated as private property. Thus, for example, the jazz musician who borrows a well-known blues melody to build something new never feels encumbered, but rather empowered to do so because he's fully invested in a shared cultural system. In this way, musicians (artists) of the African American (Black) music tradition are rewarded for their mastery of the canon as well as the uniqueness of their own individual style.

Furthermore, in the African American (Black) music tradition, the terms "new" and "original" are associated with the concept of using the the African American (Black) musical canon while adding something to it, particularly through one's own individual style, creative instincts, ingenuity, and influences. This is entirely different than the notion of purportedly doing something entirely brand new. In the African American (Black) music tradition, something "brand new" really means a *new individualized extension* of what already exists in the musical canon. Thus, historically, in the African American (Black) music tradition, musicians (artists) have simultaneously relied upon using, exploring, revising, and extending the common aesthetics, tropes, and ideas from within the tradition. In other words, what constitutes creative originality in the African American (Black) music tradition is one's ability to add their individual take — their own style, version, rendition, signature, flavor, etc. — to the works and ideas within the canon.

There are two excellent examples of the priority of this practice within the African American (Black) music tradition. In the jazz tradition, the aforementioned use of blues "standards" (well-known blues songs) as the foundation or inspiration for new jazz compositions is not only common, it's expected. To the jazz pioneers of the 1930s and 40s, some blues song standards are seen as common source stock (raw material) that is available for all to create on top of, i.e. to use as the foundation for new works. In this case, there is no overriding concern for authorial originality as U.S. copyright law might define it. And when you examine the earliest days of hip hop/rap music, you must remember that Kool Herc picked up a new style of funk DJ'ing from John Brown, an older DJ and fellow South Bronx resident. Having gotten his cue from John Brown, Herc began showcasing the new style at his parties and park jams. Soon, other DJs, most notably Grandmaster Flash and Afrika Bambaataa, keyed in on what Herc was doing and followed suit. Each DJ brought something new to the mix. For instance, Flash brought his technical precision and new style of blending record breaks, while Bambaataa brought his dubious style of imploring record breaks from a more extensive collection of records. In all three cases, Herc, Flash, and Bambaataa added their own individual style to the mix that was already there. In doing so, they extended "the mix," and added a new music tradition that was based on the key tropes and sensibilities of an older one.

It must also be noted that originality in the African American (Black) music tradition is very different from the standard European model and the mythical concept of originality that many like to believe. In the African American (Black) music tradition, distinction is achieved through one's individual mastery and unique exploration of the musical canon. Unlike the European model (as best seen in the Western classical tradition), where originality is grounded in the abstract knowledge of the composition, the African American (Black) music tradition has historically considered originality also in the context of *value-added* to the whole.

Finally, we must consider the fact that because the concept of U.S. copyright is so embedded in Western literary tradition, it can not appropriately address the African American (Black) oral tradition. Orality is central to American culture in general, but it is, and has always been, particularly important to African American (Black) culture.[147] In oral traditions, *style* is what matters most; it is what ultimately determines originality, and it is the way in which individuals distinguish themselves. Notions of authorship in oral traditions are grounded more in individual stylization than anything else. Perhaps a contemporary extension of this notion of originality can be found within the rampant use of the auto-tune, a popular vocalization device. No one can say that auto-tune *belongs* to rapper T-Pain. In fact, T-Pain was certainly not even

---

[147] Less we forget, the peculiar institution of slavery in the United States made it illegal for slaves to read and write. Thus, the significance of the oral tradition in African American culture is deeply rooted in the history of American slavery, the Reconstruction period, and the Jim Crow South.

the first person to popularize the vocoder (a device that pre-dates auto-tune); that distinction would perhaps go to the late R&B singer Roger Troutman. However, T-Pain is considered to be one of the recording artists who used this vocalization technology and technique *best*. And whether one likes or dislikes T-Pain and his use of auto-tune, he stood out because of his *individual stylization* of auto-tune. Therefore, T-Pain was rewarded because he was one of those who used the auto-tune *style* the best.

Current State Of Copyright Law as It Pertains to Sampling

The legal perception of the art of sampling that's held by most music lawyers does not take into account the conflicting views of private property rights in the American popular music tradition, which stems in large part from the African American (Black) music tradition.

Sampling, especially as it is performed and understood in hip hop/rap music, is not simply a reflection of cultural change or part of a "post-modern" sensibility, as author and copyright historian Siva Vaidhyanathan describes it. His description of sampling is a misreading of what sampling is in hip hop/rap music. And while I have no doubt that Vaidhyanathan understands communal creativity, I believe his description of sampling in this regard ignores the actual history of *sampling* (borrowing) within the African American music tradition. Sampling, in its physical form, is an extension of intellectual-appropriation, or what can best be called *virtual* sampling (like versioning or renditioning), which is an important trope and sensibility of the African American (Black) music tradition.

Furthermore, sampling does not merely exist *because of* technology, as Vaidhyanathan implies, nor is it the *invention* of technology. I prefer to see advancements in recording technology and electronic instruments as the means for opening up more possibilities for new forms of intellectual appropriation, via new technology (physical machines and software, i.e. digital sampling technology). I do not see technology as the cause of intellectual appropriation itself. As I discussed earlier, sampling is the natural evolution of what the earliest hip hop/rap DJs were doing. Thus, its roots go back further than some copyright commentators perhaps care to discuss. Moreover, the art of sampling involves any number of processes, including, most importantly, transformation, reconceptualization, recontextualization, and *intellectual* appropriation. It is the process of *intellectual* appropriation that digital sampling technology simply makes possible. In this regard, technology enables the ideas of a musician, it does not create his or her ideas and sensibilities.

Even though digital sampling transcends some of the latter practices of African American (Black) music tradition (most notably versioning, rendering, and signifying), the process of sampling itself is still an extension of the musical process which uses fragments (elements) of musical expressions and ideas to create new music. Although the advent of digital samplers has simply allowed for this process to be carried out with granularity (infinite flexibility) and greater precision, digital sampling has also allowed for the sort of wholesale, non-creative appropriation that occurs when the legitimate desire for creativity by many is trumped by the desire for rampant duplicity by a few.

Unfortunately, the perception of sampling that's held by many music lawyers and judges only seems to recognize the wholesale, less-creative type of appropriation that can occur in digital sampling. In other words, the prevailing legal view of sampling is preoccupied only with the most egregious and superficial understanding of sampling. It ignores all other notions of the art of sampling, despite its clear and obvious pedigree. This is yet another reason why sampling is misrepresented and quickly mis-labeled as "theft" and "piracy," even though such terms can't define the true meaning of the art of sampling.

Thus, it should come as no surprise that there would be a *legal* pushback against sampling by those who adhere to the property model of copyright. But to be sure, most opponents of sampling are not privy to and/or informed about the art of sampling — it's meaning, value, or necessity. Also, because of their lack of understanding of the art of sampling, these opponents are certainly not sensitive to the predilections, tropes, and fundamental concepts that are prescribed within a culture of sampling and/or the African American (Black) music tradition in general. Instead, they merely write-off sampling as simple cases of "stealing" or intellectual property "theft." Therein lies the crux of the communal creativity/copyright clash: On this side of the spectrum, you have the dominant American mainstream society, which is backed by a rather counter intuitive private property rights interpretation of copyright law, lofting the charge of "theft" at sampling, an artistic process which stems specifically from the same African-American (Black) music tradition that spawned the blues, jazz, country, rhythm and blues, soul, and rock 'n' roll.

Finally, we must remember that the original purpose of copyright law is to stimulate, motivate, and influence the creation of new works; to prompt, foster, and provoke innovation; to offer reward for such innovation and creativity; and to give incentive to create and innovate. But contemporary copyright law and policy, especially as it pertains to sampling, does just the opposite: It actually discourages the creativity of musicians (artists) who use the art of sampling (in whole or part) as the compositional process that it is.

Lawful Appropriation: When It's Not Copyright Infringement

What is Copyright Infringement and How Is It Proven?

Because the following sections explain when the threshold of copyright infringement, i.e. unlawful appropriation, isn't reached, it's necessary to first explain what copyright infringement is and how it's proven. Copyright infringement is the unauthorized use of a work under copyright. U.S. Code, 17 § 501. Infringement of copyright states that: "Anyone who violates any of the exclusive rights of the copyright owner as provided by sections 106 through 122 or of the author as provided in section 106A(a), or who imports copies or phonorecords into the United States in violation of section 602, is an infringer of the copyright or right of the author, as the case may be."[148]

"To prove copyright infringement, the plaintiff must establish that he or she owns a valid copyright, that the defendants copied a protectible expression, and that **the copying is substantial enough to constitute improper appropriation** of plaintiff's work."[149] Thus, in order for a copyright infringement claim to be successful, there are three elements that must *all* be established, or rather three things that a copyright owner must prove. First, ownership of a valid copyright must be proven. A valid copyright is established through proof of fixation, this usually means a registration of the copyrightable subject matter with the copyright office. Second, proof of copying must be established. This means that the plaintiff must prove that actual copying took place. This is established either by direct evidence of copying or by indirect evidence showing that the alleged infringer had access to the copyright owner's work. Third, *unlawful* appropriation of the copyrighted work must be established. Remember, not all appropriation/copying is unlawful. This means that after a valid copyright has been proven *and* proof of copying established, it must further be proven that the copy was *improper* under the statute, which means that the two works at issue need to be substantially similar.

In determining unlawful appropriation, the courts will engage in a substantial similarity analysis in which qualitative and quantitative factors are assessed. An allegedly infringing work is considered substantially similar when it is nearly indistinguishable from the copyrighted work it appropriated. Quantitative analysis examines whether the secondary use constituted a substantial portion of the appropriated work, NOT whether it made a substantial portion of the allegedly infringing work. Qualitative analysis considers whether the sample (i.e. copied portion) is qualitatively important to the allegedly infringed work as a whole. In other words, in terms of sampling, the analysis asks how critical, qualitatively speaking, is

---

[148] U.S. Code, 17 § 501. Infringement of copyright.
[149] *Jarvis v. A&M Records*, 827 F. Supp. 282, 290 (D.N.J. 1993), at 288, B. (emphasis added.).

the sample (the copied portion) to the appropriated work, and as a whole, how similar is the allegedly infringing song to the song it sampled.[150] Thus, something that is quantitatively insignificant may be substantially similar if the material is qualitatively important to the appropriated work. For instance, a hook from a song might be quantitatively small yet qualitatively important to the work from which it came. And note: An allegedly infringing work is considered substantially similar when it is nearly indistinguishable from the copyrighted work it appropriated.

"Proof of substantial similarity is satisfied by a two part test of extrinsic similarity and intrinsic similarity. The extrinsic test is objective in nature and requires the plaintiff to identify specific criteria which it alleges have been copied. The intrinsic test is an examination of an ordinary person's subjective impression of the similarities between the two works, and is the exclusive province of the jury." And fruther stated, "the test for substantial similarity is the reaction of a lay ear, not the reaction of the alleged infringer."[151] This test looks at each work as a whole, and considers "whether an average lay observer would recognize the alleged copy as having been appropriated from the copyrighted work."[152] Thus, the plaintiff (copyright owner) must prove that **the two works taken as a whole are substantially similar**. In *Williams v. Broadus*, the court noted that "if a secondary work transforms the expression of the original work such that the two works cease to be substantially similar, then the secondary work is not a derivative work and, for that matter, does not infringe the copyright of the original work."[153]

The more the allegedly infringing work takes from a copyrighted

[150] *Warner Bros., Inc. v. American Broadcasting Companies*, 654 F. 2d 204 - Court of Appeals, 2nd Circuit 1981. *Warner Bros., Inc. v. American Broadcasting Companies* reaffirms how unlawful appropriation is determined in the courts. Quote from Jennifer R. R. Mueller, "All Mixed Up: Bridgeport Music v. Dimension Films and De Minimis Digital Sampling," *Indiana Law Journal*, Vol. 81, Issue 1, Article 22 (2006). 442-43.
[151] Scott Hervey, "The Complexity of Proving Copyright Infringement" http://www.theiplawblog.com/archives/-copyright-law-the-complexity-of-proving-copyright-infringement.html, (accessed April, 2009); and *Jarvis v. A&M Records*, 827 F. Supp. 282, 290 (D.N.J. 1993), at 287.
[152] Mueller, 442.
[153] *Marlon Williams v. Calvin Broadus* No. 99 Civ. 10957 (MBM), 2001 WL 984714 (S.D.N.Y. Aug. 27, 2001).

work, the stronger the claim of infringement. Conversely, the less taken and the less similar the allegedly infringing work is to the copyrighted work that it appropriated, the weaker the claim of infringement. Thus, the third element in an infringement claim, unlawful appropriation, can't be established when there's a finding of de minimis or fair use.

Fair Use and De Minimis: Limitation on the Exclusive Rights of Copyright Owners and Fair Borrowing

Why Allow Fair Use? Understanding the Nature and Necessity of Fair Use

The old adage that there's nothing new under the sun is correct. All art, all intellectual activity is, in part, derivative. Since the creation of things, people have borrowed and built upon ideas. This is a permanent construct of society. "There is no such thing as a wholly original thought or invention. Each advance stands on building blocks fashioned by prior thinkers." Further, absolute ownership of any work is not what copyright law prescribes; and excessively broad protection of copyright shifts the objectives of copyright. "Notwithstanding the need for monopoly protection of intellectual creators to stimulate creativity and authorship, excessively broad protection would stifle, rather than advance, the objective" of copyright: to promote the Progress of Science and useful Arts. "Monopoly protection of intellectual property that impeded referential analysis and the development of new ideas out of old would strangle the creative process.[154]

The fair use doctrine is especially important to sample-based beatmakers for two reasons. First, because most sample-based music is largely dependent upon the use of pre-existing sound recordings as raw material, fair use gives sample-based beatmakers a core set of principles to consider when determining whether the use of a copyrighted sound recording is fair use or not. Second, fair

---

[154] Leval, 1109. 1110.

use allows sample-based beatmakers a path to creativity that does not require permission from a copyright owner or a clearance fee. Sampling that is fair use, i.e. *lawful* copying, prevents sample-based beatmakers from ever having to deal with the dreaded sample clearance system. Thus, fair use serves as a legislative safe harbor for the kind of art that sample-based recording artists create. In order to take full advantage of the protection that fair use affords, as well as improve your level of creativity in the art of sampling, here's what you need to know about fair use and how it can work for you.

What is Fair Use?

The Copyright Act grants copyright owners the exclusive control over access and use of their works, including the right to reproduce their works and to make derivative works from them, for a limited time period, just long enough to provide incentive for them and others to create new works. Fair use, a well-established judicial doctrine that is now codified in the Copyright Act, is a limitation on the exclusive right of copyright owners, as it allows others to copy/use part (or, in some circumstances, all) of a copyrighted work without permission of the copyright owner.

To determine whether an appropriation qualifies as a fair use or not, the Copyright Act includes four factors that shall be considered:

> Notwithstanding the provisions of sections 17 U.S.C. § 106 and 17 U.S.C. § 106A, the fair use of a copyrighted work, including such use by reproduction in copies or phonorecords or by any other means specified by that section, for purposes such as criticism, comment, news reporting, teaching (including multiple copies for classroom use), scholarship, or research, is not an infringement of copyright. **In determining whether the use made of a work in any particular case is a fair use the factors to be considered shall include:**
> 1. the purpose and character of the use, including whether such use is of a commercial nature or is for nonprofit educational purposes;
> 2. the nature of the copyrighted work;
> 3. the amount and substantiality of the portion used in relation to the copyrighted work as a whole; and
> 4. the effect of the use upon the potential market for or value of the

copyrighted work.[155] [emphasis mine]

On a case by case basis, whenever the proposition of fair use is raised, the courts engage in a fair use analysis, which takes into consideration the four factors specified in the statute. (Later in this chapter, I will discuss the four factors of fair use and how a fair use analysis is often applied.)

What is De Minimis?

De minimis — which is short for the Latin Maxim *de minimis non curat lex*: "the law cares not for small things" or "the law does not concern itself with trifles" — is a legal doctrine that refers to trivial matters that are not worthy of judicial scrutiny. In *On Davis v. Gap, Inc.* (hereinafter *On Davis*), the United States Court of Appeals for the Second Circuit points out that **"the de minimis doctrine essentially provides that where unauthorized copying is sufficiently trivial, 'the law will not impose legal consequences.'"**[156] Unlike fair use, the *de minimis* doctrine is not limited to copyright law; it applies in all civil cases. In *On Davis* the Second Circuit noted that "The de minimis doctrine is rarely discussed in copyright opinions because suits are rarely brought over trivial instances of copying. Nonetheless, it is an important aspect of the law of copyright." In further describing the frequency in everyday life and the ordinary, practical nature of *de minimis*, the Second Ciruit added that:

> **Trivial copying is a significant part of modern life.** Most honest citizens in the modern world frequently engage, without hesitation, in trivial copying that, but for the de minimis doctrine, would technically constitute a violation of law. We do not hesitate to make a photocopy of a letter from a friend to show to another friend, or of a favorite cartoon to post on the refrigerator. Parents in Central Park photograph their children perched on Jose de Creeft's Alice in Wonderland sculpture. We record television programs aired while we are out, so as to watch them at a more convenient hour.

---

[155] 17 U.S.C. § 107
[156] *On Davis v. Gap, Inc.*, 246 F.3d 152 (2nd Cir. 2001) (citations omitted).(emphasis mine).

> 8 Waiters at a restaurant sing "Happy Birthday" at a patron's table. When we do such things, it is not that we are breaking the law but unlikely to be sued given the high cost of litigation. **Because of the de minimis doctrine, in trivial instances of copying, we are in fact not breaking the law. If a copyright owner were to sue the makers of trivial copies, judgment would be for the defendants. The case would be dismissed because trivial copying is not an infringement.** [emphasis mine][157]

Thus, as a broad principle well recognized in common law,[158] de minimis is understood to mean usage that does not amount to actionable (unlawful) copying under the law. "Under the de minimis doctrine, some things, while technically violations of the law, are considered too petty to waste the time and resources of the court."[159] In the context of a copyright infringement lawsuit, if the allegedly infringing work makes such a quantitatively insubstantial use of the copyrighted work as to fall below the threshold required for actionable copying, courts reject the claim on that basis and find no infringement. So whether the allegedly infringing use is de minimis is considered part of the substantial similarity analysis. Thus, in a sampling context, the de minimis threshold in copyright law is the level below which courts deem the amount a musician appropriates a copyrighted work too small to be considered copyright infringement (think of something like a sample of a kick, drum, a bass-stab, or two notes from a long melodic phrase).[160]

De minimis is particularly important to understand prior to the range of fair use, because if a sample is to small (below the de minimis threshold), fair use doesn't even come into the picture. "The fair use defense involves a careful examination of many factors, often confronting courts with a perplexing task. **If the allegedly**

---

[157] *Id.*
[158] Common law (also known as case law or precedent) is law developed by judges through decisions of courts and similar tribunals rather than through legislative statutes or executive branch action.[1] A "common law system" is a legal system that gives great precedential weight to common law,[2] on the principle that it is unfair to treat similar facts differently on different occasions.[3] —http://en.wikipedia.org/wiki/Common_law
[159] Mueller, 435.
[160] For a good example of a court's description of the *de minimis* doctrine, see *Ringgold v. Black Entertainment Television, Inc.*, 126 F. 3d 70 - Court of Appeals, 2nd Circuit 1997.

infringing work makes such a quantitatively *insubstantial* use of the copyrighted work as to fall below the threshold required for actionable copying, it makes more sense to reject the claim on that basis and find no infringement, rather than undertake an elaborate fair use analysis in order to uphold a defense."[161] In this way, the de minimis concept recognizes that there are instances in which a sample is too small, too trivial to be considered copyright infringement. It's worth noting that even though sampling case law has addressed this issue (most notably in Newton v. Diamond), there is no arbitrary de minimis threshold. The circumstances of each sample is different. Therefore, in the courts, de minimis must be determined on a case by case basis.

Also, the notion of a default de minimis sample line of one, two, or three notes, or one, two, or three seconds is up for debate. But if there is ever to be any bright line threshold for what constitutes a de minimis sample, this determination should not be made by record companies, publishers, music lawyers, and the courts alone, but rather a committee that also prominently includes sample-based musicians as well.

Since de minimis is a less complicated concept to comprehend, I will leave the description of it where it is. However, a more detailed discussion of fair use is required, as it is an oft misunderstood concept that contains some gray area. Thus, what follows is a deeper examination of fair use.

Analysis of the Four Factors

The fair use statute in the Copyright Act of 1976 lists four pertinent factors to be considered when determining whether a secondary use is fair use. These factors are not to be a tally of the majority; *it's not as simple as three out of four of the factors automatically means fair use.* Moreover, one out of three factors doesn't automatically mean that a secondary use wasn't fair use. (If just one factor is satisfied, particularly the factor dealing with transformation, a secondary use may still be considered fair use.)

---

[161] *Id.*

Instead, the statutory factors should be a guide that direct courts to examine the issue from every relative angle. "Each factor directs attention to a different facet of the problem. The factors do not represent a score card that promises victory to the winner of the majority. Rather, they direct courts to examine the issue from every pertinent corner and to ask in each case whether, and how powerfully, a finding of fair use would serve or disserve the objectives of copyright."[162]

The First Factor: "The purpose and character of the use, including whether such use is of a commercial nature or is for nonprofit educational purposes"

This factor considers whether the use serves the purpose and intention of copyright law, which is to promote "the Progress of Science and useful Arts" (Art. I, § 8, cl. 8). Factor one, considered by many to be "the soul of fair use," considers whether, and to what extent, the secondary use is transformative. If quoted matter is used as raw material, transformed in the creation of new information, new aesthetics, new insights, and new understandings, then it is more likely to past the test; on the other hand, minimal creative transformation will not likely past the test: "The first fair use factor calls for careful evaluation whether the particular quotation is of the transformative type that advances knowledge and the progress of the arts or whether it merely repackages, free riding on another's creations. If a quotation of a copyrighted matter reveals no transformative purpose, fair use should perhaps be rejected without further inquiry into the other factors." Transformative uses may include: "criticizing the quoted work, exposing the character of the original author, proving a fact, or summarizing an idea argued in the original in order to defend or rebut it. They also may include parody, symbolism, aesthetic declarations, and innumerable other uses...."[163]

Factor one also raises the question of whether the use is of a

---

[162] Leval, 1110, 1111.
[163] *Ibid.*, 1111...

commercial nature or for nonprofit educational purposes. Although it has been widely held that nonprofit educational purposes tip the scale in the direction of a fair use, that a use is of a commercial purpose does not necessarily exclude it from being fair. Conversely, every use that is of a nonprofit educational purpose is not automatically fair. What is more important is whether the use of a copyrighted work fulfills the purpose and intention of copyright law. Thus, the first factor signals that a fair use of a copyrighted work is one that can show that it advances knowledge or the useful arts through transformation, i.e. the addition of something new and different. Therefore, the more transformative the use, the more likely it is fair.

The Second Factor: "The nature of the copyrighted work"

This factor looks at the type of material that copyright was designed to stimulate, i.e. whether the copyrighted work is fictional or non-fictional (facts). Creative works receive more protection than factual ones; think of a novel and telephone book. Therefore, the more creative a copyrighted work is, the more the other factors must favor the secondary user in order to earn a fair use finding. One final important note about the factor two: while the implication may be that certain types of copyrighted material are more amenable to fair use than others, the scope of fair use is not narrowed by the nature of a copyrighted work.

The Third Factor: "The amount and substantiality of the portion used in relation to the copyrighted work as a whole"

This factor considers the amount of the copyrighted work that's been used in the new work. Generally, a small amount tips the scale towards a fair use. In *Ringgold v. Black Entertainment Television, Inc.* (1997), the 2nd Circuit maintained that "the third fair use factor concerns a quantitative continuum. Like all the fair use factors, it has no precise threshold below which the factor is accorded decisive significance. **If the amount copied is very slight in relation to the work as a whole, the third factor might strongly favor the alleged infringer.**"[164] Judge Leval offers additional clarification:

> The third statutory factor instructs us to assess 'the amount and substantiality of the portion used in relation to the copyrighted work as a whole.' In general, the larger the volume (or the greater the importance) of what is taken, the greater the affront to the interests of the copyright owner, and the less likely that a taking will qualify as fair use.
>
> This factor has further significance in its bearing on two other factors. It plays a role in consideration of justification under the first factor (the purpose and character of the secondary use); and it can assist in the assessment of the likely impact on the market for the copyrighted work under the fourth factor (the effect on the market). **As to the first factor, an important inquiry is whether the selection and quantity of the material taken are reasonable in relation to the purported justification....** The more taken the greater the likely impact on the copyright holder's market, and the more the factor favors the copyright holder. **Too mechanical a rule, however, can be dangerously misleading.** One can imagine secondary works that quote 100% of the copyrighted work without affecting market potential. [emphasis mine][165]

But even a small amount may not meet the fair threshold if it can be considered the heart of the copyrighted work. Further, the third factor considers how substantial is the portion of the copyrighted work that's been used. The less substantial, or the less used in relation to the whole, the more likely the use will be considered fair under this factor.

Just as with any other copyrighted material, in the area of digital sampling, the question that would be raised is *how much was sampled*, both quantitatively and qualitatively. While extensive takings may impinge on creative incentives, the determination of an extensive — i.e. substantial — taking is based on the actual amount of appropriation, NOT how the appropriation is used.

---

[164] *Ringgold v. Black Entertainment Television, Inc.*, 126 F. 3d 70 - Court of Appeals, 2nd Circuit 1997 (emphasis mine).
[165] Leval, 1122, 1123.

For instance, most beatmakers use drum sounds that they have sampled from sound recordings. In this way, beatmakers typically use small takings as raw materials, transformed in the creation of a new aesthetic. Certainly, a single drum hit is de minimis. Thus, the copying in this instance is NOT extensive because it is looped.

Taking a de minimis fragment, looping it, then repeating it throughout a song is not what is meant by extensive/substantial. If one takes a word, phrase, or line from a poem or other literary work and repeats the quoted matter — for commentary, proving a fact, exposing the character of the original author, summarizing a point, making an aesthetic declaration, etc. — throughout a new work, this is not an examination of excessive taking. Likewise, the insistence that the looping (repeating) of a de mininmis sample is excessive is not only flawed legal reasoning, it's a grave misreading of the third statutory factor.

The Fourth Factor: "The effect of the use upon the potential market for or value of the copyrighted work"

This factor considers the likely effect upon the market of the appropriated work. It weighs the effect that the new work has on the copyright owner's right to exploit their own work. In other words, it considers whether harm would be done to the potential market of the original. "A secondary use that interferes excessively with an author's incentives subverts the aims of copyright." However, a secondary use that does not *excessively* interfere with an author's incentives does not subvert the aims of copyright, rather it achieves the very objective of copyright. Further, "The fourth factor disfavors a finding of fair use only **when the market is impaired because the quoted material serves the consumer as a substitute,** or in Story's words, 'supersede[s] the use of the original.'"[166]

This is particularly important to understand, as samples do not inherrently supersede the original. For instance, if someone samples a drum hit, horn or bass-stab, and/or brief phrase snippet from a song like "Midnight Train to Georgia" (Gladys Knight & The Pips),

---

[166] Leval, 1124 (emphasis mine).

then transforms it into an entirely new aesthetic by adding new drum sounds, a new drum framework, and vocals about a picnic in the summer, no person would reasonably believe that the new creation is the substitute for the song it took minor samples from.

In copyright infringement cases, courts often ask, in addition to the question whether the allegedly infringing use acts as a direct market substitute for the work it appropriated, whether potential market harm might exist beyond that of direct substitution. When it comes to sampling, some commentators believe that this points to the potential existence of a licensing market for *all* samples. But even this is mistaken. Every sample does not inherently require a license; any suggestion otherwise is prior restraint.

Hence, a "market" for samples that may be de minimis or fair use is no market at all. So the notion that sampling inherently interferes substantially with a copyright holder's market for licensing samples is illogical for a number of reasons. Again, all samples do not require licensing. Second, all secondary uses of samples are not locked into one type of transformation. Third, even if the notion of a market for samples was valid, not every type of market impairment goes against fair use. Fourth, "by definition every fair use involves some loss of royalty revenue because the secondary user has not paid royalties. Therefore, if an insubstantial loss of revenue turned the fourth factor in favor of the copyright holder, this factor would never weigh in favor of the secondary user. And if we then gave serious deference to the proposition that it is 'undoubtedly the single most important element of fair use,' fair use would become defunct. **The market impairment should not turn the fourth factor unless it is reasonably substantial....Not every type of market impairment opposes fair use.**"[167] Fifth, the assumption of automatic, irreparable market harm when samples are involed is greatly mistaken because hip hop/rap has proven that the transformation of a given sample is limitless. Moreover, a copyright owner does not lose his right to license samples of his work simply because a secondary use of his work has already been made, especially if the secondary use was di minimis or fair use.

---

[167] Leval, 1124, 1125 (emphasis mine).

Finally, the aforementioned notion of a potential existence of a licensing market — for samples that might likely require a license, i.e. samples that take substantially from a recording — must also be qualified. For starters, the sample licensing market in the music industry has been built largely off of sampling activity that no doubt included many de minimis and fair use appropriations. Further, the sample clearance system (which I discuss in detail in chapter 11) is so thoroughly flawed that it raises serious questions about the very existence of the music industry's current sample licensing scheme.

False Factors

In the first edition of this book, I failed to consider whether there were any additional factors that judges were applying. As it turns out, Judge Leval suggests that there are: "The language of the Act suggests that there may be additional unnamed factors bearing on the question of fair use…. the pertinent factors are those named in the statute. **Additional considerations that I and others have looked to are false factors that divert the inquiry from the goals of copyright.** They may have bearing on the appropriate remedy, or on the availability of another cause of action to vindicate a wrong, but not on the fair use defense."[168] In total, Leval maintains that there are three false factors: Good Faith, Artistic Integrity, and Privacy.

Regarding **Good Faith**, Leval offers:

> **Good Faith.** — In all areas of law, judges are tempted to rely on findings of good or bad faith to justify decisions. Such reasoning permits us to avoid rewarding morally questionable conduct. It augments our discretionary power. It provides us with an escape from confronting questions that are difficult to understand. The temptation has been particularly strong in dealing with the difficult issue of fair use. This practice is, however, misguided. It produces anomalies that conflict with the goals of copyright and adds to the confusion surrounding the doctrine.[169]

---

[168] Leval, 1125, 1126 (emphasis mine).
[169] Leval, 1126.

The problem with good faith is that, when it comes to sampling — which is often seen as morally corrupt conduct by many and especially by some judges — it tends to favor property owners above all else. The objective of copyright — to maximize the creation and publication of socially useful material — is muzzled under foot, as the property owner is empathetically seen as the injured party. But morally corrupt conduct withstanding, "copyright is not a privilege reserved for the well-behaved." It is not "a reward for goodness but a protection for the profits of activity that is useful to the public education." Further, an insistence on upstanding morality as a condition for fairness has nothing to doing with copyright. This means that a fair use inquiry "should focus not on the morality of the secondary user, but on whether her creation claiming the benefits of the doctrine is of the type that should receive those benefits. This decision is governed" by the four statutory factors — "with a primary focus on whether the secondary use is productive and transformative and whether it causes excessive injury to the market for the original. No justification exists for adding a morality test. This is of course not an argument in favor of immorality. It favors only proper recognition of the scope and goals of a body of law.... *Whether the secondary use is within the protection of the doctrine depends on factors pertinent to the objectives of the copyright law and not on the morality motives of either the secondary user or the copyright-owning plaintiff*[170]

Artistic Intergrity. This false factor deals primarily with the level of control that an author has over his work. The concept of an author having right of paternity (the right to be acknowledged as author of the work), the right to pull a work already made public, the right to determine whether or not a work is published, and the right to keep a work from change or modification. Such rights are beyond the purview of copyright in America, and they do not fit the objectives of our copyright law. Further, to have these rights forcibly placed — by judges — under the umbrella of copyright would be illogical: "it would be preposterous to permit...to claim, as an incident to copyright, the right to public acknowledgement

---

[170] *Ibid* (empahis mine).

of authorship, the right to prevent publication, the right to modify
a published work, and to prevent others from altering their work....
Our copyright law has developed over hundreds of years for a
very different purpose and with rules and consequences that are
incomparable with the *droit moral* [the French law that enforces
the aforementioned rights associated with the Artistic Integrity
false factor]."[171]

Privacy. This false factor deals with the notion of privacy
and copyright. Many people believe that copyright law protects
privacy. This is wrong. First, copyright can't generally be protected
without a *public* filing in the Library of Congress. Second, American
law already protects privacy; however, this is not the domain of
copyright law. Moreover, "...the copyright law is grotesquely
inappropriate to protect privacy and obviously was not fashioned
to do so. *Copyright protects only the expression, not the facts revealed,
and thus fails to protect privacy interest involved.*" Further, while the
right of privacy is highly regarded in the United States, free speech
is valued equally if not more. Hence, the "occasional attempt to
read protection of privacy into the copyright is...mistaken." "In
this country, a right to privacy has explicitly developed to shield
private facts from intrusion by publication," and American law...
maintains a powerful constitutional policy that sharply disfavors
muzzling speech."[172]

The Scope of Fair Use in the Statute: What's Behind the Four Factors?

What are the considerations that lie behind the fair use
doctrine's four factors of analysis? Aside from its four factors of
analysis, we can get a greater understanding of the rationale behind
fair use by examining its scope and intent as it was designed by
Congress in their report accompanying the Copyright Act of
1976. What follows in this section is a discussion of the scope of
fair use (17 U.S.C. § 107), as it's outlined in the Copyright Law

---

[171] Leval, 1128.
[172] Leval, 1129, 1130 (emphasis mine).

Revision report (H.R. Report No. 94 1476) issued by Congress to accompany the Copyright Act of 1976 (*a complete revision of the Copyright Act of 1909*).

Clarification of SECTION 107. FAIR USE begins with the reminder of the importance of fair use in copyright law:

> The judicial doctrine of fair use, **one of the most important and well-established limitations on the exclusive right of copyright owners**, would be given express statutory recognition for the first time in section 107. [emphasis mine][173]

Continuing, the report expresses that there is not just one definition of fair use, but that there is a set of criteria that helps to gauge what is a fair use, and that the rule of reason should be applied when considering whether a use is fair or not:

> Although the courts have considered and ruled upon the fair use doctrine over and over again, **no real definition of the concept has ever emerged. Indeed, since the doctrine is an equitable rule of reason, no generally applicable definition is possible, and each case raising the question must be decided on its own facts.** On the other hand, the courts have evolved a set of criteria which, though in no case definitive or determinative, provide some gauge for balancing the equities. These criteria have been stated in various ways, but essentially they can all be reduced to the four standards which have been adopted in section 107... [emphasis mine][174]

Here, Congress' call for the "rule of reason" makes clear that every fair use analysis must be reasonable. By this, it is widely understood to mean that not only should reason be applied, but also the fundamental objectives of copyright must be a guiding principle. So in a sampling context, Congress' Report indicates that it's reasonable to consider the transformative use of a small sample of a copyrighted sound recording to be fair use. Moreover, Congress' Report makes clear that it's unreasonable to consider such a tranfsormative use as inherent infringement.

Next, the report explains the specific wording of Section of 107

---

[173] U.S. House. The Committe on the Judiciary. *Copyright Law Revision*, 1976, (to Accompany S.22) *Report Together with Additional Views* (94 H. Rpt. 94-1476), p65.
[174] Ibid, 65

as the result of the related problems of fair use:

> The specific wording of section 107 as it now stands is the result of a process of accretion, resulting from the long controversy over the related problems of fair use and the reproduction (mostly by photocopying) of copyrighted material for educational and scholarly purposes. For example, the reference to fair use "by reproduction in copies or phonorecords or by any other means" **is mainly intended to make clear that the doctrine has as much application to photocopying and taping as to older forms of use; it is not intended to give these kinds of reproduction any special status under the fair use provision or to sanction any reproduction beyond the normal and reasonable limits of fair use.**
>
> **...It must be emphasized again that the same general standards of fair use are applicable to all kinds of uses of copyrighted material...** [emphasis mine][175]

This clarification is particularly revealing, as Congress makes plain that no kind of reproduction is to receive any special status under the fair use provision, which means that Congress intended for fair use to apply to any kind of use and reproduction, i.e. *any form of copying, any copyrighted material.* Thus, fair use clearly applies to the digital sampling of sound recordings, because digital sampling is just another form of copying, and sound recordings are just another type of copyrighted material. There is no "special status under the fair use provision" granted to older or new forms of use.

Next, in its report under the sub-header, "General intention behind the provision," Congress explains that Section 107. is meant to serve only as a guidance for determining fair use, not a restriction on when fair use applies:

> The statement of the fair use doctrine in section 107 **offers some guidance to users in determining when the principles of the doctrine apply.** However, **the endless variety of situations and combinations of circumstances that can rise in particular cases precludes the formulation of exact rules in the statute. The bill endorses the purpose and general scope of the judicial doctrine of fair use, but there is no disposition to freeze the doctrine in**

---

[175] Ibid, 66, 72.

> the statute, especially during a period of rapid technological change. Beyond a very broad statutory explanation of what fair use is and some of the criteria applicable to it, the courts must be free to adapt the doctrine to particular situations on a case-by-case basis. *Section 107 is intended to restate the present judicial doctrine of fair use, not change, narrow, or enlarge it in any way.* [emphasis mine][176]

Notice above the specific language that Congress used when describing the possible cases of fair use: "the endless variety of situations and combinations of circumstances." This demonstrates Congress' awareness of the infinite situations in which a use of copyrighted material could be deemed fair. It further signals Congress' intent to protect this fundamental nature of the fair use doctrine by refusing to limit it to an exact rule, or by "freezing" its scope in the statute, especially amid the constant flux of technological advancement. In other words, Congress intended for fair use to be infinitely broad and flexible, particularly because of the reality of rapidly changing technology.

Also, Congress sought to prevent changing technology from weakening or strengthening fair use. Therefore, for example, digital sampling technology should not cause a weakening of fair use. Of course, this does not mean that Congress knew that the art of sampling would blossom within two decades after its of report. But it does show that Congress understood the inevitable role that technology plays in making new useful arts possible. Moreover, the codification of fair use in the statute was intended to restate, not replace, the judicial doctrine that it was based upon. But this does not preclude courts from considering other factors in their analysis. As such, Congress recognized that a non-narrowing of the judicial doctrine of fair use helps to fundamentally fulfill the purpose of the copyright law, i.e. to promote "the Progress of Science and useful Arts" (Art. I, § 8, cl. 8).

Finally, in its report under the sub-header, "Reproduction and uses for other purposes," Congress reemphasized that although educational uses receive concentrated attention, such uses should not overshadow or exclude other uses, as fair use applies to an

---

[176] *Ibid*, p66.

exhaustive list of uses:

> The concentrated attention given the fair use provision in the context of classroom teaching activities should not obscure its application in other areas. **It must be emphasized again that the same general standards of fair use are applicable to all kinds of uses of copyrighted material,** although the relative weight to be given them will differ from case to case. [emphasis mine][177]

Differing Notions of Fair Use

Despite the long-held recognition of fair use, the four statutory factors, and a detailed Congressional report about the purpose and nature of the fair use doctrine in the Copyright Act, judges nonetheless maintain widely different opinions about fair use. The great irony of the four statutory factors is that they are broad, which leaves room for misguided interpretation. What's worse is that judges have not attempted to reconcile this great irony by establishing a cogent set of guiding principles. In fact, judges aren't in agreement on the meaning of fair use, even though they continue to make self-assured decisions when confronted with the fair use question. In other words, judges routinely make decisions that are based on individual presuppositions, not a consistent set of guided principles:

> ...judges have neither complained of the absence of guidance, nor made substantial efforts to fill the void. Uttering confident conclusions as to whether the particular taking was or was not a fair use, courts have treated the definition of the doctrine as assumed common ground. The assumption of common ground is mistaken. **Judges do not share a consensus on the meaning of fair use... Reversals and divided courts are commonplace.** The opinions reflect widely differing notions of the meaning of fair use. Decisions are not governed by consistent principles, but seem rather to result from intuitive to individual fact patterns. [emphasis mine][178]

Invariably, in the individual assessment — or ad hoc

---

[177] *Ibid*, p72.
[178] Leval, 1106, 1107.

interpretation — of fair use, justifications of fairness lean in favor of the copyright owner, as judges — not wanting to err — allow concerns of private property to weigh more favorably than the actual objectives of copyright law.

Towards a Healthy, Conistent Perception of Fair Use

There are two terribly misguided perceptions of fair use that still prevail today. First, there's the perception that fair use is just a defense. This illogical (often mean-spirited) view — one that is held predominantly by music industry lawyers — seeks to place fair use at the back doorstep of a copyright infringement lawsuit. Second, there's the perception that fair use is merely an exception (one that is grudgingly tolerated) to the rules of copyright law, i.e. to the copyright owner's rights of private property. Both perceptions are harmful. A healthy, consistent perception of fair use means not misrepresenting fair use as just a defense or as an insignificant spectacle of copyright law, but rather recoginizing fair use as a vital component and fundamental policy of copyright law. In fact, Fair use — which protects secondary creativity — is, in fact, necessary to the fulfillment of the objectives of copyright law:

> **The stimulation of creative thought and authorship for the benefit of society depends assuredly on the protection of the author's monopoly. But it depends equally on the recognition that the monopoly must have limits.** Those limits include the public dedication of facts (notwithstanding the author's efforts in uncovering them); the public dedication of ideas (notwithstanding the author's creation); and the public dedication of the right to make fair use of material covered by the copyright. [emphasis mine][179]

A healthy, consistent perception of fair use also means a recognition of the four factors that determine fair use, more specifically, how these factors must be interpreted with the objectives of copyright being the guiding principle.

---

[179] Leval, 1136.

Finally, a healthy, consistent perception of fair use requires that judges do not treat fair use as something mysterious, or dependent upon intuitive judgments. There is a reliable guide to how to govern conduct, and in this regard, the objectives of copyright remain supreme. Further, clarity in fair use is not about a bright line, but rather guiding principles. Quoting Justice Story, Leval reaffirms that a "definite standard would champion predictability at the expense of justification and would stifle intellectual activity to the detriment of the copyright objectives. We should not adopt a bright-line standard unless it were a good one — and we do not have a good one." Nor should we aim to find such a standard, as some commentators have suggested. The four statutory factors — when balanced toghether in light of the objectives of copyright — provide excellent guidance. "We can...gain a better understanding of fair use and greater consistency and predictability of court decisions by disciplined focus on the utilitarian, public-enriching objectives of copyright — and resisting the impulse to import extraneous policies."[180]

Some Important Conclusions About Fair Use, Especially as it Pertains to the Art of Sampling

When is Fair Use in Your Favor?

There are no legislative safe harbor guidelines specifically for sampling. Instead, the principles of fair use, as described earlier in this chapter, apply to all kinds of copyrighted material. But that said, below is a description of when fair use is in your favor, or rather when the sampling and use of a copyrighted sound recording is likely a fair use.

The more transformative the use of a sample, the more likely it will constitute a fair use; conversely, the less transformative the use of a sample, the more likely it will not meet the fair use threshold.

---

[180] Leval, 1135.

In other words, a 1- to 4-bar sample chopped up, pitched up or down, and combined with new drum work — and vocals over the top of the beat — is more likely to qualify for fair use than an 8- to 16-bar sample with little to no transformation and no additional music elements.

Although transformation may be subjective, when considering how transformative a sample-based beat is or isn't, ask yourself three main questions: (1) Is the way that the sample is used conceptually different from its source? (2) Is the way that the sample is used a change in context from the original? (3) How much does the sample and use sound substantially similar to the sound recording — as a whole — from which it came. These three questions should you give you a good gauge on whether a use is fair or not. But in all cases, the more that you aim for a high level of creative transformation, the more likely your sampling will meet the fair use threshold. (For a review of the standards and best practices of sampling, see the "Standards and Best Practices" section in chapter 6.)

When the amount taken is small, you're also in better shape. In a de facto context, a very small sample, like a drum kick less than one second, is de minimis, despite the *Bridgeport* ruling (more on the controversial *Bridgeport Music v. Dimension Films* case in chapter 12). Still, there is no official 1-, 2-, or 3-second rule for the amount of sampling that automatically qualifies for fair use. Instead, to meet the fair use threshold, the amount sampled and used must be considered against the whole of the copyrighted sound recording that the sample came from. Furthermore, I advise against sampling the whole "heart" (main melody, etc.) of a work. But if you do sample some or even all of the heart of a sound recording, make sure you transform it substantially.

Looking at the transformation and amount factors, there's three ways to approach the art of sampling in a way that's favorable to the fair use doctrine: (1) Sample as little as possible; (2) Transform whatever you sample, i.e. flip it to the maximum, which means transform it by changing and adding to it to create something new and substantially different; and (3) Avoid sampling the "heart" of the work or the most recognizable parts of a sound recording, but if you must, make sure that you alter it to the point that it's quite different from the work that you borrowed from.

Shifting Attitudes Regarding Copyright Protection

As I discussed in chapter 8, ideas about ownership of artistic works shifted dramatically in the twentieth century. But remarkably, ideas about fair use have remained the same. And while revolutionary advances in technology have been and continue to be made, the problems with modern copyright policy and protection, namely the romantic conception of authorship and the property concept of intellectual creativity, continues to persist. No doubt this has influenced how some people perceive art forms like sampling. This is one reason why fair use, perhaps the most important constant in copyright law, aside from the very purpose of copyright law, is critical right now.

Fair use, the "breathing room within the confines of copyright law," recognizes the realities of creativity and how new original works necessarily borrow from existing works. This legal appropriation status, if you will, that the fair use doctrine grants to transformative works that copy pieces of existing works is particularly important to the art of sampling, as the entire aesthetic is fundamentally about making new art from pieces of pre-existing sound recordings.

On the Question of Amending Fair Use and Judicial Intervention

Some commentators have suggested that Congress reduce the uncertainty surrounding fair use. The authors of *Creative License* point out, for example, that Congress "could amend section 107 of the federal copyright code, which codifies the fair use doctrine, to clarify whether a sample-based song that is not a parody can qualify as a transformative use in at least some cases."[181] However, I disagree with any such amendment or specific clarification for sampling, because fair use is codified in the copyright statute as a

---

[181] McLeod and DiCola, 243.

deliberately non-exhaustive doctrine. So there's no need for such an amendment, but rather a simple recognition that fair use applies to ALL copyrighted material — including sound recordings.

Plus, the problem with trying to clarify something that is intended to be non-exhaustive is that such an action may actually weaken fair use, by perhaps limiting instances of sampling that are fair use, and even casting aspersions on other art forms and other forms of copying. In fact, McLeod and DiCola recognize the pitfalls of pursuing such an amendment, as they point out that "Realistically, though, it is unlikely that Congress would be motivated to alter the copyright code for the benefit of such a small class of constituents — remixers — and there is no guarantee that legislators would get it right. In fact, it's quite possible that Congress could make things worse by retooling the federal copyright code, especially given the lobbying power and influence of the entertainment industries that have Congress' ear."[182]

Further, there is nothing in the statute that indicates that parody is the only transformative use, so it's useless to pursuit a course for amending the fair use doctrine to clarify non-parody transformative uses. The fair use doctrine, as codified in the Copyright Act, does not state that parody is the *only* transformative appropriation; judicial opinions in recent years make that quite clear.

Instead of altering the statute just for some clarification of what forms of copying other than parody qualify as a transformative use, I think the emphasis should be placed on educating the public on fair use. Certainly, an emphasis on fair use education is more realistic and potentially less harmful than an attempt to add other qualifying examples to the statute. Again, it's not practical to believe that Congress is going to cut open the copyright code to address the issue of music sampling. Fair use is strong enough as is. Thus, the problem isn't that the statute lacks specific language referencing sampling or more specific clarification on what forms of copying other than parody may qualify as transformative use. As Leval and the Supreme Court suggests, the solution is simple: Allow the objectives of copyright to guide any fair use inquiry, and recognize

---

[182] *Ibid.*

that no copyrighted material is immune from fair use.

As for the federal courts implementing "a clearer way to address fair use in sampling cases, perhaps by including a workable definition of transformative use for cases that don't involve parodies,"[183] I don't agree. What concerns me about the courts making this type of bright-line determination is *who* exactly would help the courts determine this workable definition of transformative use when it comes to sampling? Seriously, would there be an advisory panel to the courts on this issue? And if so, who would be on this panel? Would the advisory panel be made up of all of the most relevant groups — sample-based musicians and copyright scholars, music lawyers, music publishers, and previously sampled reocrding artists? Even if all stakeholders were at the tabel, I don't believe it's even possible to establish such a bright line, given the widely different views about creativity, or the fact that the way in which samples can be transformed is limitless.

What Matters More, Your Art or the Philosophy of Fear? On Being Motivated by Your Art, and Why You Shouldn't Be Spooked by the Sample Clearance System or the Thought of a Looming Lawsuit

The monstrous sample clearance system, which I examine in detail in the following chapter, caused many sample-based beatmakers to move away from sampling. In hip hop/rap music, this has been a deeply unfortunate thing, as its had a devastating effect on the development and overall mainstream quality of hip hop/rap music for more than a decade now. But what I find more troubling than the widespread move away from the art of sampling is the underlining philosophy of fear that the sample clearance system has fostered. This philosophy of fear — of not getting a sample cleared and, therefore, not selling beats even with samples — has caused scores of would-be samplers to avoid the sample-based compositional style and compromise their thoughts on the art of sampling, and in some cases even give up the art form altogether,

---

[183] *Ibid.*

merely because of arbitrary sample clearance issues and the pressing fear of litigation in the music industry. And the fact that fair use has been systematically buried alive in the music industry makes this philosophy of fear all the more disturbing.

I'm convinced that if there had been more awareness of fair use among sample-based beatmakers in the past two decades, this widespread shift in hip hop/rap music away from the art of sampling would never have occurred. Instead, armed with the knowledge of fair use, I think that the ranks of sample-based beatmakers who were consciously operating under the protection of fair use would have risen to such a level that the music industry would have had no choice but to deal with the issue of sampling and fair use much more favorably than they do now.

I suspect that as result of widespread fair use awareness among sample-based beatmakers, the sample clearance system would be tame by today's standard. Although it didn't happen in the past two decades, there's no reason that it can't happen now.

This is why I urge sample-based beatmakers to learn about fair use, to understand its nuances, and to uphold its importance in culture and society. Moreover, I urge sample-based beatmakers to regularly use fair use as a guiding factor in their creativity. Naturally, if you aim to sample reasonably small portions of sound recordings, and aim to be substantially transformative with your uses, then fair use will likely always be on your side. *So you should, therefore, proceed like it is on your side!* This means putting your art first. It means making creativity a priority and being guided by your creative convictions. It means understanding hip hop/rap sampling's standards and best practices and working them into your approach and skill set. Of course, it also means taking the progress of the art of sampling seriously.

Finally, here's a thought. Since we know that Negativland once took on the RIAA over fair use and won, sample-based musicians should take comfort in knowing that another fair use call to arms would be even more successful. Think about it: What did it take for the RIAA to amend its CD Plant Guidelines and publicly recognize that some sampling may in fact qualify for fair use? It took a grassroots, month-long letter-writing campaign. So what would happen if there was a month-long campaign of coordinated sample-based song releases, all of which upholding the sampling tradition's best practices and standards guidelines, and all of which accompanied by a fair use open letter to the RIAA, detailing that the samples used made fair use of existing sound recordings? What a great response to the music industry's dismissive attitude towards fair use this would be, right? More importantly, what an excellent way it would be to raise the profile of fair use in the public's eye, while also promoting the progress of the art of sampling.

Chapter 11

Fair Use, the Supreme Court, and the Music Industry

What the United States Supreme Court Says About Fair Use, and the Music Industry's View of Fair Use

Fair Use in *Campbell v. Acuff-Rose*

Campbell v. Acuff-Rose was about whether 2 Live Crew's song "Pretty Woman," a parody of Roy Orbison's song "Oh, Pretty Woman," could be fair use within the meaning of the Copyright Act of 1976, 17 U. S. C. § 107. This case wasn't about sampling *per se*; but inasmuch as "Pretty Woman" is a case about fair use — it did make use of a sample of the Orbison recording — it can, nonetheless, tell us a great deal about how fair use applies to all forms of copying and copyright material in general. So notwithstanding the fact that this case centered around parody, what's most important is that the Supreme Court's opinion in *Campbell* allows us to understand a great deal about the scope of fair use.

Very few cases involving sampling have actually made it to the courts, because in most infringement suits involving sampling, claimants and alleged infringers settle out of court. So there's nothing that we can take away about fair use in those cases. But in *Campbell*, one of the biggest fair use court cases that also indirectly involved the sampling of a sound recording, the Supreme Court made a number of things clear about the four statutory factors and the purpose and scope of the fair use doctrine. But before analyzing the Supreme Court's ruling in this landmark case and what it specifically says about fair use, it's necessary to offer a quick background on the case.

Background on Campbell

In 1989, the rap group 2 Live Crew, lead by Luther Campbell AKA Luke Skyywalker, sampled and parodied the Roy Orbison song "Oh, Pretty Woman" (1964). Roy Orbison and William Dees wrote the song and assigned their rights in it to Acuff-Rose. Before releasing the song, 2 Live Crew's manager informed Acuff-Rose of the parody, expressed that they would give all credit for ownership and authorship of the original song to Acuff-Rose, Dees, and Orbison, and indicated that they were willing to pay a fee for their use of it. Acuff-Rose refused permission, stating that they would not permit the use of a parody of "Oh, Pretty Woman."

Despite this, in July of 1989, 2 Live Crew released their album *As Clean As They Wanna Be*, which contained the song "Pretty Woman," a parody of the Orbision song. The credits on the album identified the authors of "Pretty Woman" as Orbison and Dees and its publisher as Acuff-Rose. Nearly a year later, after some 250,000 copies of *As Clean As They Wanna Be* had been sold, Acuff-Rose sued 2 Live Crew and its record company, Luke Skyywalker Records, for copyright infringement.

2 Live Crew asserted that their song "Pretty Woman" made fair use of the Orbison song. The District Court (M.D. Tennessee, Nashville Division) granted summary judgment, holding that 2 Live Crew's song did make fair use of the Orbison song, emphasizing that the commercial purpose of 2 Live Crew's song did not bar it from being fair use; that, 2 Live Crew had not taken an excessive amount of the Orbison song; and that it what was "extremely unlikely that 2 Live Crew's song could adversely affect the market for the original." Weighing these factors, the District Court held that 2 Live Crew's song made fair use of Orbison's original.

The Court of Appeals (Sixth Circuit), reversed and remanded, holding that the commercial nature of the parody rendered it presumptively unfair under the first of four factors relevant under

the Copyright Act of 1976, 17 U.S.C. § 107; and that, "by taking
the 'heart' of the original and making it the 'heart' of a new work,
2 Live Crew had, qualitatively, taken too much under the third
§ 107 factor; and that market harm for purposes of the fourth §
107 factor had been established by a presumption attaching to
commercial uses."[184]   However, the Supreme Court held that a
commercial parody may qualify for fair use and reversed the Sixth
Circuit's judgment and remanded the case for further proceedings
consistent with the Supreme Court's opinion. The Supreme Court
did not, in the end, specifically rule that "Pretty Woman" was a
parody, even though the high court's analysis left no doubt that it
was.   Nonetheless, the Supreme Court left the final determination
in the hands of the District Court, which was to apply the new
ruling to the facts. But at that point, Acuff-Rose had little hope
of winning.[185]

Analysis of the Supreme Court's Opinion in Campbell: Weighing the Four Statutory Factors Together in a Fair Use Inquiry

In coming to its opinion in *Campbell*, the Supreme Court
weighed the four statutory factors together. On the first factor, "The
purpose and character of the use, including whether such use is of a
commercial nature or is for nonprofit educational purposes...," the
Supreme Court asserted that the main clause of this factor "speaks of
a broader investigation into 'purpose and character,'" and points to
the importance of transformation, not mere verbatim duplication,
and how it figures into a fair use inquiry:

> Under the first of the four § 107 factors, "the purpose and character
> of the use, including whether such use is of a commercial nature
> . . . ," **the enquiry focuses on whether the new work merely
> supersedes the objects of the original creation, or whether and to
> what extent it is "transformative," altering the original with new
> expression, meaning, or message. The more transformative the
> new work, the less will be the significance of other factors, like**

---

[184] *Campbell v. Accuff-Rose Music*, 510 U.S. 569 (1994), p569.
[185] *Id.*, p. 594.

commercialism, that may weigh against a finding of fair use....

The central purpose of this investigation is to see, in Justice Story's words, whether the new work merely "supersede[s] the objects" of the original creation...[emphasis mine][186]

Addressing the "...commercial nature or is for nonprofit educational purposes" part of the first factor, the Supreme Court emphasized that the commercial or nonprofit educational character of a work is not conclusive. In other words, if a work is for profit, it doesn't automatically disqualify it from fair use. The commercial purpose of a work does not bar it from being fair use, likewise, a nonprofit educational purpose of a work does not make it presumptively fair use:

the mere fact that a use is educational and not for profit does not insulate it from a finding of infringement, any more than the commercial character of a use bars a finding of fairness. [emphasis mine][187]

The Supreme Court further pointed out that the more transformative the new work, the less commercial character matters:

Although such transformative use is not absolutely necessary for a finding of fair use, Sony, supra, at 455, n. 40,11 **the goal of copyright, to promote science and the arts, is generally furthered by the creation of transformative works. Such works thus lie at the heart of the fair use doctrine's guarantee of breathing space within the confines of copyright,...and the more transformative the new work, the less will be the significance of other factors, like commercialism, that may weigh against a finding of fair use.** [emphasis mine][188]

Also, with regard to transformation, the Supreme Court tells us that the transformation exhibited in the new work should be something reasonably perceived by the courts. In its inquiry of 2 Live Crew's parody, the Supreme Court reasonably distinguished the

---

[186] *Id.*, 569. 579.
[187] *Id.*, 584.
[188] *Id.*, 579.

differences between the Orbison original and 2 Live Crew's parody:

> **...we think it fair to say that 2 Live Crew's song reasonably could be perceived as commenting on the original or criticizing it, to some degree.** 2 Live Crew juxtaposes the romantic musings of a man whose fantasy comes true, with degrading taunts, a bawdy demand for sex, and a sigh of relief from paternal responsibility. The later words can be taken as a comment on the naivete´ of the original of an earlier day, as a rejection of its sentiment that ignores the ugliness of street life and the debasement that it signifies. It is this joinder of reference and ridicule that marks off the author's choice of parody from the other types of comment and criticism that traditionally have had a claim to fair use protection as transformative works. [emphasis mine][189]

On the second factor, "The nature of the copyrighted work," the Supreme Court adds no further clarity, stating simply that:

> This factor calls for recognition that some works are closer to the core of intended copyright protection than others, with the consequence that fair use is more difficult to establish when the former works are copied. See, e. g., Stewart v. Abend, 495 U. S., at 237–238 (contrasting fictional short story with factual works)...[190]

Regarding the third factor, "the amount and substantiality of the portion used in relation to the copyrighted work as a whole," the Supreme Court reminds us that this factor was born from Justice Story:

> ...the **quantity and value of the materials used**," Folsom v. Marsh, supra, at 348) **are reasonable in relation to the purpose of the copying**. [emphasis mine][191]

Also in its inquiry of the third factor, the Supreme Court asserted that the question isn't merely about the amount copied (borrowed), but the substantiality, quality, and importance of the portion copied; and that the transformative character or purpose of the first factor comes back into play if there is no transformation

---

[189] *Id.*, 583.
[190] *Id.*, 586.
[191] *Id.*, 586.

but instead a verbatim copy of a substantial portion of the original:

> this factor calls for thought not only about the quantity of the materials used, but about their quality and importance, too.
>
> ...whether **"a substantial portion of the infringing work was copied verbatim" from the copyrighted work is a relevant question...for it may reveal a dearth [lack of] of transformative character or purpose under the first factor, or a greater likelihood of market harm under the fourth;...**
>
> ...a work composed primarily of an original, particularly its heart, **with little added or changed, is more likely to be a merely superseding use, fulfilling demand for the original.** [emphasis mine][192]

In further explaining how transformation and the purpose and character figures into the third factor inquiry in Campbell, the Supreme Court pointed out that:

> Even if 2 Live Crew's copying of the original's first line of lyrics and characteristic opening bass riff may be said to go to the original's "heart," that heart is what most readily conjures up the song for parody, and it is the heart at which parody takes aim. **Moreover, 2 Live Crew thereafter departed markedly from the Orbison lyrics and produced otherwise distinctive music.**
>
> **we recognize that the extent of permissible copying varies with the purpose and character of the use**....The facts bearing on this factor will also tend to address the fourth, by revealing the degree to which the parody may serve as a market substitute for the original or potentially licensed derivatives. [emphasis mine][193]

Finally, regarding the fourth factor, "The effect of the use upon the potential market for or value of the copyrighted work," the Supreme Court emphasized that commercial gain does not presumably constitute market harm. Thus, the high court reaffirmed that a work for commercial gain does not bar a work from fair use protection, just as a work for nonprofit does not presumably make

---

[192] *Id.*, 587-88.
[193] *Id.*, 570, 586-87.

a work fair. For example, a free mixtape doesn't presumably mean that the use of samples on said mixtape are fair use. All factors must be weighed together in such an occurrence. But the verbatim duplication of a work does not favor a fair use finding. Therefore, a mixtape that uses the entire — unchanged — copyrighted song or beat of another recording artist tips the scale away from being a fair use. A beat that is *copied in verbatim* can be seen as a market substitute for the original. (Incidentally, this is why Mac Miller's verbatim use of Lord Finesse's beat for "Hip 2 Da Game" [1995] on Miller's "Kool Aid and Frozen Pizza" [2010] is not a fair use.)

So the question is, in the context of this factor: What is the likelihood that the new work will act as a substitute for the original that it sampled? If the sample (copying) is minimal and the use transformative, there is less of a chance that the new work will act as a substitute for the original. But if the copying is substantial and not reasonably transformative, then there's a better chance that the new work can act as a substitute for the original. Simply put, mere duplication for commercial purposes does not favor fair use:

> **The Court of Appeals erred in resolving the fourth § 107 factor, "the effect of the use upon the potential market for or value of the copyrighted work," by presuming...the likelihood of significant market harm based on 2 Live Crew's use for commercial gain. No "presumption" or inference of market harm...involving something beyond mere duplication for commercial purposes. The cognizable harm is market substitution, not any harm from criticism.** As to parody pure and simple, it is unlikely that the work will act as a substitute for the original, since the two works usually serve different market functions. The fourth factor requires courts also to consider the potential market for derivative works...If the later work has cognizable substitution effects in protectible markets for derivative works, the law will look beyond the criticism to the work's other elements. [emphasis mine][194]

Regarding verbatim copying of the original in its entirety, digital sampling never involves verbatim copying of a sound recording in its entirety. Although some forms of sampling may copy verbatim the heart of a recording, such instances are still distinguished by

---

[194] *Id.*, 571.

the amount and level of transformation. For example, sampling a portion of The Police's hit song "Every Breath You Take" and chopping it up, transforming it beyond recognition, is one thing. But sampling the heart of "Every Breath You Take" and doing an interpolation of it, or essentially something very close to a rap *version* of it with different lyrics, is another thing altogether. The more transformation, the less likely the new work to be seen as a market substitution for the original and, therefore, the less likely market harm to the original.

Furthermore, with regards to market harm to derivative works, the Supreme Court was not referring to "derivative works" in the sense of beats made using samples (snippets, phrases from recordings), but rather the high court was referencing genre versions (of the complete song), like a country music or rap version of "Oh, Pretty Woman.":

> 2 Live Crew's song comprises not only parody but also rap music, and the derivative market for rap music is a proper focus of enquiry, ...**the likely effect of 2 Live Crew's parodic rap song on the market for a nonparody, rap *version* of "Oh, Pretty Woman.**" [emphasis mine][195]

Thus, here, the Supreme Court was not referring to the harm of a sample licensing market. All samples are not presumably unfair, and therefore, all samples do not require permission or licensing.

What the Supreme Court Reaffirmed and Made Clear About a Fair Use Inquiry; Promoting the Purpose of Copyright Law and the Principal of Fairness a Top Concern

In its opinion in *Campbell*, the Supreme Court didn't merely express why 2 Live's Crew parody of Roy Orbison's "Oh, Pretty Woman" may be fair use or why a commercial parody (or other work) could quality for fair use, it took the opportunity to reaffirm

---

[195] *Id.*, 571, 593.

much more. First, the Supreme Court demonstrated how fair use is properly determined in accordance with the statute and common case law, i.e. the judge-made fair use doctrine, for which the statute was based on. The Supreme Court explained that the four statutory factors must be "explored and weighed together in light of copyright's purpose of promoting science and the arts," and that the four statutory factors could not be treated in isolation, one from another. All are to be explored, and the results weighed together, not in the light of equity or what's presumably fair to the copyright owner or alleged infringer, but rather in light of the purposes of copyright."[196]

Also, the Supreme Court emphasized that a fair use analysis should "avoid rigid application of the copyright statute when, on occasion, it would stifle the very creativity which that law is designed to foster." Further, the high court added that there could be no bright-line rules in the analysis, as Congress had "resisted attempts to narrow the ambit of this traditional enquiry by adopting categories of presumptively fair use, and it urged courts to preserve the breadth of their traditionally ample view of the universe of relevant evidence." The Supreme Court asserted that this was why "Congress had 'eschewed a rigid, bright-line approach to fair use."[197] Thus, the Supreme Court maintained that "the task is not to be simplified with bright-line rules, for the statute, like the doctrine it recognizes, calls for case-by-case analysis." For as the high court pointed out, Congress intended that fair use, as codified in the Copyright Act, remain within the spectrum of the judge-made doctrine from which it came:

> Congress meant § 107 "to restate the present judicial doctrine of fair use, not to change, narrow, or enlarge it in any way" and intended that courts continue the common-law tradition of fair use adjudication.[198]

The goals (objectives) of copyright law was another theme stressed by the Supreme Court in *Campbell*. Throughout its

---

[196] *Id.*, 569, 578.
[197] *Id.*, 584.
[198] *Id.*, 577. Also see H. Rpt. 94-1476.

opinion, the high court advised that courts keep in mind the goals of copyright law when conducting a fair use inquiry, reminding us that, because the fair use inquiry often requires "close questions of judgment," the goals of the copyright law, i.e. to promote the progress of science and the arts, should underscore the inquiry:

> Because the fair use enquiry often requires close questions of judgment as to the extent of permissible borrowing in cases involving parodies (or other critical works), courts may also wish to bear in mind that the goals of the copyright law, "to stimulate the creation and publication of edifying matter, are not always best served by automatically granting injunctive relief...
>
> See 17 U. S. C. § 502(a) (court "may . . . grant . . .injunctions on such terms as it may deem reasonable to prevent or restrain infringement"); Leval 1132 (while in the "vast majority of cases, [an injunctive] remedy is justified because most infringements are simple piracy," such cases are "worlds apart from many of those raising reasonable contentions of fair use" where "there may be a strong public interest in the publication of the secondary work......[199]

Thus, the Supreme Court strongly reaffirmed that the goal of any fair use inquiry is, ultimately, to serve the fundamental purpose of copyright law, not the copyright owner of the work copied or the copier who may have made fair use of the original.

Overall, what's perhaps most telling about the Supreme Court's unanimous decision in *Campbell* is not just its reaffirmation of the purpose of copyright law, but its strong reminder of the necessity, value, and purpose of fair use:

> **From the infancy of copyright protection, some opportunity for fair use of copyrighted materials has been thought necessary to fulfill copyright's very purpose, "[t]o promote the Progress of Science and useful Arts . . . ." U. S. Const., Art. I, § 8, cl. 8.5** For as Justice Story explained, "[i]n truth, in literature, in science and in art, there are, and can be, few, if any, things, which in an abstract sense, are strictly new and original throughout. Every book in literature, science and art, borrows, and must necessarily borrow,

---

[199] *Id.*, 578.

and use much which was well known and used before."[200]

Continuing, the high court expressly made clear that fair use is a "guarantee" to the public, not merely an affirmative defense to a copyright infringement claim:

> ...the fair use doctrine's guarantee of breathing space within the confines of copyright... [emphasis mine][201]

What Does the Supreme Court's Opinion in *Campbell* Tell Us About Fair Use and Sampling?

Again, *Campbell* was about whether 2 Live Crew's song "Pretty Woman," a parody of Roy Orbison's song "Oh, Pretty Woman," could be fair use within the meaning of the Copyright Act of 1976, 17 U. S. C. § 107. This case wasn't about sampling *per se*; but inasmuch as "Pretty Woman" did make use of a sample of the Orbison recording, it can, nonetheless, tell us a number of things about how fair use applies to sampling.

First, it's worth noting that the Supreme Court did not claim that the fair use doctrine does not apply to sound recordings; nor did the high court imply that sampling is presumptively barred from a fair use inquiry. In fact, the high court explained that the language Congress used in its report accompanying the Copyright Act of 1976 indicates no limitation on the sorts of copying that courts may consider in a fair use inquiry:

> Senate Report, p. 62. The text employs the terms "including" and "such as" in the preamble paragraph to indicate the "illustrative and not limitative" function of the examples given, § 101;..., which thus provide only general guidance about the sorts of copying that courts and Congress most commonly had found to be fair uses. [emphasis mine][202]

Thus, Congress gave illustrative examples, but purposely did not limit the sorts of copying that fair use may apply to. In other

---

[200] *Id.*, 575.
[201] *Id.*, 579.
[202] *Id.*, 577.

words, Congress intended for the sorts of copying that qualified for fair use to be broad and non-exhaustive:

> In determining whether the use made of a work **in *any* particular case** is a fair use the factors to be considered shall include—... [emphasis mine][203]

An opposite reading of what Congress intended, that is, an interpretation that Congress intended to *exclude* sound recordings or "any particular case" from fair use, runs counter to the purpose of copyright law. Further, in Campbell, the Supreme Court indirectly acknowledged sampling as a legitimate form of copying:

> **2 Live Crew copied the characteristic opening bass riff (or musical phrase) of the original [recording],** and true that the words of the first line copy the Orbison lyrics. **But if quotation of the opening riff and the first line may be said to go to the "heart" of the original, the heart is also what most readily conjures up the song for parody, and it is the heart at which parody takes aim.** [emphasis mine][204]

This speaks to the point that quoting (sampling) sound recordings is one of the types of copying that fair use applies to. But like all types of copying, it must work its way through all four factors of analysis with the purpose of copyright at the heart of any inquiry. The Supreme Court continued:

> **2 Live Crew not only copied the bass riff and repeated it, but also produced otherwise distinctive sounds, interposing "scraper" noise, overlaying the music with solos in different keys, and altering the drum beat. See 754 F. Supp., at 1155. This is not a case, then, where "a substantial portion" of the parody itself is composed of a "verbatim" copying of the original."** [emphasis

---

[203] *Id.*, 577.
[204] *Id.*, 588.

mine][205]

Here, the Supreme Court recognized that although the bass riff was copied and repeated, it was combined with other distinctive sounds and an original drum beat. Thus, the high court made it clear that the transformative nature of the copied (sampled) recording, rather than *verbatim copying* of the original in its entirety, meant that the use in this instance tipped the scales towards fair use.

Finally, by expressing no opinion on whether the music copied and used by 2 Live Crew was an "excessive copying," and remanding this question to the lower courts for evaluation of the amount taken, the Supreme Court signaled that fair use obviously applies to sound recordings, insofar as the high Court pointed out that the question of whether the "bass riff" sampled from the Orbison recording and repeated was excessive or not, as opposed to the question of whether a sound recording may qualify as fair use.

Thus, the Supreme Court reaffirmed that not only does fair use apply to sound recordings — just as with other copyrighted material[206] — but also that sampling a sound recording isn't presumptively excessive because a sample is repeated in the new work. (A decade after *Campbell,* The Sixth Circuit would assert the exact opposite in *Bridgeport.*) This further indicates that like other uses, when the sampling has allegedly infringed a copyrighted work, the use, i.e. instance of sampling, has to work its way through the relevant factors of a fair use inquiry.

---

[205] *Id.*, 589. A note on repetition: Repetition is a cornerstone of groove-based music; it's invaluable to the entire art form. Without repetition, there is no beat. Therefore, repetition, in and of itself, can not be considered excessive copying when the copy is an small/insubstantial portion of the original. If a poet copies a line from another poet and repeats this one line at the beginning of 12 different stanzas, each with new and original lines following it, is it reasonable to consider the use of the copied line excessive copying?

[206] H.R. Rep. No. 92-487, at 10 (1971), reprinted in 1971 U.S.C.C.A.N. 1566, 1572: **"In approving the creation of a limited copyright in sound recordings it is the intention of the Committee that this limited copyright not grant any broader rights than are accorded to other copyright proprietors under the existing title17**.

Fair Use and the Music Industry

With regards to fair use and the music industry, particularly as it pertains to sampling, there has been a huge disconnect between what fair use actually is — i.e. its fundamental purpose and what it was intended to protect— and what most music professionals commonly maintain that it is. Since the RIAA's kerfuffle with the music sampling group Negativland (I cover the incident later in this chapter), one might say that the music industry's official position on fair use and sampling is that some forms of sampling may in fact qualify for fair use. Nonetheless, this isn't the de facto position held by most in the music industry.

Since the early 1990s, the music industry has largely taken a "better safe then sorry" stance on sample licensing, mainly out of fear of copyright infringement suits. This means that common industry practice and philosophy has evolved to a position of "clear everything" whether it could be considered fair use or not. The problem with this stance, one that presumably does not allow room for the fact that some instances of sampling may qualify as fair use, is that it erodes the perception, meaning, and purpose of the fair use doctrine and copyright itself. Further, after *Grand Upright Music v. Warner Bros. Records* (the seminal sampling case involving Biz Markie's sampling of Gilbert O'Sullivan's "Alone Again Naturally; a case that I cover in greater detail in chapter 10) and especially *Bridgeport* (also covered in chapter 11), the music industry adopted an excessively conservative stance on sample clearance, and the perception of fair use further suffered in its wake.

The commonly held view of fair use by music industry lawyers and executives is that fair use is only an affirmative defense to a copyright infringement suit. Dina LaPolt, one of the most well known and respected lawyers in the music business (purportedly, she was voted the #1 music business attorney in 2011 by her peers), says that "Fair use is a misnomer. People start screaming, 'Fair use, fair use, fair use,' but *it's just a defense*, which means you have to defend it." Further demonstrating an astonishingly hostile view of fair use and a complete lack of sensitivity for — or understanding of — the objectives of copyright, she adds: "*It's a useless part of the Copyright Act. It should be just deleted.* No one gets it."[207] And in a 2007 interview at Loyola University (New Orleans), LaPolt delivered a condemnation of another area of copyright law: sound recording royalties. But she also gave a telling closeup of how the music industry has long subverted copyright law through their own "industry custom" when she said: "We have the laws, and then we have what we call 'industry custom'... **We get stuck with these laws made by the blowbags in Congress, who don't have a shit's idea what the fuck we do for a living. So they make these laws and we have to live with this crap. So they make these laws, then we turnaround — those that run the music industry — and we make up our own crap, and do what we think is right. Which is called 'industry custom.'**"[208]

Tim Quirk, another music industry insider who spoke with the authors of *Creative License*, echoed LaPolt when he said: "You ask a lawyer for a record company, which I have done — if you ask Cary Sherman, head of the RIAA {Recording Industry Association of America} — he will look at you in the eye and say, 'There is no such thing as fair use.' He will actually say that. And he will say, 'It is nothing but a negative defense to a copyright infringement claim. It doesn't exist absent a claim that you've done something wrong.'"

Such statements by LaPolt and Quirk demonstrate the music industry's hostility towards fair use. More importantly, their statements are in direct odds both with what the Copyright Act actually states and represents and what the Supreme Court strongly reaffirms about fair use in *Campbell*. The authors of *Creative License* acknowledged that "Many of those whom we interviewed between 2005 and 2008 exhibited ignorance or indifference toward this legal doctrine [fair use]."[209] This echoes my own findings, as I received the same responses from other music industry insiders as well. But what was more alarming to me was the fact that all of the beatmakers

---

[207] Kembrew McLeod and Peter DiCola, *Creative License: The Law and Culture of Digital Sampling* , (Duke University Press Books, 2011), 238, 240 (emphasis mine).
[208] "Loyola University Forum with Music Lawyer Dina LaPolt , 2007," Artists House Music (2012) http://www.youtube.com/watch?v=umonWhEdzlw, accessed June, 2012 (emphasis mine).
[209] McLeod and DiCola, 239-40.

that I interviewed acknowledged that they either knew very little or nothing at all about fair use — and several admitted that they have never even heard of fair use.

LaPolt did not mention fair use in her interview at Loyola University, nevertheless, her explanation of industry custom, proves that the music industry has established a custom of willingly subverting copyright law, especially when doing so serves their best interest. So it's easy to see how the music industry's top lawyer could so cavalierly dismiss fair use as a "useless part of the Copyright Act" that should be "deleted." To those "who run the music industry," fair use — a vital part of copyright law — is an inconvenient truth that they'd prefer to ignore, misrepresent, or purposely remain ignorant about, especially when it comes to sampling.

Of course, Ms. LaPolt and other music insiders are wrong about fair use, particularly their interpretation of it as *just a defense.* So I would ask Ms. LaPolt, is fair use really a misnomer? I would also ask her does the copyright statute, or the report Congress provided along with it, describe fair use exclusively as just a defense? I would further like to ask her, if fair use is just a defense, then why hasn't Girl Talk, someone notoriously known for sampling hundreds of recordings for the making of his albums, and someone who openly states that he considers his appropriations to be protected under fair use, been hit with an infringement claim yet? Could it be that the music industry does not want the spotlight on the facts of fair use?

Negativland Takes on the RIAA: What Does the Music Industry Officially Say About Fair Use and Sampling?

While a number of music lawyers and insiders degrade fair use, it's worth looking at what the RIAA (Recording Industry Association of America), the lobbying and enforcement arm of the Big Five multi-national entertainment companies (Sony, Time-Warner, Universal/Polygram, BMG, and EMI), officially said about fair use and sampling back in 1998.

In 1998, Negativland, a self-described experimental-music and art collective of sound collagists (sampling musicians), ran into a problem when they tried to press their CD *Over the Edge Volume 3*. Distronics, the pressing plant which they had used for four years, refused to press their CD and demanded that "Negativland provide proof that the samples on their new CD had been cleared and paid for." The plant's demands and refusal to press Negativland's CD were a direct response to the RIAA's then-recent guidelines issued to CD plants (guidelines purportedly aimed at stemming piracy) that made it clear that pressing plants are liable for infringing material, and could be fined up to $100,000 per infraction. Negativland pushed back and responded to the RIAA's guidelines with a sharply direct and legally persuasive press release entitled, "DO WE REALLY HAVE TO SUE THE RIAA????" In the press release, which threatened legal action against the RIAA, Negativland expressed deep concerns over the RIAA's attempt, via it's CD plant guidelines, to prevent the art of sampling and subvert the purpose of copyright law:

> We are now faced with the very real situation that the ENTIRE corporate music industry (via the RIAA) is **preventing an ENTIRE aesthetic, completely circumventing our legal system, and keeping the raging debate over the re-use of our common culture from ever reaching a public or legal forum.** The original intent of copyright law was to promote a public good, not a private one and no matter how valid the original intent of our nations copyright laws may have been, they are now clearly being subverted. [emphasis in the original]

> …This is now about the entire corporate music industry preventing an entire legitimate aesthetic…, completely circumventing our legal system, and keeping this raging debate over the re-use of our culture from ever reaching a public or legal forum.

> …via the RIAA, the Big Five have discovered an effective end run around the "art" barrier that prevented their omnipotent control over ALL possible uses of their very public private property. Intimidating the CD pressing plants into filtering out any and all unpaid uses prevents ANY appearance of this type of material in the marketplace which has not been cleared and paid for.

> …Anyone who can still discern a difference between art and

commerce knows that the RIAA's actions will even further reduce any form of sampling or sound collage work because artists both outside and inside corporations, or out on culture's fringe, will simply not be able to afford the going rates charged for using this stuff. Or they will be refused outright because their use annoys the sample owner. EVERY USE will be scrutinized and runs the risk of being censored prior to its coming into existence for whatever reasons might enter the unknown mind of the person listening at the pressing plant (!) who will be initially monitoring this.

…do you want to see a situation in which transnational corporations are telling manufacturers to decide what is and is not acceptable art?

…NO ONE SHOULD BE ALLOWED TO CLAIM PRIVATE CONTROL OVER THE CREATIVE PROCESS ITSELF. [emphasis in the original][210]

Negativland also used their now infamous press release to draw public attention to the difference between piracy and sampling (a form of sound collage), and the music industry's attempt to criminalize this well-known art form:

the **crucial difference between pirating or counterfeiting anothers work straight across in order to profit from the saleability of that single source, and the creative transformation of material from multiple sources into new, "original" works.** This is known in the art world as COLLAGE and it has had an undisputed legitimacy in virtually all art forms since the turn of this century. However, the owners and operators of mass marketed music, being the latest medium in which collage is being practiced, continue to naively attempt to criminalize the technique of audio collage as if it was an illegitimate intruder on originality and nothing more than a form of theft. [emphasis in the original][211]

Negativland further included a summary of the contact that they had with the RIAA prior to their initial press release:

Negativland's Mark Hosler spoke to Matt Oppenheim of the RIAA about this. Mr. Oppenheim is one of the RIAA's civil litigation

[210] "DO WE REALLY HAVE TO SUE THE RIAA????" http://www.negativland.com/archives/014riaa/, (Accessed March, 2012).
[211] *Ibid.*

attorneys and handles lawsuits against CD pressing plants. He told Mark that "the RIAA does not tell plants one way or the other what they should or should not do, but we do advise plants that they are liable if they press infringing material." So, the "experts" of the RIAA issue specific guidelines to the plants, tell plants that they could be liable for up to $100,00 per unpaid and uncleared sample infraction, consider this to be "not telling the plants one way or the other what they should or should not do" and fail to help the CD replicators distinguish between the proper and improper use of copyrighted materials.

The RIAA's position is that it's ALL copyright infringement without any room for protected speech. The CD plants are not informed that copyright law specifically permits the fair use of copyrighted material in certain circumstances and, in cases of sampling, the plants are put into the untenable position of having to act as judge and jury on all incoming releases.
In determining whether the use made of a work **in *any* particular case** is a fair use the factors to be considered shall include—... [emphasis mine]

In the rest of the half-hour long conversation with Matt Oppenheim of the RIAA, Negativland's Mark Hosler tried to describe the troubling situation that Negativland was in…Mark told him that they had taken the "offending" release to four different CD pressing plants and been turned down by them all and Mr. Oppenheim replied "Well, that tells me that we are doing our job." He then said, "This should tell you that you need to try and get this sample cleared." When Mark tried to explain that he felt that his transformative re-use of copyrighted material for parody, critical or other creative purposes was a fair use, the conversation took a nose dive. The idea that anyone could suggest that there was any possible conceivable instance in which re-using a fragment of someone else's material could be done WITHOUT getting permission and WITHOUT paying sampling clearance fees was obviously totally insane to Mr. Oppenheim. "Are you a lawyer?!," he demanded to know. "Because fair use is not a right, it's a defense!"

Clearly, the RIAA believes that their interpretation of copyright and fair use is the ONLY interpretation, and are not interested in any other point of view. Fair use IS raised as a defense when one is involved in a lawsuit for copyright infringement, but it is also one of the MAJOR EXCEPTIONS to a copyright owners exclusive monopoly of a copyrighted work….and if fair use is seen ONLY as an affirmative defense, then this interpretation of fair use creates a situation in which prior restraint and self-censorship is inevitable. When Mark suggested that what the RIAA was engaged in DID amount to an act of censorship, Mr. Oppenheim became furious. "You are making this into a political issue and accusing us of being censors!" When Mark suggested that if the RIAA could not be reasoned with, then perhaps the only thing to do was to sue the RIAA, Mr. Oppenheim hung up the phone. [emphasis in the original][212]

In addition to expressing deep concern over the RIAA's attempt to prevent the art of sampling, subvert the purpose of copyright law, and circumvent the legal system, Negativland also raised the question of whether or not the RIAA's actions, i.e. the guidelines that were "intimidating" pressing plants into not pressing CDs that contained uncleared samples on them, were, in fact, prompting CD plants to break the law. Moreover, Negativland asserted that the RIAA may have exposed itself to "Constitutional liability," and pointed out that they may be on the hook for restraint of trade, and added that their actions amounted to pre-emptive censorship:

> ...the RIAA is tarring sampling and audio collage with the same pirate brush. Negativland's CD plant was not interested in the fact that Negativland knew that their transformative re-use of the sampled material was a fair use under copyright law or that Negativland was quite willing to defend this re-use as a fair use in a court of law. They did not care that Negativland had already indemnified them or that their refusal to press the CD because of fear of the RIAA could be seen as being what is legally known as "prior restraint" and therefore illegal...Once the plants are put on notice that a particular action (like pressing a Negativland CD) is potentially infringing, they are at risk of being held liable for what is legally known as "contributory infringement". Most plants are entirely dependent on the members of the RIAA for their livelihood and dare not cross them even in the face of outrageous and oppressive behavior.

> ...a system of 'prior restraint' is any scheme which denies use of a forum in advance of its publication. The First Amendment prohibits the imposition of a restraint on a publication before it is

---

[212] *Ibid.*

published without there first being a judicial determination that the material does not qualify for First Amendment protection. Prior restraints on speech and publication are the most serious and least tolerable infringement on First Amendment rights." And The Oxford Companion To The Supreme Court Of The United States says "The prohibition on prior restraints on speech or press lies at the very core of the First Amendment....prior restraint has been equated with censorship.

...efforts to suppress the manufacture of works protected as fair use under copyright law may constitute prior restraint. (See Supreme Court Reaffirms Rejection Of Prior Restraints in CBS Inc. v. Davis, ___ U.S. ___, 114 S. Ct. 912, 127 L. Ed. 2d 358, 22 Med. L. Rptr. 1285 [1994] Justice Blackmun...).

the RIAA, by actively policing federal copyright laws on behalf of its members, is performing a governmental function, and this may expose them to constitutional liability.

In a claim of constitutional liability against the RIAA, the Courts would examine the extent to which the RIAA works with the government. Although the RIAA itself is not a governmental entity, the RIAA has, for almost 30 years, worked in tandem with law enforcement on all levels, including training and education of law enforcement personnel, supplying expert witnesses, and the preparation of legal briefs for the government to use in the prosecution of pirated recordings. This long- standing symbiotic relationship with the government, in addition to the RIAA's independent efforts to police federal copyright laws on behalf of its corporate members, opens up the RIAA to liability for constitutional violations arising from its activities.

"the actions of the RIAA may also constitute unlawful restraint of trade and interference with business and contractual relations." The RIAA heavily lobbies state and federal officials on behalf of corporate monopolies that control 90% of all recorded music in this country and thus the RIAA's abilities to suppress the manufacture and distribution of material it does not approve of is enormous.

The actions of the RIAA are an act of pre-emptive censorship. They deny musicians, record labels and music publishers the opportunity to work out issues of fair use in a court of law and create a situation in which, if they successfully intimidate both large and small CD pressing plants all over the U.S., Negativland and many others will no longer be able to press ANY of their current, future or past CD's. A truly disturbing scenario.

In effect, the RIAA is attempting to strong-arm manufacturers into seeing the issue from only its perspective, without technically violating any laws. [emphasis in the original][213]

Negativland ended its press release by calling for help from the public and launching a letter-writing (email) campaign:

This issue is far too big for Negativland to take on alone…we need someone to organize and keep track of all those folks out their who are concerned and outraged about this. Perhaps the RIAA can be reasoned with to re-think their tactics…

Music producers and consumers might need to consider organizing to bring a class action suit against the RIAA that allows them to CONTINUE their efforts to stop piracy and counterfeiting and bootlegging, but STOPS them from interfering with sampling, STOPS them from interfering with the re-use of our common culture and STOPS THEM from blocking the fair use rights the U.S. Copyright Act gives every citizen and creator. The RIAA has no business being art police.

If you are a lawyer, a label, a musician, an artist, a CD broker, a CD replicator, a writer…anybody who feels as freaked out about the implications of this as Negativland does, please add your name to our announce list (see below) to be kept informed about what happens next and how you can help….and please talk to each other and PLEASE write a thoughtful letter to the RIAA.[214]

On August 20, 1998, three days after Negativland sent its press release, the RIAA responded. Hilary Rosen, then-president and CEO of the RIAA, denied that the RIAA had any involvement with Negativland's CD *Over the Edge, Volume 3* or its prevention from being pressed. She further asserted that the guidelines issued by the RIAA to record plants were "part of its longstanding efforts to eradicate music piracy," simply "an attempt to curtail the burgeoning piracy problem that begins at the plant level." She was

---

[213] *Ibid.*
[214] *Ibid.*

careful to further add that the RIAA CD Plant Guidelines did not "mention, or make any recommendations about the use of samples in sound recordings." This was the RIAA's indirect, legalese-style denial that their CD Plant Guidelines (1) had anything to do with Negativland not being able to get its CD pressed, or (2) that they were in any way intended to curb sampling.[215]

Three days after Rosen's/RIAA's statement, Negativland responded with another press release. This time, Negativland called Rosen out for what they described as her "sadly disingenuous denial of the actual effect" RIAA guidelines "are having out here in the real world," and further added that they had talked to pressing plants and RIAA employees, "and BOTH made it clear that un-cleared samples are included in your guidelines." Negativland also sought to draw Rosen's attention to the difference between piracy and fair use appropriations, pointing out that fair use was a right, and thus, fair issues were not for the RIAA to decide. Finally, Negativland again reminded Rosen that the RIAA's actions suggested prior restraint and censorship.[216]

On September 1, 1998, less than a month after Negativland's initial press release, the RIAA announced that it had amended its CD Plant Guidelines. In a letter addressed to "Fans of Negativland," re: "Sampling and CD Plant Guidelines," Rosen conceded that "The courts, and not the RIAA, have always been the judge in determining whether any particular sample is fair use." Additionally, Rosen reprinted the amended CD Plant Guidelines, which included the new language directly addressing sampling and fair use:

> These guidelines are intended to address piracy. Some recordings presented for manufacture may contain -- as part of an artist's work -- identifiable "samples" or small pieces of other artists' well-known songs. **In some instances this sampling may qualify as "fair use" under copyright law,** and in other instances it may constitute copyright infringement. There are no hard and fast rules in this area and judgments on both "fair use" and indemnification must

---

[215] "Statement By the Recording Industry of America" http://www.negativland.com/archives/014riaa/riaa_statement_082298.html, (Accessed March, 2012).
[216] *Ibid.*

be made on a case-by-case basis.[217]

So What Does Negativland's Dealings with the RIAA Tell Us?

The major record companies largely ignore and misrepresent fair use in daily practice, but in its 1998 CD Plant Guidelines, the RIAA officially recognized what had always been true: that the sampling of sound recordings (one form of copying and one type of copyrightable material out of many) may qualify for fair use. What's with the contradiction? On the surface, it would appear that the recording industry respects (or at least acknowledges) fair use. But if we take seriously the RIAA's initial 1998 CD Plant Guidelines and their subsequent tactical denial that those guidelines did not have anything to do with thwarting sampling, even though they clearly linked any uncleared sampling to piracy, what are we to believe? Add to this equation one of the music industry's top lawyer's outrageous statement on fair use: *"It's a useless part of the Copyright Act. It should be just deleted,"* and what becomes apparent is that the "big labels hate the concept of fair use."[218]

Furthermore, while most sampling musicians who operate under the protection of fair use are ready and willing to defend their art in court, the big labels and music publishers do not want a showdown in court over the issue of fair use. The music industry isn't interested in opening Pandora's box on fair use and sampling. If many sample-based musicians prevailed in the courts on the basis of fair use, which I'm sure the major labels know is more than likely, this could mean a substantial loss in revenue for the labels in the realm of sampling (and perhaps even sync licensing). Sample clearance would be weakened and changed for ever. Most importantly, a showdown in court over fair use would end the non-factual notion that every sample used has to be cleared. Thus, the music industry is much more comfortable with misrepresenting

---

[217] "RIAA RESPONDS POSITIVELY TO NEGATIVLAND" http://www.negativland.com/archives/014riaa/positiv.html, (Accessed March, 2012).

[218] See "RIAA Thinking Of Backing Righthaven" http://www.techdirt.com/articles/20111118/11374416816/riaa-thinking-backing-righthaven.shtml, (Accessed May, 2012).

fair use and keeping it out of the scope of artists and the general public.

Chapter 12

The Sample Clearance System

How the Sample Clearance System was Born, What it Looks Like Today, and the Climate of Sampling in the Music Industry

The Beginning of the End of the "Wild West" Era of Sampling

Before hip hip/rap music made its way on to the music industry's radar, it was largely considered a fad. Never mind the runaway success of the Sugar Hill Gang's smash hit "Rapper's Delight," or the promise of Afrika Bambatta's "Planet Rock" and Run-DMC's "Sucker M.C.s;" the music industry just didn't get hip hop/rap in the beginning. On one hand, the major labels didn't consider hip hop/rap to be a viable money maker, so the majors weren't interested in backing it. On the other hand, hip hop/rap was made mostly using methods and styles that the industry wasn't entirely familiar with, so the labels were slow to invest in something that they couldn't quite understand or market. Even as hip hop/rap's profile continued to grow in the late 1980s (in spite of the big labels' initial ambivalence), sampling, the main compositional technique in hip hop/rap at the time, was still something that the major record companies were not accustomed to.

But familiarity matters little when money's being left on the table. Thus, the rise of hip hop/rap music inevitably brought with it the interest of the major record companies. As the success of hip hop/rap grew, driven in large part by sample-based records, the profile of sampling — the music technique that was integral to this success — gained new attention as well. Once major record labels, music publishers, copyright aggregators, and sampled recording artists took note of the success of sample-based music and saw that there was perhaps big money to be made in it, litigation inevitably followed. Soon, a lawsuit neurosis began to set over sampling; and thus began the end of the era that Marley Marl and others have affectionately called the "Wild West" era of sampling. What would emerge, particularly after three high profile law suits involving sampling, was the ad hoc sample clearance system that exists today.

The Lawsuits that Ended the "Wild West": What Happened When the Sugar Hill Gang, The Beastie Boys, De La Soul, Vanilla Ice, and Biz Markie All Got Sued

The Sugar Hill Gang Gets Sued by Chic

It could be argued that the beginning of the end of the Wild West era, an era in which everybody sampled whatever they wanted without ever seeking clearance, began with a case that didn't actually involve sampling at all. The Sugar Hill Gang's seminal hit song, "Rapper's Delight" (1979), did not include a sample (as commonly assumed) of the song "Good Times" (1979) by the band Chic. Instead, "Rapper's Delight" was constructed from a re-play that was built around a verbatim cover of the signature bass line from Chic's song. Although the re-performance by the Sugar Hill Records house band nixed the need for having to get a license from the copyright holder of the master recording of "Good Times," and shielded Sugar Hill Records from an infringement claim of the master recording, Sugar Hill Records was still on the hook for the composition copyright that it didn't clear. Thus, songwriters Nile Rogers and Bernard Edwards (of Chic) sued Sugar Hill Records for copyright infringement of the composition of their song. However, before a verdict could be reached, the two parties settled out of court, with Rogers and Edwards reportedly being awarded 100% of the publishing to "Rapper's Delight."

The Sugar Hill Gang's "Rapper's Delight" was the first legal conflict to involve hip hop/rap music and the appropriation of a pre-existing sound recording. And while the "Rapper's Delight" suit may not have been the first sampling lawsuit *per se*, it did, however, foreshadow the infringement law suit/settlement pattern that would emerge around sampling beginning with The Beastie Boys in 1986.

The Beastie Boys Get Sued by Jimmy Castor

In 1986, The Beastie Boys released their debut album *License to Ill*. One song in particular, "Hold it Now Hit It," contained a brief but recognizable sample of the song "The Return of Leroy, Pt. 1" (1977) by The Jimmy Castor Bunch. Songwriter/recording artist Jimmy Castor sued The Beastie Boys and Def Jam Records for unlawful taking of his song. But the parties settled out of court, with Castor reportedly receiving a sizable fee and a percentage of the sales of *License to Ill*, which sold more than 7 million copies. Castor is widely regarded as the first performer to sue over sampling, and the suit became the first to legally document the use of the word "sampling" in music.[219]

De La Soul Gets Sued by The Turtles

In 1989, De La Soul dropped their hip hop/rap classic, *3 Feet High and Rising*. Among the many influential sample-based songs on the album was a skit, not a song, called "Transmitting Live from Mars." The skit contained a sample of the song "You Send Me" by the 1960s pop group The Turtles. The Turtles sued De La Soul and their then-label Tommy Boy Records for copyright infringement. But just as in The Beastie Boys case several years earlier, the parties settled out of court, with The Turtles receiving a rumored payment of nearly $2 million; De La Soul and various commentators have suggested that the true amount was far less. Whether the big payout was a rumor or not, the labels were certainly spooked by the lawsuit and the purported figure that *was* paid out to The Turtles.

---

[219] "Artist Interview: Adrock (Beastie Boys) Deleted Scenes," http://youtu.be/abIqkjmWW4s, (Accessed October, 2010).

Vanilla Ice Gets Sued by Queen and David Bowie

For the making of his 1990 hit song "Ice Ice Baby," Vanilla Ice used a sample — the signature bass line — of the song "Under Pressure" (1981), a collaboration by the group Queen and David Bowie. "Ice Ice Baby" made use of a slight alteration (i.e. no substantial transformation at all) of the "Under Pressure" bass line, and because of this slight alteration, Ice neither sought a license or permission for the use, nor gave credit. Queen and David Bowie saw otherwise, and sued Vanilla Ice for copyright infringement. Just as The Beastie Boys and De La Soul had done, Vanilla Ice settled out of court with Queen and David Bowie for an undisclosed amount and percentage of the publishing of the song "Ice Ice Baby."

Taken together, these four cases — each settled out of court with substantial payments and publishing concessions being made to the infringed claimants — helped create the lawsuit neurosis that hangs over the use of samples to this day. But it was the verdict in the *Grand Upright Music, Ltd. v. Warner Bros. Records Inc.* case that made the labels take a more firm "clear all samples" stance going forward.

Grand Upright, More Lawsuit Fear, and the Money in Sample Clearance

There have been a number of copyright infringement cases involving the art of sampling. But perhaps no one case has impacted the sample clearance system more than *Grand Upright v. Warner Brothers Records.* In fact, it could be said that *Grand Upright* kicked off the precarious (perhaps nefarious) practice of sample clearance.

Prior to *Grand Upright*, sample-based beatmakers presumably did not have to secure a license (clearance) from the copyright owners of the songs that they sampled. At the time, the recording industry hadn't yet recognized hip hop/rap music as a legitimate and viable money maker. Moreover, beatmakers (a rapidly emerging new category of musicians) were completely unfamiliar to the record companies. In fact, as I previously stated, before the late 1980s, the major record companies widely regarded hip hop/rap music as a fluke and a fad, a defunct sub-genre of urban music that would not survive. For some people, this sentiment ran well into the early 1990s; long after hip hop/rap had proven its commercial viability. Thus, before 1991, beatmakers sampled recordings at will, without fear of legal penalty. Subsequently, the vast amount of sampling simply went unnoticed during that era. And although there were several lawsuits involving sampling and copyright infringement that were brought, none of these cases were ever decided in court, as they were all settled out of court. However, the publicity surrounding these cases alerted older artists to the possibility of big paydays in the potential sampling licensing market. Thus, "a song that had ceased bringing in royalties decades ago could suddenly yield a big check."[220]

Grand Upright was the first copyright infringement case involving digital sampling and hip hop/rap music to make it to the courts. It was a seminal event for two reasons. First, it was one of the earliest events to legally recognize and, ironically, reinforce sampling as a much-valued and common compositional practice in the hip hop/rap tradition. Second, *Grand Upright* served as the primary catalyst for the creation of one of the most ad hoc and curious systems in the history of the recording industry: the sample clearance system.

Grand Upright Background

On November 13, 1991 in New York, songwriter/recording artist Gilbert O'Sullivan filed suit against rapper Biz Markie and his then-record label Warner Bros. Records, charging that "Alone Again," a song on Markie's *I Need A Haircut* album, contained an unauthorized "digital sample" of O'Sullivan's 1972 hit song "Alone Again (Naturally).[221] Since Biz Markie and Warner Bros. did not dispute the use of a sample of O'Sullivan's song, the actual case had

[220] Vaidhyanathan, 141.
[221] Chuck Philips, "Songwriter Wins Large Settlement in Rap Suit – Pop Music: Following a court ruling, Biz Markie and Warner Bros. agree to pay Gilbert O'Sullivan for rapper's 'sampling' of 'Alone Again (Naturally),'" *Los Angeles Times*, January, 1, 1992. Also see, *Grand Upright Music, Ltd. v. Warner Brothers Records, Inc.*, 780 F. Supp. 182 (S.D.N.Y. 1991).

more to do with the validity of the rightful copyright owner than it did with the art of sampling.

The court found that Biz Markie/Warner Bros., et. al had willfully commited copyright infringement, granted an injunction against Warner Bros. to prevent further copyright infringement of Grand Upright's song "Alone Again,"and referred the defendants for criminal prosecution. But before sentencing, the parties settled out of court for an undisclosed sum.

Key Details of Grand Upright

Rather than mount a fair use defense[222] on the grounds of de minimus use or perhaps even parody, the attorneys for Biz Markie/Warner Bros. chose two ill-fated lines of defense. Their first defense was to challenge the ownership of the copyright to O'Sullivan's song. They argued that O'Sullivan himself was not the copyright holder, and therefore, he could not seek relief from the court. This was a weak defense because Markie had sent a license request for the use of O'Sullivan's "Alone Again (Naturally)" to Grand Upright long before the suit, which would indicate that Markie knew who owned the copyright or at least who to properly contact in regards to any questions of ownership. In court, Grand Upright Music, Ltd. not only produced documentation that supported their claim of ownership, Gilbert O'Sullivan testified that he had transferred ownership to them. The other defense Markie's/Warner Bros.' attorneys mounted was a "common industry practice" defense. Essentially, they argued that because so many others in the music industry were commonly engaged in "unauthorized" sampling, they should be excused. Such a defense in itself was absurd and destined to fail. In fact, it even brought on the ire of the judge.

Right from the beginning of his opinion, Judge Kevin Thomas Duffy admonished the defendants, and set the *criminalist* tone that

---

[222] Had Warner Brothers taken this approach, it is likely that the complexion of the entire sample-clearance landscape would have been dramatically different, because perceptions about digital sampling would have been more favorable; i.e. the negative stigma of *thievery* and piracy attached to sampling would not have been given much substance.

would underscore the crux of his decision (and the perception of sampling held by some commentators to this day):

> **"Thou Shall not steal."** has been an admonition followed since the dawn of civilization. Unfortunately, in the modern world of business this admonition is not always followed. Indeed, **the defendants in this action for copyright infringement would have this court believe that stealing is rampant in the music business** and, for that reason, their conduct here should be excused. [emphasis mine] [223]

Following *Grand Upright*, the art of sampling was, in effect, criminalized and assigned a stigma of "theft" and "piracy." Judge Duffy — someone who lacked any fundamental understanding of hip hop/rap music, the art of sampling, and/or the facts and complex issues before him — believed that Biz Markie and Warner Bros. were not only guilty of copyright infringement, he believed that they were also guilty of something far worse. He writes in his opinion:

> The **conduct** of the defendants herein, however, violates not only the *Seventh Commandment*, but also the copyright laws of this country. [emphasis mine][224]

That Judge Duffy shrowded United States copyright law in a biblical context (when he linked it to "Thou shall not steal," the 8th of the 10 Commandments) perhaps gives us a window into his own biases. But whatever his motivations were, Duffy not only granted the requested injunction to Grand Upright Music, Ltd. (Gilbert O'Sullivan), he referred the matter to the U.S. Attorney for the Southern District of New York "for consideration of prosecution of these defendants under 17 U.S.C. § 506(A) AND 18 U.S.C. § 2319."[225]

In the final analysis, the court's decision raised far more questions than it answered. First, Why didn't the court engage in any substantial similarity analysis, per judicial custom in any

[223] *Grand Upright Music, Ltd. v. Warner Brothers Records, Inc.*, 780 F. Supp. 182 (S.D.N.Y. 1991) (hereafter *Grand Upright v. Warner Brothers Records*).
[224] *Grand Upright v. Warner Brothers Records.*
[225] *Id.*

copyright infringement case? Second, the critical question: To what extent, if any, may an artist digitally sample another's work without infringing the sound recording's copyright, was never asked. By not considering this critical question, a great opportunity — to at least establish some broad parameters for what constitutes a permissive or fair use level of sampling — was inherently missed. According to the music industry, it wasn't until the *Bridgeport v. Dimension Films* case, 14 years later, that the legal ambiguity of sampling would presumably receive some real level of certainty. Third, Why didn't the court inquire into what exactly sampling is? That is to say, why didn't the court use this opportunity to seek an accurate, more clear definition of the practice of sampling by qualified individuals? Certainly Biz Markie didn't *pirate* O'Sullivan's recording; he did not duplicate the song in its entirety, nor did he attempt to redistribute a verbatim copy of the song in its entirety. Thus, any definition of sampling that maintained that it was piracy was deeply inaccurate.

Then there are the questions surrounding Judge Duffy's opinion itself. Why did Duffy *criminalise* sampling, without even as much as asking for a clear definition of the practice? And why did Duffy take such a stern, personal bias against Biz Markie and Warner Bros. Records and presumably the art of sampling itself? Also, why did Duffy begin his decision with *"Thou shalt not steal,"* subsequently shrouding the rest of his opinion with religious overtones? One could ask these questions and perhaps come up with any number of reasons for Duffy's slant. Either way, as I describe in the next section, the impact of *Grand Upright* was profound.

Additional Context: The Advancement of Sampling Technology and the Courts' Struggle to Keep Up

There are two critical questions of context that I have about court decisions in a number of copyright infringement cases involving sampling. First: Why has the functionality and availability of digital audio equipment increased so dramatically in the last 15 years? Is it by mistake that digital audio equipment manufacturers are developing samplers with even more functionality? And if sampling is, in effect, "illegal" for those who can't afford exorbitant and unregulated sample clearance fees (which is virtually all common beatmakers and other musicians), then *who* exactly are the audio equipment manufacturers developing and mass marketing these samplers for and to, especially when you consider that their target market is now independent pro-consumers? The affordability and availability of high powered samplers is at the best level its been since the advent of digital samplers some 26 years ago. Surely these manufacturers are bringing these products to the market for a reason. If the potential for an even bigger society of digital samplers (especially sample-based beatmakers), did not exist, it's hard to believe that digital audio equipment manufacturers would even bother to upgrade their samplers.

Second, consider this: If the courts are truly concerned with the conduct of the contemporary business structure, as Duffy implied in his ruling, why then are they not taking their lead from the top manufacturers of digital samplers? Clearly this is an example of technology being way ahead of the courts. That is to say, if the digital audio equipment manufacturers consider sampling to be a major staple in the contemporary music production process, shouldn't the courts at least look into *why* that is so? Moreover, we must assume that the courts know very well that in a market economy, product availability generally reflects consumer demand. Therefore, shouldn't the courts be concerned with why digital samplers are in such demand? Today's music is being crafted by using both traditional instruments — guitar, piano, bass, drums, etc. — as well as non-traditional instruments — EMPIs like drum machines, samplers, sound modules, sequencers, and the like. More importantly, EMPIs are increasingly becoming the chosen method of many different musicians to create, develop, and/or otherwise enhance their music. Plus, digital sampling has already been embedded deeply within the fabric of modern music production practices.

Thus, instead of trying to rewrite the fundamental themes of a free market society; and instead of trying to dictate to the American public what is and isn't art; and instead of stifling the creativity and advancement of a musical genre and art form that they do not understand; and instead of only trying to protect past artists and past art forms, the courts should be trying to preserve the objectives of copyright and the principles of a free market society.

In hindsight, the impact of *Grand Upright* was deafening. After *Grand Upright*, record companies insisted (for the most part) that *all* samples be cleared, regardless of the source and amount used. This promptly led to the solidification of the onerous and rather precarious (and perhaps nefarious) sample clearance system. A system that has gone on to more directly undermine hip hop/rap music than even *Grand Upright* itself.

So Just What Is the Sample Clearance System?

The sample clearance system has been in effect since the early 1990s. So it's no surprise that most sample-based beatmakers are familiar with the term "sample clearance." For the past two decades, there's been numerous reports of sample-based songs that were held up, reworked with live replays, or scrapped from albums altogether because a sample couldn't be cleared. Stories and rumors about exorbitant clearance fees or uncooperative copyright holders have been common for a long while. However, most sample-based beatmakers are unfamiliar with what the sample clearance system is and how it actually works. In this section, I explain what sample licensing is and how the sample clearance system works (or doesn't).

Sample Licensing Defined

To truly understand the inefficiency and unfairness of the current sample clearance system, it is necessary to breakdown how the system (or lack there of) actually works. The current procedure for clearing samples (obtaining licenses) involves a considerable amount of time and money. A copyright of a particular music performance, as it is "frozen in time" as a sound recording, belongs to whoever owns the rights to the masters of that sound recording; in most cases this means the majors. That being said, there are two sets of rights that must be obtained in the sample clearing process, they include: the sound recording copyright and the musical composition copyright. The sound recording copyright covers the fixed sounds of the recording, i.e. the captured sound performance, everything that can't be notated. The musical composition copyright covers the actual melody, harmony, rhythm, and lyrics that make up a musical work, i.e. all of the elements that can be notated/transcribed on a piece of sheet music. In many cases, in addition to these rights, the "moral approval" of the artist(s) who originally performed the recording that was sampled must be granted. Moral provisions in recording contracts stipulate an artist's right to maintain approval over types of uses of their recorded performances. Even though an artist may have a moral approval provision in their contract, labels can (and often do) work their way around this by simply persuading (paying) the artist to waive the provision.

To obtain permission and get a license to use sampled material, there are a number of different types of agreements that can be made. There's a flat fee (buyout) license agreement where a license is granted for one flat fee. There's a royalty agreement where a license is granted for a royalty percentage split, either from sales of the song that contains the sample or from sales on the song and the album that the song with the sample is contained on. There's a co-ownership agreement where a license is granted in exchange for co-ownership of the song that contains the sample. There's an assignment of rights agreement where the rights to the song with the sample are assigned to the copyright holders of the song that was sampled. Finally, there's a free license agreement where the copyright holders grant a license for free.

The Flaws of the Sample Clearance System

The Expense-Cost Factor

Although there are a number of different ways to get a sample license, normally a flat fee is made. The flat fee (usually upfront) to clear a sample can range anywhere from $100 to $200,000 per sample, with $5,000 to $15,000 being about the average range. Note: There are no standard fees or rates for samples, so the actual figures vary widely. The main reason that the price is so expensive and can range so widely is because there is no limit on the price that copyright holders can demand. Each negotiation for the use of a sample is private and takes place on a case-by-case basis, so prices can (and often do) escalate very quickly, especially for samples of well-known artists and/or hit songs. Therefore, despite any myths put forth, there is no such thing as an "industry standard flat fee" for purchasing a recording license. The asking price for clearing (licensing) a sample is at the sole discretion of the copyright owners. So they can charge whatever fee they want to. Now, whether anyone pays the asking price is a different matter, but therein lies the negotiation.

In addition to the flat fee that's paid, usually the license-seeking party must also give up a percentage of ownership in the new work's musical composition copyright. In some cases, copyright holders even demand an advance on the expected publishing revenue, as a condition to clearance. Also, the flat fee can be based on a variety of things, such as an artist's notoriety and credibility, existing negotiating history between publishers, managers, and record companies, and whether a sample might reinvigorate the back catalog of the sampled artist. Each of these factors can drive the price up or down, but in many cases the price is simply untenable, especially for independent or DIY artists. With copyright owners demanding large, often unreasonable fees, or requesting disproportionate percentages of royalties for even the most minute fragments of music, artists often just give up on clearance and move on.

Finally, there's also the sample clearance house expense. Most record labels and publishing companies won't even consider a clearance request unless you've previously done business with them, which makes clearing a sample by yourself all but impossible. This is why enlisting the services of a sample clearance house, i.e. music licensing companies with seasoned sample clearance experts with contacts and a proven track record, is almost always necessary.

They have done business with many record labels and publishing companies, and they know how to cut through the bureaucracy. Naturally, sample clearance houses charge fees for their services, as much as $300-$500 per clearance (*publishing and master clearances are separate clearances*) up front before they even begin the process. But given the minefield that sample clearance is, if you have to clear a sample, it's best to do so through a reputable sample clearance house or well-known sample clearance agent.

The Time-Cost Factor – It Can Take Forever, or At Least Long Past When You Need It

Clearing a sample takes time. Simply tracking down all of the copyright holders to both sets of copyrights isn't always easy; in fact, the search process can take months. And although the enlisted help of a skilled independent sample clearance house may speed up the search (another expense to the license-seeking party), it can still take a long time. This is especially the case when copyrights have been sold or split or transferred multiple times in the last several decades, or when the sample is from a well-known publishing catalog, etc. So even for major label artists with access to in-house sample clearance departments and sizeable budgets, this time-cost factor can be extremely taxing. So just as in the case of high flat-fee demands, artists often give up trying to clear a sample and move on simply because of the time that it takes.

Even if you're successful in finding all of the copyright holders, the negotiation itself kicks off another time clock. Remember, in most cases, the copyright holders and the performing artists have to give their permission, so the demands can be extreme. Most sampled artists, music lawyers, and publishers do not understand what goes into the making of a beat or the art of sampling, so it's no wonder that they have a remarkably limited understanding of the art of sampling, particularly how samples are actually used. And with sample-based hit songs like Puffy's "I'll Be Missing You" — which samples considerably The Police hit "Every Breath You Take" — serving as an example of sampling for many unfamiliar with the art form, the notion that sampling is a fine art that utilizes high levels of creativity is either lost on them or broadly rejected. Plus, there are other factors that can determine the full price that copyright holders and artists demand. What song was sampled? Was it a hit itself long before someone sampled it? What about how the sample was used in the new song? Bear in mind, the level of transformation may matter little to copyright holders who desire a big payday.

It's also important to remember that outright rejection always looms before a negotiation even gets started. Even if you track down all of the copyright holders and the artists, even if you have the money and are willing to pay considerably for a sample, there's still no guarantee that you'll be able to get the sample(s) cleared. One or both of the copyright holders can refuse your submission request outright, or an influential artist can nix everything. And it doesn't matter if the owner of one set of rights grants you clearance: If you're missing clearance from the other rights holder, you don't have clearance. So for instance, if the owner of the master recording copyright grants a license, but the owner of the music composition copyright does not, the sample isn't cleared. And whatever fee that you paid to the owner of the master recording copyright is gone, you don't get it back. Finally, it's widely known that there are many artists, like Prince, who do not clear samples used by hip hop/rap artists. Moreover, there are publishers who flatly deny license requests for samples used in hip hop/rap music. And again, remember this: Whatever fees that you pay to attempt to clear a sample, i.e. upfront license fees, administrative fees, etc., are not refundable.

This is all a massive headache for a sample-based beat that likely made fair use of a sound recording, no?

Side-Note: Sidemen Do Not Usually Get Paid Royalties

Some commentators have suggested that studio musicians and sidemen, i.e. hired band members and studio session players, should be paid royalties on the records that they performed on that were later sampled. Let's be clear here: Long before the art of sampling emerged, there were musicians for hire. These musicians accepted gigs, short and long stints in bands, as well as session work for pre-determined payment. Usually payment was in the form of flat fees (after the gig) or weekly salaries. Though these musicians undoubtedly contributed to the collective creative process of some of the twentieth century's best music, we can not ignore the realities of their respective arrangements with band leaders, artists, labels, and recording studios.

Therefore, when musicians like former James Brown drummer Clyde Stubblefield make claims that *they* have been robbed or not paid properly from samples of songs that they performed on, I have mixed feelings. I'm a big fan of Clyde Stubblefield. To me, he isn't just one of James Brown's drummers; there were a number of talented drummers who played in James Brown's band. Many argue that Stubblefied was the best, or most influential, of all of the James Brown drummers — most notably because of his work on "The Funky Drummer," a song often cited as being one of the most sampled in hip hop/rap history. But I propose that the role Clyde Stubblefield played in James Brown's band was not entirely different than John "Jabo" Starks' role in James Brown's band, or, for that matter, any other sidemen and studio/backing musicians who worked with let's say, Curtis Mayfield, or those who played in Motown's infamous house band, The Funk Brothers. Further, I would say that it's not too different from Dr. Dre hiring session musicians to play on his productions. Do the session musicians that Dr. Dre uses (has used) deserve a royalty for their work? Im not sure. Let's say years from now, when people sample Dr. Dre's *The Chronic*, will it be reasonable for musicians who played on *The Chronic* to claim that they were robbed or not properly paid for their work?

So is it reasonable to think that every session player that performed on a record, or every hired band member (think of all of the big jazz bands) should be paid a royalty on record sales? I don't think so. Of course, not all situations and circumstances are ever the exact same. Either way, that's a different discussion altogether. But the notion that a session member or a hired band member — albeit pivotal player like in the case of Clyde Stubblefield — has been "robbed" is one that I have trouble with. If there is any unfairness (or exploitation) in the financial arrangements that sidemen often made/make with band leaders, then that's were the blame perhaps rests, not with sample-based beatmakers or even the copyright holders of the recordings and compositions.

A Case of Burning Dollars to Make Pennies

When the recording industry first took notice of sampling, you just know that their burning question was: *How can we profit from this?* Their answer wasn't exactly a new practice in the realm of recording licenses and song usage rights. In fact, the practice of "clearing" song performances for uses in other works (most notably film and television) had been around long before the landmark *Grand Upright* ruling. However, when it came to sampling, the major record companies created an entirely new *style and form* of music rights clearance, one that sought to monetize (and perhaps penalize) sampling — the musical process that utilized fragments of old sound recordings, most of which the majors owned the rights to. Further, the major record companies, who have historically discriminated against and exploited black recording artists, also indirectly created a system of sample clearance that serves as a sort of tariff on hip hop/rap recording artists, who, at the time of *Grand Upright*, were mostly black and sample-based.

Make no mistake, this culture of sample clearance was (is) not meant to benefit those recording artists that are sampled. On the contrary, the sample clearance system was (is) designed to benefit first, the owners of the sound recording copyright, usually the record companies, and the owners of the music composition copyright, the publishers; and second, the artists that were sampled.[226] Here, the ironic thing that's worth noting is the fact that the labels did not anticipate that their sample clearance system would eventually result in them earning far less than they could have had they gone

---

[226] Combined, the major record labels own the rights to the majority of all of the master recordings of soul, blues, jazz, and funk sound recordings recorded in the late 1960s on through the mid-1970s.

the compulsory license route.

The Effects of Sample Clearance on Hip Hop/Rap Music and the Art of Sampling

Sample clearance has negatively impacted hip hop/rap music in many ways. First, sample clearance has become a means through which the record companies, in effect, control what kinds of hip hop/rap music are *allowed* to be made, manufactured, and distributed. By creating a system of harsh sample clearance practices, the labels, in their persistent quest to make as much money as they could off of the creative works of others, actually did (and still continue to do) a disservice twice over. The labels did (do) a disservice to the former recording artists whose best interest they purportedly had (have) in mind. By making the process of actually clearing samples incredibly difficult, the labels actually block these recording artists from accessing new revenue streams, both in the form of additional royalties and new sales on their reinvigorated back catalogs. Further, and more importantly, by supporting such a draconian and onerously flawed sample clearance system, the labels have helped to curb the use of sampling as a compositional method in hip hop/rap.

The sample clearance process is one of the main factors that pushed the widespread use of sampling in hip hop/rap music into second class citizenry. The "sample clearance factor" has effectively helped to make sampling a less desirable compositional method for the majority of new beatmakers (though this trend is starting to change). At the same time, sample clearance has prompted many veteran sample-based beatmakers to move away from sampling (their roots) as their chief compositional method for making beats. Thus, by insisting on an incredibly absurd and utterly flawed, top-down and one-sided sample clearance process, the labels have, in effect, dramatically decreased their opportunity to actually make much more money off of sampling.

As the art of sampling was, to some great degree, *outlawed*, partly as a result of the onerous sample clearance system, and as creativity was stiffled, via the virtual lockout on sampling that the sample clearance system placed, the value of music artistry in hip hop/rap music diminished and rampant redundancy — mostly in the form of haphazard ring-tone jingle and strip club music — emerged. Instead of seeking to bolster the art form and to distinguish themselves in terms of style and originality, many beatmakers chose to employ the synthetic-sounds-based compositional method, simply as a means for making the same redundant, cookie-cutter types of beats that all too often feature no real attempt at music artistry, but instead the jingle-rap status quo.

In fact, the broad shift away from sampling as a compositional method of hip hop/rap music led to a move away from some of the core tenets of hip hop culture. For instance, competition. The art of sampling itself has always been seen as a form of competition in the hip hop/rap tradition. It is a competition to find the rarest records; it's a competition to use and flip the illest samples. Because of this very well-understood dimension of competition and ethics among sample-based beatmakers, the practice of biting (copy-catting) was not respected; this meant that mind-numbing redundancy rarely occurred. But once the art of sampling was, in effect, outlawed, biting became much more acceptable and prevalent; and the idea of competition became more about who could *copy* the best.

Also, the move away from sampling led to a decline in the "hip hop/rap" style of musicianship and to an uptick in a rock-, EDM-, and club-pop influenced style of hip hop/rap. In these new scenarios, lyrics and lyricism became less important. Therefore, the quality of lyricism dropped dramatically (though it has been picking up to some degree in recent years), which caused a sharp decrease in the number of weighty, intelligent rhyme narratives, and in turn, prompted a rise in the number of shallow, low-quality rhymes. Even the notion of what indeed constituted a "dope" rhyme took on a bizarre new context as a result of the widespread move away from the art of sampling.

Finally, although the sample clearance system had a number of negative effects on hip hop/rap music, it must be mentioned that it also had a couple of good side-effects. Since the Electronic Drum

Machine Period (1983-1987), the third major beatmaking period, the art of sampling had been steadily evolving. But along with the emergence of the sample clearance system, came a new level of evolution in the creative processes and complexity of sampling. Also, I would argue that sampling in the hip hop/rap tradition evolved both as a result of pioneering beatmakers competing with one another and pushing the envelope, and because the sample clearance prompted — necessitated — deeper transformation of samples as well as usage of more obscure source material.

The other good side effect, for better or worse, that the sample clearance system had is trap music. There's no doubt that sample clearance contributed to the environment that led to the development of trap music, a style and sound of hip hop/rap music that shuns, or at least does not fundamentally rely on, sampling. *Whatever side of the trap music fence you sit on, there's no disputing the role that it has played in the popularity of contemporary hip hop/ rap music.*

Helpful Context: The Napster Case – The Major Labels' Biggest Mistake

Although the RIAA won their court battle against Napster, shutting down the once-mighty internet file sharing company, they effectively lost the sales war...in a big way. Thanks to their absolute ignorance of the actual flow of technology and the power of the world's most unstoppable vanguard that is the internet, the major record labels not only shot themselves in the foot, they managed to hit both ankles, a knee, and a pinky toe, while they were at it.

Soon after their Napster victory (i.e. loss), once again, in their nearsighted gluttoness, the RIAA announced plans to sue as many as 30,000 individuals for file sharing infractions. Apparently, the greedy blokes didn't realize what this would all lead to: (1) the advent of new and better music file sharing services; (2) the creation of a culture that feels *entitled* to free music; (3) declining record sales; and (4) absolute litigation hell.

It's been years since the beginning of the RIAA's infamous crusade against file-swappers, and what's the result? The music industry has been forced to deal with the reality of the culture and climate of *free* music that they themselves helped to create. The RIAA could have gone into business *with* Napster. Heck, they could have *bought* Napster, like any self-respecting, monopolistic corporation would. But to them, the upstart company did not respect *their right* to rip off artists, centralize product, and curb the quality of popular music. How dare Napster!

What Does the Napster Case and Recent RIAA Woes Signal for Sampling?

It's clear that labels are not making the money they used to. But after adapting (somewhat) to the reality of how music is bought (or not) and consumed today, the music industry — overall, not just the majors — is experiencing some success again (not exactly thriving), albeit in a smaller context. Still, today, there are 60% fewer employees at the major record labels than there were 10 years ago: The major labels have decreased employment from 25,000 to 10,000 people total. Also worth noting, over this same period, the major labels went from the 'Big Six' to the 'Big Five' (UMG buying Polygram) to the 'Big Four' (Sony and BMG merging) to the 'Big Three' of today (Universal buying EMI).[227] More importantly for the purposes of this section on the RIAA and sampling (what they still deem mostly to be "piracy"), when you look back at the RIAA's massive layoffs in 2009, it's clear that they haven't the money, the resources, and/or the man power to continue to fight any of their terror-style litigation battles.

I've long maintained the inevitable end of "fake law" in sampling; that the music industry's attitude towards sampling and sample clearance would reverse itself and lead to a final moment where most forms of sampling are considered "fair use" or something of that nature, i.e. where some forms of sampling are widely recognized as likely fair use. The RIAA's 2009 sweeping job cuts

---

[227] Mike Masnick, "RIAA Insists That, Really, The Music Industry Is Collapsing; Reality Shows It's Just The RIAA That's Collapsing," https://www.techdirt.com/articles/20120217/15023417795/riaa-insists-that-really-music-industry-is-collapsing-reality-shows-its-just-riaa-thats-collapsing.shtml (Accessed April, 2015).

is perhaps more evidence of the inevitable.

Finally, it should be understood that the RIAA's fight with Napster was, in reality, a continuum of their fight against technology, a fight that they were (are) destined to lose, and one they *should have known* that they could not win in the end. Indeed, the RIAA failed to realize that by going after Napster, instead of *working with* Napster, they helped further cripple their already broken distribution system, which, in turn, brought on the demise of countless music executives and other music insiders.

But the RIAA could have seized the opportunity of the moment, much in the same way that the film industry did 40 years ago. In the 1970s, the motion picture companies urged Congress to restrict the sale of video cassette recorders in the United States, fearing that duplication of films would limit their first-run movie profits. But after losing the anti-video battle in Congress and in the courts, the film industry embraced the technology, seized the opportunity of the moment, and opened up a whole new sector for redistributing its products: the home video market.[228] By contrast, when the major record companies stalled the introduction of Digital Audio Taping (DAT) equipment into the consumer market in the late 1980s, fearing high quality home music copying would limit compact disc sales, they did not embrace the technology or seize the moment. Instead, the RIAA saw technology — in this case digital audio recording technology — as a threat to their business. The RIAA maintained that better consumer (home) copying technology would hurt CD sales, so they fought to keep consumer digital audio recording formats, like DAT, off the market. But the RIAA's efforts ultimately failed, as Congress passed the Audio Home Recording Act (AHRA) in 1992, which enabled the release of recordable digital formats such as Sony and Philips' Digital Audio Tape without fear of contributory infringement lawsuits.[229]

If the major labels continue to work against the development

---

[228] Vaidhyanathan, 3.

[229] For further information on RIAA's fight against digital audio technology, see legislative history on the Audio Home Recording Act (AHRA)—17 U.S.C. §§ 1001–10: Senate Report 102-294; House Report 102-780; House Report 102-873 (Part 1); House Report 102-873 (Part 2).

of a real system for permissive sampling, one that is practical, fair, and just as easy as a compulsory cover license, they are going to lose big once again, because sampling's going to continue to grow in popularity, not decline.

But regardless of any policy designed to tame or cripple it, sampling will continue to play a fundamental role in the hip hop/ rap music tradition. Moreover, I anticipate that the rate of sampling will increase even more as the years stretch on, especially as more informed future beatmakers seek to incorporate sampling into their compositional processes. Further, we can't forget that other music forms are continuing to embrace sampling. Finally, as the technology that makes sampling possible continues to improve, further facilitating the ease of the technical component of sampling, the art of sampling will inevitably become a compositional process more widely used around the world. Thus, rather than criminalise sampling, the RIAA should instead try to develop a system or a simple standard procedure that fairly regulates the permissive use of it. As we already now know, the current sample-clearance system is, in effect, a non-system. It is onerous, there is no regulatory parameters, and all forms of sampling are practically outlawed, which assures that only the most resourceful and well-positioned recording artists have access to sampling "legally." And this issue of unequal access certainly stands in direct odds to the equal access that the Copyright Act, under the compulsory license for nondramatic musical works provision, already grants.

Important Conclusions About the Sample Clearance System

The present sample clearance system is a costly, heavily flawed one. It's a system that is hopelessly one sided. All of the real power belongs to the copyright holders, who hold veto power over any license request; and there is no mechanism (like a compulsory licensing scheme) in place to legally compel the copyright holders to negotiate with license seekers. Outrageous demands and outright denial by the copyright owner(s) or sampled artists can be made for any reason. And because sample clearance involves high costs, both in terms of expense and time, It's a system that puts the likelihood of clearance squarely on the side of those with greater resources. In effect, this blocks sampling from those who aren't able to pay. In other words, the present sample clearance system is rigged to favor the most successful artists with major label backing, music business connections, and extensive financial resources. Also, let's not forget that there's no regulation or Congressional oversight of the sample clearance system; all of the ground rules, ad hoc as they are, are entirely made up and enforced by the music industry alone.

Can the Sample Clearance System Be Reformed?

The music industry is notorious for hurting their own interests, so I suspect that they won't take the lead in any reform to the sample clearance system. Even though it's in the music industry's best interest to streamline the system, to make it more accessible, more affordable, and to implement change that makes it possible for all clearances to be granted (here, a compulsory license comes to mind), I doubt seriously that the music industry will do so until they're forced, either by more samplers openly claiming fair use or another court decision reaffirming that fair use applies to sampling.

In the mean time, the music industry — which prefers to live in its own delusional bubble — will continue to operate from the top-down perspective of their own biases, fears of infringement suits, and a deliberate misrepresentation of fair use. This is why clarity about existing law is especially important to sample-based beatmakers and other musicians who sample. A good understanding of the Copyright Act, and fair use in particular, gives sample-based beatmakers solid footing to sample openly.

But what if, in attempt to head off the flood gates that fair use knowledge is going to inevitably open up, the music industry came together and tried to establish its own "industry custom" parameters for what types of sampling are fair? Would that work? I don't think so. For one thing, the music industry is incapable of setting truly fair parameters. The major record companies and publishers hold all the leverage in the present system. So who exactly would be called in to help set up these parameters, and how much say would they really have? Would it be a panel of music lawyers, publishers, record company executives, and sampled artists? Would this panel include copyright scholars? More specifically, if sample-based musicians, in particular, beatmakers, were even invited to a music industry panel charged with setting fair use sampling parameters, what sort of real input would they be allowed to have? Point is, why should anyone believe that the music industry would do anything other than draft *permissible sampling parameters* that represent the thinnest concept of fair use as possible? Wouldn't the publishers and record companies, who have all the leverage, push for the lowest fair use threshold as possible? But most importantly, fair use has no bright-line test. And I join those who are against trying to establish one.

Clearance of All Samples Is NOT the Law, It's Just "Industry Custom"

Finally, it's important to remember that music executives, lawyers, and sample licensing professionals, who may or may not know that most forms of sampling in the hip hop/rap music tradition make fair use of the samples they borrow, conform nevertheless to the widely held music industry belief that *all* samples, no matter how small, must be cleared. This point of view is not grounded in a proper reading of the Copyright Act or even a tertiary look at the infamous *Bridgeport* case, the court case that famously held, "Get a license or don't sample." Instead, the reality is that the music industry insists that all samples must be cleared, not because it's the law (there is no law expressly prohibiting the sampling of sound recordings from fair use), but because it's industry custom to do so. And we can't forget the view points of the copyright owners and sampled artists, the other stake holders. Like many in the music industry, these stake holders have very little understanding of the nature or complexity of the art of sampling. They believe that all samples are created equal — they're not.

Thus, achieving a middle ground or some kind of a fair compromise in the sample clearance system can't really happen if the starting point for any such negotiation takes place from the point where we are now. The music business has leverage based on common music industry business practices, and on the misperceived authority of the *Bridgeport* ruling (in the next chapter, I discuss the flaws of *Bridgeport,* and why there is no longer any leverage because of this case). The Music industry does not, however, have leverage when it comes to fair use and what the actual statutory language of the Copyright Act stipulates, or how the United States Supreme Court has historically interpreted fair use. Thus, any middle ground or fair compromise discussion must begin with the recognition that some forms of sampling meet the fair use threshold. Only after such recognition by the music industry and all stake holders can any fair and meaningful change take place in the sample clearance system.

And consider this: If the music industry maintains that one incentive to license samples is reciprocity and revenue, might there be another incentive? Could it be that the music industry's other incentive is to maintain *the climate of illusion* that all samples must be cleared, thereby pre-empting the trouble that successful fair use defenses would cause? Perhaps. All it takes is one high-profile recording artist to get sued for copyright infringement (involving a sample), then prevail on the basis of fair use. If/when this happens, the sample clearance system will change dramatically. And this change won't be in the record labels' and publishing companies' favor.

Chapter 13

Bridgeport and the False Bright-Line
Deconstructing Sampling's Most Infamous Court Case

This chapter examines *Bridgeport Music, Inc. v. Dimension Films, LLC.*, the most important and damnatory recent copyright infringement case involving sampling. Although there has been much commentary and criticisism about the Sixth Circuit's highly flawed decision in *Bridgeport*, most (if not all) of that commentary, like the news and meaning of the *Bridgeport* case itself, has gone unnoticed by all but a few sample-based beatmakers and hip hop fans alike. Like most artists, sample-based beatmakers tend to know very little about copyright law and policy; and they know far less about the details and impact of key digital sampling copyright infringement cases like *Bridgeport*. I want to change that paradigm by introducing this case and its sigficance to a broader audience.

In this chapter, I've aimed to provide an analysis of *Bridgeport* that's rigorus yet more accessible than the typical legal/scholarly examination. This is especially important for sample-based beatmakers and other sample-based musicians — many in this community tend to be informed about *Bridgeport* and the implications it continues to hold on the art of sampling and copyright law. (*If you ever find yourself on the wrong end of a copyright infringement case in which you believe your sampling was lawful, then you better know copyright law and the flaws of the Sixth Circuit's Bridgeport decision.*) I also include an examination of *Bridgeport* in this study because I believe that it is critical to any understanding of music sampling case law and the current climate that surrounds the sample clearance system.

Bridgeport Music, Inc. v. Dimension Films: The District Court's Decision

Before looking at the Sixth Circuit's decision in *Bridgeport*, it's necessary to know the background of the case and the District court's ruling. *Bridgeport* centered around the use of N.W.A.'s song "100 Miles and Runnin'" in the 1998 No Limit Films produced/ Dimension Films distributed film "I Got The Hook Up." For part of the creation of the song "100 Miles and Runnin'," N.W.A. had sampled a two-second guitar chord from Funkadelic's tune, "Get Off Your Ass and Jam," then lowered the pitch and looped it five times in their song. This was all done without Funkadelic's permission and with no compensation paid to either Bridgeport Music, which at the time owned the publishing rights to Funkadelic's music, or to Westbound Records, which at the time owned the sound recording copyright to "Get Off Your Ass and Jam."[230]

In May, 2001, Bridgeport Music, Westbound Records, and other plaintiffs brought the issue before federal judge Thomas A. Higgins of the District Court For The Middle District Of Tennessee, Nashville Division, and Westbound specifically claimed infringement of its sound recording copyright. The defendants (Dimension Films/No Limit) argued that the sample in question was de minimis (legally insubstantial), and therefore, it did not amount to actionable (illegal) copying under copyright law. The District Court found the de minimis defense to be appropriate and granted summary judgment for the defendants. In the court's findings, Judge Thomas A. Higgins demonstrated his understanding of the complexities of the matter as it pertains to sampling and copyright law, and provided the long-held understanding of the de minimis doctrine:

---

[230] *Bridgeport Music, Inc. v. Dimension Films LLC*, 230 F. Supp.2d 830, 833-39 (M.D. Tenn. 2002) (hereinafter *Bridgeport—District Decision*).

The defendant argues that the amount of "Get Off" that is sampled is a de minimis use as a matter of law and therefore no actionable copying occurred. The defendant argues that the copied chord is neither quantitatively nor qualitatively significant to the plaintiffs' copyright interests in "Get Off" and therefore any copying of the chord is not actionable as a matter of law…

The **Sixth Circuit has recognized that the principle of de minimis…can be applied as a defense to copyright infringement if it can be shown that a substantial amount of the copyrighted work was not taken**. …The Court's role in making a de minimis analysis is a tricky one. **It must balance the interests protected by the copyright laws against the stifling effect that overly rigid enforcement of these laws may have on the artistic development of new works.** …This role becomes even more challenging when presented with works from two genres of music with which many jurists (and most likely many jurors of this District) are not familiar, and the paucity of case law on the issue of whether digital sampling amounts to copyright infringement. Further complicating the process is the lack of clear road maps for de minimis analyses from the circuit courts or the Supreme Court. Still, the case law does provide loosely-defined standards and quite a bit of legal commentary has been written on digital sampling. **The Court must also be mindful not to pre-empt the jury's role in determining factual issues…**

Legal Standards for De Minimis Analysis

Among criteria for ascertaining infringement…are whether so much has been taken as would sensibly diminish the value of the original; and whether the labors of the party entitled to copyright are substantially to an injurious extent appropriated by another.…The de minimis analysis falls under the rubric of the substantial similarity element necessary to prove a copyright infringement claim. See Ringgold v. Black Entertainment Television, 126 F.3d 70, 74 (2d Cir. 1997) (de minimis applies to copying 'at such a trivial extent as to fall below the quantitative threshold of substantial similarity'). **The plaintiff must show, in addition to proof of copying, that the copied work and the allegedly infringing work are substantially similar. …It is the plaintiff's burden to prove substantial similarity…One of the most common tests for substantial similarity is 'whether an average lay observer would recognize the alleged copy as having been appropriated from the copyrighted work.'** …The de minimis analysis is therefore a derivation of substantial similarity, where a defendant argues that the literal copying of a small and insignificant portion of the copyrighted work should be allowed....

Those courts that have addressed a de minimis defense in cases of digital sampling have focused on 'whether the defendant appropriated, either quantitatively or qualitatively, 'constituent elements of the work that are original'.'... Another court, instead of a quantitative/qualitative de minimis analysis, used Professor Nimmer's 'fragmented literal similarity' analysis to determine whether substantial similarity existed... ('this aspect of the substantial similarity test may be characterized as an inquiry as to whether the subject usage is substantial or de minimis'). Either approach in this case will result in the same outcome.[emphasis mine][231]

Thus citing the long-held judicial understanding of *de minimis* and its application in a copyright infringement case, the District Court appropriately applied the substantial similarity analysis, comparing each work as a whole, and found that the defendant's work was *de minimis*:

The sample here does not rise to the level of a legally cognizable appropriation.

The quantitative use of the plaintiffs work is only one factor in either a de minimis or substantial similarity analysis. The Court must also evaluate the qualitative use as well... '100 Miles' is a song about four black men on the run from the F.B.I. who appear to be wrongfully pursued for some unmentioned crime. The looped segment evokes the sound of police sirens; it is a background element in the song. **Qualitatively, the looped segment bears only passing resemblance to the original chord that was copied. The looped segment has been slowed down to match the tempo of the rest of '100 Miles,' which also results in a lowering of the pitch of the notes.** Instead of producing a rising sense of anticipation, the effect of the sample is to create tension and apprehension at the sound of pursuing law enforcement. This effect is amplified by the repeated use of the sample as the rapper describes the men's anger, anxiety and fatalism as the chase continues.

In comparison, 'Get Off' is a celebratory song -- it is essentially about dancing. The work as a whole is characterized by a strong

---

[231] *Id.*

dance beat and a display of intricate electric guitar playing. The only lyrics are two expletives followed by "Get off your ass and jam" repeated over and over. **There are no similarities in mood or tone between the two works.** The guitar introduction, where the sampled chord is found, can be compared to the trumpet call at the start of an anthem or march -- an attention-grabbing moment meant to create anticipation. It bears no resemblance in tone or purpose to the sound of sirens in '100 Miles.'....

The plaintiffs emphasize the importance of the sampled chord to the overall effect of 'Get Off,' and the Court does not disagree with that analysis. However, **the Court finds that the copied segment is not even recognizable to a lay observer as being appropriated from the plaintiffs' work.** The siren sounds in '100 Miles' are in the background, appear at irregular intervals, and their similarity to the guitar introduction to 'Get Off' is only apparent if one is made aware of the attribution before hearing the sample. **The Court finds that no reasonable jury, even one familiar with the works of George Clinton (the author of 'Get Off'), would recognize the source of the sample without having been told of its source. This fact, combined with the minimal quantitative copying and the lack of qualitative similarity between the works, warrants dismissal of Westbound's claims arising from infringement of its sound recording....**

The Court recognizes that the fact of blatant copying is not challenged by the defendant for the purposes of this motion, and that **the purposes of the copyright laws is to deter *wholesale plagiarism* of prior works. However, a balance must be struck between protecting an artist's interests, and depriving other artists of the building blocks of future works. Since the advent of Western music, musicians have freely borrowed themes and ideas from other musicians...If even an aficionado of George Clinton's music might not readily ascertain that his music has been borrowed, the purposes of copyright law would not be served by punishing the borrower for his creative use."**

CONCLUSION

For the reasons stated above, the motion by defendant No Limit Films for summary judgment is granted as follows: all claims based on infringement of plaintiff Bridgeport Music's interest in the musical composition '100 Miles and Runnin'' are dismissed; all claims based on infringement of plaintiff Bridgeport Music's musical composition 'Get Off Your Ass and Jam' are dismissed; all claims based on infringement of plaintiff [**37] Westbound Records' sound recording of 'Get Off Your Ass and Jam' are dismissed. The plaintiffs' motion for partial summary judgment is denied as moot... [emphasis mine][232]

Through its substantial similarity analysis, the District Court found that "the minimal quantitative copying and the lack of qualitative similarity between the works" warranted dismissal of the plaintiffs claims. Furthermore, when you carefully read the District Court's conclusion, you find that the court's focus was on reaffirming the balance that copyright law is supposed to strike and the necessity of protecting a borrower when his or her use is transformative and creative.

Finally, what distinguishes the District Court's decision is not merely the depth at which the court conducted its substantial similarity analysis — an analysis that demonstrated a decent understanding of the transformative nature of the art of sampling — but the fact that the court did not break with all relevant case law, statutory language, and legislative history. Unfortunately, the same can not be said of the Sixth Circuit. For as you will see in the following section, the Sixth Circuit's decision is distinguished precisely for its break from all relevant case law, statutory language, and legislative history.

Bridgeport Music, Inc. v. Dimension Films
The Sixth Circuit's Decision

In September, 2004, the U.S. Court of Appeals for the Sixth Circuit reversed the district court's earlier decision, finding that Westbound's claim of infringement of its sound recording was correct. In handing down their ruling, the court purportedly established what they called a "bright-line" sampling rule, which stipulated that any unlicensed sample, no matter the quantity and/or quality, was in violation of copyright law.

---

[232] *Id.*

In stating its reasons for reversing the district court's decision, the Sixth Circuit exhibited a staggeringly high level of illogical legal reasoning and offered up observations about the art of sampling, sample clearance, and the music business that were wrong or, at best, incomplete. As some other commentators have aptly noted, the Sixth Circuit's justifications for its bright-line ruling was fraught with flaws. This section explores the main flaws of the Sixth Circuit's decision in *Bridgeport*. It concludes with a discussion of the impact — real and perceived — of the Sixth Circuit's landmark ruling.

The Main Flaws of the Sixth Circuit's Decision

If Copying Is Found, Substantial Similarity Is Required to Prove Infringement

As I discussed previously in chapter 9, in order for a plaintiff to prove copyright infringement, substantial similarity must be established between the plaintiff's work and the allegedly infringing work. Therefore, in any copyright infringement case, the courts must engage in a substantial similarity analysis. And as Mueller points out, "Every circuit has held that copyright infringement requires proof of both substantial similarity and actual copying (including the Sixth Circuit in cases other than those involving sound recordings) and has rejected infringement claims where the copying was de minimis or the works were not substantially similar (also including the Sixth Circuit regarding alleged infringement of subject matter other than sound recordings)."[233] But in *Bridgeport*, the Sixth Circuit maintained that where digital sampling of a sound recording is involved, no substantial similarity analysis is necessary to prove copyright infringement:

> 1. The analysis that is appropriate for determining infringement of a musical composition copyright, is not the analysis that is to be applied to determine infringement of a sound recording. We address this issue only as it pertains to sound recording copyrights.

---

[233] Mueller, 45.

2. Since the district court decision essentially tracked the analysis that is made if a musical composition copyright were at issue, we depart from that analysis.

While the question whether an unauthorized use of a digital sample infringes a musical composition may require a full substantial similarity analysis, **the question whether the use of a sample constitutes infringement of a sound recording could end upon a determination that the sampler physically copied the copyrighted sound recording of another.** [emphasis mine][234]

First, here, the legal reasoning the Sixth Circuit applied is deeply flawed. The subject matter at question does not change the fact that the three elements of copyright infringement must be satisfied. Second, as I previously discussed in chapter 9, in order for any copyright infringement claim to be successful, the plaintiff must prove the same three elements: (1) ownership of a valid copyright; (2) proof of actual copying; and (3) proof that *unlawful* appropriation took place. For the purposes of this section, it is the third factor that must be emphasized, as appropriation itself does not automatically constitute infringement. Unlawful appropriation refers to substantial or "infringing similarity."[235] In determining unlawful appropriation, the courts must engage in a substantial similarity analysis in which qualitative and quantitative factors are assessed: "in determining whether two such works are so substantially similar as to reveal an infringement of one by the other, courts must decide whether the similarities shared by the works are something more than mere generalized ideas or themes,"[236] and the two works must considered as a whole. No copyrightable material is specified in this instruction for reason. If a work is protected by copyright, it is also subject to its limitations, which means that it is not immune to lawful takings, i.e. de minimis or fair use.

Still, the Sixth Circuit saw it differently. In its substantial similarity analysis, it did not consider the two works as a whole,

---

[234] Bridgeport Music, Inc. v. Dimension Films, 383 F.3d 390,399 (6th Cir. 2004), aft'd on reh'g, 410 F.3d 792 (6th Cir. 2005) (hereinafter *Bridgeport—Circuit Decision*).
[235] *Warner Bros., Inc. v. American Broadcasting Companies*, 654 F. 2d 204 - Court of Appeals, 2nd Circuit 1981.
[236] *Id.*

but rather it relied on the "fragmented similarity test" approach. In a fragmented literal similarity test, the "fragmented" copyrightable elements that are copied from a protected work are examined, i.e. the allegedly infringing elements are looked at in isolation to see if there is substantial similarity. Of course, applying such a test to sampling creates an immediate problem because, first, a digital sample is an exact copy; and second, because the threshold of the fragmented literal similarity test is so limited, it leads to the wrong conclusion that a factual fragment — in the case of sampling, simply proof that a sound recording was sampled — is necessarily copyright infringement. This is exactly what happened in *Bridgeport*: The Sixth Circuit essentially tossed substantial similarity to the side and concluded that a sample, however brief, *necessarily* infringes the sound-recording re-production right. Thus, using the fragmented literal similarity approach, the Sixth Circuit misapplied the substantial similarity test, which holds that substantially similarity is determined by a consideration of two works "as a whole."

Disregarding a proper substantial similarity analysis, and against explicit legislative intent, the language in the Copyright Act and judicial precedent, the Sixth Circuit broadened the protection of sound recordings, and stipulated that copyright infringement is determined differently when it involves sound recordings and digital sampling. This was a glaring error.

Neither the form of copying — in this case digital sampling — nor the category of copyrighted material changes the application of the statute, as the limitations on sound recordings are the same as all other copyrightable material: "The exclusive rights of the owner of a copyright in a sound recording are limited to the rights specified by clauses (1), (2), and (3) of section 106."[237] Additionally, during the passage of the Sound Recording Amendment of 1971, Congress explicitly stated that *"this limited copyright does not grant any broader rights than are accorded to other copyright proprietors... ."*[238] In other

---

[237] U.S. House. The Committe on the Judiciary. *Copyright Law Revision*, 1976, (to Accompany S.22) *Report Together with Additional Views* (94 H. Rpt. 94-1476) (Hereinafter House Report 94-1476). See: 17 U.S.C. §106. Exclusive rights in copyrighted works; 17 U.S.C. § 114. Scope of exclusive rights in sound recordings.
[238] H.R. Rep. No. 92-487, at 10 (1971), reprinted in 1971 U.S.C.C.A.N. 1566, 1572

words, the intent of Congress is clear: Sound recordings are not to be treated differently than any other category of copyrightable material.[239]   Yet, as Mueller and other legal commentators have correctly noted, the Sixth Circuit misinterpreted § 114(b) as an expansion of the rights of the sound recording copyright holder and "dismissed congressional intent as indicated in the House Reports accompanying the passage of the Sound Recording Amendment."[240]

Additionally, Congress expressly stated that with regards to the copyright infringement of sound recordings, "infringement takes place whenever all or any substantial portion of the actual sounds that go to make up a copyrighted sound recording are reproduced in phonorecords…"[241] Hence, Congress clearly indicated that any *insubstantial* portion of a sound recording that is appropriated is a lawful appropriation and, therefore, not actionable. So there can be no ambiguity here: The Copyright Act, and the House Reports that accompanied it, makes it quite clear that the substantial similarity analysis is to be applied in all cases of copyright infringement.[242]

De Minimis is Applicable to Every Category of Copyrightable Material; Sampling is Not Literally a "Physical Taking"

Just as substantial similarity applies to all copyright infringement cases, so does the de minimis doctrine. Furthermore, as I explained in chapter 9, the de minimis doctrine is not limited to copyright law; it applies in all civil cases, for as the Second Circuit points out, "Trivial copying is a significant part of modern life." "Because

---

[239] John Schietinger, "Bridgeport Music, Inc. V. Dimension Films: How The Sixth Circuit Missed A Beat On Digital Music Sampling," DePaul Law Review, Fall (2005) 55 DePaul L. Rev. 209, 8, citing Brief of Amicus Curiae RIAA, at 9, Bridgeport Music II (Nos. 02-6521, 02-5738 (citing 4 Nimmer on Copyright… 13.03[A][2] at 13-50). According to the Nimmer on Copyright treatise, the leading secondary source on copyright law, the "practice of digitally sampling prior music to use in a new composition should not be subject to any special analysis."
[240] Mueller, 448.
[241] House Report 94-1476.
[242] Mueller, 449. Mueller points out that "the statutory language and house reports accompanying both the Sound Recording Amendment of 1971 and the Copyright Act of 1976 make clear that Congress intended that plaintiffs would still have to demonstrate substantial similarity in sound recording infringement cases."

of the de minimis doctrine, in trivial instances of copying, we are in fact not breaking the law. If a copyright owner were to sue the makers of trivial copies, judgment would be for the defendants. The case would be dismissed because trivial copying is not an infringement."[243]

Thus, while the District Court was correct in its application of de minimis, the Sixth Circuit erred in its exclusion of the applicability of the de minimis doctrine. The fact that the Sixth Circuit relied on a misinterpretation of the statute, as well as the faulty legal reasoning that sampling is a "physical taking" rather than an intellectual one, makes this error even more alarming:

> This analysis admittedly raises the question of why one should, without infringing, be able to take three notes from a musical composition, for example, but not three notes by way of sampling from a sound recording. Why is there no de minimis taking or why should substantial similarity not enter the equation. Our first answer to this question is what we have earlier indicated. We think this result is dictated by the applicable statute. Second, even when a small part of a sound recording is sampled, the part taken is something of value. No further proof of that is necessary than the fact that the producer of the record or the artist on the record intentionally sampled because it would (1) save costs, or (2) add something to the new recording, or (3) both. **For the sound recording copyright holder, it is not the "song" but the sounds that are fixed in the medium of his choice. When those sounds are sampled they are taken directly from that fixed medium. It is a <u>physical taking</u> rather than an intellectual one.**
>
> If one were to analogize to a book, **it is not the book, i.e., the paper and binding, that is copyrightable, but its contents.**[244]

Here, the Sixth Circuit's legal reasoning is flawed on several fronts. First, and most importantly, if a work is protected by copyright, it can not be immune to de minimis or fair use, "no category of copyrighted material is either immune from use or completely without protection."[245] In other words, if a work is

---

[243] *On Davis v. Gap, Inc.*, 246 F.3d 152 (2nd Cir. 2001) (citations omitted)
[244] *Bridgeport—Circuit Decision.*
[245] Leval, 1122.

copyrighted, the public can make fair use of it. Period. There's no legal reasoning or form of semantics that can undo this fact.

Second, sampling simply constitutes a reproduction of copyrighted material. Phonorecords, digital sounds, are not to be treated differently than any other copyrighted material. This is made clear in the U.S. Code: "…the fair use of a copyrighted work, *including such use by reproduction in copies or phonorecords.*"[246] Hence, the Sixth Circuit's concept of "physical taking", as a means to exempt sound recordings from de minimis — and thereby broaden the protection of sound recordings — is in direct opposition to copyright and the fair use doctrine as codified in the Copyright Act of 1976.

Third, the type of "fixed medium of choice" is not what is copyrightable; the sounds in a recording *are* the "contents" of the recording. The wax of a vinyl record or the plastic of a CD is not what is copyrightable. An artist who samples a song doesn't literally take — i.e. physically extract — the sound out of the original recording, leaving the song with less sound than it had before it was sampled. Instead, sampling technology creates a copy that is transferred to a computer hard drive. An actual physical taking of a vinyl record would mean that after sampling a vinyl record, for instance, a digital sampler would dispense a piece of the actual vinyl record, and the original vinyl record would be missing the piece that was *physically* taken.

Further, granting copyright protection to literally every sound, every note fixed in a sound recording would be like granting protection to every word and every letter in a book or every color in a photo. Again, there is no conceptual difference between the intellectual (virtual) copying and the so-called physical (digital sampling) copying of someone's work. Both involve copying and intellectual transformation.

Here, it's worth mentioning how some commentators/lawyers have argued — perhaps prompted by *Bridgeport's* bizarre legal reasoning — that a sample is an "actual" piece of a work, and therefore, a sample without a license is inherently copyright

---

[246] 17 U.S.C. § 107.

infringement; and further, that music samples, in the abstract, represent their own market. Again, this is flawed legal reasoning. Such illogic ignores that the fact that some samples may be de minimis or fair use. Moreover, no form of copying is inherently an infringement; likewise, no appropriation is inherently infringement. (The nature and form of a copyrighted work does not make it immune to de minimis or fair use.) To insist otherwise is an example of prior restraint — censorship imposed on expression before the expression actually takes place. And while some appropriations — be they in literature, music, photography, etc. — may likely be an infringement, the actual determination of infringement must be made in a court of law on a case by case basis.

The "actual taking" double-talk also stems from an improper interpretation of a substantially similarity analysis. If you recall, an allegedly infringing work is considered substantially similar when it is nearly indistinguishable from the copyrighted work it appropriated. Some commentators have twisted the meaning of this and have come up with the idea that a sample is an *exact taking* — i.e. an actual taking — because it is an exact duplication of a piece of a sound recording. This argument is ridiculous. It's like saying that words appropriated from a book are not an *exact* copying because the pages from which words came were not taken. That any judge could ever subscribe to this legal double-talk is astonishing.

"The Legislative History is of Little Help" – The Sixth Circuit's Woefully Inaccurate Claim

The Sixth Circuit insisted that "the legislative history" was "of little help because digital sampling wasn't being done in 1971," and that if this was "not what Congress intended or is not what they would intend now, it is easy enough for the record industry… to go back to Congress for a clarification or change in the law."[247] Talk about a WTF moment? So the Sixth Circuit would have us believe that with regards to sound recordings, the intent of Congress

---

[247] *Id.*

was *unclear, "of little help."* Seriously? Further, the Sixth Circuit implied that the language in the statute, per the sound recording provisions of 1971, could be interpreted as a preemptive strike against unauthorized digital sampling. On the surface, the Sixth Circuit's claim that the intent of Congress is unclear with regards to sound recordings is alarmingly inaccurate. The House Report on the Sound Recording Amendment of 1971 that accompanied the Sound Recording Amendment identified explicitly why the amendment granting protection to sound recordings was needed:

> **The problem of record piracy has not been dealt with...We are persuaded that the problem is an immediate and urgent one, and that legislation to deal with it is needed now.** The seriousness of the situation with respect to record piracy...is unique.... **The committee agrees that it is necessary, without delay, to establish Federal legislation prohibiting unauthorized manufacturers from reproduction and distribution of recorded performances.** [emphasis mine][248]

Looking at the House Committee's report on the Sound Recording Amendment of 1971, there can be no doubt as to what the intent of Congress was, the intent was quite clear. It is also clear that digital sampling was certainly not the "immediate," "urgent," and "unique" problem that Congress was focusing on curtailing. Congress was intent, unequivocally so, on curtailing "record piracy." Any suggestions that Congress was then preoccupied with curtailing something else — including the art of sampling — are all wrong and willfully misleading. More importantly, as I previously mentioned, Congress explicitly stated that sound recordings were not to be given any more protection than any other category of copyrighted material: **"this limited copyright does not grant any broader rights than are accorded to other copyright proprietors... ."** [emphasis mine][249] So there's no ambiguity here: The legislative

---

[248] The House Report on the Sound Recording Amendment of 1971, September 22, 1971 — Committed to the Committee of the Whole House on the State of the Union. In the House Committee's report, it is clear that the legislation was aimed at "manufacturers engaged in the unauthorized reproduction of records and tapes," not individuals who now use the art of sampling as a compositional method.
[249] H.R. Rep. No. 92-487, at 10 (1971), reprinted in 1971 U.S.C.C.A.N. 1566, 1572.

history should have been of great help to the Sixth Circuit.

Additionally, in using what it called a "literal reading" of the statute to determine that substantial similarity was not applicable to copyright infringement cases involving sound recordings and digital sampling, the Sixth Circuit wrongly misinterpreted the statute. There are two points in specific that the circuit court misinterpreted. First, where the statute grants sound recording copyright holders the exclusive right "to duplicate the sound recording in the form of phonorecords or copies that directly or indirectly recapture the actual sounds fixed in the recording,"[250] the Sixth Circuit interpreted this to mean that "a sound recording owner has the exclusive right to 'sample' his own recording,"[251] because according to the Sixth Circuit, there is a distinction between the copying of books and the copying of phonorecords:

> **If one were to analogize to a book, it is not the book, i.e., the paper and binding, that is copyrightable, but its contents.** *There are probably any number of reasons why the decision was made by Congress to treat a sound recording differently from a book even though both are the medium in which an original work is fixed rather than the creation itself.* None the least of them certainly were advances in technology which made the "pirating" of sound recordings an easy task. The balance that was struck was to give sound recording copyright holders the exclusive right "to duplicate the sound recording in the form of phonorecords or copies that directly or indirectly recapture the actual sounds fixed in the recording." 17 U.S.C. § 114(b). This means that the world at large is free to imitate or simulate the creative work fixed in the recording so long as an actual copy of the sound recording itself is not made. [emphasis mine][252]

First, let's remember: Congress did not make the decision to treat a sound recording differently than a book. Second, this interpretation is an illogical reading of the statute, because the sound recording copyright protects *the sounds in the recording*, not the phonorecord, i.e. the fixed medium in which the work is fixed, itself. But clearly, in light of the Sixth Circuit's book analogy, this was a

---

[250] 17 U.S.C. § 114(b).
[251] *Bridgeport—Circuit Decision.*.
[252] *Id.*

distinction and basic understanding that the court overlooked; the House Report (1976) explicitly clarified that the "sound recording" is distinguished from the "phonorecord" (fixed medium). Note, the statute says the exact opposite of what the Sixth Circuit reasoned:

> As defined in section 101, copyrightable "sound recordings" are original works of authorship comprising an aggregate of musical, spoken, or other sounds that have been fixed in tangible form. **The copyrightable work comprises the aggregation of sounds and not the tangible medium of fixation. Thus, 'sound recordings' as copyrightable subject matter are distinguished from 'phonorecords,' the latter being physical objects on which sounds are fixed...As a class of subject matter, sound recordings are clearly within the scope of the "writings of an author"**... [empahsis mine][253]

Another problem with the Sixth Circuit's interpretation here is the fact that Congress made quite clear in its 1971 Report that rampant "piracy activity" — i.e. wholesale duplication and distribution of a copyrighted work — was the urgent (primary) motivating factor for sound recording copyright protection and the subsequent Sound Recording Act of 1971. Preventing the art of sampling was not even in part a motivating factor. Again, from The House Report on the Sound Recording Amendment of 1971:

> REASON FOR THE LEGISLATION
> The attention of the Committee has been directed to the widespread unauthorized reproduction of phonograph records and tapes. While it is difficult to establish the exact volume or dollar value of current piracy activity, it is estimated by reliable trade sources that the annual volume of such piracy is now in excess of $100 million. It has been estimated that legitimate prerecorded tape sales have an annual value of approximately $300 million .... **The problem of record piracy has not been dealt with...We are persuaded that the problem is an immediate and urgent one, and that legislation to deal with it is needed now. The seriousness of the situation with respect to record piracy...is unique.... The committee agrees that it is necessary, without delay, to establish Federal legislation prohibiting unauthorized manufacturers from reproduction and**

---

[253] House Report 94-1476.

> **distribution of recorded performances.** [emphasis mine]

Moreover, the Sixth Circuit's assertion that the statute grants the sound recording owner the exclusive right to sample their own recording is just as ridiculous as asserting that the literary work's owner has the exclusive right to borrow everything — every line, letter, or punctuation mark — from their work.

Second, the Sixth Circuit misinterpreted the definition of "remix" and "derivative works" (the proper definitions I will explain in the section below), and again dismissed Congress' clear intent — and instructions — to not treat sound recordings any differently than any other copyrightable subject matter.[254]

Even more damning to the Sixth Circuit's claim that "the legislative history is of little help" is the fact that Congress explicitly noted that "infringement takes place whenever all or any *substantial* portion of the actual sounds that go to make up a copyrighted sound recording are reproduced in phonorecords by repressing, transcribing, recapturing off the air, or any other method...."[255] Thus, digital sampling, just one method for reproducing sounds from a sound recording, is an infringement only when all or any *substantial* portion of the copyrighted sound recording is copied and used. In other words, digital sampling is likely not an infringement when any insubstantial portion of a copyrighted sound recording is copied; but infringement can't be found merely because a sound recording was sampled.

The Proper Context and Interpretation of Derivative Works Under the Statute; The "Exclusive Right to Prepare Derivative Works" Defined

Taking what it called a "literal reading approach" to the statute, The Sixth Circuit determined that sampling *per se* — i.e. just the

---

[254] Brief of Amicus Curiae RIAA, at 9, Bridgeport Music II (Nos. 02-6521, 02-5738 (citing 4 Nimmer on Copyright...13.03[A][2] at 13-50) Seen at Schietinger, 8. According to the Nimmer on Copyright treatise, the leading secondary source on copyright law, the "practice of digitally sampling prior music to use in a new composition should not be subject to any special analysis."
[255] House Report 94-1476.

activity involved in sampling, the digital duplication — amounted to copyright infringement. Specifically, the Sixth Circuit looked at section 17 U.S.C. § 114(b), which states that "The exclusive right of the owner of copyright in a sound recording under clause (2) of section 106 is limited to the right to prepare a derivative work in which the actual sounds fixed in the sound recording are rearranged, remixed, or otherwise altered in sequence or quality." Based on its so-called "literal reading," the Sixth circuit maintained that sampling was, "by definition," copyright infringement:

> In fact, the copyright law specifically provides that the owner of copyright in a sound recording has **the exclusive right to prepare a derivative work "in which the actual sounds fixed in the sound recording are rearranged, remixed, or otherwise altered in sequence or quality." A recording that embodies samples taken from the sound recording of another is by definition a "rearranged, remixed, or otherwise altered in sequence or quality."** [emphasis mine][256]

Throughout Part 2 of this study, I discussed exactly what the art of sampling is, and I specifically demonstrated why a "remix" is not equivalent to a "sample." As I pointed out in the introduction of this study, a "remix" is a version, a variant of an original sound recording. A "remix" involves using the core of the original sound recording, and always includes the lyrics of the original song, along with additional elements. Therefore, a "remix" is a derivative work of the original song. Sampling, by contrast, involves the transformative use of snippets from pre-existing sound recordings. A "sample" is just a small excerpt from a sound recording that's used in an entirely new song, one with a completely different core and new lyrics. Therefore, the new song that contains the "sample" is not a derivative work of the sound recording which it sampled. If I sample three notes from Michael Jackon's song "Thriller," then transform them. beyond recognition and combine them with a new drum beat, a new bass line, a new melody, and new lyrics depicting a rags to riches story, I have not created a derivative work

---

[256] *Bridgeport—Circuit Decision.*

of "Thriller," I've created an entirely new song, one that, as a whole, is substantially different than "Thriller."

It's further worth pointing out that 17 U.S.C. § 101 defines a "derivative work" as "a work based upon one or more preexisting works, such as a translation, musical arrangement, dramatization, fictionalization, motion picture version, sound recording, art reproduction, abridgment, condensation, or any other form in which a work may be recast, transformed, or adapted." The context of derivative work as defined by Congress is clear: A derivative work is based upon, and thus requires, the core or main theme of the original work. A small or insignificant piece of the original work that is transformed and combined with entirely new elements resulting in a new work is not a derivative work of the original work from which it borrowed.

The Sixth Circuit's General Misunderstanding of the Art of Sampling, and the Access to Pre-1972 Recordings Error

As I've hopefully demonstrated in this study, there is a tremendous aesthetic value in the art of sampling — its innovative techniques and creative processes, its historical connection, and its important place in pop culture. But it's evident that the Sixth Circuit (like many in the music business) was ignorant of this fact, as the court maintained that "if an artist wants to incorporate a 'riff' from another work in his or her recording, he is free to duplicate the sound of that 'riff' in the studio."[257]

To be certain, there is a difference, aesthetically and sonically, between sampling from old records and using studio instruments to do replays. Replays are not preferred by sample-based beatmakers, and they are not always a real substitute for the aesthetic sound of older recordings, nor are they always the best artistic solution to a clearance problem. Sample-based musicians sample for the sound and feel that's intrinsic in the source material. Therefore, replays can't always conjure up the same essence that attracts most sample-

---

[257] *Bridgeport—Circuit Decision.*

based musicians in the first place. Further, most sample-based music (like much of today's music) is made in home studios; and most sample-based artists do not have the money for or access to live musicians who can perform replays. Nothing in the Sixth Circuit's decision suggests that the court considered any of these factors.

Additionally, the Sixth Circuit considered it to be a fact that all artists who sample do so only for three reasons — to save money, to add something to the new recording, or both:

> No further proof of that is necessary than the fact that the producer of the record or **the artist on the record intentionally sampled because it would (1) save costs, or (2) add something to the new recording, or (3) both.** [empahsis mine][258]

First, sampling isn't as inexpensive as the Sixth Circuit would have the public believe. Sample-based musicians, especially those who buy used vinyl records and expensive production rigs, incur recording costs just like other musicians. Second, because of advancing technology, many artists are recording in home studios or cheaper commercial facilities, so there's not necessarily a cost advantage in this regard for sample-based musicians. Third, sampling costs a great deal of time. Diggin' for new source material takes a considerable amount of time and effort.

Finally, the Sixth Circuit claimed that "there is a large body of pre-1972 sound recordings that is not subject to federal copyright protection."[259] Certainly, this is a disingenuous justification, as the court knew very well that pre-1972 sound recordings are protected by most state laws. Thus, sample-based musicians do not have "free access" to pre-1972 sound recordings, despite what the Sixth Circuit claimed in its decision.

The Sixth Circuit's Misunderstanding of the Sample Clearance System and the Cost of Clearing Samples

In chapter 12, I discussed how clearing samples is often

---

[258] *Id.*
[259] *Id.*

extremely difficult and, in many cases, impossible. For both major label backed artists and independents, sample clearance can be expensive, time consuming, and fraught with administrative headaches. Yet the Sixth Circuit, demonstrating its total lack of understanding of the sample clearance system, asserted that sample clearance was simply a fair market value issue, and that, therefore, the sample clearance system would naturally be reformed because market forces would dictate it:

> the market will control the license price and keep it within bounds. The sound recording copyright holder cannot exact a license fee greater than what it would cost the person seeking the license to just duplicate the sample in the course of making the new recording...the record industry, including the recording artists, has the ability and know-how to work out guidelines, including a fixed schedule of license fees, if they so choose....
> [empahsis mine][260]

Huh? First off, a copyright holder can charge whaterver they want for a license to use their work. Second, Sixth Circuit's assertion that market forces would control the prices for sample licenses, and that the record industry could apply its "know-how" to improve the sample clearance system, completely misses several points. First, samples are one-of-kind. Therefore, copyright holders do not compete with each other on setting prices for the uses of their copyrighted works. This is not an example of buying, let's say, a standard set of nuts and bolts, where each hardware store in town stocks the same nuts and bolts. Second, sample-based recording artists are not interested in "duplicating" the sample; again, replays are not a preference among sample-based musicians. Third, music composition and sound recording copyright holders do not have to negotiate sample licenses at all; there is no legal path, like compulsory licenses for covers, to compel them to do so. Thus, emboldened by the Sixth Circuit's decision that all sampling is *per se* copyright infringement, these copyright holders have no incentive to improve the sample clearance system, as they can continue to charge whatever they want.

---

[260] *Id.*, at 36 and 41.

The Problems with the Sixth Circuit's Bright-Line Test: It Subverts the Copyright Act, It Doesn't Strike a Balance, It Stifles Creativity, It's Really Not a Test, and It Doesn't Lead to Judicial Economy

In detailing the "precise nature" of its decision to overturn the District Court's ruling, the Sixth Circuit further concluded that a "bright-line test" was needed going forward:

> **The music industry, as well as the courts, are best served if something approximating a bright-line test can be established.** Not necessarily a "one size fits all" test, but one that, at least, adds clarity to what constitutes actionable infringement with regard to the digital sampling of copyrighted sound recordings. [emphasis mine][261]

However, there are a number of problems with the Sixth Circuit's "bright-line test." First, the Sixth Circuit's bright-line test subverts the Copyright Act and Congressional intent, as indicated in the House Reports accompanying the passage of the Sound Recording Amendment: "In approving the creation of a limited copyright in sound recordings it is the intention of the Committee that this limited copyright not grant any broader rights than are accorded to other copyright proprietors under the existing title17."[262] By inexplicably broadening copyright protection for sound recordings, the Sixth Circuit subverted the Copyright Act and failed to recognize the clear intent of Congress to not grant any additional protection to sound recordings than are accorded to other copyrightable subject matter.

Second, the Sixth Circuit's bright-line test does not strike a balance between the interests of copyright holders and the interests of the public. The Sixth Circuit maintains that its bright-line test was "to serve the music industry and the courts," not artists or the public. How does this serve the purpose of copyright law? How does the Sixth Circuit's bright-line test "strike a balance between protecting original works and stifling further creativity?" Fact is,

---

[261] *Id.*
[262] H.R. Rep. No. 92-487 (1971).

it doesn't. Instead, the Sixth Circuit's bright-line tilts the scale decidedly towards the copyright holders of sound recordings and music compositions. There is no balance in that, as the interest of the public is ignored and dismissed.

Additionally, according to the Sixth Circuit, there was a substantial level of "uncertainty" in the music industry about what did indeed constitute actionable infringement in regards to the digital sampling of copyrighted sound recordings. Whether this is true or not, the fact remains that the RIAA was neither the plaintiff nor the defendant in *Bridgeport*. Therefore, the notion that the music industry, i.e. the interests of the major record companies, not individual recording artists, "needed clarity" is absurd. How does the music industry benefit from a test that actually stops short of "clarifying" the parameters that determine *non-infringing* forms of digital sampling? Again, let's be clear here: The Sixth Circuit's so-called "bright-line test" is a rule that stipulates that all samples constitute actionable infringement, regardless of the amount taken. That kind of "clarity" outlaws *any* sample that isn't cleared, turns the mere act of sampling into copyright infringement, and censors sample-based musicians and the art of sampling itself.

Third, the Sixth Circuit's bright-line certainly does stifle creativity. The Sixth Circuit concedes that sampling is a well-known art form, yet the court rejects the premise that de minimis applies to sound recordings (particularly in relation to digital sampling), overlooking common law de minimis and fair use adjudication. So according to the Sixth Circuit's ruling in *Bridgeport*, in order to prove copyright infringement in a digital sampling case, the only thing the copyright owner has to do is prove actual copying; the two works in question would not even have to be remotely similar. Because of higher sample clearance fees and the overall criminalization of non-cleared sampling, more people become less-inclined to produce sample-based music; record companies, wanting to keep administrative headaches to a minimum and sample clearance costs down, push for sample-free music; and artists buy into the notion that they have a better chance of being successful if they avoid sampling altogether. Collectively, all of these things point to a drop in the level of new sampling. And because of a precipitous drop in the level of contribution to the art form, the expansion of the art form slows, as creativity is indeed stifled.

This is unfortunate because the progress of the art of sampling, like any art form, requires robust (not censored) activity from artists. Just like writers, filmmakers, and other artists and creators, sample-based musicians necessarily borrow from others to create their works. But the Sixth Circuit's bright-line rule would make the art of sampling inaccessible to those sampling musicians who can not pay the fee for a license.

Fourth, it isn't really a test at all. "Get a license or do not sample." That's not a test, that's an edict that says *all* (uncleared) digital sampling of copyrighted works is copyright infringement. Of course, this is also prior restraint and censorship. A real test is the kind of examination the substantial similarity analysis already provides for. But more importantly, a bright-line test is not appropriate because copyright infringement is not determined by a bright-line test. Copyright infringement can only be determined in a court of law by a substantial similarity analysis in which qualitative and quantitative factors are assessed in effort to ascertain if the copying of a copyrighted work is substantial enough to constitute improper appropriation.

Further, sampling involves concepts of musical creativity that can't possibly be boxed in by the sort of bright-line test that the Sixth Circuit offered in its ruling. As I discussed previously in the aesthetic and instruction sections of this study, the art of sampling includes a number of different approaches. From different chopping scopes to other transformation schemes, from musical arrangement to drum pattern construction, the art of sampling relies on a variety of different methods, processes, and styles. Further, each sample-based musician utilizes his or her own individualized approach. Therefore, any real judicial test requires a level of flexibility that, on one hand, explicitly accounts for all of these factors, and on the other hand, aims to strike a balance between protecting original works and stifling further creativity. Thus, no bright-line rule could ever fairly accommodate the art of sampling.

Fifth, the Sixth Circuit's bright-line doesn't lead to judicial economy. The Sixth Circuit claimed that its decision for a bright-line test was motivated in part by judicial economy. In announcing it's bright-line, the court pointed out that the *Bridgeport* case "illuminates the kind of mental, musicological, and technological gymnastics that would have to be employed if one were to adapt a de minimis or substantial similarity analysis;" and further concedes that "The district judge did an excellent job of navigating these troubled waters, but not without dint of great effort."[263]

So let's try to understand what the Sixth Circuit has meant by this. The effort that the District judge used to reach (1) a practical, accurate application of the substantial similarity analysis; and (2) a practical understanding of the factors of an alleged infringement, was unreasonable and too time consuming? "The de minimis doctrine promotes judicial economy by ensuring that most cases involving trivial instances of copying will never result in a lawsuit at all. Where they do, they will almost certainly result in summary judgment for the defendants."[264] Copyright law, and a long history of judicial precedent in copyright infringement cases, makes it clear that a substantial similarity test must be conducted in any copyright infringement case. So in order to presumably cut down on more "great efforts" by future courts, and to subsequently increase judicial efficiency, the Sixth Circuit found that the best solution was to simply remove the substantial similarity element from copyright infringement cases involving sound recordings and digital sampling. Should we take this to mean that, with its decision in *Bridgeport*, the Sixth Circuit was simply trying to find a short cut that would enable future courts to bypass the substantial similarity analysis in copyright infringement cases involving sampling and sound recordings?

In conceding that the District Court did an "excellent job" with its substantial similarity analysis, the Sixth Circuit demonstrates its keen awareness of the amount of intellectual exercise, time, and resources expended by the District Court. So it appears then that

---

[263] *Id.*
[264] Mueller, 454.

the Sixth Circuit would have the public believe that the interest of justice is a pursuit worth taking when it doesn't require any "great effort," specifically any "mental, musicological, and technological gymnastics."

Hence, there are more reasons why the Sixth Circuit's "judicial economy" justification for its bright-line is absurd. First, the court's explanation inadvertently implies that cases of intellectual, cultural, and technological complexity are a waste of the judicial system's time and resources; and therefore, the courts are better served by a "test" that effectively ignores this complexity — purportedly in the interest of judicial economy. Huh?

Second, the notion that the adjudication of sampling cases can be simplified by a one-sided test doesn't lead to efficient litigation. As I stated previously in this section, under the Sixth Circuit's bright-line, to prove copyright infringement in a digital sampling case, all the copyright owner would have to prove is actual copying; the two works in question would not even have to be remotely similar. Therefore, this low threshold to infringement would likely mean an *increase*, not a decrease, in the number of copyright infringement cases involving sampling. This means an even bigger burden and strain on the courts, because sound recording copyright holders, now emboldened by the Sixth Circuit's bright-line rule, can bring even more action against countless sample-based recording artists, record labels, and distributors for even the smallest of samples.

Third, presumably cut off from the de minimis doctrine, sample-based musicians would now have no other legal resolve against an copyright infringement claim other than an affirmative fair use defense. And we must remember that the fair use doctrine "'permits [and requires] courts to avoid rigid application of the copyright statute when, on occasion, it would stifle the very creativity which that law is designed to foster,'" and that **"The task is not to be simplified with bright-line rules, for the statute, like the doctrine it recognizes, calls for case-by-case analysis."**[265]

So if the courts are now forced to engage in countless new fair use analyses — keeping in mind that each fair use analysis

---

[265] *Campbell v. Acuff-Rose*, p577, (emphasis mine, citations omitted).

is something much more complex and unpredictable than the substantial similarity analysis that satisfies a de minimis defense — where exactly is the judicial efficiency in that?

What We Can Take Away from the Sixth Circuit's Decision in *Bridgeport*

The Sixth Circuit's Bright-Line is an Overreach that Attempts to Subvert the Copyright Act

Simply stated, the Sixth Circuit's decision in *Bridgeport* was a judicial blunder of the highest magnitude. Presumably in its zeal to bring clarification to an area of law that was already confusing and noted for its paucity of case history, the Sixth Circuit dismissed the clear intent of Congress regarding the sound recording copyright, and it did not draw a distinction between transformative copying (legal appropriation) and piracy. Even more alarming was the Sixth Circuit's break from how copyright infringement is proven in court. In *Bridgeport*, the Sixth Circuit maintained that where digital sampling of a sound recording is involved, no substantial similarity analysis is necessary to prove copyright infringement. This, despite the fact that any copyright infringement case must satisfy the same three elements: proof of ownership, proof of copying, and proof of unlawful appropriation. What's worse? The court justified its decision to treat sound recordings differently than other copyrightable subject matter based on a bizarre reading of the statute and the House Reports that accompanied both the Sound Recording Act of 1971 and the Copyright Act of 1976.

Further, the Sixth Circuit's legal reasoning regarding the applicability of the de minimis doctrine was equally perplexing. It's well established that the de minimis concept applies to copyright law in general. The Sixth Circuit's determination that the *de minimis* doctrine doesn't apply to sound recordings, specifically as it relates to sampling, is an opinion that is at odds with the common law tradition of de minimis, sampling case law, and fair use adjudication. Moreover, wreckessly blocking sound recordings and sampling — just one particular form of copying — from access to the de minimis defense, which is essentially what the Sixth Circuit's bright-line did, not only stifles creativity by making access to the art of sampling unnecessarily difficult, it runs counter to the purpose of copyright law.

With its dismissal of Congress' clear intent and instructions for the sound recording copyright; its break from how copyright infringement cases are proven in court; its deliberate elimination of the de minimis defense with regards to the copying of sound recordings; its contrary response to all relevant case law, statutory language, and legislative history; and its highly questionable bright-line, the Sixth Circuit's decision in *Bridgeport* must be seen as a judicial overreach that attempted to subvert the Copyright Act, not to mention a long history of legal precedent in cases involving copyright infringement.

So what does this all really mean now? The damage of the Sixth Circuit's decision in *Bridgeport* is that it jeopardized the validity of transformative appropriation when it involves sound recordings. But transformative appropriation of any subject matter is a method long-practiced in the arts (particularly literature and music). A fact so well-recognized by the courts that it prompted these words by Justice Story: *"[i]n truth, in literature, in science and in art, there are, and can be, few, if any, things, which in an abstract sense, are strictly new and original throughout. Every book in literature, science and art, borrows, and must necessarily borrow, and use much which was well known and used before."* [266]

Also, the Sixth Circuit's decision in *Bridgeport* jeopardized fair and equitable access to the core of the entire sampling aesthetic itself. In effect, with it's "Get a license or do not sample" bright-line rule, the Sixth Circuit attempted to hand over the exclusive right to sample old songs — and create new art using said samples — to the copyright owners of those old songs or those who could afford to pay sample licensing fees. Not only does this setup an unequal access window to the art of sampling — as musicians without major label backing or considerable financial resources are essentially blocked

---

[266] *Id.*, 575.

from sampling because they can't afford the clearance fees — it also undermines the progress of the art form and essentially takes the art away from the artists. Thus, there is no doubt that the Sixth Circuit's decision stifles creativity and undermines the very purpose of copyright law.

Additionally, what effects has the Sixth Circuit's decision in *Bridgeport* had on the music industry's approach to the sampling quandary? For the most part, the status quo still exists. Labels, lawyers, and sample clearance houses still advise that all samples be cleared. Only now, the justification for such advocacy is embolden by *Bridgeport* — and the lawsuit neurosis that hangs over the art of sampling in the music industry is even stronger. Plus, 11 years after the *Bridgeport* decision, the music industry has not reformed the sample clearance system, and there's no reason to believe that they will do so any time soon.

And what of *Bridgeport's* effect on the art of sampling overall? Well, unlike some commentators, I've never taken the Sixth Circuit's ruling as a death knell for the art of sampling for a number of reasons. The Sixth Circuit's decision was based on improper legal reasoning, it contained key contradictions, and, most importantly, it was always at complete odds with the Copyright Act. So, I have no doubt that other courts would resoundingly reject the Sixth Circuit's opinion, especially as it broadens copyright protection for sound recordings and grants sound recording copyright holders more rights than other copyright proprietors, something the Copyright Act explicitly guards against.

Furthermore, the art of sampling has developed and will continue to develop outside of the purview of the courts, no matter what the courts say. Most sample-based musicians are unfamiliar with sampling case law, let alone the *Bridgeport* ruling, a fact I hope to change with this study. Moreover, the majority of innovative sample-based recording artists do not take their creative cues from the judicial system. Most sample-based beatmakers get their cues from the sampling tradition of hip hop/rap music itself. For sample-based beatmakers, it is the collective aesthetic, historical, methodological, and ethical aspects of the art of sampling in the hip hop/rap tradition that we take our lead from. Plus, most new sample-based artists will continue to take full advantage of the powerful sampling tools that are evermore affordable. So as long as people want to sample, and as long as the technology exists, the art of sampling will prevail.

Finally, by 2004, the sample clearance system was already well-established, and most major label-backed sampling musicians were already being encouraged not to sample, or at least get clearances for the samples that they were using. Yet, the art of sampling survived, despite a sea-size departure from the tradition by many artists.

Long Live De Minimis and Fair Use!

As my examination of *Bridgeport* in this chapter has shown, the Sixth Circuit's decision — a decision ripe with improper legal reasoning, factual inaccuracies, contradictions, and other questionable findings — was not supported by the Copyright Act or the legislative history on the sound recording copyright, nor was it in line with all sampling cases (save for *Grand Upright*) prior to its own curious "bright-line" decision. While the music industry may now consider this issue to be settled law, as it further cements the stance that the major record companies already had — i.e. that all samples, no matter how brief or insignificant or how much a musician manipulates them, require a license — the truth is, all samples do not presumably require a license.

It's important to understand that the de minimis defense is certainly alive and well outside of the Sixth Circuit's jurisdiction. In *EMI Records, LLC v. Premise Media*, the New York Supreme Court rejected the Sixth Circuit's ruling in Bridgeport:

> **A number of reasons persuade this Court against endorsing the recommendation in Bridgeport Music. Putting aside that Bridgeport Music does not represent controlling authority, this Court declines to follow the statutory interpretation of Section 114 relied upon by the court in Bridgeport Music to declare the bright line rule that a de minimis exception is not available.** The criticism of Bridgeport Music by Prof. David Nimmer best articulates this Court's basis for rejecting the holding therein.

"Indeed, had Bridgeport Music [the Sixth Circuit] consulted Section 114's legislative history instead of dismissing that history as irrelevant, it would have discovered that Congress explicitly noted in that context that "infringement takes places whenever all or any substantial portion of the actual sounds that go to make up a copyrighted sound recording are reproduced in phonorecords by repressing, transcribing, recapturing off the air, or any other method…." That excerpt debunks the court's imputation that Congress, when adopting Section 114, intended to dispense with traditional notions of substantial similarity."[267]

Equally important to remember is the fact that fair use has not gone anywhere. The unique limitation that fair use places on the exclusive rights of copyright holders is codified in the Copyright Act. The Sixth Circuit did not explore fair use in *Bridgeport*; yet another unfortunate mistake made by the court. And despite some commentators assertions that the Sixth Circuit may have eliminated the fair use defense in cases involving copyright infringement and sound recordings, the truth is, the Sixth Circuit couldn't eliminate fair use if they tried. (Incidentally, the Sixth Circuit later amended their decision, stating that No Limit wasn't barred from using a fair use defense on appeal.)

All thing considered, the Sixth Circuit's bright-line rule was an unintelligible scheme for ending the sampling quandary. Based on improper legal reasoning, a terrible misinterpretation of the Copyright Act, highly questionable and incomplete observations of the sample clearance system, and a complete misunderstanding of and a perhaps negative bias against the art of sampling, the bright-line rule did more to hurt long established principles of copyright law than it did to hinder the art of sampling from moving forward.

---

[267] *Emi Records Limited v. Premise Media Corp. L.P.* 2008 N.Y. Misc. LEXIS 7485 (N.Y. Sup. Ct. Aug. 8, 2008) See also *Lennon v. Premise Media Corp*, 556 F. Supp. 2d 310 - (Dist. Court, SD New York 2008).

Chapter 14

Post-*Bridgeport*
Five Key Developments that Signal Change in the Music Industry's Attitude Towards Sampling

Since the infmaous *Bridgeport* decision, there have been a number of developments that punctuate how and why the music industry's hostile attitude towards sampling is going to change. This chapter examines five of these developments and considers their collective role in increasing the profile of fair use.

Girl Talk and the Court Room Showdown the Music Industry Has Been Unwilling to Have

Between 2002 and 2010, Girl Talk (Greg Gillis), perhaps the most famous mashup artist to date, sampled well over one thousand different songs — many of which were/are contemporary popular hits; and none of the samples did he or his then record label Illegal Art try to clear — and used them as the bedrock for five different albums that were released in that same eight-year span. For his album *Feed the Animals* (2008), his label even listsed all of the artists and songs that were sampled per each track. That's upwards of 300 tracks, including songs by the likes of Queen, Led Zeppelin, Janet Jackson, Boz Scags, J. Geils Band, Gwen Stafani, Hall & Oates, and Jay-Z. In other words, it's not like Girl Talk and Illegal Art have been hiding. So why hasn't Girl Talk been sued yet? I mean, if the labels feel empowered by the *Bridgeport* Get-a-license-or do-not-sample-ruling, why haven't they gone after Girl Talk?

I believe it's because the major record companies (themselves pieces of large, multinational corporations) do not want a showdown in the courts over fair use and sampling because they're worried about what will happen if (when) they lose. So their stance is to carry on with the status quo, which means: 1) Reinforce the notion — through fear and lies — that all samples, no matter how small, must be cleared; and 2) Maintain some Wizard-of-Ozian fear that you will be sued if you do not clear a sample.

The underlying point here is that the labels thrive on ignorance and fear (and not just when it comes to sampling and copyright law: They have long benefited from artists not understanding their one-sided, boilerplate contracts and ad-hoc customs). They have continuously perpetuated the lie that fair use is nothing but "just a defense." In this way, they have kept the safe harbor of fair use out of the view of sample-based musicians. Further, since the mid-'90s, the labels have used a campaign of fear to pressure artists into clearing even the most minute samples; at the same they have deterred many would-be sample-based musicians from sampling.

What makes this more troubling is that the culture of fear that the labels created has now lead to a sub-culture of safety. There is no shortage of commentators willing to discuss how and why you should clear samples; and there are countless articles online detailing how to sample "safely". In the last several years, I've read many of these types of articles and all of them detail how to clear a sample or suggest doing a replay as a work around. However, none of these articles highlight the fact that: 1) Sampling is an art form; 2) That all samples do NOT require a license by law — i.e. that there is no law that holds that a musician must get a license to sample; and 3) That de minimis and Fair use are rights of the public. In other words, the safety first/how-to-clear-a-sample guides are towing the label's line and reinforcing the myth that ALL samples must be cleared. By overlooking the fact that de minimis and fair use are legitimate pathways for sample-based musicians, these safety first, how-to-clear-a-sample guides are not only painting an incomplete picture, they are helping to keep these fundamental concepts of copyright outside of public view. This is why the labels see Girl Talk as a problem they don't want to deal with; a lawsuit against him shines a bright light on issues that they'd prefer to keep in the dark.

Certainly, the music industry has never lacked an appetite for filing lawsuits against alleged copyright infringers, so it's obvious why they haven't sued Girl Talk (yet). It's not simply that Girl Talk might prevail against them; it's because a lawsuit against Girl Talk — no matter if copyright infringement is found or not — represents a watershed moment for fair use and sampling.

Some commentators have maintained that the reason that Girl Talk has avoided legal action from the labels is because he's white. But the notion that the labels have refrained from suing Girl Talk (and Illegal Art, the label that distributed his infringement-provocative works) simply because Girl Talk is white is misguided and naive. That the labels, and literally thousands of publishers/copyright holders, conspired to not sue Gillis and his label for copyright infringement because Gillis is white is conspiracy theory at it's worst. It's also inconsistent with sampling case law (the Beastie Boys, who were the target of one if the most well known infringement suits, were white).

Attempting to connect the don't-sue-Girl-Talk-for-copyright-infringement campaign to the music's industry long history of bias against and serious mistreatment of black recording artists is a big reach. The music industry's record on race, or better stated, its history of shenanigans against black recording artists, including stealing songs, song credits, and copyrights, should never be forgotten or overlooked. But this Girl Talk non-situation situation isn't about race. A broader discussion about the racial/ethnic makeup of who's doing the sampling as well as who's being sampled is an intriguing one to have, and I think it deserves more attention. But conflating that discussion (and using the DJ Drama FBI raid as evidence of the bias, as some commentators have) with the primary reason why no label has yet to sue Girl Talk for copyright infringement blurs the issue. The reason Girl Talk hasn't been sued (yet) is not because he's white; it's because he poses a serious threat to the status quo.

Since 2002, the labels have reserved their right not to sue Girl Talk. From the record companies' perspective, this is the most prudent approach. *Let sleeping dogs lie, right?* Whether they win the battle against Girl Talk or not, a lawsuit against him will open up a Pandora's box. It will not only remove the veil surrounding fair use — thereby alerting others who's sample-based works are also likely fair use — it will also diminish the music industry's role in framing the debate about the art of sampling, the implications that it holds for copyright law, and the current sample clearance system.

But, if the labels ever do sue Girl Talk for copyright infringement, he'd be smart to enlist the counsel of Karen Shatzkin.

The Rising Profile and Importance of Fair Use Crusader Karen Shatzkin

In the music and documentary film spaces, there has been no shortage of aggressive lawyers going after alleged copyright infringers. But now, the other team — i.e. the team that correctly sees fair use as it is: A vital part of copyright law and the constitution — has someone equally aggressive. Her name is Karen Shatzkin.

Karen Shatzkin, partner at Shatzkin & Mayer, P.C., is a well known and highly regarded attorney who represents numerous fiction and documentary filmmakers, designers, publishers, musicians, and fine artists. She has extensive litigation experience, particularly in the area of copyright and fair use, and thus, she holds a firm understanding of the music industry's general attitude (disdain) towards fair use and music clearance. A regular speaker on various panels covering media and doc studies and fair use, Shatzkin is a highly sought after voice in this space.

In the fall of 2015, I had the privilege of attending the Volunteer Lawyers for the Arts (VLA) "Fair Use: Current Developments Panel," at which Karen Shatzkin spoke and so graciously shared her insight and stories from the trenches. Below, I have included some quotes and highlights, both from her talk at the VLA panel as well as her 2012 talk at the New School, that demonstrate just why she's become the ultimate fair use crusader.

Karen Shatzkin On the Absurdity of Sums that Copyright Holders Feel Entitled To and the General Public's Unfamiliarity with Fair Use

"If you go to sources who own copyrighted materials, you will be shocked at the sums that they consider themselves entitled to," Shatzkin said, speaking at VLA's "Fair Use" panel. "A client of mine, who actually teaches documentary film at M.I.T., is making a wonderful documentary and wanted to use a headline. A headline from the *Chicago Tribune*, I think it was the *Chicago Tribune*. And if I'm not mistaken, my recollection is that when she called them to ask, they said it would be $7,000 to put their headline in her film. And I said, 'Did you have to get it from them?' She said, 'No.' So I said, 'Then, forget about it. You're not going to pay them $7,000, and you're gonna put it in your film. Why? Because of the doctrine of fair use."

Here, Shatzkin not only points out the absurdity that some copyright holders are willing to engage in, but just how little most people (copyright holders included) actually understand how fair use works. In Shatzkin's retelling of a situation involving a former client, the *Chicago Tribune* allegedly wanted to charge a wopping $7,000 — presumably for no reason other than the fact that they could charge any amount that they wanted to — to use a headline in a documentary. At the same time, Shatzkin's client had no idea that she did not need the paper's permission to simply use one headline of theirs in her documentary, that it was a clear instance of fair use.

Karen Shatzkin On the Key Principle of Fair Use

"Transformative is now the key principle that underlies fair use law," Shatzkin said at the VLA "Fair Use" panel. "Transformative doesn't mean that you take a scene from a movie or the text from a book and you literally alter that. It doesn't mean that in *Gone With the Wind* [the movie], she's suddenly walking up the stairs, instead of down the stairs, or that something different happens in the [new] film than what happened in [*Gone With the Wind*]. It

397

doesn't mean that you have to alter the work itself. If you add new expression, which can be your own expression about it; if you add new meaning to it, if you add a new message to it. So it means, for example, that you put it in a new context."

Here, Shatzkin is discussing how the transformative principle is what courts are now looking more closely at. For a long time, market harm was the key principle that the courts looked at. But that trend has changed, as the degree of transformation, always a major component of the four factors attached to fair use, is more and more the determining factor in cases where fair use was found.

Karen Shatzkin On Fortuitous Capture

"Often, filmmakers have substantially more negotiating power and greater rights to use pre-existing material than they initially perceive. We can often help filmmakers avoid spending countless hours and scarce dollars obtaining permissions that were totally unnecessary — or worse, excising material from their films that they have every right to include."

For instance, in detailing her dealings with the major labels when she represented the producers of the film *Prom Night in Mississippi* (2009), a documentary about a high school in Mississippi that had its first non-segregated prom in the school's history, Shatzkin discussed how the labels wanted her clients to clear all of the music that was playing in the background at the prom. "There's no way you can understand without hearing the music," Shatzkin claimed, pointing out this was an example of fortuitous capture, i.e. incidental recording."[268] "With many of the things that you film, first of all, you might not even be able to filter out music. But if you're in a restaurant, whatever's playing is actually what's part of what's actually happening there. And so, if you catch those things in your film...if you use something because it's actually part of the events that you are filming, then, that's gonna be fair use."[269]

[268] Karen Shatzkin speaking at "Fair Use: Current Developments Panel," Voluntary Lawyers for the Arts, October 6, 2015..
[269] "Karen Shatzkin On Fair Use," New School Doc Studies, (November 29, 2012) https://vimeo.com/54527399.

But "the Sony's of the world, the Universals of the world, they don't want to admit that anything is fair use. They don't care about fair use," Shatzkin said, in reference to the labels' stance that the music played by the DJ at the prom in *Prom Nigh* had to be cleared. "But what happens when the music is the subject," Shatzkin rhetorically asked, pointing out that the music, which was a representative mix of the tastes of the prom goers, was incidental even though it was critical to better understanding the story. Embolden by the law, Shatzkin says that she wrote a letter to the label after they threatened a lawsuit for copyright infringement. "I made the point that's really not in your interest…If you don't like what I'm saying, then sue me."[270]

Karen Shatzkin On Not Expecting Copyright Holders to Acknowledge Fair Use

"I'm a firm believer that if you go to sources who own materials, you will be shocked at the sums that they consider themselves entitled to…They can put any price on it that they choose…If you can get access; if you have it [access] from the owner of the intellectual property, the owner of the copyright, then, there's no point in discussing fair use. Because if you have to go to the owner to get it, they're not interested in fair use. If they charge $45 a second with a minimum of a minute, and every clip is separate, then, they're gonna charge it to you whether you think it's fair use, or I think it's fair use, or not."[271]

This issue reminds me of all the commentary about sampling music *safely*, which is essentially a euphemism for clearance. If someone's use of a snippet of a sound recording or a small audio (or visual) clip of a movie meets the transformative factor of fair use, which is to say that it's transformative inasmuch as it recontextualizes the copyrighted material it uses — i.e. it adds something new, such as a new expression or new meaning — then it's likely that said use of a sample is fair use. Still, because the

[270] Karen Shatzkin at VLA "Fair Use: Current Developments Panel."
[271] Karen Shatzkin On Fair Use," The New School's "Doc Talk Podcast," (November 29, 2012) https://vimeo.com/53536025.

fear of a copyright infringement lawsuit (a fear perpetuated by the music industry) is so pervasive, and because very little is known about fair use in the general public, the notion of sampling safely is relegated to the side of clearance, not the side of sampling in a way that's more likely to be fair use.

But, as I raised the question earlier in this study, shouldn't sampling *safely* include sampling that's done in a way that it's likely fair use, if not de minimis? I believe that Shatzkin speaks to this point, as she, theoretically speaking, suggests to documentary filmmakers that they should first look for ways to incorporate fair use, rather than first seek licenses (clearances) for things that they may not even need a license for. Similarly, I believe that sample-based musicians should first incorporate samples in ways that are likely fair use, if not de minimis, rather than be guided by a clear-first apparatus propagated by a music industry that does not like to recognize fair use.

Karen Shatzkin On Fair Use as Free Speech

"Without the fair use doctrine, copyright law would run afoul of the free speech protections afforded by the First Amendment," Shatzkin says. "It's not an invitation to poach the intellectual property of others instead of creating your own work... Fair use is the lubricant between copyright law and your First Amendment right to express yourself..." But this doesn't meant that fair use is "an invitation to poach the intellectual property of others instead of creating your own work."[272]

Here, Shatzkin reminds us that fair use is a critical component of free speech; that it is protected by the U.S. Constitution. This is the light in which fair use should be seen in by everybody. Fair use should never be dismissed, as the music industry so often prefers to do, as just a defense in a copyright infringement lawsuit.

---

[272] Karen Shatzkin at VLA "Fair Use: Current Developments Panel."

Notorious B.I.G. LLC v Lee Hutson
Proof That the Will to Test Fair Use in the Courts is Growing Stronger

It looks like the late Notorious B.I.G.'s impact on music may have a second act. Only this time, the impact will likely hold critical implications for sampling and U.S. copyright law. On March 31, 2014, in what was considered to be a preemptive lawsuit, the estate of Notorious B.I.G. filed for declaratory judgment in a California federal court, seeking relief that B.I.G's 1994 song "The What" — off of the classic album *Ready to Die* — was not a copyright infringement of the 1974 song "Can't Say Enough About Mom," performed by Leroy Hutson (co-written by Hutson and Michael Hawkins). While the suit raised the issues of valid copyright ownership, statute of limitations, and the doctrine of laches (waiting too long to file the claim), and producer indemnification, it was the fair use claim that undoubtedly had many of those on both sides of the sampling and copyright law quandary closely watching how this case would turn out.

The Complaint

According to the complaint filed by lawyers on behalf of B.I.G.'s estate, Leroy Huston "began a campaign of accusations against Plaintiff [Christopher Wallace PKA 'Notorious B.I.G.,' 'Biggie,' and 'Biggie Smalls'], claiming that the Recording ['The What,' produced by Easy Mo Bee and featuring Method Man] violated his alleged copyright in 'Can't Say Enough About Mom.'" The complaint describes Hutson's "campaign of accusations" as having began in 2012, when lawyers for Hutson sent Bad Boy Records notice of alleged copyright infringement, and having included numerous requests for financial compensation (as much as 50% of all income attributable to the recording) and part ownership (also as much as 50%); each request routinely made with the accompanying threat of a copyright infringement lawsuit.[273]

In other words, Hutson repeatedly harassed Bad Boy Records (and Atlantic Records, Warner Music Group, and EMI), likely in an attempt to force a quick financial settlement in exchange for not filing a copyright infringement lawsuit for an uncleared sample of Hutson's song. These "ongoing, intensifying, and ultimately baseless accusations," especially Hutson's recent (and second) attempt to get a "legal hold" placed on "all royalties of the Recording" and to put a stop to "all distribution of the album [Ready to Die]," are what prompted the estate of Notorious B.I.G. to file civil action for declaratory relief.

They Were Never Scared – the Law Was Always on Their Side

Rather than cave to the threat of a copyright infringement lawsuit and settle out of court (as the labels tend to do), the estate of Notorious B.I.G. retained an expert to help assist them in analysis and comparison of the two songs at question. Citing in the complaint their expert's findings and including Easy Mo Bee's (the producer of the B.I.G. track) meticulous, multidimensional description of how he composed "The What," the estate of Notorious B.I.G. — which did not deny the actual sampling — asserted in the complaint that the "use has not violated any valid copyright interest held by" Hutson, and, more importantly, that the "use" is both "de minimis and fair use." Thus, B.I.G.'s estate rejected the common infringement shakedown and balked at paying Mr. Hutson or assigning an owner percentage to him, particularly without first doing their own due diligence. Having done their due diligence, B.I.G.'s estate concluded that "The What" did not infringe upon "Can't Say Enough About Mom," and they demonstrated their preparedness to prove it in court. In other words, Hutson's infringement shakedown attempt was thwarted mainly because the estate of Notorious B.I.G. was, unlike the labels and most established artists, never scared to affirm fair use.

---

[273] *Notorious B.I.G. LLC v Lee Hutson*, 2:14-cv-02415 (3/31/14).

402

As I detailed earlier in this study, when determining unlawful appropriation, the courts engage in a substantial similarity analysis in which quantitative and qualitative factors are assessed. An allegedly infringing work is considered substantially similar when it is nearly indistinguishable from the copyrighted work it appropriated. Quantitative analysis examines whether the sample constituted a substantial portion of the appropriated work, NOT whether it made up a substantial portion of the allegedly infringing work. Qualitative analysis considers whether the sample (copied portion) is qualitatively important to the allegedly infringed work as a whole. This means how critical, qualitatively speaking, is the sample (copied portion) to the appropriated work, and as a whole, how similar are the allegedly infringing song and the song it sampled. In order to determine proof of substantial similarity in a copyright infringement case, the courts conduct a two-part test of extrinsic similarity and intrinsic similarity. The extrinsic test is objective in nature and requires the party who brought the infringement claim to identify specific criteria which it alleges have been copied.

So at question were three things: 1) As a whole, how similar is "The What" and "Can't Say Enough About Mom?;" 2) How critical, qualitatively speaking, is the sample (copied portion) to "Can't Say Enough About Mom?;" and 3) Does "The What" sample a substantial portion of "Can't Say Enough About Mom?" In my own analysis and comparison, I found no substantial similarity between "The What" and "Can't Say Enough About Mom." In fact, if there ever was a more clear cut case of fair use, I haven't heard it. Quantitatively and qualitatively speaking, the sample is a 4-second snippet of a barely audible fade out that appears — only once on the entire 5:54 long song — at the 5:50 mark. This snippet is neither substantial to the melody, rhythm, chorus, or main theme of "Can't Say Enough About Mom." And even an "ordinary person" could tell that "Can't Say Enough About Mom" is a song about a son's tribute to his mother, wherein he repeatedly professes his love and respect for his mother. Whereas "The What" is a braggadocios song about a skeptical worldview (the hook says, "Fuck the World!...")

in which the protagonists praise the values of being independent, street wise, and well armed. Certainly, the estate of Notorious B.I.G. came to a similar conclusion in their own analysis.

The Will to Test Fair Use in the Courts Continues to Grow

Whether the estate of the Notorious B.I.G. was simply shielding itself from any potential lawsuit from Leroy Hutson or aiming for some grander statement, I think it's clear that this case, one way or the other, is a watershed moment in the history of the sampling and copyright law quandary. Notwithstanding the other issues raised in the filing, namely the validity of Hutson's copyright ownership (sorry, a Wikipedia citing certainly does not establish Hutson's copyright in a song), this is a perfect test case for sampling and fair use.

On April 2, 2014, two days after the estate of the Notorious B.I.G. filed their complaint, Hutson formally filed a lawsuit for copyright infringement in the U.S. District Court, Southern District of New York, in Manhattan — *Hutson et al v. The Estate of Christopher Wallace et al* — against the estate of B.I.G., Bad Boy, EMI, Universal Music Group, and Warner Music Group. This New York case was stayed, pending a resolution of Hutson's Motion to Dismiss the California case.

On July 3, 2014, the preemptive suit brought by the estate of Notorious B.I.G. was dismissed (as perhaps it should have been, given that the California court had no jurisdiction), and legal action continued to move forward in the New York court — where the estate of Notorious B.I.G. filed a motion to dismiss on September 5, 2014 — all the way up until October 24, 2014. On December 21, 2015, the New York court filed its decision, granting B.I.G.'s estate's motion to dismiss.

However, none of the fair use issues raised by B.I.G.'s estate were addressed in the court's decision. Instead, the court held that since Hutson could not prove ownership of the copyright in "Can't Say Enough About Mom" (Hutson acknowledged a settlement that he made with Rhino and Warner Records in 2008 over Curtom

Records recordings in which he granted copyright ownership of "Can't Say Enough About Mom" and other recordings to Rhino), he lacked standing to sue B.I.G.'s estate for copyright infringement.

So what now? Does this mean that B.I.G.'s estate will face a lawsuit from Rhino for the same alleged infringement? I highly doubt it. But if they do, I can't see the defense by B.I.G.'s being any different or less persuasive. So while Judge Sullivan didn't get into the fair use issues that B.I.G.'s estate raised in its defense, this case is still important. For one thing, B.I.G.'s estate had the will to fight this copyright infringement lawsuit; their aggressive action will only serve to prompt others to do the same in the face of similar lawsuits. Second, and more importantly, the action taken by B.I.G.'s estate raises the profile of fair use and helps make the will to test fair use in other sampling/copyright infringement cases much stronger. I've long held that the infringement shakedowns in music sampling would end sooner or later. On the heels of this B.I.G. case (and the *Jay-Z TufAmerica v. WB Music Corp. et al* case, which I cover in the following section), it looks like the ending's going to be much sooner.

TufAmerica vs. Jay-Z: Who Says a Sample Can't Be De Minimis?

Ask any music industry lawyer if an unlicensed sample of a song, no matter how small or insignificant, constitutes copyright infringement or if it's illegal to sample something even as little as a kick or snare drum from a song, and chances are they'll say, "Yes." This despite the fact that 1) copyright infringement is not determined outside a court of law; and 2) no form of copying is inherently illegal (i.e. amounts to infringement simply by the act of copying). When it comes to copyright law, the labels have always had a one-sided, rights-holders-above-the-public stance. And *Bridgeport* made matters worse by emboldening this stance and helping to shape a wider misunderstanding of U.S. copyright law within the music industry and general public. But a recent ruling (December, 2014) in a high profile sampling/copyright infringement suit involving Jay Z not only shatters this long-held stance, it pushes back hard against the all-sampling-must-have-a-license myth of *Bridgeport* and further demonstrates how *Bridgeport* got it wrong.

TufAmerica Inc. v. WB Music Corp. et al:
Background and Complaint

In November, 2013, Record label TufAmerica Inc., a sampling troll (much like Bridgeport) that buys up rights to old songs then looks for samples of said songs so that they can sue people for copyright infringement, sued Atlantic Recording Corporation, Jay-Z (Shawn Carter), his entertainment company, Roc Nation LLC, Roc-a-Fella Records, LLC, WB Music Corp, and Warner-Tamberlane Publishing Corp for copyright infringement in New York federal court, claiming that they used unauthorized samples of Eddie Bo's 1969 song "Hook & Sling," which TufAmerica holds the exclusive rights to, in the hit 2009 Jay-Z song, "Run This Town," which feature guest performances by Kanye West and Rihanna, and which appeared on Jay-Z's 2009 album *The Blueprint 3* and the greatest hits compilation *The Hits Collection Vol. 1*, as well as in a music video. Specifically, TufAmerica's complaint alleged that "defendants used one or more unauthorized samples of significant portions of the Hook & Sling Master and Composition in Run This Town," and that TufAmerica did not authorize "defendants to release, exploit or publicly perform ['Hook & Sling']."[274]

In response, in September, 2014, Jay-Z filed a motion to dismiss, arguing that while he did indeed use the sample, the sample was too insignificant to warrant copyright protection: "Plaintiffs entire, misguided copyright infringement lawsuit is based on an alleged 'sample' of the most fleeting one-syllable word — 'oh' — in defendants' sound recording entitled, 'Run This Town' ('Defendants' Recording'), performed by the artist Jay-Z." But Jay-Z's lawyers also demonstrated their own misunderstanding of copyright law:

---

[274] *Tufamerica, Inc. v.. WB Music Corp. et al*, 1:13-cv-07874 S.D.N.Y. (2014)....

"Plaintiff does not allege that any musical element of Plaintiffs Works was copied - only the spoken word "oh," which appears just once in the introduction to Plaintiff's Works at approximately the 3-second mark, lasts for a fraction of a second in Plaintiffs Recording and is not repeated. Plaintiff apparently believes that it has a monopoly on the use of the word "oh" and that it can stop others from using this word in recorded form." The reality is that any element — musical or otherwise, and no matter how long it lasts — on the Eddie Bo recording was protected by U.S. copyright law. Whether the borrowing of said elements is de minimis, fair use, or copyright infringement is a separate matter altogether.

The first point that Jay-Z's lawyered argued was that "words and short phrases are simply not protectable under the Copyright Act. Thus, Plaintiff cannot state a claim based on the alleged infringement of a generic lyric such as, 'oh,' or the sound recording thereof, and Plaintiffs claims should be dismissed as a matter of law." Their second point was that "even if the word 'oh' or the miniscule portion of Plaintiffs Recording featuring the single word was somehow original enough to warrant copyright protection, the alleged copying here of a sound lasting a fraction of a second in Plaintiffs Works is de minimis and thus not actionable." That because the snippet in question "lasted less than one second, [it] is not quantitatively significant." Jay-Z's lawyers bolstered this point offering examples of where courts had found much longer sampled phrases to be not quantitatively significant, e.g. "by TufAmerica, 968 F. Supp. 2d at 605-606 (a three-second sample and a six-second sample were not quantitatively significant); Poindexter, 2012 U.S. Dist. LEXIS 42174 (concluding on a motion to dismiss that the use of a single note sounding for close to two seconds was de minimis); Newton, 388 F.3d at 1258 (a six-second sample comprising 2% of plaintiffs work was not quantitatively significant)."[275]

Another boost for Jay-Z's second point of de minimis, and perhaps most damning to TufAmerica's claim of infringement, was TufAmerica's own history in the very court they were suing Jay-Z

[275] *Id.*, see defendants' memorandum of law in support of their motion to dismiss • declaration in support of motion to dismiss 1:13-cv-07874-LAK..

407

in: **"Plaintiff is well aware that this suit is baseless because it recently suffered dismissal of similarly misguided infringement claims based on more significant phrases than the single word at issue here. Indeed, in TufAmerica, Inc. v. Diamond, 968 F. Supp. 2d 588 (S.D.N.Y. 2013), this Court dismissed several of Plaintiff's claims, including composition and sound recording infringement claims, based on the alleged sampling of the phrase, "Now I want y'all to break this down," finding such alleged infringements were quantitatively and qualitatively insignificant as a matter of law.** One would think that, faced with this decision and the host of authority upon which it is based, Plaintiff would re-evaluate its objectively weaker 'claims' herein. Yet, it has refused, without explanation, to withdraw its claims here based on the objectively less significant sound of 'oh.'"[emphasis mine][276]

The Decision

On December 8, 2014, Judge Lewis A. Kaplan dismissed the case against Jay-Z, et. al brought by TufAmerica. That's the headline. However, the real gem is Kaplan's decision itself, as it serves as both a thorough walkthrough of copyright law (particularly how copyright infringement is determined), and an emphatic (albeit indirect) smack down of *Bridgeport*.

"Not every instance of copying of a protected work is copyright infringement," Kaplan plainly states in his decision, making it clear that: 1) sampling is simply a form of copying (not "stealing" as the plaintiffs described it in their complaint); and 2) That, as a form of copying, it does not inherently constitute copyright infringement. Here, Kaplan also offers up a strong rebuke of *Bridgeport's* misguided assertion that sampling itself requires a license or that all samples of sound recordings are illegal without a license.

Kaplan struck down Jay-Z's argument that the "oh" that he sampled and used in "Run This Town" was not original, and clarified that, "with respect to the word 'oh' as it appears in the Composition,

---

[276] *Id.*

defendants almost surely are right. The word "oh" is a single and commonplace word. Standing alone, it likely is not deserving of copyright protection," but the court "assumes, *arguendo*, that 'oh,' as it appears in 'Hook & Sling Part I', is protectable," and "For purposes of this motion alone, the Court assumes that Eddie Bo's rendition of 'oh' in the Master is protectable." In other words, Kaplan correctly noted that "oh" *standing alone* was not protectable, but as part of "the master" (the sound recording master) it was protectable; and further, that whether it was protectable or not wasn't important to the resolution of the motion because the "... defendants' motion to dismiss may be decided on other grounds."[277]

The "other grounds" that Kaplan was referring to was the substantial similarity test, in which he found that "the relevant works bear no substantial similarity to one another," and thus, "It would be impermissible to conclude that defendants are liable in this case." In other words, having undergone a substantial similarity test, which Kaplan notes that both parties agreed "on the basic framework of the substantial similarity test," but "quarreled over its particulars, the court found that the sampling of "oh" in "Run in This Town" is "sufficiently de minimis to render moot whatever otherwise might have been made of the alleged copying with respect to the qualitative significance of that which was copied."[278] That is to say, the court found that the sampling of "oh" was so minor and trivial, too quantitatively insignificant, that the qualitative significance didn't matter to the resolution of the motion.

TufAmerica's argument (specifically their response to Jay-Z's motion to dismiss), which, in part, relied on the notion that because Jay-Z used the sample "42 times" in "We Run This Town," the sample was automatically quantitatively and qualitatively significant, demonstrated a common misunderstanding of copyright law in general and how quantitative and qualitative significance is determined within the substantial similarity test in particular. Thus the court took the opportunity to make some key clarifications:

"Plaintiff's tautological argument that 'oh' must be

---

[277] *Id.*
[278] *Id.*

qualitatively significant to Hook & Sling Part I and to the Hook & Sling Master because defendants' sampled it more than 40 times in Run This Town misunderstands copyright law generally and the substantial similarity test in particular… First, and most importantly, the substantial similarity test in all cases considers only 'the qualitative and quantitative significance of the copied portion in relation to the plaintiff's work as a whole.' Its significance to the defendants' works is irrelevant. Were it the other way around, a devious defendant could evade liability for copying substantial or qualitatively significant portions of another's work merely by scattering those portions within his own, lengthy work. **Such a rule would fly in the face of Justice Story's admonition more than 170 years ago that the focus of copyright law is on the original work, not the subsequent one**: 'If so much is taken, that the value of the original is sensibly diminished, or the labors of the original author are substantially to an injurious extent appropriated by another, that is sufficient, in point of law, to constitute a piracy.' Ultimately, of course, **the fact that defendants allegedly sampled 'oh' 42 times in Run This Town says absolutely nothing about the recording's qualitative significance to Hook & Sling Part I or to Eddie Bo's performance thereof in the Hook & Sling Master.**"[emphasis mine][279]

Further, in addressing TufAmerica's argument that "the bar should be set low when evaluating whether a work is or is not 'qualitatively significant' in order to protect 'impecunious artists' in the face of 'unlicensed use' of their work by 'successful artists and increasingly-large record labels and music publishers,'" the court's clarifications are again instructive:

"If the allegedly copied portion 'arguably includes a creative component,' plaintiff urges, 'it should be considered … qualitatively significant.' Were the Court to grant the motion to dismiss, plaintiff warns, would-be infringers would have an implicit license to 'use for free the work that other artists created.' **This argument too is quite wide of the mark.** Indeed, it is one thing to set a low bar. It is quite another to set no bar at all… plaintiff's argument

---

[279] *Id.*

410

necessarily — and incorrectly — assumes that every copying of any part of another artist's protected work is infringement. But as Judge Newman explained for the Second Circuit, in a case plaintiff relies upon, **factual copying and actionable copying are not coextensive concepts.** The former 'requires only the fact that the infringing work copies something from the copyrighted work; the latter ... requires that the copying is quantitatively and qualitatively sufficient to support the legal conclusion that infringement ... has occurred."[emphasis mine][280]

Thus, as I've said before in this study and as many commentators have said, the act of sampling — i.e. factual copying — is not inherently copyright infringement. With regards to *Bridgeport*, this is an especially important point to acknowledge, because when opponents of sampling and copyright infringement hawks talk of "unauthorized sampling" or argue that all samples require a license, *Bridgeport* is the case that they and many other people point to as what "the law says." But here's the big fact that gets lost in conjecture, myth, and a general misunderstanding of copyright law : There is no law in the United States code that expressly prohibits the art of sampling or any other form of copying, nor does U.S. copyright law distinguish the level of protection of or access to (i.e. de minimis, fair use) a copyrighted work based on its category. Hence, as I've stated earlier in this study, *Bridgeport* only represented one court's (terribly flawed) ruling in a private copyright infringement case; *Bridgeport* is not a "law" of the United States.

What this Decision Means Now and for the Future

The biggest reason why *TufAmerica Inc. v. WB Music Corp. et al* is a beacon for the future is because it helps firmly establish that quantitatively insignificant samples of sound recordings — i.e. very minimal samples, like that of drum kicks and snares and sound-stabs — likely fall under the scope of de minimis (small, trifle, insignificant, usages) rather than fair use, which can often be more difficult for courts to determine. Thus, *TufAmerica Inc.*

---

[280] *Id.*

411

v. WB Music Corp. et al serves as another precedent for de minimis sampling and sets up a pathway for other artists facing similar suits. *TufAmerica Inc. v. WB Music Corp. et al* also sends a strong signal that these kind of frivolous lawsuits will likely continue to be thrown out. This is a good. For one thing, as it will help deter parties, particularly sample trolls like TufAmerica and Bridgeport, from seeking out these kind of frivolous lawsuits. More importantly, it demonstrates that reason and fact, with regards to sampling and copyright law, are winning out over labels and poor-drawn conclusions in the courts.

It's been 11 years since the infamous *Bridgeport* ruling; and the brainwashing and scars of *Bridgeport* still run deep. Many people still believe that there is such a thing as "unauthorized sampling" (you do not need authorization to sample, sampling itself is not illegal); many people still believe that it's "illegal" to sample any sound no matter how insignificant or how long the sound is; many people still think that there is a "law" that expressly stipulates that you can not sample a sound recording or use any sample of a sound recording without a license from the copyright holders of both the composition and the recording. All of this is untrue of course. And *TufAmerica Inc. v. WB Music Corp. et al* further sheds light on this fact.

EMI's Sample Amnesty
How Alex Black and EMI Just Became Friends of the Sample-Based Musician Community, and How they May Have Saved an Important Piece of the Music Industry's Sample Clearance System

In September, 2015, EMI, the world's largest music publisher, announced it's sample amnesty program. Basically what EMI said to sample-based musicians was this: You have six months to come to us from out of the shadows and turn in your sample-based songs that utilize samples of songs from our Production Music Division's catalog, in return we will give you a license and we won't penalize you for unauthorized use. But here's what EMI is certainly not saying: We recognize that some sample-based works may have made fair use (or de minimis) of our catalogs, and thus you do not necessarily need a license.

In other words, EMI's amnesty offering, as forward thinking and innovative as it is, is a means to increase revenue form their Production Music Division catalog. First, the program allows EMI to expand their catalog with sample-based songs without having to grapple with adding sample-based songs that would otherwise be unobtainable due to either EMI's unawareness of their existence or EMI's unwillingness to mount a wave of copyright infringement lawsuits against musicians that they suspect have used samples from their Production Music Division's Catalog. Second, and more importantly, EMI's sample amnesty serves as a way to draw attention to their Production Music Division catalog and to invite sample-based musicians to sample songs from said catalog, which includes songs that they own both the master recording and composition copyrights to; a key point, since owning both rights allows EMI to easily and quickly clear samples.

In the press release that EMI's sample amnesty program was announced, Alex Black, EMI Production Music Global Director and the main man driving the amnesty, said, "Our vision for this amnesty is to highlight the wealth of possibilities open to producers working with samples." I take him at his word. Still, in addition to highlighting the possibilities of sampling their Production Music Division catalog, EMI is also interested in corralling perhaps a large swath of uncleared sample-based songs — songs which may have never needed to be cleared in the first place — and then monetize those "new" songs.

But, as I've previously pointed out in this study, all samples do not need a license (i.e. need not be cleared), because sampling itself (or all samples) does (do) not constitute copyright infringement. U.S. Copyright law explicitly protects de minimis (small amount) and fair-use usages of all copyrightable material. Thus, can encouraging someone to turn in a song that uses a single drum hit/

sound, a small snippet of a sampled drum break, or an "electronic segment looped" — all staples of the art of beatmaking — be seen as EMI's way of subverting U.S. copyright law? Most music industry lawyers promote the lie that "the law" says even a sample of a stand alone drum sound requires a license, even though some of them silently acknowledge that such usages are either de minimis or fair use. But, more importantly for their purposes, music industry lawyers also know that most people, especially sample-based musicians, are unaware of the de minimis and fair use doctrines.

There is a big difference between "the law" and how the law works. Copyright infringement must be proven in a court of law. Thus, pre-emption, not just a pre-emptive suit (for example, what Pharrell and Robin Thicke did in the "Blurred Lines" case), is often used to circumvent the law. So what do you do if you're EMI and you want to add many sample-based songs (including those that may have made de minimis or fair use of EMI songs) to your catalog? Offer amnesty. Smart move.

By getting people to come forward and admit use, EMI gets access to the new sample-based songs, and there's no worry of an artist claiming fair use later on. In essence, once licensed, the maker of the sample-based song has conceded that the song *needed* to be cleared, and has thus forfeited his right to argue that the song made fair use of a song owned by EMI. This concerns me deeply, as I wonder if de minimis and fair use — mainstays of U.S. copyright law — will continue to be overshadowed by yet another mechanism that further pushes all sampling towards the clearance trail, effectively obscuring the fact that the de mininis and fair use components of copyright law are critical safe harbors for sample-based musicians.

I applaud Alex Black and EMI for engaging with the sampling community in this way. It's refreshing to see their support for sample-based music, particularly their description of the art of sampling in a creative context — it's certainly a far cry from recent descriptions of sampling as "piracy". Further, the fact that EMI will offer a licensing deal at current market rates, and that they will not, however, seek back royalties for any earnings made from songs that feature samples of their catalog is great. But if we put aside the actual implications of the amnesty itself and focus on the "license" component of EMI's innovative initiative, there remains some serious questions that every sample-based musician considering EMI's proposal should want to have answered.

First, how will this amnesty actually work on the publishing splits? In exchange for coming forward, will sample-based musicians simply receive a license and no penalty? Or will they also receive a split of the publishing? Better yet, will they have to forfeit 100% of the publishing to EMI? Furthermore, what will EMI's boilerplate amnesty agreement look like? What sort of stipulations will it contain? Also, if you do come forward with a sample-based song that incorporates a sample of a song from EMI's Production Music Division catalog, will you be required to submit the song first, offering up details on which songs from EMI's catalog that you actually sampled? If you change your mind, EMI has the song and, because of you, they know the sample(s) used. Thus, if you disagree to the license and amnesty, does that mean you've now voluntarily put yourself in the position to be sued by EMI for copyright infringement?

One way to see this is: EMI has all of the leverage, all of the upside. Another way to see it is: By gaining a license, a sample-based musician now has chance to earn additional revenue by shopping the now-licensed works to artists and outlets that they previously didn't have access to. Seems to me no matter where you come down on the copyright divide, that's a good thing for sample-based musicians.

Any way you look at EMI's amnesty offer, one thing is clear: This innovative program is a strong indication of where the music industry is headed with regards to sampling. The major labels and music publishers have left (and continue to leave) a lot of money on the table by treating sampling as some sort of bandit activity that requires a license in all cases; I think EMI's move is a recognition of this fact. Moreover, I believe that Alex Black is sincere when he says that EMI's program "aims to encourage new creative use of the expansive archives of the multiple participating EMI libraries." But I also believe that Black is aware of the burgeoning realities of sampling and copyright law. As more people take part in sampling in general (what Lawrence Lessig calls an ever growing "Remix Culture"), they will inevitably learn more about copyright law and aim for making works that are likely de mininis or fair use in nature. Thus, armed with a better understanding of copyright law, as well as the knowledge of recent court cases in which fair use prevailed, these sample-based musicians will be less inclined to seek licenses for their works and less intimidated by threats of lawsuits for copyright infringement. So I believe EMI's amnesty offer — which I appreciate and support — is also the music industry's sober acknowledgement of reality. About time.

Chapter 15

Proposals
Reforming Sample Clearance and Resolving the Sampling/ Copyright Quandary

Sampling is a popular art form that offers tremendous value to the public. But it must also be acknowledged that sampling most often relies on the use of copyrighted pre-existing sound recordings. Thus, before I get into a detailed discussion about the possible solutions to the sample licensing and copyright quandary, I must preface everything by stating that the fundamental purpose of any solution presented here is to strike a balance between protecting copyright owners' interests in their works and the public's interest in furthering creativity.

How to Reform the Sample Clearance System

I suppose it's first worth asking if the sample clearance can be reformed? Sure it *could* be reformed; it certainly needs to be. But it's not likely to happen because the level cooperation needed by publishers, record companies, and artists is just too high. Publishers and record companies would have to give up much of their discretion, and they'd have to be willing to streamline the clearance process. Most notably, they'd have to standardize response times and clearance rates; and, ideally, they'd have to forfeit the right to deny permission in most cases. In theory, overhauling or streamlining the structure of the present sample clearance system could be done. But there are many in the music industry who ignore, or perhaps do not recognize, the need for an overhaul of the sample clearance system. And let's not forget that there are many copyright proprietors in the music industry who lack a proper understanding of both the art of sampling and copyright law. So, any change in the sample clearance status quo would be seen by them as an affront against their (mostly flawed) interpretation of copyright law and their common industry practices. Still, a reformed sample clearance system would add efficiency, which would make it easier to clear samples that actually need to be cleared, as well as increase the revenue record companies and music publishers receive from sample licensing. Thus, what follows below is a framework for a more efficient sample clearance system.

Centralize the Sample Clearance System; Create the Recording Industry Sample Clearance Agency (RISCA)

The first area of reform in the sample clearance system involves creating a centralized agency or clearinghouse to handle all sample clearance issues. The present sample clearance system is an ad-hoc, every-person-for-themselves mechanism where access is not equitable, pricing is not formally tiered or even capped, and the time costs are uncertain. A centralized sample clearance system, let's call it the Recording Industry Sample Clearance Agency (RISCA), could bring much needed uniformity to the sample clearance system.

Set up by a committee that would include sample-based recording artists from various genres, record companies, music publishers, and music lawyers, and acting under the authority of the RIAA, RISCA could establish a number of key components. RISCA could set tier pricing and price caps for all sample license requests for samples that fall below the predetermined length that RISCA establishes. Indie or low-budget pricing and major label pricing, including reasonable fee minimums and caps based on the major label artist's popularity, could be formally setup. Additionally, RISCA could establish standard publishing splits between parties. Further, through a mechanism much like how ASCAP and BMI operates for performance rights, RISCA could standardized publishing payments and payment schedules.

RISCA could also set time constraints for RISCA sanctioned clearances. For example, after receiving a sample license request and a RISCA "clear sheet," which would include the corresponding tier pricing and other RISCA information, a copyright holder would have 7 days to outright reject a request or permit the process to move forward. If a copyright holder permits the process to move forward, then the license seeker would have 14 days to send payment to the copyright holder. If the license seeker fails to send payment within the allotted 14 days, the transaction is terminated. However, RISCA could establish rescue remedies in such cases. Such formal pricing tiers and time constraints would create a firm transaction time window, and would thereby remove much of the unpredictability from the process.

Further, RISCA could bring about an industry-wide acknowledgement that some samples do meet the de minimis threshold. Despite the *Bridgeport* ruling, which actually has no controlling authority on the matter, not all samples are infringement *per se*. Moreover, sound recordings, like other forms of copyrightable subject matter, are not exempt from the de minimis doctrine. Therefore, one key reform to the sample clearance system would be establishing a de minimis safe harbor for some levels of sampling. RISCA could hash out the parameters for what's considered to be insubstantial copying, or more directly, what doesn't need to be cleared. For example, these parameters could include a fixed time length cap of 3 seconds, and a reasonable transformative requirement for uses of 3 to 5 seconds; anything 5 seconds or more would not be shielded by RISCA's De Minimis Standards and Best Practices. In any case, RISCA could serve as the music industry's adjudicator and assessor of all samples that do not clearly meet its own de minimis threshold.

Finally, RISCA could also create an automated system by which the entire sample clearance process is handled. For instance, on RISCA's website, license seekers could see RISCA's tiered pricing, its De Minimis Standards and Best Practices statement, and accurate information about copyright law, specifically, what constitutes copyright infringement and a detailed explanation of fair use. The hope is that this information would help license seekers determine if they even need clearance for a particular use. Also, such information would clearly outline the penalties for copyright infringement.

License seekers could also initiate the clearance process on the RISCA website by submitting a simple online form. Since the license seeker can't be expected to know the names of the copyright proprietors, menu prompts could include the name of the artist and the artist's work that the license seeker is interested in, the length of the sample, and the tier level the license seeker is making the request under, along with the name and contact information of the license seeker.

Of course such an automated system would require record companies and music publishers to sign on to RISCA. But perhaps as a recognized sub-body of the RIAA, the RIAA could stipulate that record companies are already opted in. Those companies opted in would be submitted to the RISCA online database, where license seekers could see their contact information and perhaps even current catalog. For record companies to opt out, they'd have to make a formal request, and maybe even pay for a RISCA "opt out" waiver. I'm not sure how record companies and music publishers could be compelled to sign on to RISCA, but I'm convinced that most would sign on if they understood how much revenue they'd stand to earn (more regularly) from a streamlined sample clearance system. By reforming the sample clearance system through a centralized clearing agency like RISCA, record companies, recording artists, and music publishers could tap into a shadow sampling industry. No doubt this would boost the overall amount and frequency of revenue from sample licensing. I think this would provide the incentive necessary for all concerned parties in the music industry to opt in with RISCA.

Judicial Safe Harbor: A New Sampling Test for the Courts?

With regards to sampling cases that actually reach the courts, at least one commentator has suggested that the courts could come up with a new sampling test. Mueller's test proposes that the courts could:

> consider how prominent the sample is, whether it is an organizing feature of the defendant's song, and how many times it is used. Courts should also take into account the degree to which the sample was manipulated or altered. This test would take into account the ability of sample-based artists to loop a sample, thus making it longer or more prominent in their song than it was in the original. At the same time, this test would ensure that small samples that are used merely as accent or atmospheric sounds would not be considered infringement.[282]

I strongly object to any new court test for non-actionable sampling, mainly because any such test oversimplifies the art of sampling. More importantly, there already is a test for the courts, one that is required in all copyright infringement cases, and one that has long worked well when applied: the substantial similarity test! I trust the substantial similarity test far more than I do an arbitrary test made up by someone who does not completely understand all of the mechanics of the art of sampling.

Still, to perhaps increase the ease of the court's substantial similarity analysis in cases involving digital sampling, I agree that the courts should take into account the degree to which the sample was manipulated or altered. But this isn't really a proposal *per se*, as the courts are supposed to consider the level of transformation of the copy anyway — it speaks to the substantial similarity of the two works on a whole.

In further response to Mueller's proposal, a couple of points need to be addressed here. First, Mueller either misunderstands or is misrepresenting the role of looping in all sample-based beats.

---

[282] Mueller, 459.

Looping is not merely one "organizing feature" of a sample-based beat; looping is the most basic, fundamental arrangement component to sample-based beats. By her wording, I'm not sure if Mueller quite understands how important looping is in the overall aesthetic. Looping plays a vital role in the creation of sample-based beats, but overlooking this fact, would she presumably advise the courts to grant an infringement pass to samples that are *not* looped? Plus, the preference for "small," "atmospheric," non-looped samples is misguided. As far as creativity goes, it's just as bad as a bright-line rule that outlaws every non-cleared sample, as Mueller seems to presume that looped samples, no matter the size of the sample, are more likely to be infringements than non-looped samples.

Second, her proposal in this regard runs counter to how a quantitative analysis is to be conducted, because "the relevant question in copyright infringement cases is whether the segment in question constituted a substantial portion of the plaintiff's work, not whether it constituted a substantial portion of the defendant's work."[283] Therefore, if a sample does not constitute a substantial portion of the plaintiff's work, then the copying is less likely to be an illegal appropriation, regardless how many times it's looped or not. The general principle at work is *substantial similarity*; the number of times a sample is looped does not undermine this principle.

Thus, a possible danger of this part of Mueller's proposal is that the courts would now count how many times that a sample loops, regardless of the level of transformation of the sample and its use in a new context. Such a test would add an additional burden to the substantial similarity analysis in cases involving sampling. Again, such a test runs counter to the well established substantial similarity requirement of comparing both works *on a whole*. Also, Mueller's suggested expansion of the substantial similarity test would, in effect, broaden copyright protection for sound recordings. So Mueller's proposal, which seems to rely much less on a solid understanding of the core methods of the art of sampling than it does on a simple mathematical equation, misses much of what sampling is about, particularly the importance of the break — the

---

[283] *Jarvis v. A&M Records*, at 290.

loop — and emphasizes something closer to another bright-line rule. While *Bridgeport's* bright-line rule essentially bars all samples without a license, Mueller's bright-line rule, which oversimplifies the issues sampling raises, seeks relief for non-looped samples and makes them presumptively non-infringing (fair), but blocks relief for all looped samples and makes them presumptively infringing. Indeed, both bright-lines stifle creativity. If this part of Mueller's proposal were to be adopted, all instances of looped samples, a practice found in 100% of all sample-based beats, would presumably be infringing.

Perhaps Mueller's distinction for looped samples has something to do with most legal commentators' familiarity with only those sample-based musicians who had copyright infringement claims made against them, The Beastie Boys and Public Enemy being particular darlings of legal commentators. A deeper audit and analysis of the art of sampling in the hip hop/rap music tradition — through a study of a significantly higher number of sample-based artists, not just those highlighted by infringement cases — would show how fundamental the practice of looping is to the art form, and just how marginal "atmospheric," non-looped samples are, Instead, in parts of her proposal, Mueller reverses the importance of these two practices and pushes looping to the margin, making *small* or *atmospheric*, accenting samples the presumably non-infringing kind of sampling. But if a sample is highly transformed, recontextualized, and combined with other elements to make an entirely new work, it's absurd to consider the use as an infringement because is was looped. Looping, the fundamental sequencing/arrangement method of all sample-based music, is the necessary reality of all electronic music. Thus, I think the "looping" part of Mueller's proposal would actually create more problems than it solves.

Is a Compulsory License for Sound Recordings Really the Answer?

A compulsory license is a license to use content under reasonable and non-discriminatory terms. Defined only by an act of Congress,

423

in a compulsory license, a government forces the holder of a patent, copyright, or other exclusive right to grant use to the state and/or others. Usually, the holder does receive some royalties, either set by law or determined through some form of arbitration. In the United States, the most commonly known compulsory license is for "nondramatic musical works." According to this provision of copyright law, an individual can make a "cover" (i.e. a new version of a pre-existing sound recording) of a musical work, if that work has been previously distributed to the public by or under the authority of the copyright owner. Furthermore, in covering a song, the musical composition — the artist's music in written form — is used. Under the compulsory license for nondramatic musical works provision, there is no requirement that the new recording be identical to the previous work, as the compulsory license includes the privilege of rearranging the work to conform it to the recording artist's interpretation. However, this does not allow the artist to change the basic melody or fundamental character of the work. To take advantage of this compulsory license, a recording artist must simply provide notice and pay a royalty. The notice must be sent — within thirty days of making the recording, but before distributing physical copies — to the copyright owner, or if the recording artist is unable to determine the copyright owner, he or she may send notice to the Copyright Office. If this notice is not provided as prescribed, use of the work constitutes copyright infringement.

Looking at how a compulsory license for nondramatic musical works (compositions) is handled, one could see how a similar compulsory license for sound recordings might work. In fact, copyright law, as it is often unfairly interpreted in terms of how it pertains to sampling, should not be about the proscription of sampling; instead, it should be about the recognition of sampling as an art form, a valuable music compositional process, and an example of the role existing recording technology plays in modern musical practices. In other words, the art of *sampling* should be afforded the same compulsory license treatment that is given to the art imitating or rendering a *version* of a copyrighted music composition.

There are three fundamental reasons why a compulsory license for the sampling of sound recordings might be useful: (1) to update copyright law so that it reflects the realities of digital sampling, twenty-first century music compositional methods, and existing recording technology; (2) to end the current ad-hoc, onerous sample clearance system; and (3) to help to restore a creative balance and a higher level of artistic integrity to hip hop/rap music.

The purpose of copyright law and policy is to *promote,* not *stifle,* creativity. Moreover, the entire premise of copyright law and policy was born upon the fundamental understanding of the fact that all creativity, consciously and subconsciously, depends on the use, consideration, supplementation, and criticism of previous works. Therefore, the framers of the Constitution, specifically the leaders of copyright legislation, James Madison and Thomas Jefferson, recognized the need for creative works (or expressions) to enter into the public domain as soon as reasonably possible. Thus, the initial copyright protection term was just 14 years, renewable by *one* additional 14-year term. Altogether that's 28 years. Worth noting, given the fact that in hip hop/rap music, the overwhelming majority of sound recordings that are sampled have been recorded more than 35 years ago. Because Congress can enact any legislation that best promotes the arts, and because in order to update copyright law and bring it inline with the realities of digital sampling, twenty-first century music compositional methods and existing recording technology, a compulsory license for the sampling of sound recordings could be highly effective if it were implemented.

A compulsory license for the sampling of sound recordings could also put an end to sample-clearance as we now know it. The current sample clearance process is an ad hoc, one-sided, complicated, inefficient, unpredictable, totally unreasonable, incredibly contentious, and time-consuming system that truly benefits no one but publishing and sound recording copyright holders, older recording artists, and well-funded recording artists, who typically have the backing and power to actually get clearance for the samples they use. But rank-and-file and/or up-and-coming recording artists, who lack the funding and backing of a well-resourced record company, do not benefit from the existing sample clearance system. So, they are essentially denied equal access to sampling and, subsequently, hampered in their efforts to compete with recording artists who enjoy a privileged access to sampling. Furthermore, the numerous recording artists (both familiar and obscure) from the past, who would stand to gain from sampling are, in effect, blocked from the new revenue streams and notoriety that sampling could ultimately grant them. Why? Because as there is less *above ground* sampling being done these days, very little music is actually even being cleared.

We must also remember how the ad-hoc and ineffective sample clearance system fostered a steep decline in the use of the art of sampling in hip hop/rap music — a development that many agree has played a significant role in the overall decline in the creativity and quality of hip hop/rap music in recent years. Taken together, all of the points outlined here demonstrate how the current sample clearance system actually does more harm than good. Thus, one thing that could end the existing sample clearance system is a compulsory license for the sampling of sound recordings.

Finally, a compulsory license for the sampling of sound recordings could be useful because it is one of the best ways to help restore the creative "balance" (parody) and a higher level of artistic integrity to hip hop/rap music. The de facto outlawing of the art of sampling by the contentious sample-clearance process led to a diminished value of music artistry in hip hop/rap music, along with a rampant level of redundancy. Further, the broad shift away from the art of sampling as a major compositional method of hip hop/rap — caused in great part by sample-clearance — also led to a decline in quality lyricism and a widespread move away from some of the core tenets of hip hop culture itself. Although there are certainly a number of solutions that could help restore the high value of music artistry that hip hop/rap music once had, *decriminalizing* the art of sampling is among the most critical ones. Therefore, to achieve this goal, one step might be to enact a compulsory license for the sampling of sound recordings.

PROPOSALS

The Primary Benefit of a Compulsory License for Sampling Sound Recordings

A compulsory license for sampling sound recordings fundamentally serves the public good. A compulsory license for sampling sound recordings adheres to the original purpose of United States copyright law, in that it gives incentive for the creation of original works, encourages alternative forms of creative expression, and protects the rights of those who hold copyrights to sound recordings by ensuring compensation for use.

Futhermore, a compulsory license for sampling sound recordings would eliminate the ad-hoc, heavily flawed sample clearance system. This is significant, as it gives the average rank-and-file musician an equal and fair opportunity to compete. By granting an non-negotiated, automatic right to sample recordings for a fixed fee, the inequity created by the existing sample clearance system — which was bolstered by the false bright-line of Bridgeport — would be eliminated. Moreover, it places a value on older sound recordings and the artists that record them;[284] and indeed, this opens up opportunities for new revenue streams for these artists, both from the royalties a compulsory license would command as well as from a new market of listeners.[285] The public further benefits greatly from this because it preserves important music history as a permanent part of the present musical narrative, giving us all access to music ideas and developments that we might not otherwise be exposed to.

The Caveat for a Compulsory License for the Sampling of Sound Recordings

Before I present my proposal for what a compulsory license for sampling could look like, I want to point out that I doubt seriously any legislation for a compulsory license for sound recordings

---

[284] Black artists, or the executors of the estates of those artists, should not only welcome such a system, they should lead the call for it..

[285] "Sampling in hip-hop increases the recognition of the original work, often leading to significant boosts in album sales and publishing revenue for the original work's copyright holders... It is, therefore, not in either party's economic interest to make a sample difficult to clear." Norek, 85.

(especially as it pertains to the permissibility of defined levels of sampling) would ever happen. Although sampling technology and the art of sampling itself has seemingly dictated the need for a compulsory license for sound recordings, I'm not convinced that Congress is aware of the problem. And in the slim chance that there are more sampling-friendly Congressmen like Representative Mike Doyle (D-Pittsburgh, PA),[286] I question just how sensitive they are to the complexity of the situation — the popularity of the art of sampling in culture; the unfairness and inefficiency of the sample clearance system; the illegalization of sampling; and the blunder of *Bridgeport*.

Even still, I'm not even sure that I would want a compulsory license for sound recordings at this point. My biggest concern is: What will happen to the perception of fair use in the music industry if a compulsory license for samping is created? Right now, much of the sampling done in the hip hop/rap music tradition falls well within the standards and best practices that I described in chapter 6. Would a compulsory license for sound recordings lead most sample-based recording artists to pursue the compulsory license path by default? Moreover, given the security of a compulsory license for sound recordings, will sampling take a dip in creativity, as more sample-based beatmakers seek to create in terms of what the compulsory license allows? Before any change to the statute, I would first stress the need for emphasizing a more accurate interpretation and understanding of fair use.

Another one of my concerns is who would Congress consult

---

[286] House Subcommittee on Telecommunications and the Internet at "The Digital Future of the United States: Part II-- The Future of Radio" (2007). Congressman Doyle signaled his understanding of sampling as a transformative art form that should not be arbitrarily deemed as copyright infringement: "I want to tell you a story of a local guy done good. His name is Greg Gillis and by day he is a biomedical engineer in Pittsburgh. At night, he DJs under the name Girl Talk. His latest mash-up record made the top 2006 albums list from Rolling Stone, Pitchfork and Spin Magazine amongst others. His shtick as the Chicago Tribune wrote about him is 'based on the notion that some sampling of copyrighted material, especially when manipulated and recontextualized into a new art form is legit and deserves to be heard.'... maybe mash-ups are transformative new art that expands the consumers experience and doesn't compete with what an artist has made available on iTunes or at the CD store. And, I don't think Sir Paul asked for permission to borrow that bass line, but every time I listen to that song, I'm a little better off for him having done so."

with for such a compulsory scheme? Music industry lawyers and academics? All proposals that I'm aware of have thus far been made by lawyers and academics, not actual sample-based recording artists, especially sample-based beatmakers. Without sample-based beatmakers in the conversation, I fear that the art of sampling, and the issues that it raises, will be oversimplified. So what assurances are there that any possible Congressional committee (on the compulsory license for sound recordings) would consult sample-based beatmakers, rather than lawyers, academics, and legal commentators alone? But, in the unlikely event that any legislation for a compulsory license for sound recordings did go forward, I hope that Congress and the music industry consults the following proposal beforehand.

The BeatTips Proposal for a Compulsory License for the Sampling of Sound Recordings

Before I delve into the specific details of the BeatTips Proposal for a Compulsory License for the Sampling of Sound Recordings (hereinafter the BeatTips Proposal), I will outline the necessary elements for a proper compulsory license plan.

First, a proper plan for a compulsory license for sampling sound recordings should be on par with the scheme that copyright law already stipulates for "covers" of nondramatic musical works (compositions). A similar compulsory license for sampling sound recordings would bring about fairness in the eye of the law. Second, a compensation scheme that is fair and reliable to both copyright holders and samplers must be included. Finally, a proper plan should remove any obligation of a license when the appropriated portion of a copyrighted sound recording is substantially and qualitatively different.

Material Scope of the BeatTips Proposal

The material scope of the BeatTips Proposal would build, in small part, off of the compulsory license proposal made by

Michael L. Baroni,[287] in that it would give any person the right to sample from any sound recording or audiovisual work that has been distributed to the public in the United States under authority of the copyright owner, and from any publicly broadcast television program (whether received through traditional, cable, or satellite transmissions), and to make and distribute phonorecords embodying such samples. Thus, one could sample from any sound recording, whether it contains, for example, pop songs, sound track or film score music, or any other copyrighted sound recording. But unlike Baroni's proposal, the BeatTips Proposal would not exclude "voices" from a compulsory license, particularly because voices and moans (not necessarily recognizable) are often pivotal parts of some samples used in hip hop/rap music.

Usage

Here, I should note that since it is widely understood by musicians, consumers, the courts, and the music industry that (1) hip hop/rap music first popularized and developed sampling as it's commonly known, and (2) the overwhelming majority of digital sampling that has taken place in the past 30 years occurred and still occurs in hip hop/rap music, then it's appropriate to formulate usage parameters based on compositional practices in the hip hop/rap music tradition, first and foremost. In hip hop/rap, most sample-based beats are based on a 2- or 4-bar (looped) phrase, and the average duration (i.e. length) of a typical sample is just about 4 seconds, often less. Thus, under the BeatTips Proposal, the compulsory license for sampling sound recordings would give individuals the right to sample a sound recording indefinitely for the use of "one" new musical work, up to 16 total seconds (non-looped). For instance, one could sample the same record four times, up to 16 total seconds (non-looped) for the use of only one new song. Use of the same or different samples from the same song in a new work would, therefore, require one to obtain a new compulsory license for sampling sound recordings. Furthermore,

---

[287] Baroni, 94.

this compulsory license would give individuals an unlimited right of manipulation of the samples they appropriate. That is to say, that samplers could alter the sample (the sound sampled) in any conceivable manner, now or hereafter known, and make it a part of any new musical arrangement. Next, usage must fall under three levels of usage: **transformative/non-substantial similarity**, **transformative/substantial similarity**, or **non-transformative/ substantial similarity**. Set mechanical fees would correspond to each level of usage. (See Payment breakdown below.)

Purpose

Individuals would be permitted to use only the compulsory license for sampling sound recordings if one's primary purpose was to distribute nondramatic musical works embodying the sample to the public for private use. In other words, for the purpose of creating new works (beats) that include the appropriated elements of the copyrighted sound recording.

Notice Requirements

Just as with the existing compulsory license for a nondramatic music work (composition), the person seeking to use the compulsory license for sampling sound recordings would have to serve upon the copyright owner of the sound recording appropriated a Notice of Intention to Obtain a Compulsory License for the Use of a Sample in Making and Distributing Phonorecords.[288]

Fee

Under the current compulsory license system for covers (at the time of this publication and printing), an artist desiring to re-record a song that has already been commercially released obtains

---

[288] This is similar to the designation provided for by 37 C.F.R. § 201.18(c) — the existing mechanical compulsory license.

a mechanical license[289] and pays, per track sold to the original work's publisher, "either 9.1 cents or 1.75 cents per minute of playing time or fraction thereof, whichever is greater" (an amount those in music publishing circles consider to be much too low).[290] Sampling differs from a cover, in that it incorporates only *fragments* of sound recordings, never a complete composition or recording. Below is the provision of the existing compulsory license for nondramatic musical works (compositions):

> "§ 115. Scope of exclusive rights in nondramatic musical works: Compulsory license for making and distributing phonorecords
>
> In the case of nondramatic musical works, the exclusive rights provided by clauses (1) and (3) of section 106, to make and to distribute phonorecords of such works, are subject to compulsory licensing under the conditions specified by this section.
>
> (a) Availability and Scope of Compulsory License. —
>
> (1) When phonorecords of a nondramatic musical work have been distributed to the public in the United States under the authority of the copyright owner, any other person, including those who make phonorecords or digital phonorecord deliveries, may, by complying with the provisions of this section, obtain a compulsory license to make and distribute phonorecords of the work. A person may obtain a compulsory license only if his or her primary purpose in making phonorecords is to distribute them to the public for private use, including by means of a digital phonorecord delivery. A person may not obtain a compulsory license for use of the work in the making of phonorecords duplicating a sound recording fixed by another, unless:
>
> (i) such sound recording was fixed lawfully; and
>
> (ii) the making of the phonorecords was authorized by the owner of copyright in the sound recording or, if the sound recording was

---

[289] Mechanical royalties are paid to the owner of the copyright of the composition (not sound recording) of a song. To do a "cover" of someone's song, one does not need permission of the copyright owner to the song; however, one must obtain a compulsory mechanical license as well as pay a mechanical royalty payment to the owner of the copyright of the music composition (publishing) of the song.
[290] U.S. Copyright Office CARP (Copyright Arbitration Royalty Panel): Mechanical Royalty Rate (2014 — last updated December 31, 2007), see: http://www.copyright.gov/licensing/m200a.pdf.

fixed before February 15, 1972, by any person who fixed the sound recording pursuant to an express license from the owner of the copyright in the musical work or pursuant to a valid compulsory license for use of such work in a sound recording.

(2) A compulsory license includes the privilege of making a musical arrangement of the work to the extent necessary to conform it to the style or manner of interpretation of the performance involved, but the arrangement shall not change the basic melody or fundamental character of the work, and shall not be subject to protection as a derivative work under this title, except with the express consent of the copyright owner.[291]

Here, I maintain that if U.S. copyright law stipulates that anyone has the freedom to do a cover of a musical composition and recording at a reasonable price — a set compulsory scheme — then sample-based recording artists should have a similar degree of freedom to use small portions of existing recordings at a similar cost, or perhaps even lower since only a fragment of the recording is being used, not covered. Finally, as with other compulsory licenses, the fee would be established by the Copyright Royalty Tribunal, along with input from sample-based recording artists, recording artists who've had their work sampled before, record companies, and music publishers.[292]

Payment and Usage

Each phonorecord (commercial unit) sold and distributed to the public that embodies the sample would require payment of the compulsory license fee. Using the usage parameters previously discussed, payment would breakdown like this:

- For a **transformative/non-substantial similarity** sample up to 7 seconds, looped or non-looped: no fee;
- For a **transformative/non-substantial similarity** sample

[291] 17 U.S.C § 115 (U.S. Code, Title 17: Copyrights, Section 115).
[292] Section 801 of the Copyright Act establishes the Copyright Royalty Tribunal and defines its purpose. It states that royalty rates for compulsory licenses shall be calculated to achieve four objectives:..." Baroni, 97.

7.1-12 seconds, looped or non-looped: 4 cents per distributed phonorecord;

- For a **non-transformative/substantial similarity** sample 7.1-12 seconds: 8 cents per distributed phonorecord;

- Any **transformative/non-substantial similarity** sample longer than 12 seconds would be charged at a rate of 8 cents per distributed phonorecord, plus .0025 cents for every additional two seconds, up to a limit of sixteen seconds (non-looped).

- Any **non-transformative/substantial similarity** sample longer than 12 seconds: 12 cents, plus 1 cent for every additional two seconds, up to a limit of twenty seconds (non-looped).

Label Credit

As a condition of the compulsory license for the sampling of sound recordings, one would also be required to disclose the name of the copyrighted song the sample(s) was appropriated from. In addition, the names of the recording artist who performed and wrote the song would be credited.

Compulsory License Integrity

Individuals would be prohibited from combining a compulsory license for sampling sound recordings with a mechanical compulsory license for nondramatic works (compositions). Likewise, one using a mechanical compulsory license for nondramatic works (compositions) would be prohibited from using a compulsory license for samples for the same song. For example, if an artist obtained a mechanical license for nondramatic works to record a cover of the Curtis Mayfield song "We the People Who are Darker than Blue," the artist would be prohibited from using any samples from the recording of that song unless they also obtain a compulsory license for sampling.

"Fair Use" Exception for Some Forms of Sampling

Irrespective of a compulsory license for sampling sound recordings, and excluding the need for a fair use defense against an infringement claim that can be proven as de minimis or fair use, I contend that there should be fair use "exceptions" extended to some forms of sampling. First, there will always be forms of sampling in which the appropriated source material is simply unrecognizable. Plus, the way in which most sample-based beatmakers use recorded music is mostly transformative *and* transgressive — that is to say, the new works that are created by sample-based beatmakers are usually substantially different than the work(s) which they sample. In cases such as these, the notion of obtaining a compulsory license is simply impractical.

Second, the source material/music that sample-based beatmakers overwhelmingly prefer most could be narrowed down to the years between 1965 and 1975. In other words, sampling, as it's typically done in hip hop/rap music, reinvigorates musical works that are long past their commercial prime. Therefore, there is no threat of direct competition in the market place. Moreover, sampling provides a greater good to the public, in that it helps restore interest in forgotten, and in some cases, passed over, art-works from the past. This, in turn, broadens the current palette of creative influence from which new authors, artists, musicians, and the like can draw from to create new works of art, thereby achieving the objectives of copyright. Hence, for those reasons, it's practical to extend fair use exceptions to transformative uses of samples that are either: (a) beyond recognition to an ordinary person's subjective impression of the similarities between the two works, or (b) below 7 seconds in length. To do otherwise would not only be impractical, it would be a contradiction to the original intent and spirit of United States copyright law and policy.

435

Afterword

Beatmaking, a tradition that grew out of the broader hip hop culture and hip hop/rap music tradition, has changed modern music forever. Some 40 years after it first emerged, it has substantially reconfigured the approach to modern music-making. Specifically within the last quarter of the twentieth century, the hip hop/rap music and beatmaking traditions have brought forth a number of pivotal developments that have both transcended and built (ingeniously) upon previous musical approaches. Of these developments, few have been as dynamic and complex as the art of sampling.

For those who engage in the art of sampling, it's not only important to have a detailed knowledge of its history, mechanics, priorities, and standards and best practices, it's also important to have a fundamental understanding of copyright law. Although the vast majority of sample-based beatmakers will likely never deal with the sample clearance system; still, it's helpful to understand how the system works (or for that matter how it doesn't) and what copyright law actually stipulates.

In this book, I have aimed to provide deep insight into the sampling tradition of hip hop/rap music as well as some of the most notoriously complex issues of copyright law, especially as it pertains to the art of sampling. I have not compromised the complexity of these issues, but rather, I've attempted to discuss them in a way that is much more accessible to sample-based beatmakers and the public in general. In this study, I've shown how the art of sampling in the hip hop/rap tradition contains its own aesthetic priorities, recording practices, philosophies, standards and best practices, and specific nuances. I've shown the art of sampling in the hip hop/rap music tradition as one that maintains and adheres to its own cultural predilections and musical goals. Further, I've demonstrated how the art of sampling in the hip hop/rap tradition makes use of revolutionary technology in its own way, directly in accordance to the sensibilities of its tradition.

Sample Clearance: The Curse and the Gift

Although the sample clearance system had a number of negative effects on hip hop/rap music, it must be mentioned that it also had one good side-effect. Since the Electronic Drum Machine Period (1983-1987), the third major beatmaking period, the art of sampling had been steadily evolving. But along with the emergence of the sample clearance system, came a new level of evolution in the creative processes and complexity of sampling. Also, I would argue that sampling in the hip hop/rap tradition evolved both as a result of pioneering beatmakers competing with one another and pushing the envelope, and because the sample clearance prompted (necessitated) deeper transformation of samples as well as usage of more obscure source material.

The Art of Sampling is Here to Stay, Fair Use is the Future, and Forcing an Attitude Change About the Art of Sampling in the Music Industry

The more informed sample-based beatmakers are about the art of sampling, the more the art form will progress. Likewise, the more informed sample-based beatmakers are about copyright law, the more fair use sample-based beats will make their way to the public. Plus, the more informed we all are — not just musicians — about copyright law, the more the original intent and purpose of copyright law shines through for the public.

The art of sampling is here to stay. As a music technique, sampling will only grow and become commonplace in the future. But this growth depends, in part, on the ability of all sample-based recording artists to challenge the music industry's status quo on copyright law. This means embracing the idea that when it comes to the art of sampling, copyright law is, more often than not, on the side of sample-based recording artists — this, despite what the music industry would otherwise have the public believe. Thus, in the future, I suspect that more sample-based beatmakers will successfully pursue the fair use path.

Furthermore, recent history shows us that the music industry is very slow to adapt to the realities of culture and technology. Typically, the music industry doesn't change until it's forced to; and often by then, it's too late. (Let's remember, the music industry could have been ahead of the file sharing problem if they had embraced P2P technology early on and made it work for them.) So, it's not likely that the music industry will take the lead on fixing the sample clearance system. It's even less likely that the music industry will lobby for a more accurate understanding of and more open discussion on fair use. Therefore, any real and lasting attitude change about sampling in the music industry can only happen if sample-based recording artists take the lead. Sample-based recording artists must advocate for their own interests, not leave it up to the music industry. They must educate themselves about copyright law, in particular the area of usage rights and the limitations placed on the exclusive rights of copyright owners; and they must identify the ways in which the music industry commonly ignores or misrepresent these rights.

More importantly, sample-based recording artists must understand that as the ranks of fair use-minded sample-based recordings artists grow, the music industry will have no choice: It will have to change the sample clearance system. Of course, by then it may be too late for the music industry, because there will be far more sample-based recording artists who will be aiming for fair use than those seeking clearance. Thus, once again, the music industry will be stuck behind culture and technology.

Regarding Copyright Law

Ideas about the ownership of artistic works shifted dramatically in the twentieth century. And while revolutionary advances in technology have been and continue to be made, exposing the problems with modern U.S. copyright law and policy, the romantic conception of authorship, and the property concept of intellectual creativity continues to persist, no doubt influencing how people perceive art forms like sampling, which necessarily borrow from pre-existing copyrighted material.

Today, considerations of public policy that underlie the current statute of copyright protection are not born out of what benefits the public good. On the contrary, such considerations are formulated from views that are based on attitudes about copyright law that are extreme and at odds with the original purpose of copyright. But I suspect that as more people move from the ranks of consumers and into the ranks of producers and content makers, be it as sample-based music makers or not, there will be another widespread shift in ideas about the ownership of artistic works. As this happens, I believe that the art of sampling will only continue to grow. Moreover, I firmly believe that copyright terms will eventually be rolled back to where copyrighted works enter the public domain sooner. Given the beautiful collision of culture, art, and technology, what alternative will there be?

The ability to record and release music today is easier than ever before; and with more musicians doing exactly that, pretending that sampling isn't a part of the equation for a growing number of these musicians is irrational. Also, as more musicians move towards a business model that relies less on direct music sales, musicians will place less creative restraints on themselves. This means, just as musicians will increasingly ignore "traditional" or legacy record company business and recording practices, they will also ignore traditional stigmas against the usefulness of the art of sampling. Further, I believe attitudes towards copyright law, particularly as a restraint against sampling, will fade. As more musicians grow to fully understand how copyright law actually protects and encourages the very kind of borrowing that the art of sampling is based upon.

Finally, let's remember that the primary purpose of copyright is not to protect the creator of a work from infringement; nor is the primary purpose of copyright to compensate the creator of content. The primary purpose of copyright is to promote the progress of Science and the useful Arts.

Appendix

Canon of Hip Hop/Rap Sample-Based Beatmakers
A List of Sample-Based Beatmakers to Study

Every art form has its own canon of artists. But when it comes to the sample-based beatmaking tradition of hip hop/rap music, most legal commentators and scholars have tended to focus on those sample-based musicians who had copyright infringement claims made against them (The Beastie Boys and Public Enemy being particularly popular among legal commentators). However, the canon of sample-based beatmakers in the hip hop/rap music tradition runs much deeper than that. So in order to get a better understanding of hip hop/rap's sample-based tradition, it's important to be familiar with this canon. Thus, in the following list, I have included a list of 100+ sample-based beatmakers that have all helped (in some way) to shape hip hop/rap's sample-based canon. Each beatmaker on this list, mentioned in no particular order, is worthy of some degree of study.

> *Kool Herc, Grandmaster Flash, Afrika Bambaataa — grandfathers of modern beatmaking.[293]

> DJ Premier • Marley Marl — father of modern beatmaking[294] • The RZA • Pete Rock • Large Professor (Example of Paul C.'s biggest influence) • True Master • Paul C • The Bomb Squad (Hank Shocklee, Eric "Vietnam" Sadler, Keith Shocklee, Chuck D) • J Dilla • Just Blaze • Prince Paul • Buckwild • DJ Shadow • The Beatnuts • Dr. Dre • Nottz • Q-Tip and Ali Shaheed Muhammad (of A Tribe Called Quest) • Kev Brown • Rick Rubin • Kanye West • Showbiz[295] • Havoc (of Mobb Deep) • Bronze Nazareth • Marco Polo • 9th Wonder • The Alchemist • DJ Clark Kent (from Brooklyn) • DJ Quik • Erick Sermon • D.R. Period • Diamond D •

---

[293] Arthur Baker does deserve some level of honorable mention for his contributions to early sampling and his early work with Afrika Bambaataa.

[294] Since 1986, every beatmaker (producer) who's ever made a beat stands on the shoulders of Marley Marl.

[295] Who was chopping samples like Showbiz, before Showbiz? Without Showbiz, no DJ Premier, no Buckwild, and no Minnesota, as we know them.

Lord Finesse • Ced Gee • Ski AKA Ski Beatz • Hi-Tek • Salaam Remi • The Hitmen (D-Dot, Nashiem Myrick, Chucky Thompson, Stevie J, Carlos "6 July" Broady, Sean C) • Easy Mo Bee • Bink • No I.D.[296] • DJ Scratch • DJ Muggs • EZ Elpee • Madlib • DJ Khalil • Rockwilder • Steinski • Emile • Da Beatminerz • !llmind • Trackmasters • Ayatollah • Jake One • Mel-Man • Battlecat • Statik Selektah • Minnesota • The Heatmakerz • Mathematics • El-P • K-Def • Lil Fame (of M.O.P.) • Black Milk • Scram Jones • Ty Fyffe • 88-Keys • Megahertz • DJ Jazzy Jeff • Focus • Exile • Ant Banks • Oddisee • Dan the Automator • Domingo • L.E.S. • Apollo Brown • J-Zone • DJ Pooh • Amadeus • Jimi Kendrix • Dante Ross • Don Cannon • Sha Money XL • J-Swift • The Awesome 2 (Teddy Ted and Special K) • MF Doom • Jam Master Jay • RJD2 • 4th Disciple • Mark the 45 King • Domino • Herbie "Luv Bug" Azor • J-Rawls • Rick Rock • Mahogany • Cool & Dre • Juicy J • DJ Paul • Danger Mouse • Kay Gee • A Plus • RJD2 • Sean C and LV

Interviews

DJ Premier • Marley Marl • Buckwild • True Master • 9th Wonder • Marco Polo • Rich Keller • Rsonist (of The Heatmakerz) • Minnesota • EZ Elpee • !llmind • DJ Supa Dave • Steve Sola • DJ Toomp • John King • Dame Grease • Ari Raskin • DJ Clark Kent • Bangout • Reefa • D.R. Period

Discography

Hip Hop/Rap

2 Live Crew. *As Nasty As They Wanna Be* (Luke, 1989); *Banned in the U.S.A.* (Luke, 1990).

3rd Bass. *The Cactus Album* (Def Jam, 1989).

9th Wonder [also see Little Brother]. *The Dream Merchant, Vol. 2* (6 Hole, 2007).

50 Cent. *Get Rich or Die Tryin'* (G-Unit, Aftermath, Shady, Interscope, 2003); *The Massacre* (G-Unit/Aftermath/Shady/Interscope, 2005); *Curtis* (G-Unit/Aftermath/Shady/Interscope, 2007).

A Tribe Called Quest. *People's Instinctive Travels and the Paths of Rhythm* (Jive, 1990); *The Low End Theory* (Jive, 1991); *Midnight Marauders* (Jive, 1993); *Beats, Rhymes and Life* (Jive, 1995).

A.Z. *Doe or Die* (EMI, 1995); *Pieces of A Man* (Virgin, 1998); *Aziatic* (Motown, 2002); *A.W.O.L.* (Quiet Money, 2005); *The Format* (Quiet Money/Fast Life, 2006).

Afrika Bambaataa. "Jazzy Sensation" (Tommy Boy, 1981); "Planet Rock" (Tommy Boy, 1982); "Looking for the Perfect Beat" (Tommy Boy, 1982); "Renegades of Funk" (Tommy Boy, 1983).

The Alkaholiks. *21 & Over* (Loud, 1993); *Coast II Coast* (Loud, 1995); *Likwidation* (Loud, 1997).

Akinyele. *Vagina Diner* (Interscope/Atlantic, 1993); *Put It In Your Mouth* (Stress/Zoo/BMG, 1996).

BDP (Boogie Down Productions). *Criminal Minded* (B-Boy, 1987); *By Any Means Necessary* (Jive/RCA, 1988); *Ghetto Music: The Blueprint of Hip Hop* (Jive/RCA, 1989); *Edutainment*

---

[296] Without No I.D., no Kanye West!

(Jive/RCA, 1990).

Beanie Sigel. *The Truth* (Roc-A-Fella, 2000); *The Reason* (Roc-A-Fella, 2001); *The B. Coming*, (Dame Dash Music Group/Def Jam, 2005).

Beastie Boys, The. *Licensed to Ill* (Def Jam, 1986); *Paul's Boutique* (Capitol, 1989).

Beatnuts, The. *Intoxicated Demons: The EP* (Relativity/Violator, 1993); *Stone Crazy*(Relativity/Violator/Epic/Sony, 1997).

Big Daddy Kane. *Long Live the Kane* (Cold Chillin', 1988); *It's A Big Daddy Thing* (Cold Chillin', 1989).

Biz Markie. *Goin' Off* (Cold Chillin'/Warner Bros., 1987); *The Biz Never Sleeps* (Cold Chillin'/Warner Bros., 1989); *I Need A Haircut* (Cold Chillin'/Warner Bros., 1993).

Black Moon. *Enta Da Stage* (Nervous, 1993).

Black Sheep. *A Wolf in Sheep's Clothing*, (Mercury/Polygram, 1991).

Black Star (Mos Def and Talib Kweli). *Mos Def & Talib Kweli Are Black Star* (Rawkus, 1998).

Bumpy Knuckles (aka Freddy Foxxx). *Industry Shakedown* (Landspeed, 2000).

Cam'Ron. *Confessions of Fire* (Untertainment/Epic, 1998); *Come Home With Me* (Diplopmat/Roc-A-Fella/Def Jam, 2002).

Clipse. *Lord Willin'* (Star Trak/Arista, 2002).

The Cold Crush Brothers. "Fresh, Fly, Wild, and Bold" (1984); "Cold Crush Brothers Battle Tape," Pts. 1-5 (Ca.

1981). [CCB music only on cassette between 1978-1979]

Cormega. *The Realness* (Legal Hustle, 2001); *The True Meaning*, (Legal Hustle, 2002); *Legal Hustle* (Legal Hustle/Koch, 2004).

Common (previously known as Common Sense). *Can I Borrow a Dollar* (Relativity, 1992); *Resurrection* (Relativity, 1994); *One Day It'll All Make Sense* (Relativity, 1997); *Like Water for Chocolate* (MCA/Universal, 2000); *Be* (G.O.O.D./Geffen, 2005); Finding Forever (G.O.O.D./Geffen, 2007).

Cypress Hill. *Cypress Hill* (Ruffhouse/Columbia, 1991).

The D.O.C. *No One Can Do It Better* (Ruthless, 1989).

De La Soul. *3 Feet High and Rising* (Tommy Boy, 1989); *De La Soul Is Dead* (Tommy Boy, 1991); *Buhloone Mindstate* (Tommy Boy, 1993); *Stakes Is High* (Tommy Boy, 1996).

DMX. *It's Dark and Hell Is Hot* (Ruff Ryders/Def Jam, 1998); *Grand Champ* (Def Jam, 2003).

Dilated Peoples. "Worst Comes to Worst" (Capitol, 2001).

Diamond D. *Stunts, Blunts and Hip Hop* (Chemistry/Mercury, 1992).

Double X Posse. "Not Gonna Be Able to Do It" (Big Beat, 1992).

Doug E Fresh (with the Get Fresh Crew). "The Show" (Reality, 1985); "La Di Da Di" (Reality, 1985).

Dr. Dre. *The Chronic* (Death Row, 1992); *2001* (Aftermath, 1999).

EPMD. *Strictly Business* (Fresh/Sleeping Bag, 1988); *Unfinished Business* (Priority, 1989); *Business As Usual* (Priority, 1990); *Business Never Personal* (Def Jam, 1992).

Ed O. G and Da Bulldogs. *Life of a Kid in the Ghetto* (PWL/Mercury, 1991).

Eminem. *The Slim Shady LP* (Aftermath, 1999); *The Marshall Mathers LP* (Aftermath, 2000).

Eric B & Rakim. *Paid In Full* (4th & B'way, 1987); *Follow the Leader* (Uni/Mercury, 1988); *Let the Rhythm Hit 'Em* (MCA, 1990); *Don't Sweat the Technique* (MCA, 1992).

Fat Boys, The. *Fat Boys* (Sutra, 1984).

Fat Joe. *Represent* (Relativity, 1993); *Jealous One's Envy* (Terror Squad/Relativity, 1995).

Freeway. *Philadelphia Freeway* (Roc-A-Fella, 2003).

Funky Four (aka Funky Four Plus One). "That's the Joint" (1981); "Rappin' & Rockin' the House."

The Game. *The Documentary* (Aftermath/G-Unit, 2005); *Doctor's Advocate* (Geffen, 2006).

Gang Starr. *No More Mr. Nice Guy* (Wild Pitch, 1989); *Step in the Arena* (Chrysalis, 1991); *Daily Operation* (Chrysalis, 1992); *Hard to Earn* (Chrysalis, 1994); *Moment of Truth* (Noo Trybe/Virgin, 1998); *Full Clip: A Decade of Gang Starr* (Noo Trybe/Virgin, 1999); *The Ownerz* (Virgin, 2003).

The Geto Boys. *We Can't Be Stopped* (Rap-A-Lot, 1991).

Ghostface Killah [also see Wu-Tang Clan]. *Iron Man* (Razor Sharp/Epic, 1996); *Supreme Clientele*

(Razor Sharp/Epic, 2000); *Bulletproof Wallets* (Epic, 2001); *The Pretty Toney Album* (Def Jam, 2004); *Fishscale* (Def Jam, 2006); *The Big Doe Rehab* (Def Jam, 2007).

Grandmaster Flash. *The Adventures of Grandmaster Flash on the Wheels of Steel* (Sugar Hill, 1981).

Grandmaster Flash and the Furious Five. *The Message* (Sugar Hill, 1982).

Grandmaster Melle Mel. "White Lines" (Sugar Hill, 1983).

The GZA [also see Wu-Tang Clan]. *Liquid Swords* (Geffen, 1995); *Beneath the Surface* (MCA, 1999).

House of Pain. *House of Pain* (Tommy Boy, 1992).

Ice Cube. *AmeriKKKa's Most Wanted* (Priority, 1991); *Death Certificate* (Priority, 1991); *The Predator* (Priority, 1992).

Ice T. *Rhyme Pays* (Sire/Warner, 1987); *Power* (Sire/Warner, 1987); *O.G. Original Gangster* (Sire/Warner, 1991).

Inspectah Deck [also see Wu-Tang Clan]. *Uncontrolled Substance* (Loud, 1999).

Jadakiss. *Kiss Tha Game Goodbye* (Ruff Ryders, 2001); *Kiss of Death* (Ruff Ryders, 2004).

Jay-Z. *Reasonable Doubt* (Roc-A-Fella, 1996); *In My Lifetime, Vol. 1* (Roc-A-Fella, 1997); *Vol. 2... Hard Knock Life* (Roc-A-Fella, 1998); *Vol. 3... Life and Times of S. Carter* (Roc-A-Fella, 1999); *The Dynasty: Roc La Familia* (Roc-A-Fella, 2000); *The Blueprint* (Roc-A-Fella, 2001); *The Blueprint²: The Gift & The Curse* (Roc-A-Fella, 2002); *The Black Album* (Roc-A-Fella, 2003); *Kingdom Come* (Roc-A-Fella, 2006); *American Gangster* (Roc-A-Fella, 2007).

Jeru the Damaja. *The Sun Rises in the East* (Pay Day/FFRR, 1994).

Jurrassic 5. "What's Golden" (Interscope, 2002).

Juvenile. *400 Degreez* (Cash Money, 1998).

Kanye West. *The College Dropout* (Roc-A-Fella, 2004); *Late Registration* (Roc-A-Fella, 2005); *Graduation* (Roc-A-Fella, 2007); *808s & Heartbreak* (Roc-A-Fella, 2008).

KMD. *Mr. Hood* (Elektra, 1991).

KRS-One [also see BDP]. *Return of the Boom Bap* (Jive, 1993).

King Tee. *Act a Fool* (Capitol, 1988); *At Your Own Risk* (Capitol, 1990).

Kool G Rap & DJ Polo. *Road to the Riches* (Cold Chillin', 1989); *Wanted: Dead or Alive* (Cold Chillin', 1990); *Live and Let Die* (Cold Chillin', 1992).

Kurtis Blow. *Kurtis Blow* (Mercury, 1980);

LL Cool J. *Radio* (Def Jam, 1985); *Bigger and Deffer* (Def Jam, 1987); *Walking with a Panther* (Def Jam, 1989); *Mama Said Knock You Out* (Def Jam, 1990); *14 Shots to the Dome* (Def Jam, 1993); *Mr. Smith* (Def Jam, 1995).

Large Professor [also see Main Source]. *1st Class* (Matador, 2002).

Leaders of the New School. *A Future without a Past* (Elektra, 1991).

Lil Jon & the East Side Boyz. *Get Crunk, Who U Wit: Da Album* (Mirror Image, 1997); *Kings of Crunk* (TVT, 2002); *Crunk Juice* (TVT, 2004).

Lil Wayne. *Tha Block is Hot* (Cash Money, 1999); *Tha Carter* (Cash Money, 2004); *Tha Carter III* (Cash Money/Young Money, 2008).

Little Brother. *The Listening* (ABB, 2003); *The Minstrel Show* (Atlantic/ABB, 2005).

The Lox. *Money, Power & Respect* (Bad Boy, 1997).

MC Hammer. *Let's Get It Started* (Capitol, 1988).

MC Lyte. *Lyte As a Rock* (First Priority, 1988); *Eyes On This* (First Priority, 1989).

M.O.P. *To the Death* (Select, 1994); *Firing Squad* (Relativity, 1996); *First Family 4 Life* (Relativity, 1998); *Warriorz* (Loud, 2000).

Madlib (as Quasimoto). *The Further Adventures of Lord Quas* (Stones Throw, 2005).

Madvillain [Madlib with MF Doom]. *Madvillainy* (Stones Throw, 2004).

Main Source. *Breaking Atoms* (Wild Pitch, 1991).

Marley Marl. *In Contol* (Cold Chillin', 1988).

Method Man [also see Wu-Tang Clan]. *Tical* (Def Jam, 1994); *Tical 2000: Judgement Day* (Def Jam, 2000).

Method Man and Redman. *Blackout* (Def Jam, 1999).

Mobb Deep. *Juvenile Hell* (4th & B'Way, 1993); *The Infamous* (Loud, 1995); *Hell On Earth* (Loud, 1996); *Murda Muzik* (Loud, 1999); *Infamy* (Loud, 2001); *Blood Money* (G-Unit, 2006).

Mos Def. *Black on Both Sides* (Rawkus, 1999).

N.W.A. *Straight Outta Compton* (Ruthless, 1988); *100 Miles and Runnin'* (Ruthless, 1990); *Niggaz4Life* (Ruthless, 1991).

Noreaga. *N.O.R.E.* (Penalty, 1998).

NYGz. *Welcome 2 G-Dom* (Year Round, 2007).

Nas. *Ilmatic* (Columbia, 1994); *It Was Written* (Columbia, 1996); *I Am* (Columbia, 1999); *Nastradamus* (Columbia, 1999); *Stillmatic* (Ill Will/Columbia, 2001); *Nasir Jones: God's Son* [aka God's Son] (Ill Will/Columbia, 2002); *Street's Desciple* (Ill Will/Columbia, 2004); *Hip Hop Is Dead* (Def Jam, 2006).

Nature. *For All Seasons* (Track Masters, 2000).

Naughty By Nature. *Naughty By Nature* (Tommy Boy, 1991); *19 Naughty III* (Tommy Boy, 1993).

Notorious B.I.G. [aka Biggie Smalls]. *Ready To Die* (Bad Boy, 1994); *Life After Deathi* (Bad Boy, 1997).

O.C. *Word...Life* (Wild Pitch, 1994); *Jewelz* (Payday, 1997).

Ol' Dirty Bastard [also see Wu-Tang Clan]. *Return to the 36 Chambers: The Dirty Version* (Elektra, 1995); *Nigga Please* (Elektra, 1999).

Onyx. *Bacdafucup* (Def Jam, 1993).

Outkast. *Southernplayalisticadillacmuzik* (LaFace, 1994); *ATLiens* (LaFace/Arista, 1996); *Aquemini* (LaFace/Arista, 1998); *Stankonia*, (LaFace/Arista, 2000); *Speakerboxxx/The Love Below* (LaFace/Arista, 2003).

The Pharcyde. *Bizarre Ride II the Pharcyde* (Delicious Vinyl, 1992); *Labcabincalifornia* (Delicious Vinyl, 1995).

Public Enemy. *Yo! Bum Rush the Show* (Def Jam, 1987); *It Takes a Nation of Millions to Hold Us Back* (Def Jam, 1988); *Fear of a Black Planet* (Def Jam, 1990).

Q-Tip [also see A Tribe Called Quest]. *Amplified* (Arista, 1999).

Raewkon [also see Wu-Tang Clan]. *Only Built 4 Cuban Linx* (Loud, 1995); *Immobilarity* (Loud, 1999); *Only Built 4 Cuban Linx... Pt. II* (Ice H2O, 2009). *Reflection Eternal* [Talib Kweli and Hi-Tek]. *Train of Thought* (Rawkus, 2000).

Redman. *Whut? Thee Album* (Def Jam, 1992); Muddy Waters (Def Jam, 1996).

Rich Boy. "Throw Some D's," 2006.

Royal Flush. *Ghetto Millionaire* (Blunt, 1997).

Royce Da 5'9. *Street Hop* (M.I.C./One, 2009).

Run-DMC. *Run-DMC* (Profile, 1984); *King of Rock* (Profile, 1985); *Raising Hell* (Profile, 1986); *Tougher Than Leather* (Profile, 1988).

The RZA [also see Wu-Tang Clan]. *Bobby Digital in Stereo* (Gee Street/V2, 1998).

Salt-N-Pepa. *Hot, Cool & Vicious* (Next Plateau, 1986); *A Salt with a Deadly Pepa* (Next Plateau/London, 1988).

Scarface [also see The Geto Boys]. *The Diary* (Rap-A-Lot, 1994); *The Fix* (Def Jam South, 2002).

Screwball, *Y2K The Album* (Tommy Boy, 2000); *Loyalty* (Landspeed, 2001).

Sean Price. *Monkey Barz* (Duck Down, 2005); *Jesus Price Supastar* (Duck Down, 2007).

Showbiz & AG. *Runaway Slave* (Payday, 1992).

Slum Village. *Fantastic, Vol. 2* (Good Vibe, 2000).

Slick Rick. *The Great Adventures of Slick Rick* (Def Jam, 1988).

Smif N' Wesson. *Dah Shinin'* (Wreck, 1995).

Smoothe Da Hustler. *Once Upon a Time in America* (Profile, 1996).

Snoop Doggy Dog. *Doggytyle* (Death Row, 1993); *Tha Doggfather* (Death Row, 1996).

Soulja Boy Tell 'Em. *souljaboytellem.com* (Collipark/Stacks on Deck/Interscope, 2007).

Souls of Mischief. *93 'til Infinity* (Jive, 1993).

Special Ed. *Youngest In Charge* (Profile, 1989).

Spoonie Gee. "Love Rap" (ca. 1979/80).

Styles P. *A Gangster and a Gentleman* (Ruff Ryders, 2002); *Super Gangster* (Extraordinary Gentleman) (Koch, 2007).

T.I. *I'm Serious* (Ghett-O-Vision/LaFace, 2001); *Trap Muzik* (Grand Hustle/Atlantic, 2003); *Urban Legend* (Grand Hustle/Atlantic, 2004); *King* (Grand Hustle/Atlantic, 2006); *T.I. vs. T.I.P.* (Grand Hustle/Atlantic, 2007); *Paper Trail* (Grand Hustle/Atlantic, 2008).

Talib Kweli [also see Reflection Eternal]. *Quality* (Rawkus, 2002).
Three Six Mafia. *When the Smoke Clears: Sixty 6, Sixty 1* (Loud, 200); *Da Unbreakables* (Columbia, 2003); *Most Known Unknown* (Sony, 2005).
Too Short. *Born to Mack* (Dangerous/Jive, 1987); *Life Is…Too Short* (Jive, 1988).
Treacherous Three. "Feel The Heartbeat" (1981).
Tupac. *2Pacalypse Now* (Jive, 1991); *Strictly 4 My N.I.G.G.A.Z.* (Atlantic, 1993); *Me Against the World* (Atlantic, 1995); *All Eyez On Me* (Death Row, 1996).
Whoodini. Escape (Jive, 1984).
Wu-Tang Clan. *Enter the Wu-Tang* (36 Chambers) (Loud, 1993); *Wu-Tang Forever* (Loud, 1997); *The W* (Loud, 2000); *Iron Flag* (Loud, 2001); *8 Diagrams* (SRC, 2007).
Young Jeezy. *Let's Get It: Thug Motivation 101* (Corporate Thugz Entertainment/Def Jam, 2005); *The Inspiration* (Corporate Thugz/Def Jam, 2006); *The Recession* (Corporate Thugz Entertainment/Def Jam, 2008).
Yo Yo. *Make Way for the Motherlode* (East West America, 1991).
Young Black Teenagers. *Dead Enz Kidz Doin' Lifetime Bidz* (MCA, 1993).

Blues

Dixon, Willie. *Willie's Blues* (Bluesville, 1959).
Hooker, John Lee. "Hobo Blues" (Modern, 1948); "Boogie Chillen" (Modern, 1948).
Howlin' Wolf. *Moanin' in the Moonlight* (Chess, 1959); "Spoonful" (Chess, 1960); "Shake It For Me" (Chess, 1964).
King, B.B. *Singin' The Blues* (Crown, 1956); *The Blues* (Crown, 1958); *My Kind of Blues* (EMI, 1961).
Little Walter. "Juke" (Chess, 1952); "My Babe" (Chess, 1955).
Muddy Waters. "Rollin' Stone" (Chess, 1950); "Hoochie Coochie Man" (Chess, 1954); "Got My Mojo Working" (Chess, 1956); *The Best of Muddy* (Chess, 1958); *Waters* (Chess, 1958).
Smith, Bessie. "Downhearted Blues" (ca. 1923); "Ain't Nobody's Business" (ca. 1925).
T-Bone Walker. "Mean Old World" (Capitol, 1942); "Call It Stormy Monday (But Tuesday Is Just as Bad)" (1947).
Turner, Big Joe. "Roll 'Em, Pete" (1938); "Shake, Rattle, and Roll" (1954); *The Boss of the Blues* (Atlantic, 1956).

Jazz

Armstrong, Louis. "St. Louis Blues" (1929, Okeh); "All of Me" (Columbia, 1932); *Louis Armstrong Plays W. C. Handy* (Columbia, 1954); Porgy and Bess (Verve, 1958); "Hello Dolly!" (Kaap, 1964); "What a Wonderful World" (ABC, 1968).
Blakey, Art (with the Jazz Messengers) *Art Blakey with the Original Jazz Messengers* (Columbia, 1956); *Moanin'* (Blue Note, 1958).
Count Basie. *Swinging the Blues 1930-1939* (Jazz Legends, 2004) [orignal recordings 1930-1939].
Count Basie [with Joe Williams]. *One O'Clock Jump* (Verve, 1957).
Coltrane, John [also see Miles Davis Quintet, I]. *Coltrane* (Prestige, 1957); *Blue Train* (Blue Note, 1957); *Soultrane* (Prestige, 1958); *Giant Steps* (Atlantic, 1960); *My Favorite Things* (Atlantic, 1961); *Coltrane Plays the Blues* (Atlantic, 1962).
Davis, Miles. *Birth of Cool* (Capitol, 1949); *Blue Haze* (Prestige, 1954); *Miles Davis and the Modern Jazz Giants* (Prestige, 1956); *Miles Ahead* (Columbia, 1957); *Milestones* (Columbia, 1958); *Porgy and Bess* (Columbia, 1958); *Kind of Blue* (Columbia, 1959); *Sketches of Spain* (Columbia, 1960);
Davis, Miles Quintet (I). *Miles: The New Miles Davis Quintet* (Prestige, 1956); *Cookin' with The Miles Davis Quintet* (Prestige, 1957); "So What" (Robert Herridge Theater [television show] "The Sound of Miles of Davis" CBS, 1959).

Davis, Miles Quintet (II). *E.S.P.* (Columbia, 1965); *Miles Smiles* (Columbia, 1966); *Miles in the Sky* (Columbia, 1968); *Filles de Kilimanjaro* (Columbia, 1969).

Ellington, Duke. "Mood Indigo" (Brunswick, 1930); *It Don't Mean a Thing* (If It Ain't Got That Swing) (Brunswick, 1932); Take the "A" Train (1939).

Fats Waller. "Honeysuckle Rose" (1929); "This Joint Is Jump'in'" (ca. 1934).

Hancock, Herbie [also see Miles Davis Quintet, II; also see The Headhunters]. *Inventions and Dimensions* (Blue Note, 1964); *The Prisoner* (Blue Note, 1969); *Fat Albert Rotunda* (Warner, 1969); *Sextant* (Columbia, 1973).

Holiday, Billie. "Strange Fruit" (Columbia, 1939); "God Bless the Child" (Okeh, 1942); "Mack the Knife" (Columbia, 1955); *Lady Sings the Blues* (Verve, 1956); "Ain't Nobody's Business" (Decca, ca. 1945).

Jamal, Ahmad. *The Awakening* (Impulse, 1970).

Jones, Quincy. *The Quintessence* (Impulse, 1961); *Walking in Space* (A&M, 1969); *Body Heat* (A&M, 1974).

Klemmer, John. *Blowin' Gold* (Cadet, 1969).

Monk, Thelonius. *Monk* (Prestige, 1954); *The Unique Thelonious Monk* (Riverside, 1956); *Thelonious Monk with John Coltrane* (Milsesone, 1957); *Thelonious Himself* (Riverside, 1959).

Parker, Charlie. "Ko-Ko" (Savoy, 1945); "Ornithology" (Dial, 1946).

Roach, Max (with Miles Davis). *Birth of Cool* (Capitol, 1949).

Rollins, Sonny. *The Bridge* (Bluebird, 1962).

Gospel

Caravan, The. "Swing Low, Sweet Chariot" (1958).

Clara Ward Singers, The. "How I Got Over" (1950); "Didn't Rain" (ca. 1952); "Swing Low, Sweet Chariot" (ca. 1952).

Dixie Hummingbirds, The. "When the Gates Swing Open" (ca. 1950s); "Holding On" (ca. 1950s).

Dorsey, Thomas A. "Take My Hand, Precious Lord" (aka "Precious Lord, Take My Hand") (ca. 1932).

Franklin, Aretha. *Aretha Frankilin Amazing Grace (with James Cleveland and the Southern California Community Choir)* (Atlantic, 1972).

Golden Gate Quartet (aka The Golden Gate Jubilee Quartet). "The General Jumped at Dawn" (1944); "Golden Gate Gospel Train" (Ca. early 1940s); "Joshua Fit the Battle" (1949).

Jackson, Mahalia. Bless This House (Columbia, 1956).

Sister Rosetta Tharpe. "Down By The Riverside" (ca. 1944); "Didn't It Rain" (ca. 1964).

Soul Stirrers. "Wade in the Water" (ca. 1946); "I'm A Pilgrim" (ca. 1947).

Soul Stirrers with Sam Cooke. "Nearer to Thee" (ca. 1950); "Peace in the Valley" (Specialty, 1950).

Ward, Clara [also see The Clara Ward Singers]. "When the Gates Swing Open" (ca. 1949).

Country

Autry, Gene. "Back in the Saddle Again" (Columbia, 1939).

Cash, Johnny. "I Walk the Line" (Sun, 1956); *Now Here's Johnny Cash* (Sun, 1968).

Rodgers, Jimmie. "Blue Yodel No. 1" (T for Texas) (Victor, 1927).

Williams, Hank. *Moanin' the Blues* (MGM, 1952); *Ramblin' Man* (MGM, 1954).

Rhythm & Blues

Brown, Ruth. "Teardrops From My Eyes" (Atlantic, 1950); "(Mama) He Treats Your Daughter Mean" (Atlantic, 1952).

Charles, Ray. *Hallelujah I Love Her So* (Atlantic, 1957); *What'd I Say* (Atlantic, 1959); *Ain't Nobody Here But Us Chickens* (Atlantic, 1960). *The Genius Hits the Road* (ABC, 1960); *Dedicated to You* (ABC, 1971).

Cooke, Sam. *Ain't That Good News* (RCA, 1964).

Otis, Johnny. "Willie and the Hand Jive" (Capitol, 1958).

Jordan, Louis. "Ain't Nobody Here But Us Chickens" (1946); "Let the Good Times Roll" (1946); "Beans and Cornbread" (1949); "Saturday Night Fish Fry" (1949).

Thomas, Rufus. *Walking the Dog* (Stax, 1963).

1950s Rock 'n' Roll

Berry, Chuck. "Maybellene" (Chess, 1955); "Roll Over Beethoven" (Chess, 1956); "No Particular Place to Go" (Chess, 1964).

Bill Haley and His Comets. "Shake, Rattle and Roll" (Decca, 1954) [originally recorded by Big Joe Turner]; "Rock Around the Clock" (Decca, 1954).

Fats Domino. "The Fat Man" (Imperial, 1949); "Hide Away Blues" (Imperial, 1950); "Ain't That a Shame" (Imperial, 1956); "My Blue Heaven" (Imperial, 1956); "Blueberry Hill" (Imperial, 1956); "I'm Walkin'" (Imperial, 1957).

Soul

Brown, James. *Please, Please, Please* (King, 1956); *Prisoner of Love* (King, 1963); Out of Sight (Smash, 1964).

Cooke, Sam. *Sam Cooke* (Keen, 1957); *Night Beat* (RCA, 1963); *Ain't That Good News* (RCA, 1964).

Chaka Khan, *Chaka* (Warner, 1978); *Naughty* (Warner, 1980).

Charles, Ray. *Hallelujah I Love Her So* (Atlantic, 1957); *What'd I Say* (Atlantic, 1959); *Ain't Nobody Here But Us Chickens* (Atlantic, 1960); *The Genius Hits the Road* (ABC, 1960); *Ingredients in a Recipe for Soul* (ABC, 1963).

Connors, Norman. *You Are My Starship* (Buddah, 1976).

Delfonics, The. *La La Means I Love You* (Philly Groove, 1968); *Sound of Sexy Soul* (Philly Groove, 1969); *The Delfonics* (1970).

Dells, The. *Love Is Blue* (Cadet, 1969); *Like It Is, Like It Was* (Cadet, 1971); *Sweet As Funk Can Be* (Cadet, 1972); *Give Your Baby a Standing Ovation* (Cadet, 1973); *The Dells* (Cadet, 1973); *The Mighty Mighty Dells* (Cadet, 1974); *The Dells vs. The Dramatics* (Cadet, 1975).

Dramatics, The. *Whatcha See Is Whatcha Get* (Volt, 1972); *A Dramatic Experience* (Volt, 1973); *The Dells vs. The Dramatics* (Cadet, 1975).

Earth, Wind & Fire. *That's the Way of the World* (Columbia, 1975); *Gratitude* (Columbia, 1975); *Spirit* (Columbia, 1976).

Emotions, The. *So I Can Love You* (Stax, 1970); *Untouched* (Stax, 1972); *Flowers* (Columbia, 1976).

Franklin, Aretha. *I Never Loved a Man the Way I Love You* (Atlantic, 1967); *Lady Soul* (Atlantic, 1968); *Soul '69* (Atlantic, 1969); *Aretha's Gold* (Atlantic, 1969); *The Girl's In Love With You* (Atlantic, 1970); *Spirit in the Dark* (Atlantic, 1970); *Young, Gifted and Black* (Atlantic, 1972); *Hey Now Hey* (The Other Side of the Sky) (Atlantic, 1973); *Let Me in Your* Life (Atlantic, 1974); *You* (Atlantic, 1975); *Sparkle* (Atlantic, 1976).

Green, Al. *Let's Stay Together* (Hi, 1972); *I'm Still In Love With You* (Hi, 1972).

Harold Melvin and The Blue Notes featuring Theodore Pendergrass. *I Miss You* [aka If You Don't Know Me by Now] (Philadelphia International, 1972).

Hathaway, Donny. *Everything is Everything* (Atco, 1970); *Donny Hathaway* (Atco, 1970); *Come Back, Charleston Blue* (Atco, 1972); *Roberta Flack & Donny Hathaway* (Atlantic, 1972); *Extension of a Man* (Atco, 1973).

Hayes, Isaac. *Hot Buttered Soul* (Enterprise, 1969); *The Isaac Hayes Movement* (Enterprise, 1970); … *To*

Be Continued (Enterprise, 1970); *Shaft* (Enterprise, 1971); *Black Moses* (Enterprise, 1971).

Hutch, Willie. *Soul Portrait* (RCA, 1969); *Fully Exposed* (Motown, 1973); *The Mack* (Motown, 1973); *Foxy Brown* (Motown, 1975).

Impressions, The. *The Impressions* (Paramount, 1963); *Keep on Pushing* (Paramount, 1964); *People Get Ready* (Paramount, 1965); *Ridin' High* (Paramount, 1966); *We're a Winner* (Universal/MCA, 1968); *This Is My Country* (Curtom, 1968); *The Young Mod's Forgotten Story* (Curtom, 1969).

Intruders, The. *The Intruders Are Together* (Gamble, 1966); *Cowboys to Girls* (Gamble, 1968); *When We Get Married* (Gamble, 1970); *Save the Children* (Gamble, 1973).

Jackson, Michael [also see The Jackson 5 and The Jacksons]. *Off The Wall* (Epic, 1979); *Thriller* (Epic, 1982).

Jackson 5, The. *ABC* (Motown, 1970); *Third Album* (Motown, 1970); *Maybe Tomorrow* (Motown, 1971); *Lookin' Through the Window* (Motown, 1972); *Dancing Machine* (Motown, 1974).

Jacksons, The. *The Jacksons* (CBS, 1976); *Goin' Places* (CBS, 1977); *Destiny* (CBS, 1978).

James, Etta. *At Last* (Chess, 1961).

Kendricks, Eddie. *Peoople...Hold On* (Motown, 1972); *Eddie Kendricks* (Motown, 1973).

Gladys Knight & The Pips. *If I Were Your Woman* (Motown, 1971); *Neither One of Us* (Motown, 1973); *Imagination* (Motown, 1973); *Claudine* (Buddah, 1974).

Marie, Teena. *Wild and Peaceful* (Motown, 1979); *Lady T* (Motown, 1980); *Irons in the Fire* (Motwon, 1980); *It Must Be Magic* (Motown, 1981); *Robbery* (Epic, 1983); *Starchild* (Epic, 1984).

Mayfield, Curtis [also see The Impressions]. Curtis (Curtom, 1970); Roots (Curtom, 1971); Super Fly (Curtom, 1972); *Back to the World* (Curtom, 1973); *Sweet Exorcist* (Curtom, 1974); *There's No Place Like America Today* (Curtom, 1975).

Moments, The. *A Moment with the Moments* (Stang, 1970); *Those Sexy Moments* (Stang, 1974).

O'Jays, The. *Back Stabbers* (Philadelphia International, 1972); *Ship Ahoy* (Philadelphia International, 1973); *Survival* (Philadelphia International, 1975); *Family Reunion* (Philadelphia International, 1975); *Message in the Music* (Philadelphia International, 1976).

Paul, Billy. *360 Degrees of Billy Paul* (Philadelphia International, 1972).

Redding, Otis. *Pain in My Heart* (Atco, 1964); *Otis Blue: Otis Sings Soul* (Stax, 1965).

Ripperton, Minnie. *Perfect Angel* (Epic, 1974); *Minnie* (Capitol, 1979).

Rufus (aka Rufus featuring Chaka Khan) *Rags to Rufus* (ABC, 1974); *Rufus Featuring Chaka Khan* (ABC, 1975).

Scott-Heron, Gil. *Winter in America* (Strata-East, 1974).

Sly and The Family Stone. *Dance to the Music* (Epic, 1968); *Stand!* (Epic, 1969); *There's a Riot Goin' On* (Epic, 1971).

Smokey Robinson. *A Quiet Storm* (Tamla, 1975).

Staples Singers, The. *Be Attitude: Respect Yourself* (Stax, 1972); *Let's Do It Again* (Curtom, 1975).

Stevie Wonder. *Innervisions* (Tamla, 1973); *Songs in the Key of Life* (Tamla, 1976); *Hotter than July* (Tamla, 1980).

Taylor, Johnnie. "Who's Making Love" (Stax, 1968); "Jody's Got Your Girl and Gone" (Stax, 1970); "Doin' My Own Thing" (Stax, 1972); "Cheaper to Keep Her" (Stax, 1973).

Wilson, Jackie. "Lonely Teardrops" (Brunswick, 1958); "That's Why (I Love You So)" (Brunswick, 1959).

Pre-Hip Hop Rap/Spoken Word

Last Poets, The. *The Last Poets* (1970); *This Is Madness* (Douglas, 1971).

Lightnin' Rod. *Hustler's Convention* (United Artist, 1973).

Scott-Heron, Gil. *Small Talk at 125th and Lenox* (Flying Dutchman, 1970); *Pieces of a Man* (Flying Dutchman, 1971); *Winter in America* (Strata-East, 1974).

African Soul/Afrobeat

Fela Kuti. *Why Black Man Dey Suffer* (Wrasse, 1971); *Open & Close* (Wrasse, 1972); *Expensive Shit* (Wrasse, 1975).

Hugh Masekela. *The Promise of a Future* (Uni, 1968); *Masekela Uni*, 1968); *The African Connection* (Impulse, 1973).

Funk

Bar-Kays, The. *Soul Finger* (Votl, 1967); *Gotta Groove* (Volt, 1969); *Black Rock* (Volt, 1971).

Baby Huey. *The Baby Huey Story: The Living Legend* (Curtom, 1970).

Bataan, Joe. *Mr. New York & The East Side Kids* (Fania, 1971); *Sweet Soul* (Fania, 1972); *Saint Latin's Day Massacre* (Fania, 1972); *Salsoul* (Mericana, 1973).

Beginning of the End, The. *Funky Nassau* (Alston, 1971).

Blackbyrds, The. *The Blackbyrds* (Fantasy, 1973).

Black Heat. *Black Heat* (Atlantic, 1972); *No Time to Burn* (Atlantic, 1974).

Black Ivory. *Don't Turn Around.* (Today, 1972); *Baby, Won't You Change Your Mind* (Today, 1972).

Black Nasty. "Party on 4th Street" (1972).

Booker T. & the MGs. *Soul Limbo* (Stax, 1968); *The Booker T. Set* (Stax, 1969); *McLemore Avenue* (Stax, 1970); *Melting Pot* (Stax, 1971); *The MGs* (Stax, 1973).

Boris Gardiner Happening, The. *Is What's Happening* (Dynamic, 1973).

Brown, James. *Out of Sight* (Smash,1964); *Papa's Got a Brand New Bag* (King, 1965); *Cold Sweat* (1967); *Say It Loud—I'm Black and I'm Proud* (King, 1968); *It's a Mother* (King, 1969); *Sex Machine* (King, 1970); *On the Good Foot* (Poyldor, 1971); *The Payback* (Polydor, 1973); *Hell* (Polydor, 1974).

Byrd, Bobby [also see James Brown]. "I Need Help" (1970); "I Know You Got Soul" (1971).

Carbo, Chuck. "Can I Be Your Squeeze" (1970).

Collins, Lynn. *Think* (About It) (People, 1972).

Counts, The (aka The Fabulous Counts). *What's Up Front That Counts* (ca. 1971).

Creative Funk. "Moving World." (ca. early 1970s).

Cymande. Cymande (Janus, 1972); *Second Time Around* (Janus, 1973); *Promised Heights* (Janus, 1974).

David Batiste & The Gladiators. "Funky Soul" (Soulin', ca. 1971).

Dayton Sidewinders. *Let's Go Down To Funksville* (1972).

Dells, The. *Sweet As Funk Can Be* (Cadet, 1972).

Dynamics, The. *What A Shame.* (Black Gold, 1973).

Earth, Wind & Fire. *That's the Way of the World* (Columbia, 1975); *Gratitude* (Columbia, 1975); *Spirit* (Columbia, 1976).

Eliminators, The. *Loving Explosion.* (1974).

Fabulous Originals, The. "It Ain't Fair But It's Fun" (1971).

Fabulous Three. "Answer Me Softly" (Psycho, ca. 1972).

Freddie and the Kinfolk. "Mashed potato popcorn" (ca. 1972).

Gaturs, The. "Gator Bait" (1970); *Wasted* (1970).

Harvey & The Phenomenals. *Soul & Sunshine* (1971).

Headhunters, The. *The Head Hunters* (1973); *Thrust* (Columbia, 1974).

Hitson, Herman. "Ain't No Other Way" (Sweet Rose, 1972).

Honey Drippers, The. "Impeach the President" (1973).

Huck Daniels Co., The. "Foolish Man (Pt.2)" (Kent, 1971).

Identities, The. "Hey Brother" (1970).

Jackson 5, The. *Dancing Machine* (Motown, 1974).

Jimmy Castor Bunch, The. *It's Just Begun* (RCA, 1972).

Kool and The Gang. *Kool and The Gang* (De-Lite, 1969); *Music Is the Message* (De-Lite, 1972); *Good Times* (De-Lite, 1973); *Wild and Peaceful* (De-Lite, 1973).

Latin Breed, The. "I Turn You On" (ca. 1971).

Lucien, Jon. *I Am Now* (RCA, 1970); *Rashida* (RCA, 1973).

Majestics, The. "Funky Chick" (ca. 1969).

Meters, The. *The Meters* (Sundazed, 1969); *Look-Ka Py Py* (Josie, 1969); *Struttin'* (Josie, 1970).

Mobile Blue, The. "Puffin'" (1969).

Mohawks, The. "The Champ" (Contillion, ca. 1969).

New Birth. *The New Birth* (RCA, 1971); *Ain't No Big Thing, But It's Growing* (RCA, 1971); *Birth Day* (RCA, 1973); *It's Been a Long Time* (RCA, 1974); *Blind Baby* (Buddah, 1975).

Nite-Liters, The [also see New Birth]. *Nite-Liters* (RCA, 1970); *Morning, Noon & the Nite-Liters* (RCA, 1971); *Different Strokes* (RCA, 1972).

Ohio Players, The. *Paint* (Westbound, 1972); *Pleasure* (Westbound, 1972); *Ecstacy* (Wettbound, 1973); *Skin Tight* (Mercury, 1974); *Fire* (Mercury, 1974); *Honey* (Mercury, 1975) .

Reid, Clarence. "Funky Party" (ca. 1971); "Winter Man" (ca. 1973).

Nina Simone. "Ain't Got No...I've Got Life;" (RCA, 1970); *Black Gold* (RCA, 1970).

Sexton, Ann. "You're Losing Me" (1973).

Skin Williams and the Soulfadelics. "Skins Funk" (ca. early 1970s).

Skull Snaps. *Skull Snaps* (GSF, 1974); "It's a New Day." (1973); "All of Sudden" (1974).

Sly and The Family Stone. *Dance to the Music* (Epic, 1968); *Stand!* (Epic, 1969); *There's a Riot Goin' On* (Epic, 1971).

Thomas, Rufus. "Do That Breakdown Chillin'" (Stax, ca. 1973); "The Funky Chicken" (Stax, ca. 1973).

Yellow Sunshine. "Yellow Sunshine" (1973).

Dub

Big Youth. *Screaming Target* (Gussie/Jaguar, 1972).

Upsetters, The. *Musical Bones* (DIP, 1975).

U-Roy. "Earth's Rightful Ruler" (1969); "Wake the Town" (1970).

60s and 70s Rock/Progressive Rock/Art Rock/Hard Rock/Southern Rock

Allman Brothers, The. *The Allman Brothers Band* (Capricorn/Atco, 1969); *Idlewild South* (Capricorn/Atco, 1970); *Eat a Peach* (Capricorn, 1972); *Brothers and Sisters* (Capricorn, 1973).

Band, The. *Music from the Big Pink* (Capitol, 1968); *The Band* (Capitol, 1969).

Beatles, The. *Please, Please Me* (Parlophone, 1963); *Meet the Beatles* (Capitol, 1964); *The Beatles' Second Album* (Capitol, 1964); *A Hard Day's Night* (Parlophone, 1964); *Beatles '65* (Capitol, 1964); *Beatles VI* (Capitol, 1965); Revolver (Capitol, 1966); *Sgt. Pepper's Lonely Heart Club Band* (Capitol/Parlophone, 1967); *Magical Mystery Tour* (Capitol/Parlophone, 1967); *The Beatles* (aka "The White Album") (Capitol/Apple/Parlophone, 1968); *Yellow Submarine* (Apple/Capitol, 1969); *Abbey Road* (Capitol/Parlophone, 1969); *Let It Be* (Apple/Capitol, 1970).

Bluesbreakers with Eric Clapton. *Bluesbreakers with Eric Clapton* (Decca, 1966).

Clapton, Eric. *Eric Clapton* (Atco, 1970); *461 Ocean Boulevard* (RSO, 1974).

Cream. *Fresh Cream* (Atco, 1966); *Disraeli Gears* (Atco, 1967).

Doobie Brothers, The. *The Doobie Brothers* (Warner, 1971); *Toulouse Street* (Warner, 1972); *The Captain and Me* (Warner, 1973); *What Were Once Vices Are Now Habits* (Warner, 1974); *Takin' It to the Streets* (Warner, 1976).

Hendrix, Jimi. *Are You Experienced* (Track, 1967); *Electric Ladyland* (Reprise, 1968).

Joel, Billy. *Piano Man* (Columbia/Family Productions, 1973); *Streetlife Serenade* (Columbia/Family Productions, 1974); *Turnstiles* (Columbia/Family Productions, 1976).

Jethro Tulle. *This Was* (Reprise, 1969); *War Child* (Chrysalis, 1974).

Joplin, Janis. *Pearl* (Columbia, 1971).

Led Zeppelin. *Led Zeppelin* (Atlantic, 1969); *Led Zeppelin II* (Atlantic, 1969); *Led Zeppelin III* (Atlantic, 1970); *Led Zeppelin IV* (Atlantic, 1971); *House of the Holy* (Atlantic, 1973); *Physical Graffiti* (Swan Song, 1975).

Morrison, Van. *Astral Weeks* (Warner, 1968); *Moondance* (Warner, 1970).

Rolling Stones, The. *The Rolling Stones* (Decca, 1964); *The Rolling Stones No. 2* (Decca, 1965); *Out of Our Heads* (London, 1965); *Aftermath* (London, 1966); *Between the Buttons* (London, 1967); *Their Satanic Majesties Request* (London, 1967); *Beggars Banquet* (London, 1968); *Let It Bleed* (London, 1969); *Exile on Main Street* (Rolling Stones/Atlantic, 1972).

Santana. *Santana* (Columbia, 1969); *Abraxas* (Columbia, 1970); *Santana [aka Santana III]* (Columbia, 1971); *Borboletta* (CBS, 1974).

Toussaint, Allen. *Toussaint* (Scepter/DJM, 1970).

The Yardbirds [also see Eric Clapton]. *For Your Lovei* (Epic, 1965); *Having a Rave Up* (Epic, 1965); *Roger the Engineer* (Epic, 1966); Little Games (Epic, 1967).

Punk/British Ska/New Wave/80s Pop Rock

Beat, The (aka The English Beat). *I Just Can't Stop It* (Go Feet/Sire, 1980); *Wha'ppen* (Go Feet/Sire, 1981); *Special Beat Service* (Go Feet/IRS, 1982).

Clash, The. *The Clash* (CBS, 1977); *London Calling* (CBS, 1979); *Combat Rock* (Epic, 1982).

Police, The. *Outlandos d'Amour* (A&M, 1978); *Reggatta de Blanc* (A&M, 1979); *Zenyattà Mondatta* (A&M, 1980); *Ghost in the Machine* (A&M, 1980); *Synchronicity* (A&M, 1983).

Specials, The (aka The Specials AKA). *Specials* (2 Tone, 1979); *More Specials* (2 Tone, 1980).

Talking Heads. *Talking Heads: 77* (Sire, 1977); *More Songs About Buildings and Food* (Sire, 1978); *Fear of Music* (Sire, 1979); *Remain in Light* (Sire, 1980).

Western Classical

Beethoven, Ludwig van. *Beethoven Symphony No. 5 in c minor; Symphony No. 9 in d minor;* performed by The Philadelphia Orchestra (2005).

Mozart, Wolfgang Amadeus. *Piano Concerto No. 24,* performed by Philharmonia Orchestra of London (1997).

Copland, Aaron. *Symphony no. 3 (aka Third Symphony),* performed by the New York Philharmonic (Deutsche Grammophon, 1990).

Bernstein, Leonard. *Serenade for Solo Violin, Strings, Harp and Percussion (after Plato's "Symposium"),* performed by New York Philharmonic. From the album Bernstein: *Symphony No. 2; Serenade after Plato's Symposium* (Sony, 1998).

Bibliography

Bailyn, Bernard. *The Ideological Origins of the American Revolution,* Enlarged Edition. Cambridge: Harvard University Press, 1990.

Berman, Marshall. *All That Is Solid Melts Into Air: The Experience of Modernity.* New York: Simon and Schuster, 1982.

Burnim, Mellonee V. and Portia K. Maultsby. *African American Music: An Introduction.* New York: Routledge, 2006.

Chang, Jeff. *Can't Stop Won't Stop.* New York: St. Martin's Press, 2005.

Chapple, Steve and Reebee Garofalo. *Rock 'N' Roll Is Here to Pay: The History and Politics of the Music Industry.* Chicago: Nelson/Hall, 1978.

Chernoff, John Miller. *African Rhythm and African Sensibility.* Chicago: University of Chicago Press, 1979.

Demers, Joanna. *Steal This Music: How Intellectual Property Law Affects Musical Creativity.* Athens: the University of Georgia Press, 2006.

Fitch, Robert. *The Assassination of New York.* New York: Verso, 1993.

Flash, Grandmaster with David Ritz. *The Adventures of Grandmaster Flash: My Life, My Beats.* New York: Broadway Books, 2008.

Floyd, Jr., Samuel A. *The Power of Black Music: Interpreting Its History From Africa to the United States.* New York: Oxford, 1995.

Gates, Jr., Henry Louis. *Black Literatue & Literary Theory*. New York: Methuen, 1984.

Hager, Steven. *Hip Hop: The Illustrated History of Break Dancing, Rap Music, and Graffiti*. New York: St. Martin's Press, 1984.

Hebdige, Dick. *Cut 'N' Mix: Culture, Identity and Caribbean Music*. New York and London: Metheun, 1987.

Heller, Michael. "The Groove Robbers' Judgement; Order on 'Sampling' Songs May Be Rap Landmark," *Washington Post*, December 25, 1991, d1.

Holloway, Joseph E. *Africanisms in American Culture*. Bloomington: 1990.

McLeod, Kembrew and DiCola, Peter. *Creative License: The Law and Culture of Digital Sampling*. Durham and London: Duke University Press, 2011.

Miller, Michael. *The Complete Idiot's Guide to Music Theory, Second Edition*. New York: Penguin, 2005.

Mueller, Jennifer R. R. "All Mixed Up: Bridgeport Music v. Dimension Films and De Minimis Digital Sampling," Indiana Law Journal, Vol. 81, Issue 1, Article 22 (2006)

Neal, Mark Anthony. *Soul Babies: Black Popular Culture and The Post-Soul Aesthetic*. New York: Routledge, 2002.

Norek, Josh. "'You Can't Sing Without the Bling': The Toll of Excessive Sample License Fees on Creativity in Hip-Hop Music and the Need For a Compulsory Sound Recording Sample License System," 11 *UCLA Ent. L. Rev.* 83, 90 (2004).

Patterson, Lyman Ray, *Copyright in Historical Perspective*. Nashville: Vanderbilt University Press, 1968.

Perkins, William Eric. *Droppin' Science: Critical Essays on Rap Music and Hip Hop Culture*. Philadelphia: Temple University Press, 1996.

Poe, Randy. *Music Publishing:: A Songwriter's Guide, Revised Edition*. Cincinnati: Writer's Digest Books, 1997.

H. Raine. 'US Housing Program in South Bronx Called a Waste by Moynihan.' *New York Daily News* 20 Dec 1978, p. 3.

Rose, Tricia. *Black Noise: Rap Music and Black Culture in Contemporary America*. Hanover: Wesleyan University Press, 1994.

'Text of the Moynihan Memorandum on the Status of Negroes.' *New York Times*, 30 January 1970, p. 3.

'Taki 183 Spawns Pen Pals.' *New York Times*, 21 July 1971.

"Plunderphonics: An Interview with John Oswald, Norman Ingma, *Retrofuturism Magazine*, Jan. 1990, no. 12, 1533-38.

Ramsey, Jr., Guthrie P. *Race Music: Black Cultures From Bebop to Hip Hop*. Berkeley: University of California Press, 2003.

Said, Amir "Sa'id". *The BeatTips Manual: Beatmaking, the Hip Hop/Rap Music Tradition, and the Common Composer*. Brooklyn: Superchamp Books, 2009.

Schloss, Joseph. *Making Beats: The Art of Sample-Based Hip-Hop*. Middletown: Wesleyan University Press, 2004.

Schietinger, John. "Bridgeport Music, Inc. V. Dimension Films: How The Sixth Circuit Missed A Beat On Digital Music Sampling," DePaul Law Review, Fall (2005) 55 DePaul L. Rev. 209.

Small, Christopher. *Music—Society—Education: An Examination of the Function of Music in Western, Eastern and African Cultures With Its Impact On Society and Its Use In Education*. New York: Schirmer Books, 1977.

Snead, James A. "On Repetition in Black Culture." In *Black American Literature Forum*, vol. 15, no. 4, 1981.

Southern, Eileen. *The Music of Black Americans: A History*. New York: W.W. Norton & Company, 1971.

Toop, David. *The Rap Attack: African Jive to New York Hip Hop*. New York: Pluto Press, 1984.

Vaidhyanathan, Siva. *Copyrights and Copywrongs: The Rise of Intellectual Property and How It Threatens Creativity*. New York: New York University Press, 2001.

Wallace, Deborah and Rodrick Wallace. *A Plague On Your Houses: How New York Was Burned Down and National Public Health Crumbled*. New York: Verso, 1998.

Legal Cases

Bridgeport Music, Inc. v. Dimension Films LLC, 230 F. Supp.2d 830, 833-39 (M.D. Tenn. 2002).

Bridgeport Music, Inc. v. Dimension Films, 383 F.3d 390,399 (6th Cir. 2004), aft'd on reh'g, 410 F.3d 792 (6th Cir. 2005).

Campbell v. Accuff-Rose Music, 510 U.S. 569 (1994).

Cariou v. Prince, 714 F. 3d 694 (2d Cir. 2013)

Grand Upright Music, Ltd. v. Warner Brothers Records, Inc., 780 F. Supp. 182 (S.D.N.Y. 1991).

Jarvis v. A & M Records, 827 F. Supp. 282 - Dist. Court, D. New Jersey 1993.

Lennon v. Premise Media Corp., 556 F. Supp. (2d 310 - Dist. Court, SD New York, 2008)

Marlon Williams v. Calvin Broadus No. 99 Civ. 10957 (MBM), 2001 WL 984714 (S.D.N.Y. Aug. 27, 2001).

Newton v. Diamond. 388 F.3d 1189 (9th Cir. 2003).

On Davis v. The Gap, Inc., 246 F.3d 152 (2nd Cir. 2001).

Ringgold v. Black Entertainment Television, 126 F.3d 70, 74 (2d Cir. 1997).

Warner Bros., Inc. v. American Broadcasting Companies, 654 F. 2d 204 - Court of Appeals, 2nd Circuit 1981.

Index

455

W

Acknowledgements

Amir and Qamar, *Salaam Aikum wa Rahmatullah, wa-Baraktahu.* Thank you for patiently listening to me talk about the origins of hip hop, developments in hip hop/rap music, science, philosophy, culture, mathematics, politics, and history; the discussions we shared always helped me gain new levels of clarity. The support, patience, advice, and, most importantly, the love and respect of both of you is something that I thank Allah for.

Amir Ali Said, my son, best friend, and Superchamp co-founder — Thank you for your friendship, knowledge, courage, and curiosity, and also for your always smart, enthusiastic, and timely copy editing. Remember, all the answers are in three places: Q, S, and YT. Samir Arts next.

Qamar, my son's mother — Your love, belief, and support through the years has meant (and will always mean) something incredibly special to me. Thank you.

Insight and information has been contributed to this study by many individuals. Therefore, I have not attempted to cite in the text all the authorities and sources consulted in the preparation of this study. To do so would require more space than is available. The list would include various beatmakers (producers), recording artists, recording engineers, A&Rs, lawyers, librarians, music retailers (owners, managers, associates), music writers, and other well-known "music people". However, I would like to single out the following individuals, in particular, for their continued help, thoughts, encouragement, and overall support:

Mariella Gross, thank you for your unwavering commitment and timely copy editing. To EVERYONE I've ever interviewed or built with, you have my deepest gratitude. Among those that I've interviewed, I would especially like to thank: **DJ Premier,** good-lookin' out, Preme. Your word is gold with me; **Buckwild; Minnesota; True Master; D.R. Period; John King** (founder of Chung King Studios); **Rsonist** (of The Heatmakerz); **Rich Keller; EZ Elpee; DJ Clark Kent; Steve Sola; 9th Wonder; DJ Toomp;** and **Marley Marl.**

Finally, I would also like to extend my respect and gratitude to Eileen Southern and to every unknown architect and pioneer who played a role in hip hop's foundation. Thank you.

About The Author

Amir Said (aka "Sa'id") is a writer, publisher, beatmaker/rapper, and father from Brooklyn, NY (now making his home in Paris). In addition to writing, making beats, and managing the BeatTips Network of music education websites, Said also runs Superchamp Books, an independent publishing company. Equally adept at translating the beatmaking themes and sounds of every beatmaking period since 1973, Said has been able to help scores of different beatmakers (producers) develop their overall production level and music-business understanding. While he's committed to the advancement of hip hop studies worldwide, he's also dedicated to raising public awareness about copyright law.

Sa'id, Dec. 1993

Lightning Source UK Ltd.
Milton Keynes UK
UKHW020654171022
410608UK00018B/1059